DEBATING EDUCATION IN INDIA

Issues and Concerns

DEBATING EDUCATION IN INDIA

Issues and Concerns

Edited by
MAYA JOHN

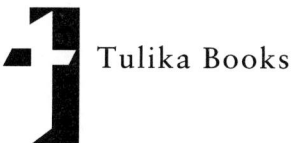

Tulika Books

Published by
Tulika Books
44 (first floor), Shahpur Jat, New Delhi 110 049, India
www.tulikabooks.in

First edition (hardback) 2023

ISBN: 978-81-956392-4-3

Printed at Chaman Offset, Delhi 110 002

On behalf of my co-authors, I dedicate this book to the struggles for quality public-funded education accessible to the last person in the line

Contents

Acknowledgements   ix

Introduction
MAYA JOHN   1

1 Elusive India: Lost in the National Education Policy 2020?
  KUMKUM ROY   37

2 'Low-cost' Schooling for the Poor in India:
  Contemporary Concerns
  GEETHA B. NAMBISSAN   49

3 Policy Shifts in School Education: A Critical Analysis
  JYOTI RAINA   69

4 Academic Heretic: A Reflexive Teacher–Educator
  ANTHONY JOSEPH   99

5 Progress of Education among the Muslims of Lakshadweep
  L.R.S. LAKSHMI   116

6 Reclaiming Education Policy for Equality and Social Justice
  MADHU PRASAD   127

7 Continuity amidst Changes: *Longue Durée* of Educational
  Apartheid in India
  MOHD. BILAL   151

8 Construction of a State-regulated Market for Indian
  Higher Education Reform: A Reflection on NEP 2020
  SAUMEN CHATTOPADHYAY   182

9 'Blending' the Futures of Higher Education: Digital Capital
and the Indian University
DEBADITYA BHATTACHARYA 201

10 Citizen, Consumer, User: Covid-19, the Platform University
and Higher Education in India
ROHAN D'SOUZA 234

11 Higher Education in NEP 2020: Rhetoric and Realities
MAYA JOHN 261

Notes on the Contributors 287

Acknowledgements

This book was brought together at a time when many were still coming to terms with the disruptions unleashed by the Covid-19 pandemic-cum-lockdowns. I am, hence, extremely grateful to all the scholars who have generously spared the time to contribute and make this publication possible. Each of the contributors is a noted academician and is concerned about the marked problems with educational structures and policies. When I requested them to write for the e-journal of Jesus and Mary College, *The JMC Review*, of which I was the editor in 2020, they readily agreed. In light of the National Education Policy (NEP) 2020 being rolled out and a spate of policy measures being hectically imposed, I subsequently requested reworked, updated chapters for a book-length publication. Each of the contributors promptly responded with their chapters. Their enthusiasm and promptness have always been encouraging.

Sadly, during the finalizing of the book one of the contributors and an esteemed colleague, L.R.S. Lakshmi, was not keeping well. She is unfortunately no longer amongst us. Amidst routine work, one was unaware of her fast-deteriorating condition. In retrospect, learning of her condition, I am humbled and have come to further appreciate her forbearance, patience and goodwill.

I take this opportunity to thank a valuable friend from the trade union movement, Comrade Alok Kumar, for his critical inputs, thought-provoking questions and consistent encouragement of socially meaningful research. My gratitude also extends to youth activists across Delhi, Haryana, Punjab, Assam, Manipur and other parts of the country, who have laid the field for many pertinent struggles for greater equity and access to quality education. In this regard, I would like to thank Dinesh, Harish, Bilal, Bhim, Mudita, Prithviraj, Virendra, Vikram, Jyoti, Chinglen, Madhuri, Mandvi and several other young activists whose work on the ground constitutes the base on which such a book could materialize. Indeed, their efforts have enabled a synergy on the education question of our times, which this book strives to encapsulate.

I am thankful to Indu Chandrasekhar and the team at Tulika Books for agreeing to a timely publication, and for their commitment in seeing this through. A word of appreciation for Nilanjana Dey whose meticulous copy-editing has been a respite for those of us who had given up on quality copy-editing in recent times. With respect to the cover, I thank the designer Alpana Khare for providing an image which captures the spirit of the book so aptly.

Introduction

Maya John

The contemporary conjuncture of the twenty-first century has been identified by academics, educationalists and activists as a moment of 'crisis' in education. Yet others have questioned this emphasis on a 'crisis', given the continuities between existing and earlier education systems and paradigms. To take these discussions forward, the current volume offers critical perspectives from historical, sociological, philosophical and other social science disciplines. Several of the essays speak to each other and elicit much-required introspection on the arguments claimed about India's educational experience. Reflecting on the importance of formal public-funded mass education, this volume strives to highlight the crucial fault lines of contemporary educational policy in India, as well as the long trajectory of educational inequalities against whose backdrop the recent policy paradigms need to be assessed.

Historically speaking, the idea of formal mass education and the attempts for its gradual realization in the Indian subcontinent can be traced to the modern era of colonial conquest, anti-colonial struggles and post-colonial state formation. There was, nonetheless, a diversity in the provisioning of 'indigenous' education, which was imparted at home, in temples, *tol*s, *chatuspadi*s, *gurukul*s, *makhtab*s and *pathshala*s that together offered education in religiously endowed as well as secular subjects. In this regard, we have evidence of a diversity of reputed centres of learning which were funded by royal grants and other public donations. Likewise, local communities pooled resources to financially support village schools or *pathshala*s that offered basic/elementary education to select social groups. Such education was mostly suited to the local requirements of parents and students.

Beyond the Politics of Knowledge: Bringing Back the Issue of Equality

Domains of skilling and the creating and disseminating of knowledge as well as wisdom emanated from varied forms of society which did *not* turn to religious bodies – formal institutions of learning or textual traditions for the imparting of knowledge and skills. Typically, 'tribal', pastoral-nomadic, 'lower-caste' groups, etc., nurtured their own distinct forms of learning in the Indian subcontinent. Of course, a sharp hierarchy developed in premodern times between orality and textual traditions. Those who did not convert their knowledge forms into canonized texts were increasingly marginalized. Yet, far from being purged, subaltern forms of knowledge persisted and were part of the complex interface that unfolded between indigenous forms of knowledge production and the expanding colonial state which sought to reconfigure knowledge into a singular form by reducing the epistemic diversity of the colonized people. As aptly argued by the decolonial theorist, Boaventura de Sousa Santos, 'throughout the world, not only are there very diverse forms of knowledge of matter, society, life and spirit, but also many and very diverse concepts of what counts as knowledge and criteria that may be used to validate it' (de Sousa Santos 2015: 192).

As a *diverse* premodern society and *indigenous knowledges* encountered colonial modernity through an extremely complex relationship, some hierarchies were tweaked, at times reproduced, alongside the crystallizing of new hierarchies. In the process, there emerged under the aegis of the colonial state, a hegemony of knowledge or what came to be counted as legitimate knowledge to be acquired. Colonialism benefitted from this politics of knowledge as the colonial knowledge system was envisaged in a way in which the colonized were supposed to be disassociated from their histories, languages, social relations and their own ways of thinking, feeling and interacting with the world in the process of generating an 'acceptance' for the supremacy of European modernity. Needless to say, the process was a contested one.

Accompanying this politics of knowledge in the colonial context was a marked development whereby access to hegemonic knowledge increasingly translated into concrete access to new forms of power, posts and positions in society. This, in turn, propelled aspirations as well as numerous struggles for such access. Against this colonial backdrop, we see a churning amongst 'upper-caste' groups to modernize certain aspects of their life so as to gain access to modern education. In the domain of their 'private' sphere and appended social relations, such thrusts of change towards modernity were, of course, much slower, if not missing. In addition to upper-caste aspirations were the assertions by less privileged segments of Indian society, who were increasingly compelled to confront yet also sought access to hegemonic knowledge being perpetuated through colonial institutions in the larger quest to avail new opportunities and upward mobility.

Consequently, in the genealogy of our present, a marked assertion by lower-caste groups has always existed. In the distinct contestation over knowledge, lower castes threw up new readings of the canon, that is, texts and supporting traditions of the dominant sections of society. In this way, historically speaking, the subaltern take on the politics of knowledge has posed a very important corrective. Indeed, premodern society comprised a distinct continuum in which there co-existed shades of hierarchy as well as egalitarianism.

Turning to the institutionalized forms of indigenous learning, we find several positive accounts (Dharampal 1983; Dibona, ed. 1983). Yet we have adequate scholarship that reveals the limitations of premodern education, especially its reproduction of social hierarchy and appended inequalities (Acharya 1978; 1996). The entrenchment of hierarchy and inequality is further substantiated by the historical evidence extractable from various written sources for ancient and medieval Indian history. A tradition of inequality and exclusion in Indian society is nearly impossible to dismiss, and as henceforth discussed, is a phenomenon that persists in new forms even in modern times. In this regard, the present volume seeks to highlight the contentious past, the ambivalent present and the uncertain future of education.

A reading or revisiting of traditions and old canons by lower-caste groups does not augur well with glorified accounts of ancient systems of learning in the Indian subcontinent. In this way, Eklavaya's story becomes allegorical to understanding the question of access of subalterns to dominant knowledge and the spheres of learning. The legend of Ekalavya is a well-known one, though awkwardly blinkered out by the valorizing discourses on Indian tradition that the ruling elites nurture. Such discourses speak of a supposedly unequivocal glorious past, involving great 'gurus' and much-sought-after centres of learning in ancient times. Conveniently concealed is the exclusion and violence unleashed on those who sought access to established learning centres, new skills and the *shastras* in contravention of the norms of hierarchy. As the legend goes, Ekalavya was the son of Hirnadhanu, who was a king of a forest-dwelling community. Such tribal origins usually translated into a lower *varna* and lower-caste status within the Brahminical ordering of society. Ekalavya has thus been ascribed the status of a Nishada (low-caste) in several sources of ancient history. According to one such source, that is, the *Mahabharata*, Ekalavya sought an education in archery from the best instructor of the art, Guru Dronacharya, who of course refused to teach Ekalavya because of his non-Kshatriya status. Undeterred by Dronacharya's staunch assertion of Kshatriya privilege or 'dharma', Ekalavya proceeded to set up an idol of the master and follow a path of rigorous self-study that transformed him into a greater archer than Dronacharya's famed Kshatriya pupil, Prince Arjuna of the Pandavas. Stumbling upon Ekalavya's abilities, a threatened Arjuna voiced his disapproval to Dronacharya, accusing his teacher of reneging on his promise of making Arjuna the uncontested master of archery. As the legend goes, on learning of Ekalavya's path of self-study that was inspired by his own person, Dronacharya demanded Ekalavya's right thumb as *gurudakshina,* that is, an offering given to a teacher in respect and gratitude. The legend valorizes Ekalavya's obliging and respectful obedience to a claim that ensured he could no longer challenge the superiority of prince Arjuna; hinting simultaneously at the ignobility of elite social groups who monopolized traditional education and imparting of coveted skills.

The politics of difference within which the parable is located indicates just how socially disabling and violent the system of caste hierarchy was in earlier times. The story also makes evident that access to ancient forms of learning was strictly denied to the *majority* because of its potential to change inherited circumstances and destabilize the status quo. Correspondingly, the skills and learning acquired by the *privileged few* came to breed an erroneous idea of *merit* which, in real terms, was firmly anchored in the systemic *denial* of equitable opportunities to scores of able men and women.

The present times are replete with similar instances of exclusion and hollow meritocracy. Crumbling government/public-funded schools; limited seats in public-funded universities, exclusionary admission policies, burgeoning enrolment numbers in poorly funded, badly managed *informal* education, heavy concentration of working-class youth in vocational learning and low-ranking institutions, skewed funding structures that breed inequality between educational institutions, and the steady privatization of the education sector, together manufacture scores of Ekalavyas on a daily basis. This tragedy is embodied in the collapsing dreams of millions of youths who aspire for access to good schools, affordable college education, and consequently, better paying jobs. As highlighted by several contributors to this volume, important questions for modern education include how distanced the bottom quantiles of Indian youth are from quality education, and how much of the distance has been covered by bridging the gap. The following essays amply highlight that education as a component of cultural inheritance remains a contentious issue. Representing the transfer of knowledge, skill endowment, and so on, education harbours the tendency to support and reproduce social hierarchy, as well as the countervailing propensity towards amelioration of vulnerable socio-economic groups.

Navigating the *Zeitgeist*: Equality and its Discontent

Departing from the classical and medieval intellectual legacies that were imbricated in religion, the eighteenth century onwards witnessed an efflorescence of general theories on social inequality which were anchored in the principles of 'natural law' rather than a divine scheme. These diverse theories on the causes, persistence and role of social inequality undoubtedly helped fashion concepts and interventions in education. These social theories prove significant as they embodied the logic of changing social relations and state formation from the eighteenth century onwards. Navigating through the varied perspectives and their assessments of whether or not education could remedy the widespread inequality plaguing society, a lot can be gleaned about the emancipatory and reproductionist aspects of modern education.

In the west, a watershed moment in the conceptualization of social inequality was the eighteenth century wherein the ideas of the Enlightenment, with their emphasis on human reason and 'natural rights', slowly chipped away at the traditionalism informing the arts, philosophy, state power and politics. The works of the French philosopher, Jean-Jacques Rousseau, are particularly noteworthy for their firm assertion of a distinction between natural inequalities stemming from individual physical differences, and the moral and political inequality that he attributed to privileges stemming from the unequal division of private property. For Rousseau, education was crucial for removing the children of the rich from the corrupting influence of society and for their moral uplift. For him, the poor tended to learn adequately from their life. Moreover, considering that Rousseau attributed social inequality to the unequal division of private property and its political impacts, the education of the poor was not per se considered an effective remedy against social inequity. Consequently, within the Rousseanian paradigm of social reform, quality education for the masses was overshadowed by the desire to use enlightened education to sensitize the privileged elite about the problems of inequality and their obligation to contribute to the common good. This Rousseanian paradigm of social reform is aptly captured in his *Emile* or *On Education* ([1762]1991), wherein the protagonist is a youth from an affluent family, who is educated in keeping with the principles of natural man.

The late eighteenth and early nineteenth century also witnessed other interventions that emphasized the importance of schooling and education for the moral betterment of society. These included the work of a staunch advocate of mass education for the poor, that is, the Swiss educational reformer, Johann Heinrich Pestalozzi, who developed teaching methods designed to strengthen the student's own abilities. Committed to teaching the poor how to live self-respecting lives, Pestalozzi helped construct educational programmes that eradicated illiteracy in places like Switzerland by the 1830s. His efforts at running the orphanage in Stans in 1799 and his repeated attempts at establishing industrial (poor) schools point to his espousal of education as an important form of alleviation in the context of extreme poverty (McKenna 2010).

Advocating that the poorest of the poor were the responsibility of the state, he strove to work with orphans, destitutes, impoverished peasant children, etc. Nevertheless, similar to Rousseau, Pestalozzi also realized that even if such education salvaged a few youths, in itself such an education was incapable of eradicating systemic poverty and destitution in society. In other words, schooling for the poor could nurture the moral betterment of society, but it could *not* dismantle material inequality or facilitate the reordering of society via education-based enhanced social mobility.

However, as the nineteenth century progressed, educational reform came to be increasingly promoted as a remedy for crushing material inequality. Many such interventions marked a crucial shift away from critiques of private property and the prevailing intuition about the limits of public education for eradicating social inequality. Seeking to explain the major source of social inequality not so much in terms of private property but unequal access to it, social theorists like Gustav Schmoller, Emile Durkheim, John Stuart Mill, and many others, instead drew attention to the increasing division of labour, defining it as the cause rather than the consequence of social inequality. Such theoretical approaches essentially focused on the horizontal division of labour (along the lines of skills) and appended social differentiation that accompanied the vertical social stratification of society along the lines of rank, estates, classes, etc. Promoting the idea that social inequality could be overcome by social mobility that allowed for greater social cohesion, such theorists did not envisage the need for revolutionary change, and instead, worked within the logic of reform. In this light, they valued education and the state's role in guaranteeing free access to it. The German political economist, Gustav Schmoller, for instance, argued that the root cause of social conflict is not the unequal distribution of property but the dissonance in the access to and degree of education. All social reform has to start at this point. It has to improve the attitude towards life, the character, knowledge, and skills of the lower classes (Schmoller [1890] 1993).

He vocally supported better public education in general and supported vocational training for the lower classes in particular. Similarly, the utilitarian thinker, John Stuart Mill, spoke favourably of the state's role in ensuring equal opportunities, and thereby, social justice and social cohesion. Advocating compulsory education, Mill argued that the state could leave this to private initiative 'and content itself with helping to pay the school fees of the poorer classes of children, and defraying the entire school expenses of those who have no one else to pay for them' (Mill [1859] 1978).

By the early twentieth century, a certain reading of the division of labour, hierarchy of skills and their coalescing with vertical social stratification came to assert that given differentiations are generally acceptable and essential to the functioning of society. Talcott Parsons (1940), for example, argued that differential positions like those of engineers, scientists, surgeons, teachers, politicians, etc., have their role in society, but not all these positions require the same degree of skill endowment and proficiency. Arguing that social stratification and inequality were inherent to society and its functioning, Parsons laid a framework which projected that the role of education was not to overcome social inequality but to strengthen the differential valuation of given hierarchies of skills and professions. In the same vein, normalizing social inequality and social stratification, Niklas Luhmann (2012) projected the education system as a functional subsystem of society that simply served as a channel for the transfer of skills which was essential for society. Such positions have subsequently come to be reflected in neoliberal policy discourses that have increasingly shifted the focus away from state investment in enhancing access to education so as to facilitate greater social mobility. Working with an engrained disinterest and dismissal of the ameliorative tendencies of education systems, the technical and skills-driven approach to education has justified reduced state intervention and promoted market-driven education models, which simply reinforce inherited educational and other social inequalities. In the more specific Indian context, the ruling discourse on education in present times reflects a confluence of neoliberal policy frameworks, functional perspectives of sociology, and caste hierarchy and biases. This confluence reproduces the marginalization of the majority among lower castes and reverses the gains of movements for social justice.

A markedly alternative perspective has been provided by Marxist theory. In their writings on education, Marx and Engels offer a nuanced dialectical approach to education, which highlights the twin role of the educational process. At one level, they recognize the role of education in reproducing the hegemony of the ruling elites. Accordingly, Marx sharply criticized the 1875 Gotha Programme of the Socialist Workers' Party of Germany for bestowing trust in the school system of the imperial German state (Marx [1875] 1970). At another level, the writings of Marx and Engels drew attention to the role of free, compulsory uniform public education in the fundamental battle of consciousness that would displace knowledge monopolies, bring up children under less unequal conditions, as well as weaken the hold of traditional institutions (like the family) which kept at bay the socializing force of the community. Drawing on such observations, successful revolutionary educational policies were introduced in Russia after the October Revolution and during other socialist experiments. Marxist interventions thus identify that a counter-hegemony of education is possible through the struggles for access. In the process of such struggles for access, the ideological moorings of education systems are correspondingly also transformed as both the materiality and ideas of education are co-constituted. In the Indian context, such tendencies can also be seen in Dalit-Bahujan thoughts, which continue to emphasize the issue of access and the nature of upper-caste hegemony on education.

Emergence of the Education Question: The Colonial Period

A scrutiny of crucial developments since the colonial era into contemporary times is helpful in comprehending the realities of modern public education in India. Overall, a tenuous process of the spread of modern (English) education in India can be traced to the eighteenth-century initiatives of individual Company officials, Christian missionaries and local elites (Frykenberg 1986; More 2020). Yet, a more formal policy with respect to education surfaced more concretely in the nineteenth century. From thereon, a territorially advancing and more expansive colonial state, which was experimenting with new forms of governance, revenue management, surveys, enumeration and classification, triggered a process of complex and relatively contentious encounters with indigenous arrangements of education.

At one level, these encounters included the gradual absorption of indigenous schools into the evolving governmental system of education. This was achieved through financial grants and other supporting resources that were extended on the basis of results (Shukla 1959); the introduction of teacher training and the corresponding curbs on teachers' autonomy (Kumar 1991); and the construction of new kinds of learning environments in classrooms that proved disjunct from the lived experiences of enrolling students (Kumar 2007). The new schools offering English education increasingly outbid the colonial state's earlier endeavours of setting up educational institutions that promoted 'classical' learning in Sanskrit, Bengali, Persian and so on.

At another level, the gradual proliferation of English education from the 1830s aided specific political objectives of the colonizers. These objectives ranged from moulding the 'natives' in ways that facilitated their approval of foreign rule (Viswanathan 1990) to their absorption into western-style administration and their incorporation into new forms of production that served metropolitan markets (Carnoy 1974) and necessitated social changes which synced with western notions of work and interpersonal relations. These new roles for the colonized served the interests of the colonial state and the elites of the metropole, but were roles that were eventually ascribed, through unequal education, to a select segment of 'natives'. Avoiding the provision of free compulsory primary education and the establishment of an expansive network of educational institutions, modern English education under the colonial state catered largely to the *indigenous elites*.

Notably, mass primary education and higher education were viewed with suspicion even though some higher colonial officials believed enhanced literacy was a crucial tool for good administration. Lord Curzon, in particular, actively propagated primary education over higher education and believed it expedient to shift the emphasis of government resources from urban to rural areas, the justification being the popularly held misconception that opposition to British rule had emerged mainly from the educated classes in the cities rather than from the illiterate peasantry. With such views in circulation, the colonial regime began to spend a lot more on primary education from 1907 onwards, resulting in a substantial increase in the number of students pursuing primary education (H. Sharp 1914).

Nevertheless, the colonial state stalled the process of appropriate legislative action on the enhanced expenditure on primary education. Gopal Krishna Gokhale's resolution for free and compulsory elementary education was shot down by the Council of the Governor-General in 1910, and Gokhale was assured by the Home Member that the requisite investigation into the issue was being pursued. The next year when Gokhale introduced a bill to the effect of free and compulsory elementary education, the government opposed it. Meanwhile, the Government of India did refer the question of free and compulsory primary education to the local governments, most of who ended up opposing Gokhale's Bill. The Governor of Bombay, for example, argued that certain nationalists were agitating for elementary education since a literate peasantry would be further open to their influence through the vernacular press (A. Basu 1971).

Given the imperial government's hesitation, the initiative to press forth legislative action for free and compulsory primary education came from individuals in the provincial legislative assemblies. The first Primary Education Act was passed in 1918 by the Bombay Legislative Assembly. The act was the outcome of a private bill that was circulated and lobbied for by Vithalbhai Patel. Similarly, other provinces like the United Provinces, Bengal, Bihar and Orissa also saw the introduction of private bills which culminated in Primary Education Acts in June 1919, May 1919 and February 1919, respectively. Unfortunately, despite the fact that seven provinces pushed through such legislation, the scope of their respective acts was very limited. For instance, the acts of Bombay and the United Provinces were applicable only to the municipalities. Moreover, the acts assigned local bodies the authority to decide whether any area under their control warranted compulsory primary education. A two-thirds majority of the local body had to pass a resolution to this effect and prepare a scheme for its implementation before the concerned provincial government could intervene. Not surprisingly, very few local bodies took the initiative (Richey 1923). The piecemeal provision of educational infrastructure and opportunities under this structure of colonial governance propelled important struggles by 'untouchable' communities (Constable 2000; Nambissan 1996; Zelliot 2002, 2014) as well as paved the way for some initiatives in the domain of female education (Forbes 1999; Minault 1998).

The social and educational uplift of untouchable communities progressed despite virulent opposition from the custodians of caste hierarchy, particularly due to radical movements that emerged from the ranks of 'untouchables' and other 'low'-caste groups. A certain measure of educational uplift can also be traced to the efforts of the first generation of educated untouchables and the initiatives taken by a broad spectrum of social reformers. While prominent social reformers included figures like Ayyankali, Jotirao Phule, Savitribai Phule, the Maharaja of Kolhapur, Ishwar Chandra Vidyasagar, Dr B.R. Ambedkar, among others, there were many lesser-known Dalit and non-Brahmin activists across the country who established educational institutions for discriminated caste groups (Zelliot 2014). This apart, the network of schools opened for untouchables by the Arya Samaj and Christian missionaries also came into existence. However, the schooling imparted through these institutions, especially so in the cases of Arya Samaj schools, was subordinated to the endeavour of inculcating subservient Dalit youth. Instruction was anchored on promoting 'industriousness', 'morality', 'cleanliness' and docility' in Dalit children as they continued to be perceived as labouring bodies (Kumar 2019).

Given the public and private initiatives in the sphere of education, the colonial government's records expectedly reflect an increase in the enrolment of untouchable youth in schools. However, the records tend to conceal the fact that in villages where the majority of untouchables[1] resided, the kind of education imparted to them was such that the possibilities of them moving into secondary education and hence higher segments of occupations were very limited. Rural instruction in India was managed by either public or private agencies, with the latter often outnumbering the former type of school. A large number of schools for untouchables were below the normal standard (Richey 1923: 206), and even in the 'common' village schools, high-caste teachers refused to instruct untouchable children 'unless paid a rupee or so per month per ward' (Singh 1947: 145).

Indeed, a duality or ambiguity informing the colonial state's education policy was evident in the way its grants-in-aid system supported the establishment of not only special schools for untouchables but also separate schools for those castes that objected to any association between children of caste Hindus and those of untouchables. Similarly, the duality of the state's education policy was reflected in its projected receptivity to the inclusion of untouchable children in its aided schools, which was ironically accompanied by special instructions issued by district school boards regarding separate seating arrangements for untouchable students (Nambissan 1996).

In addition to the obstacle of poor-quality special schools, limited access to and discrimination within 'common' village schools was the oppression unleashed by the upper-caste landholding class in villages. Realizing the loss of labour that they would incur due to the spread of educational facilities in the villages, landlords dissuaded untouchables from educating their children and often sought to tempt them by offering their children employment (Singh 1947: 146).

Within this matrix of crushing inequality and competing aspirations, the specific recommendations and measures taken for the amelioration of the educational condition of untouchables reflected a predominant pattern of restraint/moderation. In other words, ameliorative measures were built on the principle of proportionate representation wherein educational rights were extended to a fixed number of untouchable youths in proportion to their community's demographic weight in the total population. By extension, such intervention imbibed notions of merit and downward filtration in the bid to rationalize the competition over limited seats and scholarships. Such interventions also reproduced the assumption that *vocational* education best suited the youth of untouchable communities and other labouring groups.

Therefore, most local governments, important untouchable and non-Brahmin leaders sought to: (1) provide a fixed number of scholarships to untouchable children and youth based on some notion of merit; (2) constitute some form of fee reduction and fee waiver for untouchable children at the level of primary schools and for the vernacular final examination instead of abolition of school fees;[2] (3) provide for reservation of a certain number of seats in teacher training institutes; (4) provide for reservation of some seats in government secondary schools and colleges, and (5) open institutes for industrial and technical education for these classes in order to encourage industrial pursuits within them.

TABLE **Number of Depressed Classes (boys and girls) under instruction by stages and provinces**

Provinces	Primary Stages	Middle Stages	High Stages	Collegiate Stage
Madras	224, 873*	2,647**	...	47
Bombay	58,651* (a)	730***	...	9
Bengal	310,398	8,787	5,996	1,670
United Provinces	88,383	1,367	42	10
Punjab	14,284	914	110	Nil
Bihar and Orissa	24,574	52	7	Nil
Central Provinces	33,123	1,022	59	16

Notes: * Number in primary schools only; ** number in the middle and high stages; ***
number in primary, middle and high stages of secondary schools.
Source: Interim Report of the Indian Statutory Commission: Review of Growth of Education
in British India by the Auxiliary Committee Appointed by the Commission, September 1929.

Since these education welfare measures were based on numbers and
ideas of merit, the majority of untouchable youth could not benefit from
them. The number of untouchables entering the fold of education was, consequently, concentrated at the level of primary education.

Taken together, the aforementioned ameliorative measures worked
towards creating a layer of better-educated untouchables who could enter
a wider range of occupations (teaching, law, etc.). Simultaneously, these
measures rendered the majority of untouchables as less skilled workers who
could be pushed into various kinds of stigmatized work as cleaners, farm-
hands, and so on.

It is thus important to recognize that colonial rule did not simply
unleash a contest between the high-caste, English-educated elites and discriminated caste groups who were provided mostly vernacular, substandard education. What was also unleashed by unequal access to education
nurtured through ameliorative measures that were based on the principle of
proportionate rights coalesced with the concept of merit was the monopo-
lization of the avenues of social and educational uplift by the better-off
segments within underprivileged social groups. In this way, education in
the colonial era did not improve the economic status of the majority of
working-class Dalits and instead fostered an articulate middle-class Dalit
intelligentsia. This intelligentsia, itself, continued to envisage ameliorative
educational measures within the paradigm of merit and proportionate representation in educational institutions. Competitive examinations for avail-
ing scholarships, hostel accommodation, accessing secondary education,

etc., are the most apt examples of the entrapment of the Dalit intelligentsia within the idea of merit and within the assumption that educating a few 'able' untouchable youths satiated the educational aspirations and changed the life circumstances of the wider Dalit community (John 2016).

By factoring in evolving class formation within the caste groups, a more realistic picture emerges with respect to education's reproduction-ist role in colonial times. Considering the socio-economic disadvantages in which the majority of untouchables were trapped, ameliorative measures of the colonial state were not just inadequate but also geared towards produc-ing and reproducing a hierarchy of skill endowment through a hierarchized education system. Hence, rather than an education which was exclusively literary in its bent, the focus of the state's education policy moved steadily towards imparting skills that helped secure a greater variety of occupations.

This push towards vocational/industrial and technical education accompanied the emerging needs of the industrial and commercial sectors, as well as the colonial state's efforts to appoint untouchables to the subor-dinate ranks of state service in a context of significant transformations in the traditional avenues of livelihood. In other words, education provided to the majority of untouchables was with the purpose of creating additional skills that would enable them to move into other kinds of craft produc-tion as traditional village industries steadily declined. Industrial/vocational education was also geared towards facilitating the transition of untoucha-bles into certain kinds of skilled wage labour in the cities like in tanneries, presses, the textile, and leather industries, etc. (ibid.).

The majority of village-based untouchable youth were unable to make much of the newly acquired skills imparted through the government's efforts to spread vocational education (ibid.). More than an unwillingness of untouchables to acquire or to put into practice any new industrial train-ing they may have accessed, it was the precarious livelihoods, the high costs of special (industrial) training, the extremely limited educational opportu-nities offered by the government,[3] the lack of better-paying jobs in villages and the paucity of resources to put their vocational training into practice that combined to press untouchable families to be trapped in the web of traditional avocations.

In the colonial context, another thrust towards piecemeal voca-tional education in the form of factory schools surfaced alongside the unfolding process of state regulation of child labour (the 'half-timer') employed in industrial enterprises (John 2018). Talk of imparting basic education, that is, writing, reading, mathematics and technical skills, to child labourers developed within circles of social reformers. Such education was also advocated by individual employers and certain employer lobbies.[4]

Of course, both reformers and employers focused on *vocational* education. According to them, such education inculcated greater industriousness in the child worker; the only difference being that reformers spoke more in terms of children working and studying together so as to lessen the alienation brought on by mechanical industrial activity, and employers spoke in more direct terms of the need to create a competent manufacturing class from within existing half-timers.[5] The marked instrumentalism involved in churning out efficient workers from the factory schools was often asserted repeatedly despite falling attendance. In fact, there are instances where attendance to such schools was made compulsory by the factory management in the context of their unpopularity. Lacking teaching aides, furniture and even paper, these 'schools' came to stand out more as disciplining centres than truly educational ones. Meanwhile, the few factory schools that were run more systematically simply reproduced class inequality by luring workers' children into a form of education which, by promising them future employment in the industrial enterprise, trapped them in the same class position as the *worker*.

Inequality was also reproduced by the colonial state through its differential allocation of funds for female education and minimal involvement in this domain (Bhattacharya, Bara and Yagati, eds 2001). Female education, consequently, remained dependent on non-state actors for its funding, which hampered its growth. As highlighted in Bhattacharya, Bara and Yagati, eds (2001), the colonial state's low investment in this domain of education was driven by the concern of higher per capita costs of girls' schooling, which in turn was linked to the practice of hiring female teachers for separate girls' schools wherein enrolment was extremely limited and thus the per-child expenditure on a teacher worked out to be much higher. Unwilling to bear the cost of separate girls' schools, as well as disinclined towards reducing this cost by converting separate girls' and boys' schools into co-educational ones, the colonial state reproduced educational inequality along the gender axis. Further, as one moved beyond primary schools, very few secondary schools and higher educational institutions worked towards restraining female education to largely the primary level.

Making of Modern Ekalavyas

Evidently, the development of modern public education in India has been fraught with contradictions, which involved both the colonial state and non-state actors. Many contradictions are linked to the fact that education has meant different things to different sections of Indian society. A pervasive, mainstream view has restricted education, particularly quality education, to the 'talented' and 'meritorious' across various strata of society. In more specific terms, such an approach asserts that the unfolding of mass public education cannot be at the cost of 'talent'. Correspondingly, artificial categories of 'merit' and the 'deserving' proliferate the discourse and inform several policy measures in education. For example, dictating the parameters of quality education, the dominant classes and ruling elites have nurtured and defended an educational policy framework that consciously combines quality with exclusivity, or essentially, limited intake.

Shunning the idea and demands for a common schooling model, educational inequality has been bred by successive regimes right from the school level. When it comes to schooling, we have seen children of agrarian workers and poor peasants being relegated to village-level government schools or Charvaha vidyalayas/Ekal schools, while children of agrarian elites – through competitive entrance tests – are provided access to quality public-funded schooling via a limited network of prestigious Jawahar Navodayas Vidyalayas. Likewise in cities, running parallel to expensive private schools that are based on exclusive admission procedures and cater to the well-to-do, a network of Sarvodayas or run-down government schools is the mainstay of children of the urban working masses. Meanwhile, well-funded and equipped Sainik schools and Kendriya Vidyalayas (Central Schools) provide equality schooling to a select few, that is, children of central government employees who comprise the middle-class and a small segment of working-class families.

Building on this dual (public/private) education model and the above-mentioned segmented school education structure, an entrenched hierarchy and segmentation in the higher education sector have been perpetuated. In this way, the landscape of higher education is sprinkled with 'centres of excellence'/'institutes of eminence'. The premium status of these 'centres of excellence' is preserved by limiting the number of seats for admission and by allocating them the lion's share of government funding. The hierarchy has strengthened the hold of the privileged classes on elite (central government-funded) metropolitan universities through competitive entrance tests and the ruthless 'cut-off' system; relegated the lower-middle-class to second-grade regional universities and private institutes; and has kept the majority of impoverished youth out of the university system altogether, while pushing a segment of such youth into poorly funded regional universities, B-grade private institutes and the Open and Distance Learning (ODL) mode offered by some public-funded universities.

In many ways then, universities have become enclosures of knowledge which appropriate the world for knowledge production while reducing society simply to passive objects of study. Moreover, the obverse relationship between marginalization and access to the university system makes universities almost like gated colonies where entry is jealously guarded, and where only a small section of elites can acquire knowledge so as to gain leadership and power in different fields. The guarded access to knowledge, in turn, influences to a significant extent the form and content of what is counted as knowledge. In turn, the lack of this hegemonic knowledge tendentially locks the marginalized in a state of powerlessness.

Historically speaking, the monopoly of the elites on quality education and the ideological justification of restricted access to education reflect a perplexing continuity from colonial into post-colonial times. Further, a survey of the historical trajectory of modern public education reveals a close association between evolving structures of education on the one hand and the needs of a *segmented* labour market on the other. Various measures of the late colonial state, and subsequently, of the post-colonial state, have bred a close connection between education and the segmented labour market whereby the structure of the dual mode of school education[6] and the rigidities of admission procedures in the (purely) academic stream of higher education have largely excluded the majority of poorer youth from quality higher education in general, and compartmentalized such youth into vocational education in particular. Rarely able to cross over to full-time academic or university education, youth from the ranks of the urban and rural poor, consequently, remain locked within particular kinds of (lower segment) jobs. Thus, a long-standing failure to equalize educational access has essentially allowed higher education to render 'hidden services' to the old order by 'concealing social selection under the guise of technical selection and legitimating the reproduction of the [old] social hierarchies by transmuting them into academic hierarchies.'[7]

Accordingly, if we are to transcend the mere reification of the university as a harbinger of democratization and the consequent idolization of such institutions as enclaves of excellence, we need to inject a greater measure of materiality into the very idea of a university. The materiality on which the edifice of university education rests entails a segmented educational structure coalescing and reproducing the segmented job market. Correspondingly, a truly inclusive and radical envisioning of the university would naturally mean forging a more organic link with the educational needs and aspirations of the millions of less privileged youths standing on the margins, if not outside the very high walls of existing universities. Such restructuring, which expands access to the marginalized, serves to make them part and partners of what knowledge does to them as well as to larger society. Further, enhanced access to quality university education is not just about the upward mobility gained but also about the critical knowledge(s) facilitated.

However, four-fifths of India's youth in the age bracket of eighteen to twenty-three years do not enter the ambit of formal university education; translating into a monopoly over higher education by elite sections of society. An entry-level barrier or iron ceiling to university education clearly exists as a very limited number of underprivileged youth after their senior secondary schooling moves into higher education; in particular, regular-mode university education. The exclusion includes a vast number of young women who, unable to cross the iron ceiling upholstered by competitive entrance tests, high cut-offs, etc., are compelled to leave education altogether so as to become full-time unpaid labour for their households. Even the few students from the ranks of the urban and rural poor who have been trickling into public-funded universities have seen high drop-out rates due to financial difficulties and the lack of institutional support like remedial classes. With this, their chances to move into higher-rung jobs are obliterated.

Inequity in access to quality education and the consequent obstacles to attaining better-paying jobs is a process that has triggered penchant criticism and resistance. At important conjunctures, the use of education to reproduce wider inequality has been vocally criticized by many progressive social forces. We have, for example, powerful critiques offered by leaders of the non-Brahmin movement in the nineteenth century, such as Jotirao Phule. In the introduction to the English edition of his work, *Gulamgiri*, Phule highlighted the skewed inverse relationship between human labour performed and access to education when he argued that the colonial taxation system channelized resources away from the labouring masses towards the wealthy elites in the form of education. Armed with such education, the elites easily hegemonized government jobs. However, despite such trenchant criticism and the popular yearning for equality exemplified by lower-caste movements and anti-feudal struggles, the post-colonial state took more than 60 years to consecrate the right to education as a fundamental right. The propensity for this delay in a post-Constitution era is, in fact, traceable to the founding moment of the independent nation-state. Notably, during the framing of the Constitution, the right to education as a fundamental right was shifted in the process of Constituent Assembly debates from a 'justiciable right' to a 'non-justiciable right' in the final text of the Constitution (Mondal 2022).

In real terms, the Indian state since itsformative years has nurtured a graded system of education which relegates the toiling masses to the margins of quality education right from the level of schooling. As a result, class, caste, community, gender, family and regional-level disadvantages continue to be inadequately addressed; more so with the provisioning of poor-quality education to those already struggling with inherited poverty and inequalities. Such provisioning of education does not guarantee that the poor will be able to change their circumstances in life.

The Republic and Public Education: Promissory Estoppel

On the eve of Independence, the country's literacy level was an abysmal 15 per cent. At the time, 84 per cent of boys and 92.1 per cent of girls had no schooling (Kaur 2008). These realities demanded unwavering state investment and intervention at *all* levels of education. The immediate years after Independence were significant in terms of the tenuous process of socio-economic transformations and skewed trajectories of development that unfolded and were closely linked to certain constitutional provisions being adopted. These developments were also closely aligned with the post-colonial state's economic policy, which drew heavily on the Bombay Plan (1944–45). The Plan was tabled by leading Indian capitalists, who sup-ported – for an interim period – the idea of a substantially interventionist state and an economy with a sizeable public sector. This was part of their bid to strengthen the indigenous industries that they owned and could not immediately face foreign competition in the domestic market. Contrary to the socialist rhetoric in circulation in the early decades post-Independence, India's political elite pushed through a model of economic planning and the expansion of the public sector that did not hinder but rather facilitated the capitalist model of development. Private investment and involvement in the social sector persisted.

Trends in School Education

Against this backdrop, the private sector in education expectedly remained intact and flourished. The idea of the common school system was repeatedly sidestepped, even as it surfaced in certain policy documents like the Report of the Education Commission (1964–66) [better known as the Kothari Commission] and the National Policy on Education, 1968 (Government of India [GoI] 1968). The commitment towards expansive social uplift of the marginalized sections of the Indian population through state-backed education appeared accommodative of the status quo, given the Constituent Assembly's decision to place free primary education in the Directive Principles of State Policy, that is, the non-justiciable section of the Indian Constitution. The concerned Article 45 of the Constitution stipu-lated a period of ten years within which the state was to provide education to all children up to the age of fourteen years. However, formal legisla-tion, the Right to Education Act (RTE) (2009), materialized only with the passing of the 86th Constitutional Amendment in 2002, which made the right to education a Fundamental Right by inserting Article 21-A in the

Constitution. The implications of such a measure within a broader context of steady withdrawal of the state from public provisioning of school education is an issue I will return to.

The accommodation with inherited circumstances was further apparent in the new Constitution's reproduction of the overall administrative framework. Education continued to be the prime responsibility of the state governments, while the union (central) government continued to assume responsibility for the coordination of educational facilities and the maintenance of appropriate standards in higher education, research and scientific and technical education. Within such a federal structure, pre-primary and primary schooling, by and large, took a backseat. With access to fewer revenue sources than the central government, state governments were less likely to roll out an expansive network of government schools that synced with the dismal literacy levels and actual needs of the people; more so in the case of less affluent/poorer states.

Within the federal structure that placed the subject of education in the state list, the central government on the one hand minimized its intervention, more specifically with respect to expanding primary education. Paradoxically, on the other hand, it actively intervened through the constitution of education commissions and the five-year planning model[8] to draw greater attention to and channelize a lion's share of funds towards higher education. The formative years, for example, saw the constitution of two important commissions that focused on higher and secondary education, that is, the University Education Commission (1948–49) [also known as the Radhakrishnan Commission on Higher Education] which tabled recommendations on the reorganization of courses, techniques of evaluation, media of instruction, student services and the recruitment of teachers; and the Secondary Education Commission (1952–53)[better known as the Mudaliar Commission] which focused mainly on secondary and teacher education.

The 1960s were characterized by a visible challenge to the authority of the ruling elites[9] at the centre. To a significant extent, this development took off with the country's escalated food crisis from the late 1950s into the 1960s, and the rise of a regional bourgeoisie[10] which fuelled the growth of regional parties and electoral alliances that came to pose a threat to the ruling national party, the Congress. In the case of food shortages, the undermining of the authority of India's ruling elites combined with the growth of American dominance and arm-twisting through its PL-480 programme, as well as the entry of multinational capital due to the massive expansion of imports of chemical fertilizers and pesticides necessitated by genetically modified crop production. As land hunger persisted in large parts of the country due to a chequered history of land reforms, and the indebtedness of small peasants intensified under the new circumstances unleashed by genetically modified crop production, radical peasant and Adivasi movements surfaced as a major challenge to the projected claims of development under economic planning. In many ways, these social movements laid bare the poor condition of the social sector and the limited reach of the state's socio-economic 'reforms'. Against this backdrop, there emerged the scope for a revisitation of the lacunae in the country's education policy, that is, the preoccupation of the planning technocracy with higher education in its bid to create a self-reliant industrial economy and an indigenous base in modern fields of knowledge. The need for a comprehensive education policy that addressed the disbalance between school and higher education, thus, came to be recognized. The Kothari Commission (1964–66) was constituted to look into *all* aspects and levels of education, and some of its recommendations were drawn on to formulate the National Education Policy of 1968.

School education correspondingly began to expand in the 1960s, with the most spectacular growth being witnessed in the 1970s. Importantly, the 1970s marked another crucial conjuncture of contestations over state-supported capitalism in the country. These contestations stemmed from the assertions of the marginalized sections as well as from the conflicts *within* the Indian capitalist class. Desperate to remain politically relevant, keen to be seen as curbing monopolies and the excesses of Indian business houses and compelled to address the slow-down of economic growth since the mid-1960s, the Congress regime at the centre responded with a slew of radical measures. These included the taking over of the privy purses of Indian princes and the nationalization of crucial sectors like banking, coal production, steel, cotton textiles, insurance and so on. What followed in the education sector was the 42nd Constitutional Amendment, introduced in 1976. Consequent to this, education was shifted from the state list to the Concurrent list – a manoeuvre which enabled the central government to steadily intervene in and determine education policy at the state level.

Nevertheless, the 1970s witnessed the continued redirecting of resources away from the common school system and a steady growth in informal education for first-generation learners from labouring backgrounds. In particular, it was under the Janta government at the Centre (1977–79) that the focus of the education policy framework shifted sharply towards adult literacy programmes and non-formal education. These policy thrusts resonated with the 'structural adjustment programmes' promoted by powerful financial and regulatory agencies like the World Bank, International Monetary Fund (IMF), etc., that were dictating the terms of further integration of India's economy into the capitalist world economy (Sadgopal 2013).

These agencies had begun aggressively promoting adult literacy missions and pilot projects on informal modes of imparting basic literacy to the poor.

By the 1980s there was a slowing down in the expansion of government schools. Further, the model of the common school system was buried by the 1986 National Education Policy (GoI 1986). To elaborate, the policy created a layer of elite government-funded schools, distinct from the above neighbourhood government school. These were the central schools (Kendriya Vidyalayas) in urban areas and the Navodaya Vidyalayas in rural areas. This apart, the policy created, below the neighbourhood government school, a layer of poor quality non-formal centres for inculcating literacy among child labourers and underprivileged girls mostly from discriminated caste groups. This hierarchical structure was based on the crowding of resources within elite government schools while the ordinary government schools were steadily starved of funds. As a consequence, the infrastructure and teaching–learning standards of the average government school declined rapidly.

Following close on the heels of the National Education Policy 1986 (ibid.) was the comprehensive 'reform' package that was imposed on India in the early 1990s by agencies like the World Bank and IMF. Essentially, the reforms tabled and incrementally implemented were geared towards reduced per capita allocation of funds for health, education and state subsidies. Such structural adjustment rapidly materialized in India as it was made the prerequisite for further loans from these agencies. From the 1990s onwards, enhanced deregulation and promotion of autonomous educational institutions have become the buzzwords in policy framing.

The overall withdrawal of the state from the public provisioning of education was accompanied by the worsening of state finances, a reduced quantum of funds released by the centre to states and curtailments on increasing public expenditure, as imposed by laws like the Fiscal Responsibility and Budget Management Act. Expectedly, such restructuring of the budget allocation for the social sector provided a substantive impetus to the private sector in school and higher education.

The push for the private sector in school education was in fact the first priority of transnational advocacy networks and their pro-market organizations within the country. Private players[11] came to reap the benefits of the country's growing demand for education through poorly equipped, low-cost private schools offering English medium and catering to low-income groups, as well as through premium private schools with exorbitant fee structures whose consumers were largely the upward mobile middle class.

A policy paradigm anchored on the logic of *dual* education, as well as enhanced privatization of education, has only worked towards widespread non-compliance with the norms of the RTE. As per official reports available before the Covid-19 pandemic-cum-lockdowns, only 25.5 per cent of elementary schools were compliant with the 10 RTE indicators (GoI 2020b). Furthermore, measures implemented by directorates of education (DoE) in several states continue to dilute the key provisions of the RTE Act. Even in a state like Delhi where the local government's populist propaganda claims that the government school system has been resurrected, close to 100 neighbourhood government schools have either been closed or merged since April 2022, as per the directives from the DoE, Government of Delhi. The measure comes in the wake of the implementation of the National Education Policy 2020 (NEP 2020), which justifies the withdrawal of the state from the education sector and promotes the spread of non-formal education through dictums like 'multiple pathways of learning' (GoI 2020a).

In real terms, the current policy thrust of 'multiple pathways of learning' seeks to push the poor more and more into the clutches of informal education like distance learning. To elucidate, for some years now, changes in the criterion for admission to classes 10 to 12 in Delhi's government schools have resulted in the flushing out of so-called under-performing students; compelling their families to enrol them in the distance learning mode under the National Institute of Open Schooling (NIOS). These drop-out figures can be expected to grow with the closure and merging of government schools, given the rapid implementation of the provisions of the NEP 2020 which seek to equate formal and non-formal modes of teaching-learning. Notably, a development like this represents not so much a matter of non-compliance, but rather the fallout of the prized RTE policy itself. The RTE legislation erroneously restricts access to free, compulsory education only up to the upper primary level, relegating to the margins the issue of access to secondary education. Moreover, the RTE policy keeps intact the private school system by merely mandating private schools to reserve 25 per cent of seats for the economically weak sections. It is then important to recognize that by its very nature, RTE has been allowing ample room for governments to field exclusionary measures and privatization with relative ease.

Trends in Higher Education

Eventually, the same matrix of transnational advocacy networks and their pro-market lobbies within India have increasingly pushed for higher levels of privatization and commercialization of higher education. Correspondingly, on the one hand, there has been a proliferation of B-grade private colleges and training institutes that target under-privileged youth from government or low-cost private schools, who lack the marks to apply to the coveted public-funded universities due to the poor quality of schooling. On the other hand, we have seen growth in top-ranking private/autonomous colleges and universities, which cater to the higher-income groups. Overall, such privatization has reproduced sharp inequalities along class lines as affluent families send their children to premium private schools that equip them to compete more successfully in the intensely competitive admission processes of top-ranking public-funded Indian universities. If unable to secure a seat in the public-funded universities of their choice, the elite private schooling and superior financial status still allow such youth to enter into programmes of their choice in prestigious private universities, including universities abroad.

Privatization of higher education has been a prevailing phenomenon since the formative years post-Independence, with the most spectacular growth in the number of private colleges and universities being reported in the fields of engineering, medicine, management and information and communications technology (ICT) (S. Basu 2012).The overall growth of private institutions in higher education has been traced to compromised enforcement of regulatory standards for this sector.

In addition to private colleges and universities, trajectories of privatization have unfolded even within public-funded higher educational institutions, wherein the market principles of cost recovery gradually made their way from the 1970s and 1980s with the introduction of self-financed courses (Varghese 2012). Current times have seen a meteoric rise in self-financed courses, which are mostly taught by contractual teachers whose salary costs are directly linked to the fee structure imposed on enrolling students. This apart, we have seen the emergence of several other forms of financial privatization in public-funded institutions. These include the aggressive promotion of institutional tie-ups between public-funded colleges/universities and industry that are now increasingly being used as parameters for claiming higher rankings; the linking of an educational institution's high ranking with its bid for autonomy or delinking from a public-funded university; and the gradual replacement of the system of governmental grants with loans that are to be accessed from a new crop of financial agencies.

Not only have private colleges and universities of dubious quality proliferated (Sudarshan and Subramanian 2012) but public–private partnerships (PPPs) in public-funded institutions, that is industry and higher education institutional tie-ups, have also been steadily increasing. The latter trend has been justified on the grounds that the state cannot meet the growing demands for resources from public-funded institutions and that such linkages expand access, improve quality, promote efficiency and facilitate greater employability. Each of these projections has been amply questioned by a rich body of scholarship which reveals the inability of PPPs to fulfil their objectives mostly due to the lack of sync between the two very disparate systems (Chattopadhyay 2012; Tilak 2014).

It has been observed that the PPP model generally tends to transform public universities and colleges into institutions which are preoccupied with revenue-generating ventures and cost-recovery to the extent that they nurture detrimental changes. These changes include a disbalanced expansion of courses and research in fields which are seen to be more market-oriented; the undermining of long-standing practices that ensure social justice or a more inclusive intake of students/researchers; and drastic modifications in hiring practices that nurture a new hierarchy of differentially placed faculty whose service conditions and pay are shrouded in opacity. In actual terms, PPPs in higher education have facilitated the transfer of crucial resources of public institutions to private players. Typically, the private party gains access to a public institution's primely located land, well-established infrastructure (laboratories, libraries, playgrounds, classrooms, auditoriums, etc.), brand name, reputed faculty, research scholars and so on. In turn, it uses these resources to fund research of specific interest to it and for the benefit of its own profit motives. The private player also uses the public institution's resources to launch courses – at subsidized establishment costs – which eventually provide the private player easier access to a workforce qualified in desired skills.

The influence of the private sector on India's higher education has been keenly felt even in terms of the consistent endeavours of industry and pro-market lobbies to get the educational bureaucracy to restructure the curriculum framework of public-funded universities. Evidently, in the past three decades, eager to earn profits through investment in the high-demand education sector, the major corporates of India and the world have reached a consensus on a required roadmap for educational 'reforms'. The inclusion of education in the General Agreement on Trade in Services (GATS) indicates just how seriously the ruling elites of different countries are coordinating with each other to further the scope of profitable private investment in the education sector. Moreover, in the highly globalized capitalist world, the demands of the global labour market have triggered the need for a homogeneous education and uniform educational degrees across countries (John 2013). Importantly, then, a four-year undergraduate programme with multiple exit options, 'multidisciplinary' undergraduate education, cluster innovation centres, knowledge hubs, semesterization, a growing emphasis on vocational education, etc., represent models that now exist across the world.

In addition to the needs of the global labour market, the current context is characterized by the domestic manufacturing and service sectors' rapidly changing organizational practices, which are geared towards greater flexibility and multi-tasking. The key requirement of the manufacturing and service sectors are, namely, workforces that can perform different tasks. This has fuelled the aggressive lobbying for more and more skill-based education that helps reduce the training costs of the industry-corporate combine.

Against the aforementioned backdrop to attain 'global standards' and meet the new workforce requirements of employers' lobbies, the curriculum restructuring process in central universities has been continuous, and in fact, relatively disruptive of sound academic functioning. Prime metropolitan public universities like Delhi University have, for example, been undergoing regular curriculum revision for the past decade, with each new curriculum framework lasting not more than two to four years before the next wave of revisions makes its way.[12] With regard to curriculum restructuring, the supporting discourse within official policy circles has gained huge ground with the implementation of the NEP 2020. Typically, the current policy paradigm emphasizes the four-year undergraduate programme based on the multiple entry-exit system and the need for premium public universities to sync their syllabi with the prevailing market needs so as to impart more practical learning, to facilitate (unpaid) internships and apprenticeship by enrolled students, etc.

Online Education

It is precisely in this flow of things that the pandemic-induced lockdown period was (mis)used to launch another of the key provisions of the NEP 2020, that is, online learning. Indeed, the Ministry of Human Resources Development (MHRD), University Grants Commission (UGC), and various university administrations have used the period of the pandemic-cum lockdowns to impose online learning as an integral component of university education. The most recent regulations of the UGC post the introduction of NEP 2020 have directed central universities to adopt the 'blended' mode of education which entails offering up to 40 per cent of the syllabi of courses in the online mode. Factoring in provisions like inter-institutional credits transfer under the system of the Academic Bank of Credits announced by the UGC, it is expected that high-ranking public universities will be increasingly pushed into offering a much higher percentage of their course curriculums in the online mode. This is expected given that off-campus students from across the country would seek to collect credits from educational institutions with a brand name, especially in order to make up for the poorer quality education offered by the institutions where they are actually enrolled. Overall, as discussed in some of the essays of this volume, the promotion of online education has several fallouts, including hidden costs for the learner, and is ultimately a development that benefits the private sector in substantial ways rather than one which enhances the public provisioning of higher education.

In recent years, the shortage of quality public-funded educational institutions has translated into enhanced business for ed-tech companies. Touted as an online revolution in education, the courses offered by ed-tech companies have only added to the existing educational disparities along the lines of the digital divide between urban and rural India and the digital divide across class, caste and gender axes (Kalidasan and Goyal 2021). Using predatory marketing strategies, these companies have been targeting mostly middle-class urban households that are in constant search for training/exposure which equips their children for competitive examinations and entrances to professional courses.

Nonetheless, in the expanding market for education, even some segments of lower-income households in tier-one and tier-two cities are drawn towards the online courses offered by such companies in a desperate bid to make up for the poor quality of education imparted in government schools. The boom in the business of ed-tech companies is, thus, phenomenal. As highlighted by the member of Parliament Karti Chidambaram in his Lok Sabha address, the net worth of some ed-tech companies is even higher than the country's entire education budget.[13] The regulation of the quality of the online courses offered by these companies is, of course, conspicuous by its very absence. Such lack of regulation is expected, given the persistent endeavour of the state to absolve its responsibility of meeting the rising demand for the expansion of educational facilities and enhancement of quality.

Clearly, rather than paving the way for expansive and equitable school and higher education that challenge inherited inequalities, successive regimes post-Independence have consciously restrained the rate of growth of public-funded educational institutions. As a result, there exists a widening gap between the constrained supply and the burgeoning demand for quality public-funded education. Justifying the lacunae, policy discourses have continually evolved, more so from the late 1980s, wherein the idea of common schooling was altogether pushed out from the policy frame. The current policy framework declares as the 'new normal', the clustering and closing down of public educational institutions and the corresponding expansion of informal modes of education like online education, distance learning, etc. The biggest beneficiary of this unfortunate development has been the profit-driven private sector. In reality, the unfolding of this skewed process has reduced education in India largely to the role of reproducing inequalities.

A Theatre of Dialogue: Essays in this Volume

Almost all the contributions in the current volume engage closely with substantive realities and contextualize policy frameworks, in particular, the NEP 2020, whilst addressing other concerns. A special reference thus exists with respect to the discrimination and inequity that is evident along several axes. Examining the case of Muslims of the Lakshadweep Islands who constitute a Scheduled Tribe, L.R.S. Lakshmi traces an interesting exception to the generalized trajectory of educational backwardness of Muslims in post-colonial India. As a case study, her work draws ample attention to the benefits of consistent state investment in educational uplift through quality government schools and affirmative action at the level of university education. Interestingly, she highlights that given the status of the islands as a union territory, the Muslims of the Lakshadweep Islands gained from the positive interventions made by the central government, as well as from the proximity of the region to the state of Kerala, which has been reported as the most literate state of the country.

The chapter by Anthony Joseph is another useful case study. It highlights the fault lines in teacher education and the potential for their exacerbation under the NEP 2020, which purportedly seeks to transform the teaching-learning process and build a 'new' India as a 'knowledge society'. This chapter builds on the concept of the reflexive teacher educator, who is the key to the construction of knowledge and education that is holistic, creative and critical. Joseph argues that as 'academic heretics' who are sensitive to social contexts, marginalization and the tyranny of orthodoxy and tradition, teacher educators are up against a huge challenge; namely, the burgeoning ethos of economism masquerading as nation-building. Engaging critically with the ethos resonating from the NEP 2020 policy document, the chapter indicates the breeding of a process that replaces the reflexive teacher-educator with a technocratic instructor.

Kumkum Roy's chapter offers a succinct critical overview of the monolithic reading of 'Indian knowledge' that the NEP 2020 promotes, and which, she argues, takes us further away from an inclusive envisioning of education in India. She questions the selective privileging of the Sanskrit knowledge system and its assumed universal and undying appeal. She does so on the basis of the history of divergent and conflictual knowledge traditions that co-existed in the Indian subcontinent, as well as on the basis of the specificities of present-day challenges. Roy also draws attention to the inherent contradictions between democratic Constitutional values, and concepts like the hierarchical 'Vishwa Guru' model of teacher-pupil relations that the policy framework valorizes. Read against the contemporaneous context of growing inequalities and political differences, Roy argues that the policy reflects an uncanny de-centring of key constitutional values like justice, liberty, equality and fraternity, and the corresponding prioritization of certain 'traditional' values. The chapter aptly highlights the effacing of vibrant interactions between co-existing civilizations and those of the Indian subcontinent in the making of knowledge systems, as well as the eclipsing of medieval educational institutions and knowledge creation (through contestation) by non-literate groups.

The chapter by Madhu Prasad offers an important survey on the evolution of modern learning and its interface with widespread inequalities, oppression and exclusion. The chapter highlights that neglecting the civilizational evolution of the country, NEP 2020 reflects a perspective obsessed with the supposed purity of an almost mythical 'ancient' past. More specifically, Madhu Prasad asserts that a historical survey is crucial, considering the silences in the NEP 2020 regarding the impact of the caste system on the 'Indian ethos', the repercussions of colonial rule on educational initiatives, as well as the role of the anti-colonial struggle in envisaging democratic education for all and an egalitarian social transformation of the country. According to Madhu Prasad, the aspirations for egalitarian social transformation found expression in an earlier education policy, but these met with failure due to the resistance offered by the landlord-bourgeois ruling elites. Further, she argues that NEP 2020 reveals itself as a market-oriented education policy that is the carrier of historically entrenched exclusions and contemporary neoliberal inequalities. It betrays the promise of the egalitarian alternative, and in this way, departs from the constitutional guarantee of the right to education as a fundamental right.

The chapter by Mohd. Bilal is an insightful overview of the colonial and post-colonial trajectories of educational inequalities that lays bare the blindspots – in particular, the elitist class bias – within the reformist and nationalist envisionings of modern education. The exposition of the subversion of quality mass education by several anti-caste reformers themselves is extremely revealing. The longue durée of exclusion and inequality in education is highlighted to reveal the continuities between educational schemes of the colonial and post-colonial periods and to assert that the educational crisis, which is usually associated with the current context of heightened privatization, has been a long-standing one. Talking in terms of educational apartheid that has long plagued the labouring masses, the chapter questions the overt emphasis on neoliberal policies to which the commodification of education is attributed. Hence, Mohd. Bilal aptly points to the fact that the education system in India has evolved hierarchically even prior to the so-called neoliberal phase, and has been contributing to the reproduction of labour for a deeply segmented job market.

Jyoti Raina's chapter is a focused study of policy shifts and their repercussion on equitable elementary school education in the post-colonial era. It emphasizes that in contrast to the constitutional policy wisdom with which educational development began, school education has unfortunately turned into a category of social division. Raina works with three distinct phases when tracing policy shifts that accentuated differentiation and exacerbated structural exclusion in the school education system. She identifies the phase from 1947 to the mid-1980s, which according to her, was characterized by a policy framework anchored on egalitarianism and a substantial role of the state in establishing school education as a public good. The second phase is associated with the launch of the NEP 1986 and into the period of rapid liberalization of the economy. This phase features the retreat of the state, the increased presence of non-state actors, incremental growth in private schools, and the 'neoliberalization' of education. The chapter highlights the period since 2016 as marking a distinct third phase wherein graded schooling hierarchies have been normalized, the neoliberalization of education has intensified, and the neoliberal logic, in general, has gained much ground.

An extremely rich overview of low-cost schooling for the poor from the early 2000s is provided in Geetha Nambissan's chapter. Nambissan situates low-cost schooling within the larger context of rising aspirations of the poor for good quality education for their children and the abdication of the state in this regard. Pertinently, the chapter highlights that while the state's neglect of public-funded education is one of the reasons for the decline of government schools, the disillusionment of the poor with government schooling is also attributable to the failure of teacher education programmes to equip teachers with a critical perspective and an understanding of pedagogies that address poverty and social disadvantage within a rights and social justice framework.

Of course, low-cost schooling cannot fill the vacuum in any meaningful way because the deskilled teacher and narrow curriculum are key elements in its standardized profit-inclined business model. Importantly, Nambissan traces how the discourse on market-oriented solutions to the educational problems of the poor has not only redefined education for the poor but are constantly shaping 'reforms' in government schooling as well. A separate section on the discourse and endeavours that have surfaced since the Covid-19 pandemic disrupted the direct teaching mode, is particularly revealing. Nambissan rightly questions the technology and digitization-driven forms of low-cost education that are being peddled since the pandemic set in. She does so on the grounds of the digital divide that shapes the educational experiences of the poor, and on the basis that technology-driven low-cost education amounts to highly individualized and person-alized learning packages which simply enhance the business of ed-tech companies, and corporate and venture philanthropic organizations.

The chapters by Saumen Chattopadhyay, Rohan D'Souza and Debaditya Bhattacharya are a lucid, critical engagement with what NEP 2020 entails when it comes to the higher education sector. Chattopadhyay focuses on provisions of NEP 2020 that seek to rejuvenate the Indian higher education system by overhauling the entire structure of regulatory interven-tion, namely, by granting autonomy to the students, teachers and universi-ties. Pointing to the neoliberal thrust of the NEP's provisions that appear to coexist with its supposed claims for increased public funding, Chattopadhyay argues that there is an undeniable push towards greater private participation and the construction of a quasi-market for higher education which fosters competitiveness within the higher education system. This is a development that actually restricts the scope for autonomy for both teachers and insti-tutions, as envisaged by the NEP. Delineating the present context within which higher education restructuring is being pursued, the chapter shows why the neoliberal form of governance reform need not necessarily guaran-tee quality unless faculty are empowered to realize their goals. In this regard, Chattopadhyay asserts that if public funding is not adequately augmented, the proposed fostering of competition among higher educational institutions (HEIs) will prove unfair. In the absence of a level playing field, many HEIs will struggle to compete and survive under the new system of accreditation.

Debaditya Bhattacharya's chapter delves into the various facets of the now prominent discourse that projects the public university as a fail-ing project. As per the NEP 2020 and related policy directives issued by the current regime, the one-step reform or 'antidote' for the supposedly crisis-ridden public university system is mass online transitioning of the teaching-learning process. Arguing that the transition entails the introduc-tion of a private equity model within higher education, Bhattacharya points to the dangerous possibility of huge quantums of academic and non-aca-demic labour being designated as unwanted surplus. Furthermore, the push towards online education is also explained in the context of fast-retreating protections of the state and ruthless competition in a free market wherein waged labour in the private sector is desperately trying to boost its produc-tivity through part-time stints at skill upgradation. Bhattacharya projects that because many of the new entrants into college education – aspiring to achieve the status of knowledge workers from being merely skilled wage labour – will have to balance work commitments alongside their academic pursuits, there will be a continuous demand for online courses from reputed universities at minimal costs.

While discussing the compromising of social justice by NEP 2020, Bhattacharya highlights the sinister silence of the new policy framework on the question of caste-based reservation mandated by the Constitution. He argues that a casteist bias informs the policy, considering the repeated references to 'merit-appointments and career progression', concerns about 'quality and engagement of faculty' and talk of constituting statutory bodies with 'persons having high expertise'. Another parameter by which the NEP 2020 envisions higher education is the overt emphasis on a multidisciplinary curriculum, which conveniently effaces, of course, the actual instances of interdisciplinary social science practice within public universities. Bhattacharya rightly asserts that skilling in the multidisciplinary framework reproduces the conditions for the survival of a recessionary economy, that is, an order of multi-tasking labour which flourishes on cheap, semi-skilled, informal job contracts.

Rohan D'Souza's chapter argues that the higher education story of recent years alerts us to the emergence of a larger game plan for university education. He identifies that a crucial component of this game plan is the dismantling of the public university system, and its replacement by the private university ecosystem. This agenda has been set in motion not only through a spate of regulations and via the corporate university model most recently spelt out in the NEP 2020, but even more aggressively through violence. To this effect, the chapter offers a close examination of ideological and physical attacks on Jawaharlal Nehru University, a premium public university harbouring a vibrant political culture. The larger point being made through this particular example is the scope provided by public universities – in contrast to private universities – for radical intellectual and political possibilities that challenge the undermining of social justice in the country; in particular, the prevalence of caste violence. D'Souza thereby asserts that by eroding the public university's capacity to produce (critical) political citizenship, the current regime is apparently striving to radically reconfigure the scope and mission of higher education.

Elaborating on the spurt in online education in the context of the Covid-19 pandemic and lockdowns, D'Souza also discusses the crystallizing of the notion of the 'platform university', that is, a new unity between computer hardware, software and education theory. Going beyond the usual arguments on digital infrastructure entering the domain of the teaching-learning process in significant ways, D'Souza highlights a more damning impact of online education, which is the creation of the 'student-user'. Herein, the chapter argues that university students, by default, are transitioning into, both, virtual learners and a 'source of raw material' for the harvesting of metadata.

The present author's chapter asserts that the key thrusts of NEP 2020 reveal their sharp contradiction with the aspirations for quality education that the vast majority of youth harbours. Arguing that the fulfilment of such aspirations depends on unfettered access to public-funded education, the chapter offers a close reading of the NEP 2020 against the backdrop of existing educational inequalities and the hierarchical, segmented education structure; thereby indicating the hollowness of the policy framework's repetitive rhetoric on 'increased access, equity, and inclusion'. To overcome the farcical repetition of inherited educational inequalities that confront the socially and economically marginalized sections of society, the overview presented emphasizes the importance of the common school system, equal allocation of resources to bridge the pre-existing disparity among central and regional universities, as well as the necessity of creating more public-funded universities with *equitable* funding to facilitate genuine massification of higher education through the formal or regular mode of education.

As a body of work, this volume recognizes the limitation of a book to call for a contemporary Mahabharata which seeks justice for Ekalavyas. However, it is an important endeavour to understand the need for drastic transformations. As an honest testimony of its times, this collection of essays will hopefully become an archive for future generations, and also act as a clarification for those seeking to remake present times.

Notes

[1] 'Untouchables' were identified as the 'Depressed Classes' in several colonial records.

[2] The Government of India's reluctance to abolish school fees led to the introduction of a scale of standard-linked school fees, with students being compelled to pay more fees for each class they progressed to. Several government officials tended to fight the clause of *free* primary education on the grounds that it would reduce the moral value of such an education. For this official opinion, see Government of India, Selections from the Records, Department of Education, Serial 1, no. 448, 1911, Calcutta, pp. 330–50. Also see G.O. 271, dated 21 May 1910, Madras Education Department Proceedings, 1910, TNSA and G.O. 178, Madras Education Department Proceedings, 1916, p. 6.

[3] In 1921–22, there were a total of only 276 technical and industrial schools out of which 199 were for men and 77 for women. Of these 57 were government schools, 37 were managed by boards and 182 were under private management, all but 20 of them receiving aid from public funds. See Report on Vocational Training in Primary and Secondary Schools.

[4] The Bombay Government in 1913, for example, constituted a committee on factory education comprising prominent mill owners. The government accepted the recommendation of the committee. We also find evidence of the fact that the Bombay Mill Owners Association (BMOA) was itself in favour of factory education. See the Report of the Bombay Mill Owners Association for the Period Ending on 31 October 1912.

[5] The leather factory Cooper, Allen and Co., for example, opened a factory school in

Cawnpore in 1908. Similarly, a school was opened in 1904 for the sons of workers and for workers belonging to two mills owned by Binny and Co. in Madras. In this school, the children were taught the basic skills of reading, writing, arithmetic, as well as technical skills to make them 'efficient' mill-hands.

[6] Dual school education refers to the prevalence of both government and private schools.

[7] Bourdieu and Passerson (1977) quoted in Deshpande (2013), p. 1.

[8] According to some assessments, the increased allocation of resources to higher education under the five-year plans is most evident in the first three plans. Others trace this trend up to the Sixth Five Year Plan (Tilak 1987).

[9] The term 'ruling elites' here refers to the political and economic dominant segments at the all-India level. This would mean the Congress-led governments and the national bourgeoisie. The latter reaped the lion share of benefits under Congress rule at the centre and state levels in the initial decades post-Independence.

[10] For an elucidation of the rise of a regional bourgeoisie in post-colonial India and its relation to revitalized regionalism, see Baru (2000).

[11] While a crop of private schools had long been existence, the 1990s onwards saw the entry of many new private players in this sector.

[12] In Delhi University, curriculum frameworks have been under constant revision since 2010–11 when the university transitioned into the semester mode. Thereafter, the university launched a pilot initiative by introducing a four-year undergraduate programme in 2013–14, which was subsequently withdrawn a year later. In 2015, the UGC imposed the Choice-based Credit System (CBCS) and a new curriculum on all central universities. Under the CBCS, these universities were allowed only 30 per cent variation in the curriculums that they framed. Again in 2019, Delhi University introduced curriculum revision as part of its compliance with the UGC's Learning Outcomes-based Curriculum Framework (LOCF). Under the NEP 2020, the university launched the four-year undergraduate programme for which massive curriculum revision has been introduced in 2021–22. In the supposed bid to sync with policy-level directives on multidisciplinary education and practical learning, the university has floated new skill enhancement courses. While the number of skill enhancement courses to be taught has increased in the first two years of the undergraduate programme, the weightage and content of the disciplines-specific core courses have been reduced. This points to the dilution of the academic content of the university's otherwise rich undergraduate curriculum.

[13] 'Sivaganga MP Karti Chidambaram Urges Centre To Monitor Companies Providing Online Courses', *Indian Express News Service*, 14 December 2021, available at https://indianexpress.com/article/cities/chennai/sivaganga-mp-karti-chidambaram-urges-centre-to-monitor-companies-providing-online-courses-7672126/, accessed on 9 November 2022.

References

Primary Sources: Reports
Report of the Bombay Mill Owners Association for the Period Ending on 31 October 1912, Bombay: Times Press, 1913.
Interim Report of the Indian Statutory Commission: Review of Growth of Education in British India by the Auxiliary Committee Appointed by the Commission, Calcutta: Central Publication Branch, September 1929.
Report on Vocational Training in Primary and Secondary Schools and Consequent Reorganization, Bombay, Bombay: Government Central Press, 1938.

Secondary Sources

Acharya, P. (1978), 'Indigenous Vernacular Education in Pre-British Era: Traditions and Problems', *Economic and Political Weekly*, vol. 13, no. 48.

——— (1996), 'Indigenous Educations and Brahminical Hegemony in Bengal', in N. Crook, ed., *The Transmission of Knowledge in South Asia: Essays on Education, Religion, History and Politics*, Delhi: Oxford University Press.

Baru, S. (2000), 'Economic Policy and the Development of Capitalism in India: The Role of Regional Capitalists and Political Parties', in F. Frankel, Z. Hasan, R. Bhargava and B. Arora, eds, *Transforming India: Social and Political Dynamics of Democracy*, New Delhi: Oxford University Press.

Basu, A. (1971), 'Indian Primary Education, 1900–1920', *Indian Economic and Social History Review (IESHR)*, vol. 8, no. 3, July.

Basu, S. (2012), 'Private Sector in Education: An Overview', in *India Infrastructure Report: Role of Private Sector*, New Delhi and London: IDFC Foundation and Routledge.

Bhattacharya, S., J. Bara and C.R. Yagati, eds (2001), *Development of Women's Education in India: A Collection of Documents (From 1850 to 1920)*, New Delhi: Kanishka.

Carnoy, M. (1974), *Education as Cultural Imperialism*, London: Longman Inc.

Bourdieu, P. and Jean-Claude Passerson (1977), *Reproduction in Education, Society and Culture*, London: Sage.

Chattopadhyay, S. (2012), 'The Emerging Market for Higher Education: Rationalizing Regulation to Address Equity and Quality Concern', *India Infrastructure Report*, New Delhi and London: IDFC Foundation and Routledge.

Constable, P. (2000), 'Sitting on the School Verandah: The Ideology and Practice of "Untouchable" Educational Protest in Late Nineteenth-Century Western India', *Indian Economic and Social History Review (IESHR)*, vol. 37, no. 4.

de Sousa, Santos B. (2015), *Epistemologies of the South: Justice Against Epistemicide*, New York: Taylor & Francis.

Deshpande, S. (2013), 'Introduction: Beyond Inclusion', in S. Deshpande and U. Zacharias, eds, *Beyond Inclusion: The Practice of Equal Access in Indian Higher Education*, New Delhi: Routledge.

Dharmapal (1983), *The Beautiful Tree: Indigenous Indian Education in the Eighteenth Century*, New Delhi: Biblia Impex Private.

Dibona, J., ed. (1983), *One Teacher One School*, New Delhi: Biblia Impex Private.

Forbes, G. (1999), *Women in Modern India*, Cambridge: Cambridge University Press.

Frykenberg, R.E. (1986), 'Modern Education in South India, 1784–1854: Its Roots and Role as a Vehicle of Integration Under Company Raj', *American Historical Review*, vol. 91, no. 1.

Government of India (GoI) (1966), *Report of the Education Commission (1964–66): Education and National Development*, Ministry of Education, Government of India, Delhi.

——— (1986), *National Policy on Education*, available at https://www.education.gov.in/sites/upload_files/mhrd/files/document-reports/NPE-1968.pdf, accessed on 2 July 2022.

——— (2020a), *National Education Policy 2020*, available at https://www.mhrd.gov.in/sites/upload_files/mhrd/files/NEP_Final_English_0.pdf, accessed on 30 October 2020.

——— (2020b), Unified District Information System for Education Plus (UDISE+), 2019–20, Ministry of Education, Government of India, available at https://www.education.gov.in/sites/upload_files/mhrd/files/statistics-new/udise_201920.pdf, accessed on 15 January 2023.

John, M. (2013), 'Critiquing Reforms in Higher Education', *Social Scientist*, vol. 41, nos 7–8, July–August.

—— (2016), '(De)skilling Caste: Exploring the Relationship between Caste, State Regulations and the Labour Market in Late Colonial India', in R.P. Behal and S. Bhattacharya, eds, *The Vernacularization of Labour Politics*, New Delhi: Tulika Books, 2016.

—— (2018), '"The 'Half-timer'": Colonial Indian Regulation of Child Labourers', in S. Beynon-Jones and E. Grabham, eds, *Law and Time*, London: Routledge, Social Justice Book Series.

Kalidasan, V.K. and Tanya Goyal (2021), 'Ed-tech companies won't create a more egalitarian educated India', *The Wire*, 31 December, available at https://thewire.in/education/ed-tech-companies-wont-create-a-more-egalitarian-educated-india, accessed on 10 November 2022.

Kaur, H. (2008), *Development of Education in India*. New Delhi: Commonwealth Publishers.

Kumar, A. (2019), 'The "Untouchable School": American Missionaries, Hindu Social Reformers and the Educational Dreams of Labouring Dalits in Colonial North India', research paper available at the Nottingham Research Repository, 3 September, available at https://core.ac.uk/download/pdf/265451542.pdf, accessed on 20 October 2022.

Kumar, K. (1991), *Political Agenda of Education: A Study of Colonialist and Nationalist Ideas*, New Delhi: Sage Publications.

—— (2007), 'Education and Culture: India's Quest for a Secular Policy', in K. Kumar and J. Osterheld, eds, *Education and Social Change in South Asia*, New Delhi: Orient Longman.

Luhmann, N. (2012), *Theory of Society*, Vol. 1, translated by Rhodes Barrett, Stanford, California: Stanford University Press.

Marx, K. and F. Engels (1970), *Selected Works*, Vol. 3, Moscow: Progress Publishers.

McKenna, M.K. (2010), 'Pestalozzi Revisited: Hope and Caution for Modern Education', *Journal of Philosophy and History of Education*, vol. 60.

Mill, J.S. (1978), *On Liberty*, Indianapolis and Cambridge: Hackett Publishing Company.

Minault, G. (1998), *Secluded Scholars: Women's Education and Muslim Social Reform in Colonial India*, New Delhi: Oxford University Press.

Mondal, A. (2022), 'Dynamics of Transformation of Right to Education in India from Directive Principle to Fundamental Right: A History of Denial', *Journal of Social Inclusion Studies*, vol. 8, no. 2, November.

More, J.B.P. (2020), *Pondicherry, Tamil Nadu, and South India under French Rule: From François Martin to Dupleix 1674–1754*, Delhi: Manohar.

Nambissan, G. (1996), 'Equity in Education? Schooling of Dalit Children in India', *Economic and Political Weekly*, vol. 31, no. 16/17.

Parsons, T. (1940), 'An Analytical Approach to the Theory of Social Stratification', *American Journal of Sociology*, vol. 45, no. 6.

Richey, J.A. (1923), *Progress of Education in India, 1917–1922: Eighth Quinquennial Review*, vol. 1, Calcutta: Superintendent Government Printing.

Rousseau, J. (1991), *Emile*, or *On Education*, London: Penguin Classics.

Sadgopal, A. (2013), *Shiksha Mein PPP: Sarvajanik-Niji Sanjhedari ya Navudarwadi Loot?*, Hoshangabad: Kishore Barati.

Schmoller, G. (1890), *Zur Sozial- und Gewerbepolitik der Gegenwart*, Leipzig: Duncker & Humblot; cited in Manfred Prisching, 'Schmoller's Theory of Society', *History of Economic Ideas*, vol. 1/2, no. 3/1, Special Issue: Essays on Gustav Schmoller, 1993/1994, pp. 117–42.

Sharp, H. (1914), *Sixth Quinquennial Review of Education in India, 1907–12*, Volume I, Calcutta: Superintendent Government Printing.

Shukla, S.C. (1959), *Elementary Education in British India During Later Nineteenth Century*, New Delhi: Central Institute of Education.

Singh, M. (1947), *The Depressed Classes: Their Economic and Social Condition*, Bombay: Hind Kitabs Ltd.

Sudarshan, A. and S. Subramanian (2012), 'Private Sector's Role in Indian Higher Education', *India Infrastructure Report*, New Delhi and London: IDFC Foundation and Routledge.

Tilak, J.B.G. (1987), *The Economics of Inequality in Education*, New Delhi: Institute of Economic Growth and Sage Publications.

——— (2014), 'The Privatization of Higher Education', *Economic and Political Weekly*, vol. 49, no. 40, 2014.

Varghese, N.V. (2012), 'Private Higher Education: The Global Surge and Indian Concerns', *India Infrastructure Report*, New Delhi and London: IDFC Foundation and Routledge.

Viswanathan, G. (1990), *Masks of Conquest: Literary Study and British Rule in India*, London: Faber and Faber.

Zelliot, E. (2002), 'Experiments in Dalit Education: Maharashtra, 1850–1947', in S. Bhattacharya, ed., *Education and the Disprivileged: Nineteenth and Twentieth Century India*, New Delhi: Orient Longman.

——— (2014), 'Dalit Initiatives in Education, 1880–1992,' in P.V. Rao, ed., *New Perspectives in the History of Indian Education*, New Delhi: Orient Blackswan.

1

Elusive India

Lost in the National Education Policy 2020?

Kumkum Roy

The National Education Policy (NEP) 2020 has been opened up to intense scrutiny and discussion, even as its implementation has already begun. While there are several dimensions of the policy that have attracted attention, I focus here on the notion of India and 'Indian' as either taken for granted or elucidated in the text of the policy. Although this may seem to be of less immediate importance – in a situation where the policy and its implementation have assumed priority – it may be useful in providing some insights into the context for the provisions that are laid down and can, thus, enable us to respond to its challenges more effectively.

There are at least two intersecting levels at which the notion of India is invoked – one, in an increasingly globalized environment, of India vis-à-vis the wider world, and the second, of an India that is held up for the consideration of and emulation by those who claim to be or are recognized as Indians. We will attempt to explore both these levels, dwelling more on the latter. In doing so, we will focus on the place accorded to the Constitution, the privileging of Sanskrit and the understanding of traditions of knowledge production, transmission and circulation.

India and the World

One of the very first statements of the NEP document (GoI 2020: 3)[1] is as follows: 'Providing universal access to quality education is the key to India's continued ascent, and leadership on the global stage in terms of economic growth, social justice and equality, scientific advancement, national integration, and cultural preservation.'

Let us compare this claim with India's ranking in terms of the Human Development Index (HDI). On 17 December 2020, the *Economic Times* noted that India ranked 131 out of 189 countries in the world, having slipped down one point in the order from its position of 130 in the previous year. Given that the impact of the second wave of Covid-19 that had hit the country earlier that year remains to be factored in, it is unlikely that there has been any dramatic improvement. Therefore, it would appear that our performance in terms of the HDI does not quite substantiate the claim to 'continued ascent and leadership on the global stage' as claimed in the NEP.

More specifically, in terms of gender, about 11.7 per cent of parliamentary seats are held by women in India, well below the average of 17.1 per cent for South Asia as a whole. Further, only 39 per cent of adult women have attained education up to the secondary level, in contrast to 63.5 per cent of men. In terms of poverty, it was estimated that about 28 per cent of the 1.3 billion poor in the world were in India. It is unlikely that this scenario has improved in the course of the pandemic and the lockdown(s) that we have witnessed since March 2020. In such a situation, the claims of global leadership in terms of social justice and equality seem far-fetched and unrealistic, to say the least.

The NEP occasionally acknowledges a near-crisis situation within the educational scenario:

> [Various] governmental, as well as non-governmental surveys, indicate that we are currently in a learning crisis: a large proportion of students currently in elementary school – estimated to be over 5 crore in number – have not attained foundational literacy and numeracy, i.e., the ability to read and comprehend basic text and the ability to carry out basic addition and subtraction with Indian numerals. (GoI 2020: 2.1)

That the situation is particularly grim for those designated as SEDGs (socially and economically disadvantaged groups, a catch-all phrase for girls/women, minorities, Scheduled Tribes and Scheduled Castes and the disabled, amongst others) is also admitted in the document:

> According to U-DISE 2016–17 data, about 19.6% of students belong to Scheduled Castes at the primary level, but this fraction falls to 17.3% at the higher secondary level. These enrolment drop-offs are more severe for Scheduled Tribes students (10.6% to 6.8%), and differently-abled children (1.1% to 0.25%), with even greater declines for female students within each of these categories. The decline in enrolment in higher education is even steeper. (Ibid.: 6.2.1)

It is in this context that we need to examine the following aspiration: 'India will be promoted as a global study destination providing premium education at affordable costs thereby helping to restore its role as a Vishwa Guru' (ibid.: 12.8). What exactly does 'restoring' India to the role of Vishwa

Guru mean? It assumes that there was a time when India functioned and was acknowledged as a Vishwa Guru, one of the many unsubstantiated and perhaps not substantiable claims in which the document abounds. The second, perhaps more problematic issue is whether, in fact, if we dream of a democratic world, the model of the 'guru–shishya parampara', based on the exercise of almost unbridled power and authority on the part of the guru and unquestioning obedience and subservience on the part of the disciple, is an ideal worth pursuing. Perhaps there are other goals and destinations beyond that of unswerving loyalty and more suited to 'cultivating critical thinking', one of the catchphrases that the document resorts to time and again.

There is a more realistic assessment of the relationship between India and the world towards the end of the document (ibid.: 22), which provides an insight into some of the central concerns of the policy – combining profit, privatization and commercialization with the promotion of culture as a commodified good for the 'betterment' of the world as well as of the country. We are informed that 'India is a treasure trove of culture' and that 'crores of people from around the world partake in, enjoy, and benefit from this cultural wealth daily'. This is acknowledged as being 'truly important for the nation's identity as well as for its economy' (ibid.: 22.1). And yet, while there is an intense desire to mesh and merge identity with the economy, this is a source of tension within the policy. While these inconsistencies may appear as irritants, they may also be indicative of spaces that are susceptible to intervention. Having said that, let us turn to the ways in which identities are envisaged, especially within the country.

Decentring the Constitution

It may be useful to begin the discussion by flagging the space or the lack of space accorded to the Constitution within the document. One would have assumed that the Constitution in its entirety would provide a focal point for what is being projected as a long overdue intervention in educational policy. However, this assumption is sadly belied. To cite just one instance, in the context of school education, we are told:

> As consequences of such basic ethical reasoning, traditional Indian values and all basic human and Constitutional values (such as seva, ahimsa, swachchhata, satya, nishkam karma, shanti, sacrifice, tolerance, diversity, pluralism, righteous conduct, gender sensitivity, respect for elders, respect for all people and their inherent capabilities regardless of background, respect for environment, helpfulness, courtesy, patience, forgiveness, empathy, compassion, patriotism, democratic outlook, integrity, respon-

sibility, justice, liberty, equality, and fraternity) will be developed in all students. (Ibid.: 4.28)

As many as twenty-nine words/phrases are listed within brackets. One would assume that some of these are related to ethical reasoning, some to traditional Indian values, some to basic human values and some to constitutional values. Given that constitutional values figure at the very end, and are best identified with the last four terms of the long list, it is unlikely that either teachers or learners will consider these as a priority. Second, the other values are so diverse, and even amorphous, that teachers and learners would probably have a tough time classifying them and engaging with them. Faced with this situation and given that the list begins with a long series of terms derived from Sanskrit, it is most likely that there would be a tendency to privilege these as 'traditional Indian values' and prioritize them. This may in itself seem unexceptional – after all, what is wrong with service, non-violence, cleanliness, truth, selfless performance of duty and peace? Are they incompatible with justice, liberty, equality and fraternity?

The actual question that we need to pose is about the context within which these values are hierarchized. In a situation where socioeconomic, cultural and political differences and inequalities have become sharper, concerns with justice and equality cry out for prioritization in our understanding and are likely to be of immediate concern to future generations of learners. Tucking them into the tail end of a long list of values does little to address this situation. In other words, retrieving and focusing on constitutional values is likely to prove an uphill task for those who are confronted with this formidable list.

Sanskrit Knowledge Systems

The attention devoted to Sanskrit in the NEP has been commented on earlier and insightfully (see, for instance, Narayanan 2020). An entire subsection (GoI 2020: 4.17) in the recommendations on school education is devoted to Sanskrit, in which Sanskrit knowledge systems are mentioned. This use of the plural is a striking departure from the tendency to reduce multiplicities to uniform, singular categories, which we will discuss later. The plural terminology used in the present instance is a tacit acknowledgement of developments within the wider academic universe.

The idea of Sanskrit knowledge systems derives from an ambitious and complex project, initiated by Sheldon Pollock and a team of scholars, which attempted to explore the state of Sanskrit in what the team defined as the early modern period, specifically between 1550 and 1750. The website of the project describes these two centuries as 'one of the most innovative eras in Sanskrit intellectual history'. We are also informed that:

> Sanskrit continued to be used exclusively in such major disciplines as language analysis (*vyakarana*), hermeneutics (*mimamsa*), logic-epistemology (*nyaya*), moral-legal-political discourse (*dharmasastra*). The emerging regional languages were largely restricted to religious poetry, sometimes theology, and practical arts such as medicine. Persian (Urdu would not become a language of scholarship until the mid-nineteenth century) inhabited a separate knowledge sphere, where inspiration for ways of making sense of and inscribing the world derived from sources altogether different from those of Sanskrit (some exact sciences excepted, where both groups relied in part on Greek sources).

The project was described as 'an attempt to grasp at once the remarkable strengths of the Sanskrit disciplines and their remarkable weaknesses in the face of European colonial modernity'. Interestingly, while the name of the project is appropriated within the NEP, there is little or no attempt to engage with the problem with which the project attempted to grapple or the multilingual and multicultural milieu it envisaged. In other words, the NEP abstracts Sanskrit out of its many contexts of transmission and circulation to create an almost ahistorical understanding of what is projected as its almost universal and eternal appeal.

This leads to a simplistic and naively celebratory understanding of Sanskrit and its resources, which does little justice to the complexity of a rich historical tradition. Unfortunately, sterile as this may be, it is this understanding that is likely to be promoted insistently. As much seems evident in the detailed provisions for ensuring the centrality of Sanskrit:

> Due to its vast and significant contributions and literature across genres and subjects, its cultural significance, and its scientific nature, rather than being restricted to single-stream Sanskrit Pathshalas and Universities, Sanskrit will be mainstreamed with strong offerings in school – including as one of the language options in the three-language formula – as well as in higher education. It will be taught not in isolation, but in interesting and innovative ways, and connected to other contemporary and relevant subjects such as mathematics, astronomy, philosophy, linguistics, dramatics, yoga, etc. Thus, in consonance with the rest of this policy, Sanskrit Universities too will move towards becoming large multidisciplinary institutions of higher learning. Departments of Sanskrit that conduct teaching and outstanding interdisciplinary research on Sanskrit and Sanskrit Knowledge Systems will be established/strengthened across the new multidisciplinary higher education system. Sanskrit will become a natural part

of a holistic multidisciplinary higher education if a student so chooses. Sanskrit teachers in large numbers will be professionalized across the country in mission mode through the offering of 4-year integrated multidisciplinary B.Ed. dual degrees in education and Sanskrit. (Ibid.: 22.15)

Whether this should be a priority in a situation where access to education itself remains a distant dream for many is a question that is not even raised, let alone addressed.

Circumscribing the 'Indian'

The document occasionally mentions 'Knowledge of India'. One of the first references to this knowledge, and its purported uses, is found in the introduction: 'Instilling knowledge of India and its varied social, cultural, and technological needs, its inimitable artistic, language, and knowledge traditions, and its strong ethics in India's young people is considered critical for purposes of national pride, self-confidence, self-knowledge, cooperation, and integration' (ibid.: 4). 'Knowledge of India' also figures in the context of teacher training, especially for those who undergo the four-year programme which is projected as the norm for the future (ibid.: 15.5). This begs the question: what exactly would knowledge of India mean? Consider a paragraph from the introduction, a long paragraph that has been retained, with slight modifications, from the earlier draft documents, even as the present policy document itself has shrunk drastically from over 400 pages in the draft versions to a slim 66-page document at present:

> The rich heritage of ancient and eternal Indian knowledge and thought has been a guiding light for this Policy. The pursuit of knowledge (Jnan), wisdom (Pragyaa), and truth (Satya) was always considered in Indian thought and philosophy as the highest human goal. The aim of education in ancient India was not just the acquisition of knowledge as preparation for life in this world, or life beyond schooling, but for the complete realization and liberation of the self. World-class institutions of ancient India such as Takshashila, Nalanda, Vikramshila, Vallabhi, set the highest standards of multidisciplinary teaching and research and hosted scholars and students from across backgrounds and countries. The Indian education system produced great scholars such as Charaka, Susruta, Aryabhata, Varahamihira, Bhaskaracharya, Brahmagupta, Chanakya, Chakrapani Datta, Madhava, Panini, Patanjali, Nagarjuna, Gautama, Pingala, Sankardev, Maitreyi, Gargi and Thiruvalluvar, among numerous others, who made seminal contributions to world knowledge in diverse fields such as mathematics, astronomy, metallurgy, medical science and surgery, civil engineering, architecture, shipbuilding and navigation, yoga, fine arts, chess, and more.

Indian culture and philosophy have had a strong influence on the world. These rich legacies to world heritage must not only be nurtured and pre-served for posterity but also researched, enhanced, and put to new uses through our education system. (Ibid.: 4)

There are several features of this paragraph that are striking. Note, for instance, the consistent use of the singular for many of the categories and concepts that are thrown in. These include Indian thought and philosophy, 'the aim of education' and, later in the paragraph, 'the Indian educational system'. Amongst other things, the constant and repeated usage of the singular erases and obliterates memories of the multiplicity and diversity of Indian traditions and replaces them with a monolithic, uniform frame of reference. What happens, one wonders, to the conventional six schools of philosophy, the *sad-darshana*, mentioned within Sanskritic traditions? Where would Buddhism, perhaps one of the most influential philosophical systems to emanate from the subcontinent and spread through Asia, feature within this scheme? One is also left wondering why there is an urge to reduce differences and contentious as well as vibrant debates to create a bland, homogeneous, almost stifling view of the past. The strategy of encapsulating all these possibilities within the seemingly unexceptionable frames of *jnan*, *pragyaa* and *satya* leaves little room for grappling with distinctive and even conflicting understandings. And, while the importance of critical thinking is acknowledged time and again in the document, this detailed invocation of an imagined monolithic tradition does not leave space for it.

Also, this perspective implicitly denies the multi-directional flows of knowledge both into and within the subcontinent that have been as, if not more, important than the outward flow from the subcontinent for centuries, if not millennia. So, contacts with China, Southeast Asia, East Africa, West Asia, Central Asia and the Mediterranean world in the pre-colonial context as well as the complex colonial encounter – which enriched and transformed knowledge systems within the subcontinent – find no space within this framework. That this heritage needs to be constructively and critically evaluated and assessed, rather than ignored, is obviously beyond the purview of the policy.

The reliance on the singular resurfaces in specific contexts such as school education as well. Here we learn that part of the purpose of such education will be 'imbibing the Indian ethos through integration of Indian art and culture in the teaching and learning process at every level' (ibid.: 4.7).

We could, if we wanted to, dismiss these usages as rhetorical, but the choice of rhetoric is perhaps significant and worth reflecting on. Also important to note is that these statements are occasionally repeated in a document that is often terse, if not cryptic. So, we find the following statement:

> Moving to large multidisciplinary universities and HEI [higher educa-tion institution] clusters is thus the highest recommendation of this policy regarding the structure of higher education. The ancient Indian universities Takshashila, Nalanda, Vallabhi, and Vikramshila, which had thousands of students from India and the world studying in vibrant multidisciplinary environments, amply demonstrated the type of great success that large multidisciplinary research and teaching universities could bring. India urgently needs to bring back this great Indian tradition to create well-rounded and innovative individuals, and which is already transforming other countries educationally and economically. (Ibid.: 10.2)

This culminates in a claim that the roots of a liberal education lie within the 64 *kalaa*s or arts mentioned in Sanskrit literature:

> India has a long tradition of holistic and multidisciplinary learning, from universities such as Takshashila and Nalanda, to the extensive literatures of India combining subjects across fields. Ancient Indian literary works such as Banabhatta's Kadambari described a good education as knowl-edge of the 64 Kalaas or arts; and among these 64 'arts' were not only subjects, such as singing and painting, but also 'scientific' fields, such as chemistry and mathematics, 'vocational' fields such as carpentry and clothes-making, 'professional' fields, such as medicine and engineering, as well as 'soft skills' such as communication, discussion, and debate. The very idea that all branches of creative human endeavour, including math-ematics, science, vocational subjects, professional subjects, and soft skills should be considered 'arts', has distinctly Indian origins. This notion of a 'knowledge of many arts' or what in modern times is often called the 'lib-eral arts' (i.e., a liberal notion of the arts) must be brought back to Indian education, as it is exactly the kind of education that will be required for the 21st century. (Ibid.: 11.1)

I have discussed the contents of the 64 *kalaa*s and their incongruence with current notions of liberal education elsewhere (Roy 2020). The list, as available in the *Kamasutra* (I.3.15; Doniger and Kakar 2002: 14–15) is as follows:

> Singing, playing musical instruments, dancing, painting, cutting leaves into shapes, making lines on the floor with rice powder and flowers, arranging flowers, colouring the teeth, clothes and limbs, making jew-elled floors, preparing beds, making music on the rims of glasses of water,

playing water sports, unusual techniques, making garlands and stringing necklaces, making diadems and headbands, making costumes, making earrings, mixing perfumes, putting on jewellery, doing conjuring tricks, practising sorcery, sleight of hand, preparing various forms of vegetables, soups and other things to eat, preparing wines, fruit juices and other things to drink, needlework, weaving, playing the lute and the drum, telling jokes and riddles, completing words, reciting difficult words, reading aloud, staging plays and dialogues, completing verses, making things out of cloth, wood and cane, woodworking, carpentry, architecture, the ability to test gold and silver, metallurgy, knowledge of the colour and form of jewels, skill at nurturing trees, knowledge of ram-fights, cock fights, and quail fights, teaching parrots and mynah birds to talk, skill at rubbing, massaging and hairdressing, the ability to speak in sign language, understanding languages made to seem foreign, knowledge of local dialects, skill at making flower carts, knowledge of omens, alphabets for use in making magical diagrams, alphabets for memorising, group recitation, improvising poetry, dictionaries and thesauruses, knowledge of metre, literary work, the art of impersonation, the art of using cloths for disguise, special forms of gambling, the game of dice, children's games, etiquette, the science of strategy and the cultivation of athletic skills.

The advocacy of spurious connections between this list and the present-day understanding of liberal education does not inspire confidence in the document or its implications.

Another noteworthy element, here and elsewhere, is the elimination of the medieval. We move swiftly and seamlessly from the ancient to the present. So, there are no references, even rhetorical, to medieval educational institutions, be it *matha*s or *madrasah*s, which thrived in different regional centres of the subcontinent. Further, this narrative has no space for the complex negotiations through which modern universities have evolved – through dialogue and contestation with religious institutions, state structures and corporatization, processes which are by no means smooth or, fortunately, complete.

To return to the eradication of the medieval, noted earlier. This happens in more than one instance. The introduction (ibid.: 6) refers to 'ancient and modern culture and knowledge systems and traditions'. Further, in the context of school education, we are told (ibid.: 4.27) that 'Knowledge of India' will include knowledge from ancient India and its contributions to modern India.

Once again, the medieval is elided over in silence. This is reinforced by adding in the same context that 'video documentaries on inspirational luminaries of India, ancient and modern, in science and beyond, will be shown at appropriate points throughout the school curriculum' (ibid.).

This ellipse is repeated in the discussion on languages in the context of school education, where we learn: 'India's languages are among the richest, most scientific, most beautiful, and most expressive in the world, with a huge body of ancient as well as modern literature (both prose and poetry), film, and music written in these languages that help form India's national identity and wealth' (ibid.: 4.15). Note the absence of any reference to medieval literature. What, one wonders, will happen to the vast repertoire of devotional literature, within diverse strands of Bhakti, Sufi and Sikh traditions, amongst others, which emerged during this period? Are they all to be consigned to oblivion because of their diversity and the fact that they cannot be reduced to or confined within a monolithic framework?

Returning once more to the introductory paragraph, the third element, again noteworthy, is that an assortment of men (and a couple of women) has been mentioned as being produced by the 'Indian education system'. This statement is misleading, to say the least. We know virtually nothing of the education that these men received, and to project them as the products of an education system, as if they were alumni of a university or a college, is at best, a comforting illusion. But whether it lives up to the claims of *satya*, mentioned a couple of sentences earlier, or not, remains doubtful.

In the very rare instances where traditions preserve narratives about how any of these deservedly acclaimed men and women acquired knowledge, what is noteworthy is the absence of access to anything resembling a formal system. In this context, the story of Maitreyi and her husband, the philosopher Yajnavalkya, preserved in the *Brihadaranyaka Upanishad* (2.4, 4.5; Olivelle 1998: 66–71, 126–31) is illustrative. When the sage was planning to enter into a different, non-domestic stage of life, he offered to make arrangements for the material support of Katyayani and Maitreyi, the wives he would be leaving behind. While the former was satisfied with the arrangement, Maitreyi, we are told, asked him to impart the knowledge that might lead to immortality, which she thought would be more valuable than wealth. The text goes on to record the dialogue that ensued between the husband and the wife, as the former imparted knowledge to the latter. This mode of transmission was clearly not part of any formal, institutionalized educational system, even as it may have been effective.

A fourth issue, which I have raised and discussed elsewhere (Roy 2019), is the mismatch between the two lists that are part of the long, central sentence of this paragraph. Briefly, the unwary reader may be led into believing that Charaka and Susruta contributed to mathematics and astronomy rather than medicine if they innocently tried to match the two lists. But these are, perhaps, minor inaccuracies that we should overlook.

Far more important is a fifth issue, which I will highlight by drawing on Kancha Ilaiah's work (2007). In this book, meant for young readers, Ilaiah highlights the enormous range of knowledge and skills developed, transmitted and possessed by non-literate people. Consider just two examples to illustrate the insights he arrives at, those of the Adivasis and barbers.

This is what Ilaiah says about the Adivasis:

> The adivasis introduced most of the basic food items to the plainspeople. Not curd-rice or pizza, but pineapple, jackfruit, mango, melons, custard apple (*sitaphal*), various types of bananas and scores of fruits were first discovered by the adivasis. They also discovered the sourness of wild lemons and used them as an additive to food. They were the first to gather wild honey that has medicinal properties. Most vegetables, fruits and flowers we cultivate today have their origins among the adivasis. They are, therefore, our first teachers.
>
> Having risked their limbs and lives in order to develop our basic food culture, the adivasis shared such knowledge with others. They also orally passed this knowledge from generation to generation, through songs and stories. Several medicinal plants used in ayurveda and siddha were originally identified by adivasis. The adivasis were also the first to discover the gums, resins and dyes that are commercially produced today. We not only have to respect adivasis, but we also have much to learn from them. (Ilaiah 2007: 12, 15)

About the barbers, Ilaiah writes:

> Among the medical sciences, the cutting of hair occupies a significant place in history. Cutting the hair that grows on our heads and other parts of the body needs skill and tools of precision – sharp blades and scissors. The barbers, in several societies, also doubled up as the world's first doctors and surgeons. . . . They tended to battlefield injuries because of their expertise in handling the razor. Surgery, in fact, is organically linked to barbering. The presence of hair on the part of the body where surgery is to be performed can cause infection. The clean removal of hair is therefore mandatory before surgery. This practice continues to this day. The barbers can therefore be called the earliest social doctors of India. (Ibid.: 78, 80)

What Ilaiah alerts us to through these and other examples is the fact that knowledge is produced in diverse sites – and is by no means a monopoly of the 'high' tradition. In fact, if anything, the 'high' tradition appropriates and monopolizes much of the knowledge that is generated through other, less hierarchical modes and, in the process, displaces or marginalizes those who may have arrived at the original insights through painstaking experiments, trial and error and through preserving and transmitting knowledge through generations.

How would a new education policy look if these roots were acknowledged centrally rather than tucked into the margins of the document? While we can raise the question, answering it imaginatively, creatively and constructively would demand disinvesting in the exalted 'great' traditions that we are conditioned to celebrate and acknowledging far more complex relationships of dependence and support. It would compel us to question the social, political and economic hierarchies, in terms of gender, castes, communities, tribes and regions that are naturalized and normalized at present and push us out of our comfort zones. Whether we and, more importantly, those in charge of designing and implementing the NEP are prepared to move in this direction or not is the question. Till then, those described by Shereen Ratnagar (2004) as *The Other Indians* will remain on the margins of the NEP.

Note
[1] All references to pages and sections of the NEP are from the document available on the website of the Ministry of Human Resource Development, Government of India.

References

Doniger, W. and S. Kakar, trans. (2002), *Kamasutra,* Oxford: Oxford University Press.

Government of India (GoI) (2020), *National Education Policy 2020,* New Delhi: Ministry of Human Resource Development, Government of India, available at https://www.education.gov.in/sites/upload_files/ mhrd/files/NEP_Final_English_0.pdf, accessed 8 November 2020.

Ilaiah, K. (2007), *Turning the Pot, Tilling the Land: Dignity of Labour in Our Times,* New Delhi: Navayana.

Narayanan, M. (2020), 'Whose Sanskrit Is It Anyway?', *Frontline,* available at https://frontline.thehindu.com/cover-story/whose-sanskrit-is-it-anyway/article32306029.ece, accessed 29 October 2020.

Olivelle, P. (1998), *The Early Upanishads: Annotated Text and Translation,* Delhi: Munshiram Manoharlal Publishers.

Ratnagar, S. (2004), *The Other Indians,* New Delhi: Three Essays Collective.

Roy, K. (2019), 'Examining the Draft National Education Policy, 2019', *Economic and Political Weekly,* vol. 54, no. 25.

—— (2020), 'NEP 2020 Implementation and Timeline Worries', *Frontline,* available at https://frontline.thehindu.com/cover-story/timeline-worries/article32305885.ece, accessed 29 October 2020.

Sanskrit Knowledge Systems, available at http://www.columbia.edu/itc/mealac/pollock/sks/proposal.html, accessed 13 October 2020.

Special Correspondent (2020), 'India Drops Two Ranks in Human Development Index', *The Hindu,* 16 December, available at https://www.thehindu.com/news/national/india-ranks-131-in-2020-un-human-development-index/article33348091.ece, accessed 16 December 2021.

2

'Low-cost' Schooling for the Poor in India

Contemporary Concerns

Geetha B. Nambissan

Low-fee/cost[1] private schooling for the 'poor' – also called 'afford-able learning' (AL) – has been flagged as a key market in the global education industry (GEI) (Verger, Lubienski and Steiner-Khamsi 2016). It is projected as the panacea that will 'help provide millions of the poorest children in the world with quality education, in a profitable and sustained manner'.[2] In barely a decade and a half, for-profit schooling has become normalized in policy discourses on education for the poor. It has spawned a whole new language around education markets that evoke social responsibilities and moral concerns of the private sector which is increasingly engaged in 'impact or social investing' (Ball 2019: 30). Here, the role of powerful advocacy and business networks in the construction of problems around the education of the poor and their solution through the market has been particularly important. The attempt is to show that markets in schooling, profits and quality education for the poor and marginalized can be realized together.

Focusing specifically on India, this essay maps the trajectory of low-cost schooling for the poor from the early 2000s, highlighting, in particular, the building of discourse(s) around poverty and for-profit school-ing. I revisit my earlier writings on the theme (Nambissan and Ball 2011; Nambissan 2012, 2014) and subsequent scholarship (Verger, Lubienski and Steiner-Khamsi 2016; Ball 2019; Riep 2019) to map this trajectory and highlight some of the key concerns as they emerge in the last almost two decades. I show that the advocacy of low-cost education and the busi-ness around it has redefined education for the poor and is shaping reforms in government schooling as well. I argue that it is important to seriously engage with the discourses, practices and actual evidence in relation to pri-vate education and the complicit role of the state in the growth of this sector. Such an engagement, I believe, is especially important in the time of Covid-19, as the low-cost education model is technology-driven, and technology (and digitization) is being projected as the way not merely to address the impact of the pandemic on schooling but to 'reimagine' education (Williamson and Hogan 2020). I foreground education as a site of competing aspirations and interests. I point to the rising aspirations of low-income families for good quality education for their children, the increasing abdication of the state in this regard and growing business interests around schooling. I keep in mind that powerful networks and relationships are being mobilized to dominate the field of education and make schooling a profitable business and thereby change the very paradigm of education. I emphasize the importance of research that is informed by a perspective of social justice and public purpose of education.

Low-cost Education: Early Advocacy

It is important from the vantage point of discourses constructed around the promise of 'low-cost schooling/affordable learning' to revisit the early years when James Tooley first made public his 'discovery' of 'high performing', unrecognized schools in India (more specifically in the city of Hyderabad) and published a study in 2005 (Tooley, Dixon and Gomathi 2007). More than five years earlier, he was in the city conducting an International Finance Corporation (World Bank)-funded study on the possibility of private education in developing countries. The study was published in 1999 under the title, *The Global Education Industry* (Tooley 1999). The pro-market Centre for British Teachers (CfBT) with which he was associated already had a base in Hyderabad, and Pauline Dixon, his future collaborator, was doing her doctorate on regulatory systems and private schooling in Andhra Pradesh around the same time. Tooley subsequently established the Educare Trust through which he carried out his study (2003–05) on 'low-fee' private schooling for which he was generously funded by the conservative John Templeton Foundation based in the United States. At the global level, the World Bank had by 2000 begun to frame a new agenda of privatization in education based on private partnerships with the state in school education (Robertson and Verger 2012). In fact, the World Bank, International Finance Corporation and CfBT were part of the initial group that in the 1990s itself had 'started considering partnerships in education as an evolution of the privatization agenda' (ibid.: 13). The advocacy for markets in education and the focus on the poor, which appeared to suddenly emerge with Tooley's 'discovery' around 2005, must be seen in relation to larger global economic and political interests informed by a neoliberal agenda in education and its major planks: destatalization, privatization and extending markets in schooling (Nambissan and Ball 2011).

Tooley claimed on the basis of his study that 'unrecognized' (unregulated) private primary schools (UPS), hitherto viewed as illegal 'sub-standard teaching shops',[3] were better performing (in terms of learning achievement) and more cost-effective (teacher salaries being extremely low) as compared to government primary schools. Renaming UPS as low-fee private schools (LFPS), he also highlighted that since they charged low tuition fees ($1–2 a month at the time), they were accessed by the poorest families who aspired to English-medium private education for their children (Tooley, Dixon and Gomathi 2007). Equally important was that LFPS yielded profits and hence could be attractive for education business as well (Tooley 2009)

It is often forgotten that what Tooley was actually proposing as a good business proposition was not a revamped UPS that would help them compete with the reputed public/private English-medium schools or sought-after government schools such as the KendriyaVidyalayas. Instead, he visualized a qualitatively different model that would be targeted at poor children – low-budget, standardized education that would be scalable with appropriate technology through branded school chains and yield profit. For such a model to work, it was necessary to bring about changes in education policy – for instance, deregulation, permitting profits in schooling which was illegal in India as well as providing state-supported vouchers to enable 'parental choice' of schools for their children.[4] Led by Tooley, a transnational advocacy network (TAN) for low-cost education for the poor was built from around 2005. The TAN comprised pro-market organizations, foundations and think tanks from the US and UK as well as local organizations such as the Centre for Civil Society, Educare Trust and Liberty Institute (Nambissan 2014). TAN proactively constructed and circulated discourses around failing government schools, non-performing and absentee teachers on the one hand, as against 'high quality', 'world class' education that could be provided at a low cost to the poor and yield profits on the other. A narrow base of evidence was used for this purpose (Tooley, Dixon and Gomathi 2007; Kremer *et al.* 2005). Low-cost school chains were established by some corporate houses/their philanthropic foundations in Hyderabad around 2009, but the venture was abandoned within a couple of years. In fact, the lowest-fee market segment of UPS was soon viewed as not profitable since school owners did not fall in line with branding and standardization of schools and raising of fees necessary for a profitable business (Kamat, Spreen and Jonnalagadda 2016). The higher-fee unrecognized schools, which were named 'affordable' private schools and educational services were seen as more attractive markets (Nambissan 2012).

Bridge International Academies (BIA), a for-profit multinational school chain established in Kenya in 2009, presents the low-cost education business model in terms of discourses and practices. The BIA website showcased its ambitious aims: to *'revolutionize access to affordable, high quality* primary education for *poor* families across Africa' with a 'network of *ultra low-cost for-profit* primary schools' and claimed that 'its schools *profitably deliver high-quality education for less than $4 per child per month*, enabling local school managers to operate their school businesses *profitably*, while creating a *highly successful business at the central level*'[5] (emphases here and through the chapter are mine).[6] What is on offer in BIA is 'scripted schooling' where 'every step of the learning process is remotely directed' (Stewart 2015). Professionally untrained teachers, usually high school graduates employed on low salaries, are directed through nook readers and tablets (referred to as 'teacher computers') to transact standardized and digitalized content. Teaching is reduced to simple tasks that are closely monitored with a focus on learner outcomes through regular testing. Further, Bridge Academies (and chains such as Omega) do not reach the poorest (as they claim to) as their fees comprise a significant proportion of the daily income earned by wage workers in these countries (Riep 2014; 2019).

Research on Bridge schools has shown that they are technology-driven to enable cost-cutting and increase profits. But this has transformed the paradigm of education for the poor (Riep 2019). As Riep says 'the BIA model has leveraged technology to drive down operating costs, resulting in a profoundly standardised, automated, and mechanised form of provision that is strikingly similar from one context to another' (ibid.: 7; see also Riep and Machacek 2016). The detrimental implications for the quality of learning offered to children who attend these schools, as reflected in the curriculum and pedagogy on offer, can be seen in Riep's elaboration of the Bridge (Academy-in-a-box) model:

> It is a pre-fabricated model designed for replication and rapid scalability ... instructional (e.g. curriculum, pedagogy, lessons) and non-instructional activities (e.g. admissions, accountancy, administration) are standardised and automated using internet enabled devices. On the instructional side, pre-programmed curriculum is developed by BIA at corporate headquarters abroad and then sent electronically to each school site using web-enabled smartphones that transfer curriculum to tablet e-readers, which is then read out verbatim, word-for-word, to students by unqualified staff referred to as 'Learning Facilitators'. (Riep 2019: 8–9)

The BIA has come under considerable criticism for the sub-standard infrastructure it provides and the poor quality of instruction offered by deskilled teachers/instructors who work under exploitative conditions. These were among the reasons why BIA was ordered to shut shop in Uganda in 2016. It is significant that Bridge Academies are funded by powerful philanthropic foundations established by global corporates such as Pearson, Gates and Google among others, and lauded by organizations such as the World Bank and DfID.

'Affordable' Learning and Edu-business

'Affordable learning' (AL) as a solution to what is projected as the 'learning crisis' in society was flagged by Pearson in 2012 when the Pearson Affordable Learning Fund (PALF) was established. The corporate giant had morphed into a 'Learning Company' which sought to expand its multi-billion-dollar business focusing on education. PALF had a $15 million fund to 'help improve access to *quality education for the poorest families in the world*' (PALF). In 2015, the fund was increased to $65 billion in capital 'to expand PALF's work within emerging markets'. Its mandate was *'to invest in companies that can build quality, scalable education solutions to meet a growing demand for affordable educational services across Africa, Asia and Latin America'*.[7] Within a few years, affordable learning became what Verger (2012: 109) terms a 'programmatic idea', constructed as the dominant but flexible paradigm and embedded in 'practice communities' (advocacy and business) that presented it as the solution to high-quality education for the poor and profitable for edu-business – in other words, a win-win sector. Affordable learning includes a range of profitable ventures for 'learning' informed by the low-cost school model. The shift to individualized 'learning' is significant as the quality of education is reduced to narrow learning outcomes of individual students.[8]

PALF offers to support education entrepreneurs with 'scalable and profitable education solutions' for the 'low income segment' and emphasizes 'efficacy and learner outcomes' as indictors of quality (ibid.). Also included is 'investment in low-cost private school chains and service providers for low-cost private schools (such as 'teacher development solutions') and 'other low income focused ventures that use technology to create scalable, quality solutions' (ibid.).[9] K-12 schools for the poor also form part of the PALF investment portfolio. In other words, AL is an umbrella category that includes diverse institutional arrangements for 'learning' that are low cost and use technology to create scalable services that yield profit and focus on 'efficacy and learner outcomes' as indictors of quality (ibid.).

Affordable learning is also embedded in transnational networks. However, the affordable learning advocacy networks are qualitatively different from TAN (discussed earlier) in that they are not merely channels for advocacy but bring together a range of powerful business interests to 'grow' new markets in education. In other words, these are affordable learning advocacy and business networks (ALABN). Ball (2016) has followed the building of networks in which advocacy and edu-business are enmeshed and shows the new 'transnational and intra-national spaces' that they have penetrated, including policy infrastructure with changing modes of governance. He points to the discursive coherence and 'shared epistemic sensibility' that has been built among network actors as they work in tandem through diverse strategies and synergies to build global discourses that construct educational problems of the poor and the solutions that should follow (ibid.). These are new social relations and strategic alliances, processes and practices that are not easily visible and require innovative methodologies to identify, name and understand. The ALABN has within it powerful corporate houses that are today 'growing' low-cost 'learning' markets and an enabling 'eco-system' for this purpose. These are corporates that are active in education policy changes at the global level and within nations where they find profitable business opportunities (ibid). There are new nodal organizations and key individuals within India (Centre Square Foundation [CSF] for instance) that build synergies among private actors within and between networks and also help strengthen linkages with the state(s).

Post-2015, a whole new language has developed around edu-business targeted at the 'bottom of the pyramid' (Prahalad and Hart 2001). This is now called 'impact' and 'social investing' with an emphasis on 'social outcomes' that 'benefit' the underprivileged (Ball 2019). New moral narratives and discourses have emerged that locate the private sector within the social sphere where it is projected as addressing concerns of equity and inclusion that were formerly within the purview of the state and civil society. This is what is called 'soft capitalism' where edu-business is not only 'doing well' but also 'doing good' (Hogan *et al.* 2016: 234; Ball 2019: 33). Corporate players who have a global presence and are building markets in countries such as India are leading these processes through their philanthropic foundations or social enterprises, facilitated by international development and finance organizations.

Kamat, Spreen and Jonnalagadda (2016) provide a window into the expanding low-cost/affordable learning market in India. Focusing on Hyderabad, they point to the rapid expansion of the high-profit unregulated markets for pre-schooling, tuition and 'coaching' made available to families at 'affordable' prices, depending on what they can pay. The picture they paint is one of pro-active 'growing' of markets for edu-business, funding and support (ibid.). For instance, PALF supports educational entrepreneurs who are 'creating *scalable and profitable education solutions for the low income segment'.*[10] In India, the early ventures that PALF identified and launched included Sudhiksha pre-schools (*affordable* early childhood education through *low-cost* preschool centres), Experifun science gadgets (*affordable* and *cost-effective solutions* for schools) and Zaya (*blended learning solutions* accessed through software and tablets sold to schools).[11] As can be seen, edu-business is launched within the framework of AL: cost-effective, technology-based solutions with an emphasis on 'affordability' for consumers who are poor or from low-income families and their schools.

Srivastava (2016) is sceptical of the actual scalability of low-cost private school chains and points out that they (including BIA) comprise only a minuscule proportion of public provision in the few countries where they operate. However, as discussed, AL comprises much more than school chains and includes a range of cost-effective, profitable educational ventures. The unregulated pre-schools, higher-fee unrecognized schools (called 'affordable' private schools), tutorial or coaching centres, as well as new pedagogies for learning using technology (digital content, scripted lessons, smartphones and tablets) and a range of school improvement services are likely to see expanding markets. Services such as testing and assessment of students and schools are integrated into AL markets as learning outcomes are increasingly projected as indicators of teacher effectiveness and school quality. Teacher development, alternate certification as well as school leadership are also new spheres of edu-business. In the last few years, education markets have expanded, especially in relation to education technology, which pervades all aspects of school education from curricular modules, pedagogy, assessment of students, self-learning, testing and monitoring of teachers, school governance and so on.

Ball (2019) draws attention to a major corporate group foundation, the Michael and Susan Dell Foundation (MSDF), which is a key player in the business of, and reform in, schooling in India. He discusses at length the intricate and dynamic web of networks that have evolved in which global investors and financial organizations link with local enterprises and start-ups in the education business. 'Edu-start-ups' are embedded in these networks and a whole 'eco-system' is being set in place to enable the rapid growth of what is viewed as emerging profitable education markets targeted at lower income groups. For instance, there are now 'edcubators' that incubate promising ventures and enable the growth of what are being called 'social enterprises' (ibid.). Global networks and platforms circulate the ideology and practices of new markets in schooling and offer opportunities for innovative businesses that tie in with internationally set goals in education (Sustainable Development Goal 4 [SDG4]), for instance, and national obligations in this sphere that private players offer to effectively meet (Ball 2019).

It is important to draw attention to what appears to be the major goal of edu-business in India – the reform of publicly funded education and making it the site of new markets in schooling. The over one million government primary schools across India offer a vast site for advocacy and edu-business in the name of the poor.

Public–Private Partnership, School Reform and the Poor

Public-private partnership (PPP), as mentioned earlier, was part of the privatization agenda in education mooted since the late 1990s led by the World Bank, International Finance Corporation, CfBT and other pro-market organizations (Verger 2012). 'Partnership' was seen as more appealing than privatization as the former suggested processes of dialogue and democratic decision-making. Philanthropic foundations of multinational corporates are key players in education PPPs (ePPP). This is what Saltman (2010) calls 'new philanthropy' or 'venture philanthropy' (VP). In his study of the foundations of Google, Walmart and Dell, Slatman draws attention to the power of venture philanthropies in influencing education policy and privatizing public schooling (ibid).

Since 2010, ePPP is embedded in education policy in India and is seen by governments at the centre and in the states as necessary for reforms to improve the quality of education for the poor (Nambissan 2014). I have drawn attention to a range of early interventions by private sector organizations in government schools that focused on 'quality improvement' – by bringing IT to schools and computer-aided learning and training of teachers (ibid.). Since 2009/2010, private sector and non-state organizations have been given schools/sections within them to improve the quality of education and meet growing aspirations for learning English. These include handing over of underperforming government schools to corporate foundations (for instance, the Bharati Foundation of Airtel in Rajasthan in 2009); the establishment of schools by giving land at cheaper rates and other incentives (Adarsh Schools in Punjab, again in 2009); the School Excellence Programme (SEP) in 2010 where 148 primary schools under the Brihanmumbai Municipal Corporation (BMC) in Mumbai were handed over to a group of organizations including McKinsey, Michael and Susan Dell Foundation, Save the Children, Naandi Foundation, Akshansha/Teach for India and UNICEF 'to improve attendance and learning outcomes and reduce drop out'.[12]

The rationale for ePPPs and the terms of partnership are not transparent, nor are they brought within structures of democratic decision-making. The interventions are focused on learning-outcome targets which frame out other dimensions of education. Independent evaluations of ePPPs are also lacking and programmes are usually assessed in-house of by pro-market scholars. It was through a newspaper report that the public learnt that after an expenditure of Rs 100 crore, the MBC decided to close down SEP 'on account of the poor improvement in students; performance till 2012', and the programme had to 'hand the schools under its management back to the civic body'.[13] The details are not available and no questions appear to have been asked. Teach for India (TFI), which is part of the global Teach for All network, is another programme that has been brought into schools in some of India's major cities. TFI creates separate English-medium sections within government elementary schools where professionally unqualified volunteers teach and manage children under more conducive norms. Alternative certification is integral to teacher development for school markets. By creating alternative paths for uncertified teacher–fellows/volunteers as well as exclusive spaces within publicly funded schools, organizations such as TFI compound the growing de-professionalization of teaching and stratification and differentiation within institutions that cater mainly to the poor.

I draw attention to a few PPPs that have been initiated since around 2010 as they provide a window to the privatization agenda in publicly funded schools in the name of education reform. The organizations that lead them are embedded in networks that have a global reach. In 2012, STIR (Schools and Teachers Innovating for Reform) was created as a global forum with a focus on India.[14] On its Board[15] are powerful organizations and individuals who are part of the ALABN and are today in positions where they can influence education policy processes at the national level and within individual states in India and easily enter into PPPs as well. STIR for instance states on its website that it has entered into PPPs with the governments of Uttar Pradesh and Delhi and plans to 'spread across India'. STIR's solution to raising the quality of education in government primary schools is simplistic. Its emphasis is on 're-igniting intrinsic motivation' in teachers and 'changing mind-sets' through 'building teacher networks' where they share their work. Rather than address the diverse social and pedagogic contexts of educational inequality, it seeks to merely identify, *test* and *scale* 'promising school and teacher "micro-innovations" to *improve educational outcomes for the poorest children*'.[16] Eight years on, STIR explains that it has extended its work to some other Indian states which seem to have bought into its model. The 'cost-effectiveness' of the reform is underscored. In 2012, STIR offered to bring about reform for as 'as little as $70 per teacher, or $2 per child, per year'. In 2020, the going rate offered for reform is much lower: 'our average annual cost per child in India is less than $0.50, and falling. Every $1 invested yields governments $7 in improved efficiencies'.[17]

Absolute Return for Kids (ARK) entered into a 'partnership' with the South Delhi Municipal Corporation in 2015 and adopted one of its schools. ARK's claim was that if successful, it 'hopes to open a network of primary schools in south Delhi, which could, in turn, provide a model for education reform across India'.[18] The model proposed for the PPP is one where the government provides 'infrastructure staff and utilities', and ARK and other organizations provide 'academic management, TLM (teaching and learning material) and accountability for outcomes'.[19] It comes as no surprise that ARK was part of TAN and also the ALABN. It initiated a pilot voucher scheme in schools in east Delhi in 2010–11. The organization created the Global Schools Forum (BIA and STIR are members) and is on the advisory board of STIR. It has also made inroads into policy spaces. ARK is the founding partner of the Education Alliance along with MSDF and CSF. The Alliance is registered as Network for Quality Education Foundation 'to facilitate PPPs' which are called Government-Partnership Schools or 'G-Partnership Schools'.[20] The attempt appears to blur the private in the PPP and highlight only the partnership (with the government), suggesting that it is forged to discharge social responsibilities. This is in tune with the building of moral discourses around the market mentioned earlier.

The most contentious of PPPs is the entry of the for-profit (still illegal in India) BIA into government schools in Telangana in 2015. The then Chief Minister of Andhra Pradesh invited BIA 'to *strengthen* delivery of early childhood education and primary education in the state . . .'. He was quoted as saying that 'the group could use *low-cost technology* it has pioneered, to *radically improve learning outcomes through accountable delivery*'.[21] This was Bridge speaking through a Chief Minister who appeared to be oblivious to the intense criticism that these chain schools were facing in Africa. Will BIA attempt to work with its charter school model in India? It must be remembered that charter schools and vouchers are part of neoliberal school choice policies associated with the privatization and commercialization of public schools in the US (Saltman 2010). Riep observes that 'the second market opportunity identified by Bridge involves a US\$179 billion publicly funded charter school market in low-income countries (BIA n.d.). This market venture involves partnering with governments in the Global-South to operate charter schools that are publicly funded' (Riep 2019: 8).

What we are seeing are familiar elements of the privatization of education in the name of school reform through a partnership with the state. As seen in the cases of ARK, STIR and BIA and earlier mentioned ePPPs, publicly funded schools are being opened up to private organizations on their terms. There is no transparency in PPP processes, nor have measures of accountability to the concerned children and parents been set in place in case it does not perform. This is in the nature of what Ball and Youdell (2007) call 'hidden privatisation in public education' where the private sector/its practices (marketization and managerialism as well as behaviouristic pedagogies) are brought into government schools, almost by stealth, ostensibly to improve the quality of education for the poor.

Poverty in India is a complex social reality that is intersected by a range of marginalities including caste, ethnicity, as well as gender and other identities. This is reflected in government schools, especially at the primary stage, where children enrolled largely belong to families in the lowest economic quintile (Desai *et al.* 2010). Further, over 80 per cent of Dalit and Adivasi children attend government schools and the proportion of girls enrolled exceeds that of boys (ibid.). The majority of children in these schools also the first generation to receive a formal education in their families. Though low-cost schooling advocacy claims to provide education to the poorest, neither the earlier chain schools nor the UPS reached children from the most economically and socially vulnerable strata (Nambissan 2012).

Despite relentless shaming of government schools and denigration of its teachers by private advocacy and business networks, there is little robust evidence today to show a clear private advantage in the schooling of the poor when the relevant background variables are controlled for (Day *et al.* 2014). Akmal, Crawfurd and Hares's review of studies on low-cost schools between 2014 and 2019 also finds that 'any difference between public and private schools is marginal at best and learning outcomes across both sectors are woefully low'. Significantly, they conclude that 'As things stand, there is not sufficient evidence to suggest that the private sector is a viable route to reach the poorest children' (Akmal, Crawfurd and Hares 2019).

Two pilot voucher schemes were carried out in rural Andhra Pradesh (2008–09 to 2011–12) and east and north-east Delhi (2010–11 to 2015–16). An experimental (RCT) study was also put in place in each site to study the impact of school vouchers on learning outcomes and hence the rationale for state-supported private school choice policy.[22] However, the findings from both studies showed that the voucher schemes failed to realize higher learning outcomes expected of students who won a voucher lottery and exercised the option to study in private schools as compared to their peers who remained in government schools (Karopady 2014; Crawfurd, Patel and Sandefur 2019). Karopady observes that the Andhra voucher pilot study shows that 'private schools add no value to children in terms of learning outcomes as compared to government schools. Children shifting to private schools under a scholarship programme perform no better than their government school counterparts even after five years of private schooling' (Karopady 2014: 46). Crawfurd, Patel and Sandefur have a similar story to tell from their analysis of data from the Delhi voucher scheme study anchored by ARK and referred to earlier: 'A year after the end of primary school, we find no impact of vouchers on English or math, and small negative effects on Hindi' (Crawfurd, Patel and Sandefur 2019: 1). It is important to mention that in both pilot studies, it was not UPS but private-recognized (regulated) schools that were included. The advocacy for schools for the poor emphasized that UPS which included lower-fee markets performed better than government schools. Pro-market scholars have attempted to rework their analysis and arguments in the light of less-than-favourable findings from these studies (see Tooley 2016; Muralidharan and Sundararaman 2015). The instrumental use of 'evidence' in the advocacy of private schools for the poor needs serious attention.

Children from poor and marginal communities predominate in government primary schools. These are under-resourced schools where teaching and learning are often carried out under abysmal conditions. However, for the majority of the poor in India, and particularly those actually at the bottom of the economic and social hierarchy, it is government schooling that is most accessible. They are tuition-free, mid-day meals are provided, there is special support for marginalized groups and, importantly, they are available in most of rural and urban India. These are the schools that are today the site for improvement under PPPs through affordable learning ideology and practices.

Scholars who have carried out research on poverty and education (Connell 1994; Darling-Hammond 2001 and Gorski 2013, among others) and teacher educators who have taught in high-poverty schools (Delpit 1988) point to the harsh effects of poverty on children's health and their ability to learn, as well as on their active participation in school activities. While foregrounding the complexity of poverty and a range of intersecting social inequalities, scholars have drawn attention to the fact that children from such families also lack the required cultural capital (language and other social skills) that schools demand.

Decades ago, Bernstein (1972) underscored the importance of creating meaningful and challenging learning environments within the classroom for children from poor and disadvantaged backgrounds if schools are serious about responding to the inequalities in society. He pointed out that a teacher must understand the sociocultural contexts of children which include specific marginalities, cultural diversity, and social and emotional concerns that constitute their life worlds. Delpit also underscores that 'teachers must teach all students the explicit and implicit rules of power as a first step to a just society' (Delpit 1988: 280). The implication is that teachers and schools themselves must be equipped to play this larger role.

The growing commodification and marketization of education and the preoccupation with cost-cutting and global scaling to reap profits has little in common with the concerns of social justice, the rights of children and the larger purpose of education. While the neglect of publicly funded education by the state has been mentioned as one of the reasons for the decline of government schools, the failure to ensure that teacher education programmes equip teachers with a critical perspective and an understanding of pedagogies that can address poverty and social disadvantage within a rights and social justice framework is also a reality. By its very framing, low-cost schooling that is being advocated cannot even begin to address these concerns because the deskilled teacher and narrow curriculum are key elements in its standardized for-profit business model. On the other hand, publicly funded education is informed by the Right to Education (RtE) 2009 which has laid down norms to ensure the right to equitable education to all children and hence has the potential to do so.[23]

Contemporary Challenges: Some Reflections

Since early 2020, the world has seen the devastating impact of Covid-19 on schooling. Globally, 'hundreds of millions of students' are said to have been affected by school closures (UNESCO 2020). In India as well, formal schooling has come to a standstill. The poor have borne the brunt of the pandemic, as seen in the massive dislocation of their lives and loss of livelihoods. This has also placed the education of their children at grave risk. In such a situation, we need to look more closely at the calls, globally and within India, for ways to minimize the disruption of children's education.

Online learning, education technology and digital resources are seen as the solution to the current crisis and the way to effectively tide over it. It must be remembered that education technology, digitization and datafication are the key drivers of the global education industry (for more on GEI, see Verger, Lubienski and Steiner-Khamsi 2016; Ball 2019). Since around 2015, scholars have pointed to expanding markets in this sector as well as efforts of industry (mainly ed-tech companies), international organizations and states to bring together synergies from technology that will enable 'disruption' and innovations seen as necessary for the qualitative transformation of systems of education (ibid.). Thus, well before Covid-19, education technology was the main thrust of the GEI with global corporates as major players in this booming business.

Education technology business has received a fillip and private actors have mobilized resources and consolidated networks not merely to construct 'solutions' to meet the challenge posed by Covid-19 but to 'reimagine' an education based on technology and artificial intelligence. It is this agenda and its unfolding that need to be looked at more closely. For instance, by mid-2020 itself, the Asia Venture Philanthropic Network (AVPN)[24] which has more than 600 members (corporates, philanthropic foundations and development organizations) had already organized events around 'Re-Imagining Education post-Covid-19'. A post on the AVPN website observes that 'this might be the *start of an era that necessitates the convergence of technology and education in a way that has never been witnessed before*'.[25]

Social impact bonds were already being floated in India to mobilize Corporate Social Responsibility (CSR) and other funds which were to be offered to organizations that were prepared to meet learning outcome targets for further funding. MSDF, for instance, has the 'Quality Education India Development Impact Bond' (QEIDIB).[26] Social Finance India (Ashish Dhawan of CSF is on the Board) has the 'Indian Education Outcomes Fund' and aims to 'bring together service providers, investors and funders to set-up scalable outcomes focussed solutions addressing India's pressing education challenges'.[27] Covid-19 has provided enormous opportunities for the ed-tech business that was already looking towards transforming the paradigm of education and enabling increasingly profitable markets. We can expect to see for-profit, low-cost narrow solutions couched in discourses suitably tweaked to flag the enormity of the Covid-19 crisis and the urgent imperative of technology to 'effectively' ensure equitable and inclusive education.

Reports have highlighted the vulnerability of children, especially from poor and marginalized communities, as a result of the Covid-19 pandemic (Jha and Ghatak 2020). The adverse impact on their education has been highlighted by early reports and a few studies. A survey of 1,400 children was carried out across fifteen states and union territories in India in August 2021 (The School Team 2021). The children lived in rural hamlets and urban poor settlements 'inhabited by underprivileged families' (ibid: 1–3). The findings of the survey are disturbing. They reveal that during the 500 days of school closures in India the overwhelming majority of rural (72 per cent) and urban (53 per cent) children covered in the survey were studying from 'time to time' or 'not studying at all' (ibid.: 2). It concludes that 'only a minority of privileged children were able to study online in the comfort and safety of their home' (ibid.: 1).

Digital inequality and lack of teacher preparedness in relation to online learning have been raised as key issues during the pandemic in India and are concerns that will have to be addressed in the short run.[28] However, the larger agenda of powerful corporate and venture philanthropic organizations to put in place individualized and personalized for-profit learning packages as education needs to be interrogated. Williamson and Hogan's observation from internet searchers in mid-2020 is worth citing in detail:

> A 'global education industry' of private and commercial organisations has played a significant role in educational provision during the Covid-19 crisis, working at a local, national and international scales to insert edtech into education systems and practices, It has often set the agenda, offered technical solutions for government departments of education to follow and is actively pursuing long-term reforms whereby private technology companies would be embedded in public education systems during the recovery from the Covid-19 crisis and beyond it in new models of 'hybrid' teaching and learning. (Williamson and Hogan 2020: 1)

Williamson and Hogan add that 'this instantiation of the global education industry produced and circulated powerful ideas about Covid-19 as a novel "opportunity" to "reimagine" education. . . . It established the crisis as a catalytic opportunity for educational transformation' (ibid.). This chapter has already discussed the technology-driven narrow, standardized, scalable business model of education being advocated and marketed as high-quality education for the poor. What is important is that discourses constructed and circulated through powerful advocacy networks camouflaged the democratic deficit that characterized this school model. This must alert us to critically interrogate post-Covid discourses and practices around new education imaginaries led by business interests (Nambissan 2020).

The National Education Policy on Education was announced mid-2020. A close reading of the policy document reveals that it is couched in the language of flexibility and choice and encourages the privatization of education including in government institutions. The NEP lists 'fundamental principles that will guide the education system' that include 'flexibility, so that learners have the ability to choose their learning trajectories' as well as the 'extensive use of technology in teaching and learning' and the facilitation of 'philanthropic and community participation' (GoI 2020: 5–6). Also mentioned is that 'the requirement for schools will be made less restrictive' and that 'Other models for schools will also be piloted such as public–philanthropic partnerships' (ibid.: 11). The CSF report on private schools in India (Centre Square Foundation 2020) released in 2020 appears to be speaking to the NEP when it calls for state-funded vouchers to access private schools (large numbers had shut down following Covid-19) and a separate private school regulatory authority. Improvement of government schools through PPP as well as the charter school model is also among the solutions offered (ibid.). The report flags for the first time the poor quality of learning in low-cost private schools. However, it continues to focus on learning outcomes and reform of government schools through managerial and market principles.

Covid-19 has seen the shutting down of private schools catering especially to low-income families and the return of children to government schools in large numbers. This poses an enormous challenge to publicly funded education – a system that has suffered decades of neglect and denigration and has been subject to increasing privatization. Covid-19 has drawn attention to the institutionalized space of schooling and provided an opportunity for critical reflection on public education.

There is a need for a deep and complex understanding of the implications of Covid-19 for the deprivations and disadvantages suffered by the poor, keeping in mind prior inequalities as well as new marginalities that are emerging. The adverse impact of the pandemic on the education of children as well as on the capabilities of schools in coping with the crisis has become clear. It is unlikely that technological fixes will be able to address the structural and institutional roots of inequalities in education that have been compounded during the pandemic. Collaborative networks of researchers and interdisciplinary conversations are urgently required to systematically study and critically engage with the extremely complex processes that are unfolding and to which I have attempted to draw attention. Such research must also inform advocacy, which is long overdue, for the 'public' in education – that is, one which is equitable and informed by the rights of all children. A public education that foregrounds the critical role of social and pedagogic relations and practices that are mindful of the complexity of poverty, diversity and the range of marginalities that children bear because of the iniquitous social structure in which their families are located. It also means revisiting the public purpose of education and engaging with how to realize and strengthen it.

Notes
[1] A number of terms have been used to signify private education that can be accessed by poor/low income families. The term 'low-fee' school was used in the early advocacy of edu-business and subsequently 'affordable learning'. I prefer to use low-cost/low-budget schooling as this indicates that the cost of provision of such education is low.
[2] See the PALF website: https://www.affordable-learning.com/about.html, accessed December 2017.
[3] http://www.delhidistrictcourts.nic.in/Feb08/Social%20Jurist%20Vs.%20GNCT.pdf. All unrecognized schools were given until 2013 to meet the required norms and gain recognition or close down under the Right to Education Act, 2009. See

https://legislative.gov.in/sites/default/files/A2009-35_0.pdf, accessed January 2017.

4 Vouchers are a key plank of neoliberal school choice policies being implemented in the US, Chile and Argentina.

5 https://www.omidyar.com/news/bridge-international-academies-launches-affordable-schools-kenyaOmdiyar, accessed January 2014.

6 The Omega chain of schools in Ghana, which is owned by Tooley and entrepreneur Ken Donkoh, have similar aims: 'to bring quality education to as many children as possible'. They claim that 'it is possible for a private company to educate the poor at a profit . . . and provide high quality education at the lowest cost possible'. See https://olbios.org/pay-a-little-only-if-and-as-you-learn/, accessed July 2021. For a critique of Omega schools, see Riep (2014).

7 https://www.pearson.com/news-and-research/announcements/2016/11/pearson-affordable-learning-fund-makes-investment-in-indonesian-.html, accessed December 2017.

8 https://www.affordable-learning.com/about.html, accessed December 2017.

9 Biesta (2010) laments the dominance of what he calls 'learnification' in educational discourses and practices.

10 https://www.affordable-learning.com/about.html, accessed December 2017.

11 Ibid. See also respective company websites.

12 https://indianexpress.com/article/cities/mumbai/civic-body-to-scrap-school-excellence-programme/, accessed March 2018.

13 Ibid.

14 See website for details about STIR: http://stireducation.org/, accessed July 2020.

15 The Global Advisory Board includes 'the World Bank's Chief Education Economist; chief advisor to UN Education Special Envoy Gordon Brown; Professors James Tooley and Eric Hanushek; a global director at Pearson; the co-founder of Teach for All; and the former Permanent Secretary for Education for Uganda'. The 'India Advisory Board includes the CEOs and Directors of some of India's most progressive education reform organizations—Central Square Foundation, Bharti Foundation, JPAL, Pratham and Akanksha' . . . 'STIR is fortunate to be funded by some of the world's leading foundations and development agencies, including USAID, the Macarthur Foundation, the Mastercard Foundation and the Draper Richards Kaplan Foundation', http://stireducation.org/pdf/Senior-Programme-Manager-Karnataka.pdf, accessed July 2020. In 2020, there were many more funders. See updated website http://stireducation.org/, accessed July 2020.

16 http://stireducation.org/, accessed July 2020.

17 https://stireducation.org/our-learning/, accessed July 2020.

18 http://arkonline.org/news/new-school-model-south-delhi-could-transformeducation, accessed July 2020.

19 http://arkonline.org/news/new-school-model-south-delhi-could-transformeducation, accessed September 2017.

20 http//.www.theeducationalliance.org/, accessed December 2019.

21 http://www.business-standard.com/article/pti-stories/bridges-international-to-partner-with-ap-state-government-115090901472_1.html, accessed September 2017.

22 The Andhra Pradesh voucher pilot programme was 'implemented and evaluated' by the 'Indian state of Andhra Pradesh, working with the Legatum Institute, the Azim Premji Foundation, and under the technical leadership of the World Bank' (World Bank 2016: 1). The Delhi voucher programme was 'administered by the UK-based charity Absolute Return for Kids (ARK) and the Centre for Civil Society' (Crawfurd, Patel and Sandefur 2019: 6).

23 It is important to keep in mind that the publicly funded school system includes reputed and sought after institutions such as the Navodaya and Kendriya Vidyalayas,

indicating that the state can also provide high-quality education. The RtE aims to ensure that all children have access to such education as a matter of right.

[24] https://avpn.asia/about-us/, accessed August 2000.

[25] https://avpn.asia/event/re-imagining-education-post-covid-19/, accessed August 2020.

[26] https://qualityeducationindiadib.com/wp-content/uploads/2019/08/Quality-Education-India-DIB-Case-Study.pdf, accessed July 2020.

[27] https://socialfinance.org.in/india-education-outcomes-fund-2/, accessed June 2020.

[28] Jha and Ghatak (2020) show how significant challenges and constraints in online learning vary for children in different social contexts. See also The School Team (2021).

References

Akmal, M., L. Crawfurd and S. Hares (2019), 'Low-cost Private Schools: What Have We Learned in the Five Years Since the DFID Rigorous Review', available at https://www.cgdev.org/blog/low-cost-private-schools-what-have-we-learned-five-years-dfid-rigorous-review, accessed July 2020.

Ball, S.J. (2016), 'Following Policy: Networks, Network Ethnography and Education Policy Mobilities', *Journal of Education Policy*, vol 35, pp. 549–66.

———— (2019), 'Serial Entrepreneurs, Angel Investors and Capez Light Edu-business Start-ups in India: Philanthropy, Impact Investing, and Systemic Educational Change', in M. Parreira do Amaral, G. Steiner-Khamsi and C. Thompson, eds, *Researching the Global Education Industry: Commodification, the Market and Business Involvement,* pp. 23–46, London: Palgrave Macmillan.

Ball, S.J. and D. Youdell (2007), 'Hidden Privatisation in Public Education', Preliminary report prepared for the Educational International 5th World Congress, available at https://pages.ei-ie.org/quadrennialreport/2007/upload/content_trsl_images/630/Hidden_privatisation-EN.pdf, accessed December 2017.

Bernstein, B. (1972 [1970]), 'Education Cannot Compensate for Society', in D. Rubenstein and C. Stoneman, eds, *Education for Democracy,* second edition, Middlesex: Penguin, pp. 104–16.

Biesta, G.J. (2010), *Good Education in an Age of Measurement: Ethics, Politics, Democracy.* New York: Routledge.

Centre Square Foundation (2020), *State of the Sector Report on Private Schools in India,* available at https://www.centralsquarefoundation.org/state-of-the-sector-report-on-private-schools-in-india/, accessed August 2020.

Connell, R.W. (1994), 'Poverty and Education', *Harvard Educational Review*, vol. 64, pp. 125–50.

Crawfurd, L., D. Patel and J. Sandefur (2019), 'Low Returns to Low-cost Private Schools: Experimental Evidence from Delhi' (preliminary draft).

Darling-Hammond, L. (2001), *Inequality in Teaching and Schooling: How Opportunity is Rationed to Students of Color in America,* available at https://www.ncbi.nlm.nih.gov/books/NBK223640/, accessed August 2020.

Day, A.L., C. Mcloughlin, M. Aslam, J. Engel, J. Wales, S. Rawal, R. Batley, G. Kingdon, S. Nicolai and P. Rose (2014), *The Role and Impact of Private Schools in Developing Countries: A Rigorous Review of the Evidence. Final Report. Education Rigorous Literature Review,* Department for International Development, available at http://r4d.dfid.gov.uk, accessed November 2017.

Delpit, L.D. (1988), 'The Silenced Dialogue: Power and Pedagogy in Educating Other People's Children', *Harvard Educational Review*, vol. 58, no. 3, August, pp. 280–98.

Desai, S., A. Dubey, B.L. Joshi, M. Sen, A. Shariff and R. Vanneman (2010), *Human Development in India: Challenges for a Society in Transition,* New Delhi: Oxford University Press.

Gorski, P.C. (2013), *Reaching and Teaching Students in Poverty: Strategies for Erasing the Opportunity Gap*, New York: Teachers College Press.

GoI (Government of India) (2020), *National Education Policy 2020*, Ministry of Human Resources Development, Government of India.

Hogan, A., S. Sellar and B. Lingard (2016), 'Commercializing Comparison: Pearson Puts the TLC in Soft Capitalism', *Journal of Education Policy*, vol. 31, no. 3, pp. 243–58.

Jha, J. and N. Ghatak (2020), 'What a Survey of Children in Bihar Revealed about Online Schooling', *The Wire*, 25 May, available at https://thewire.in/education/online-school-education, accessed July 2021.

Kamat, S., C.A. Spreen and I. Jonnalagadda (2016), *Profiting from the Poor: The Emergence of Multinational Edu-businesses in Hyderabad, India*, available at https://download.ei-ie.org/Docs/WebDepot/ei-ie_edu_ privatisation_final_corrected.pdf, accessed November 2017.

Karopady, D.D. (2014), 'Does School Choice Help Rural Children from Disadvantaged Sections? Evidence from Longitudinal Research in Andhra Pradesh', *Economic and Political Weekly*, vol. 49, no. 51, pp. 46–53.

Kremer, M., N. Chaudhury, F.H. Rogers, K. Muralidharan and J. Hammer (2005), 'Teacher Absence in India: A Snapshot', *Journal of the European Economic Association*, vol. 3, pp. 658–67, retrieved from doi:10.1162/jeea.2005.3.2-3.658

Muralidharan, K. and V. Sundararaman (2015), 'The Aggregate Effect of School Choice: Evidence from a Two-stage Experiment in India', available at https://econweb.ucsd.edu/~kamurali/papers/Published%20Articles/The%20Aggregate%20Effects%20of%20School%20Choice%20Full%20(10%20February%202015).pdf, accessed September 2017.

Nambissan, G.B. (2012), 'Private Schools for the Poor: Business as Usual?', *Economic and Political Weekly*, vol. 47, no. 44, pp. 51–58.

—— (2014), 'Poverty, Markets and Elementary Education in India', in Working Papers of the Max Weber Foundation's Transnational Research Group India: 'Poverty Reduction and Policy for the Poor between the State and Private Actors: Education Policy in India since the Nineteenth Century', London: German Historical Institute (also on http://www.perspectivia.net/publikationen/trg-working-papers/nambissan_markets).

—— (2020), 'Caste and the Politics of the Early "Public" in Schooling: Dalit Struggle for an Equitable Education', *Contemporary Education Dialogue*, vol. 17, no. 2, pp. 126–54.

Nambissan, G.B. and S.J. Ball (2011), 'Advocacy Networks, Choice and Private Schooling of the Poor in India', in M. Lall and G.B. Nambissan, eds, *Education and Social Justice in the Era of Globalization: Perspectives from India and the UK*, New Delhi: Routledge, pp. 161–80.

Prahalad, C.K. and S.L. Hart (2001), *The Fortune at the Bottom of the Pyramid*, available at http://www.stuartlhart.com/sites/stuartlhart.com/files/Prahalad_Hart_2001_SB.pdf, accessed September 2017.

Riep, C.B. (2014), 'Omega Schools Franchise in Ghana: "Affordable" Private Education for the Poor or For-profiteering?', in I. Macpherson, S. Robertson and G. Walford, eds, *Education, Privatization, and Social Justice:Case Studies from Africa, South Asia, and South East Asia*, Oxford, UK: Symposium Books, pp. 259–77.

—— (2019), *What Do We Really Know about Bridge International Academies? A Summary of Research Findings*, Brussels: Education International, available at https://www.researchgate.net/publication/343510376_Commercialisation_and_privatisation_inof_education_in_the_context_of_Covid-19, accessed December 2020.

Riep, C.B. and M. Machacek (2016), *Schooling the Poor Profitably: The Innovations and Deprivations of Bridge International Academies in Uganda*, Brussels: Education International, available at file:///E:/DATA%20C/Documents/Privatisation_Markets_March%202020/Riep%202019_EI_Research_GR_BIA_corr.pdf, accessed July 2020.

Robertson, S.L. and A. Verger (2012), 'Governing Education through Public–Private Partnerships', Bristol: Centre for Globalisation, Education and Societies, University of Bristol, available at http://susanleerobertson.com/publications/, accessed July 2017.

Saltman, K.J. (2010), *The Gift of Education: Public Education and Venture Philanthropy*, New York: Palgrave Macmillan.

Srivastava, P. (2016), '*Questioning the Global Scaling* Up of Low-fee Private Schooling: The Nexus between Business, Philanthropy and PPPs', in A. Verger, C. Lubienski and G. Steiner-Khamsi, eds, *The World Yearbook of Education 2016: The Global Education Industry*, New York: Routledge.

Stewart, C. (2015), 'Bridge International Academies: Scripted Schooling for $6 a Month is an Audacious Answer to Educating the Poorest Children across Africa and Asia', available at http://www.independent.co.uk/news/world/africa/bridge-international-academiesscripted- schooling-for-6-a-month-is-an-audacious-answer to-educating-10420028.html, accessed August 2017.

The School Team (2021), *Locked Out: Emergency Report on School Education*, available at https://ruralindiaonline.org/en/library/resource/locked-out-emergency-report-on-school-education/, accessed December 2021.

Tooley, J. (1999), 'The Global Education Industry', IEA Hobart Paper No. 141, 1999/ SSRN: https://ssrn.com/abstract=681181 or http://dx.doi.org/10.2139/ssrn.681181

—— (2009), *The Beautiful Tree: A Personal Journey into How the World's Poorest People are Educating Themselves*, New Delhi: Penguin/Viking.

—— (2016), 'Extending Access to Low-cost Private Schools through Vouchers: An Alternative Interpretation of a Two-stage "School Choice" Experiment in India', *Oxford Review of Education*, vol. 42, no. 5, pp. 579–93, DOI: 10.1080/03054985.2016.1217689

Tooley, J., P. Dixon and S.V. Gomathi (2007), 'Private Schools and the Millennium Development Goal of Universal Primary Education: A Census and Comparative Survey in Hyderabad, India', *Oxford Review of Education*, vol. 33, no. 5, pp. 539–60.

UNESCO (2020), *Education: From Disruption to Recovery*, available at https://en.unesco.org/covid19/educationresponse, accessed August 2020.

Verger, A. (2012), 'Framing and Selling Global Education Policy: The Promotion of Public–Private Partnerships for Education in Low-income Contexts', *Journal of Education Policy*, vol. 27, no. 1, pp. 109–30.

Verger, A., C. Lubienski and G. Steiner-Khamsi (2016), *World Yearbook of Education 2016: The Global Education Industry*, New York: Routledge.

Williamson, B. and A. Hogan (2021), *Commercialisation and Privatisation in/of Education in the Context of Covid-19*, Education International.

World Bank (2016), 'India: Do Kids in Private Schools Learn More?', in *From Evidence to Policy*, available at https://smartnet.niua.org/sites/default/files/resources/105178-revised-public-e2p-india-vouchers-redo-read.pdf, accessed August 2020.

3

Policy Shifts in School Education

A Critical Analysis

Jyoti Raina

Elementary education in India was envisioned as a leveller to combat the prevailing systemic inequalities through policies aimed at the inclusive development of our stratified society. Article 45 in Part IV of the Constitution is a provision for equitable elementary education directing the Indian state to provide free and compulsory education for all children until they complete the age of fourteen years. The companion Article 46 further directs the state to promote with special care the educational and economic interests of the Scheduled Castes (SCs), Scheduled Tribes (STs) and other disadvantaged sections of society. These provisions were enablers of social justice, inclusivity and scholastic development in the nation's educational imagination. It was assumed that an equitable school education system would have the potential to attenuate inequities through access to knowledge leading to emancipatory possibilities for all sections of society.

Has the Indian state attempted to actualize such a vision of inclusive development through an equitable system of schooling that attempts to transcend inherited inequality? Could the Indian state have fared better? What does faring better imply? Is our elementary education system just, inclusive and equitable, serving an enabling role in democratizing society? What would such a system look like, in a basic normative sense? What is the direction of cumulative policy shifts in post-independent India? Has school education attenuated region-specific social divisions of class, caste and gender? If not, is course correction with specific policy prescriptions possible now when almost all aspects of our social and political life are neoliberalized?

This essay is a commentary on these posers. Based on an analysis of school education policy shifts in post-independent India, the history of school education is divided into three phases. A critical analysis highlights how policy shifts in each phase have accentuated differentiation, firmed up social divisions, exacerbated inequality and magnified structural exclusion in the Indian school education system. School education has distorted into entrenched multilayered hierarchies of access consisting of different types of schools.

Study of Policy Development

The study of education in India has been demarcated into pre-Jomtien and post-Jomtien phases (Sadgopal 1994). The Government of India's (GoI's) concurrence to the Jomtien Declaration (1990), euphemistically termed *World Declaration on Education for All,* ostensibly to meet the basic learning needs of all children and youth, was a major policy departure in independent India's history of education. The constitutional vision of elementary education for all children up to eight years was reduced in the Jomtien programme documents to five years, along with the term elementary education replaced by primary education. The main features of Indian education policy in the latter phase were: increasing abdication by the state, trivialization of educational aims, fragmentation of knowledge and a dilution of policy commitment to a public education system (ibid.: 110–117). In another policy analysis, two divisions in the phases of policy change have been identified. The first, beginning with the introduction of the National Policy on Education (NPE) in 1986 and the second with the international donor agency-led structural adjustment programmes (SAPs) following the liberalization of the Indian economy in 1991 (Velaskar 2010: 70).

Furthermore, in another perspective aimed at understanding the changes in the educational policy framework in post-Independence political economy of education, three phases in the post-Independence period are delineated. The first constitutional welfarism phase from 1947 to 1968 recognizes a 'state-supported capitalism' albeit one in which the public sector dominated the private. The years 1968–1991 are regarded as the second phase where the balance of forces between the public and the private sector in education was a crisis for state-supported capitalism. The third neoliberalism phase is from 1991 to date (Sadgopal 2009: 13–14). This represents the 'neoliberal phase of state-supported capitalism when the private sector incrementally established its dominance over the public sector, with the public sector becoming subservient to the demands of the private sector (Sadgopal 2021: 655).

In the present essay, the author proposes three phases to the study of policy development in post-independent India. Each of these phases is characterized by a distinct direction of aims, shifts and policymaking processes with identifiable concerns. The three phases are as follows. The period from

Independence till 1986 is viewed as the first phase. This phase was located in the constitutional framework of policymaking aimed at egalitarianism that was followed by a 'just' state, which looked at school education as a public good. The second phase begins with the announcement of the NPE in 1986 marking the beginning of increased non-state stake holding and consequent neoliberalization of education. This phase extends into the economic reforms of 1991 characterized by the dilution of policy thrust on providing social infrastructure and public goods like elementary education. The direction of policy change was rooted in an economistic framework derived from the ideology of neoliberalism that became dominant in shaping social and economic practices. The third phase from 2016 onwards marks not just an intensification of the neoliberalization of school education but essentializes the neoliberal common sense. This is a completely altered policy scenario with wider social, political and educational consequences.

Phase I: Policy Wisdom of Early Post-Independent Years: Egalitarian Visions

Pre-colonial Indian society was characterized by exclusions based on economic status, caste and gender while colonial education 'sought to legitimize the privileges of colonizers' (Kumar 2006: 15). Yet there emerged historic countercurrents of an egalitarian imagination. Two of the significant trajectories in this direction were: Rajarshi Shahu Maharaj (1894–1922) in the erstwhile princely state of Kolhapur established India's first state-funded public education system based on freedom from discrimination in the early twentieth century (Bagade 1982). The second countercurrent was the contest of British hesitance to universalize elementary education in 1911 by Gopal Krishna Gokhale's Free and Compulsory Education Bill, which aimed at free and compulsory primary education for all children in a phased process. Gokhale even raised the demand for specific proposals in this regard before the Imperial Legislative Council (Dasgupta 1993: 124). The freedom movement inherited this radical social imaginary – an imagination of a society in which all the sections of the population, including children belonging to various social backgrounds, had claims on the state in accordance with the principles of equality, justice and protective discrimination. The role of the state determines the nature of rights availed by the citizenry and has been the basis of intellectual, social and educational development in the history of human civilization (Prasad 2020: 177). The first goalpost of educational planning 'towards reversing the long history of structural exclusion and creating equal opportunity in education' (Velaskar 2021: 576) was to provide basic educational provision of quality elementary education.

Post-independent India's agenda of educational development for our emerging nation-state was shaped by this progressive vision. The Preamble to the Constitution reflects an aspiration of democratic citizenship for a socialist, egalitarian and just society, envisioning education to be the moral force to build a new inclusive society. Article 45, by directing the state to provide free and compulsory education to all children till fourteen years of age, aimed to actualize this constitutional morality. The Preamble set out the policy development framework according to which education was a process to build citizenship for a democratic society with a guarantee of equality as well as equality of opportunity. Equitable elementary education that reached out to children from diverse social, linguistic and economic backgrounds was constitutionally imagined as a public good in our stratified society.

Be that as it may, early decades of educational development in post-Independence India ignored an actual policy thrust on elementary education (Sadgopal 2010; Bhatty 2014). The University Education Commission (1948–49), which looked into the aims and scope of higher education, and the Secondary Education Commission (1952–53) were constituted first in the Indian state. Both held limited terms of reference, focusing on the higher and secondary levels of education respectively.

The Indian Education Commission (IEC), popularly known as the Kothari Commission, aimed at a comprehensive review of the state of education in the country and was set up as late as 1964. It submitted its report in 1966 on the general pattern of education being necessary for nation-building. The IEC envisioned education to be integral to national development, thus, it titled its report *Education and National Development*. The recommendations of its voluminous report included: provisioning for free and compulsory elementary education, reconstructing a uniform educational structure of 10+2+3 all over the country, strengthening teachers' education, developing regional languages, publishing quality textbooks, relating education to productivity, with a thrust on scientific education, provisioning adult education, modernizing the methods of teaching and equalizing educational opportunity by the establishment of a common school system (CSS) of public education (GoI 1966).

The tonality of the report aligned with an optimistic sociology of education typifying the 1960s era of redistributive policymaking for inclusive development through public education. The sociological framing underlying the policy prescriptions believed that the relationship between education and social change was that education could harbinger democratic transformative processes. In the spirit of constitutional morality, the report of the commission was critical of the classist access to school education through differential arrangements of schooling for children belonging to different sections of society. The commission's report lamented that this was turning schools into oppressive instruments of the perpetuation, legitimization and entrenchment of a class divide (NCERT 1970: 449). To gradually abolish this divide that becomes a barrier to the social integration of certain advantaged socioeconomic sections from the rest of the community, the recommendation for the establishment of the CSS to attenuate the systemic inequities between public and private schools was seminal. According to the recommendation made,

> [the] existing segregation in the educational system in which the well-to-do educate their children in a small minority of private schools that charge high fees and maintain good standards while the masses are constrained to send their children to the vast bulk of publicly maintained and free (or charging comparatively lower rates of fees) but poor quality schools, should be brought to an end; and the objective of educational policy should be to evolve a common school system of public education. (Naik 1969: 5)

Such a state-funded school system would be open to all children irrespective of their social background, making quality education universally accessible while mitigating glaring systemic inequalities. Based on the report of the commission, the seven-and-a-half-page NPE 1968 was released. It accepted the recommendation of CSS for the twin goals of equalizing educational opportunity and promoting social cohesion and national integration among the country's children (GoI 1968). The system was not meant to be a uniform school system in terms of curricula, pedagogy or learning but 'common' for children belonging to different sections of society in a vision of egalitarian education.

The notion of equality was bestowed great importance by the state, in principle, as education came to be perceived as a right and not a privilege (Kumar 2006: 22). The stance of the state recognized equitable elementary education as a public good. Policymaking emphasized the concerns of equality, social justice, equal access to educational opportunities and direct delivery of elementary education as values underlying the inclusive state agenda.

State action however bellied policy intent since NPE 1968 offered a 'broad framework only without delineating the specific necessary organizational and financial support structures this requires from the state' (Raina 2020b: 73). The constitutional vision of state-funded education for children from different sections of society did not turn into a reality, and the 'early decades of Independence witnessed a continuous deferral of achievement targets for universal elementary education' (Mukhopadhyay and

Sarangapani 2018: 9). The Indian state failed at the implementation process that was simply passed over without even an analysis of why policies remained rhetoric. This neglect of the state sorely underwrites Article 45, the only constitutional provision with a time frame that ended in 1960, far from its actualization.

Different social processes in post-colonial Indian democracy acted towards the maintenance of autonomy between institutions (state schools) and the norms (equality) that are supposed to inform their participation in society (Bhargava, Reifeld and Stiftung 2005: 40). The self-aggrandizing interests of private schools as a social group retained autonomy from institutional arrangements of school education even in the face of contrarian policy 'norms' like CSS as mandated by NPE 1968.

'Has the Indian state earnestly attempted inclusive development through an equitable system of schooling?' is arguably one of the most important research problems in post-colonial educational studies. Yet this cardinal problem – the failure of the state and its minutiae – has not received the attention it merits. In particular, a question apposite to the first phase, which has slipped under the radar, is that in an era when vital industries like steel, coal, airlines and copper were nationalized, when another major institution of our society, banks, were also nationalized in the name of nation-building, why were our schools not nationalized? This was the crucial historical juncture when,

> in principle, there was only one officially acknowledged, planned and financially supported stream in Indian education (that is, the government, local body and government-aided schools of comparable quality), the relatively minor streams of private unaided schools (erroneously called public schools) and Kendriya Vidyalayas (or Central Schools) notwithstanding. (Sadgopal 2006: 97)

The ground was fertile in such a landscape to institutionalize equality in education for all by nationalizing schools. This would render classrooms inclusive, deepen democracy and ameliorate the life chances of vulnerable socioeconomic groups. The neglected research-worthy question that begs consideration is whether it was an absence of political will, resistance among dominant hegemonic social quarters for an inclusive childhood for their children, influential advocacy networks of elite private schools or simply the immiserating rule of private capital because of which the prospects of school nationalization were not even raised in the years even though the policy thrust was on establishing a CSS. In the first phase of policy development, there was ample scope for the state to fare better since faring better simply meant actualizing the policy solution of setting up a CSS. The state could have thereby fared so much better at turning education into a leveller. In hindsight, the state missed a historical opportunity.

Phase II: Heralding Non-State Stakeholding

The release of the second policy – NPE 1986 – begins the second phase of policy development. NPE 1986, along with the Programme of Action (POA) 1986, as also their modified versions of 1992, undertook policy initiatives like the introduction of non-formal education (NFE) which added another stream to the school education structure. NPE 1986 also introduced, under the category of pace-setting schools, a stream that was supposedly above the formal school, that is, for children with special talent 'by making good quality education available to them, irrespective of their capacity to pay for it' (GoI 1986: 13). Both these initiatives institutionalized discriminatory parallel streams and multi-tracks in school education. These tracks were layered below and above the mainstream system. On the policy concerns of equalizing educational opportunities as well as strengthening CSS, NPE 1986 policy text merely restated the earlier recommendations briefly but again passed over matters of detail or implementation. These ignored aspects included specific proposals on the commitment of public funds, measures to mitigate disparities and region-specific thrust on school planning and management.

Non-formal education was now the flagship programme to universalize elementary education. It was touted as comparable in quality to formal schooling simply because of special provisions for girls in afternoon centres and boys in the evening. The policy text uses the word 'resolve' (GoI 1986: 17) in addressing the problem of children dropping out of school and retaining them in school with coordination with non-formal centres but via the emergent system of NFE. Non-formal education proliferated as the Indian state had evaded its responsibility of providing free elementary education for all children as stated in the directive principles of state policy decade after decade. The Acharya Ramamurti Committee Report (GoI 1990) pointed out that at the time of the adoption of NPE in 1986, the number of 'out of school' children in the country was almost half the total number of school-going children.

At the time of the introduction of the international donor agency-led SAP in 1991, the funding organizations had pointed out that India's adult literacy rate (calculated for persons over seven years of age) was a mere 52 per cent. This was of course considerable progress from the time of Independence when the literacy rate was around 15 per cent. Even our counterparts in East Asia – Thailand and South Korea – with literacy rates at 68 and 71 per cent, respectively, in 1961 fared substantially better

(World Bank 1997: 15). We were rather closer in this regard to sub-Saharan Africa's literacy rate of 50.3 per cent (Grindle 2004: 29). By 1991, we were home to large numbers of illiterates: 127 million males and 197 million females (World Bank 1997: 16). Also, educational development was very uneven with caste-, gender- and class-based overlapping inequities, with some variations across states. It is therefore not surprising that policy analysts have highlighted that by the early 1990s, India's school education 'was in dire need of a new direction with respect to both policy and operational programmes' (Priyam 2016: 160).

The assumption underlying the new direction of policy formulation was that a formal school is not necessary for every child, unabashedly recognizing that those who were already out of the system could make do with a non-formal centre of learning in the name of elementary education. Anil Sadgopal elaborates,

> The most visible structural distortion of the school system comprised the introduction of a non-formal (NFE) stream of educational facilities (not schools!) of inferior quality for more than half of the nation's children below the school system. The 1986 policy also introduced a layer of expensive residential Navodaya Vidyalayas above the school system for a handful of children (about 80 children per district per year). The Navodaya Vidyalaya was justified, among others, on the untenable ground of acting as 'pacesetting schools' for the ordinary government schools in its neighbourhood – an objective that turned out to be entirely misconceived. (Sadgopal 2010: 4)

Both the policy texts of NPE 1986 and its companion document, POA 1986, were approved by the Parliament in May and November 1986, respectively. The Parliament revised NPE 1986 in 1992, which stated the rationale for the legitimization of this structural distortion:

> Given the present condition of schools in general, the challenges before the school system are many, e.g., enrolling and retaining children who cannot afford to attend school regularly; a harmonious interaction with community around; improving the infrastructure, quality and learning environment; and ensuring that every student acquires minimum levels of learning. These challenges are daunting enough and it does not seem desirable to overload the school system with yet another formidable challenge of meeting the educational needs of children with severe para-educational constraints. (GoI 1992: 9.13)

The school education structural landscape at the time of the release of NPE 1986 comprised government, government-aided and private schools (unaided by the government) but the 1986 policy proposed other streams that were both parallel to and above the mainstream formal school education system. The previous policy, NPE 1968, had attempted to at least course-correct this structural distortion through the policy imperative of the CSS. NPE 1986 camouflaged a commitment to the ideal of CSS with the policy text stating that effective measures will be taken in the direction of CSS (GoI 1986), even though it made contradictory policy shift(s) in the opposite direction by legitimizing the differentiations in the school system by institutionalizing multiple tracks of 'higher' and 'lower' to mainstream schools. It can be read as the beginning of a distinct new phase of policy change or a new policy cycle:

> . . . it was the first policy-level acknowledgement since independence that elementary school education of *comparable quality* will *not* become available to all children of India in the 6 to 14 age group. The notion of education of *comparable quality* for all children, irrespective of their class, creed, caste, gender, linguistic or cultural background or physical/mental disability, was clearly implied in the Constitution. (Sadgopal 2006: 96, emphasis in original)

There is no gainsaying that the policy significantly 'diluted notions of inequality in education' (Velaskar 2021: 586).

Another major feature of NPE 1986 was the introduction of new policy proposals for community participation, including generating community resources and involving non-government organizations. In the section, 'Resources and Review', the policy text states,

> Resources to the extent possible will be raised by mobilising donations, asking the beneficiary communities to maintain school buildings and supplies of some consumables, raising fees at the higher level of education and effecting some saving by the efficient use of facilities. Institutions involved with research and the development of technical and scientific manpower should also mobilise some funds by levying a cess or charge on the user agencies, including government departments and entrepreneurs. (GoI 1986: 47)

The direction of the policy shift was 'in favour of privatization (or non-state stakeholding), reducing the role of the state and its commitment to public education' (Raina 2020d: 2). This was a policy departure that acknowledged a non-state stakeholding in the public financing of a constitutionally mandated public infrastructure good – elementary education. Is it any different from 'camouflage' (Sadgopal 2006: 105) when NPE 1986 pays lip service to the recommendation of enhancing the total outlay of education as follows:

The National Policy on Education, 1968, had laid down that the investment on education will be gradually increased to reach a level of 6 per cent
of the national income as early as possible. Since the actual level of investment has remained far short of that target. . . . While the actual requirements will be computed from time to time on the basis of monitoring and
review, the outlay on education will be stepped up to ensure that during
the Eighth Five Year Plan and onwards it will uniformly exceed 6 per cent
of the national income. (GoI 1986: 38)

The increased outlay has never become a reality (a mere 3.84 per cent was
allocated to education even as late as 2013) yet an era of a shift towards
serious non-state stakeholding in policymaking had begun.

Neoliberal Restructuring

In methods of policy analysis, an important tool distinct to education
is viewing policies in the broader continuum of cumulative policy changes.
This enables a sharper focus on 'the *character of the policy* itself' (Sadgopal
2006: 125, emphasis in original). It is often looked at as if the constitutional
policymaking era continued till NPE 1986 and the neoliberalization of education was ushered in suddenly with the opening of the Indian economy
in 1991. On the contrary, the cumulative policy shifts towards non-state
stakeholding, privatization and pruned public financing had already begun
post-NPE 1986 and prior to the opening of the economy. The policy shifts
heralding non-state stakeholding prepared a fertile ground post-NPE 1986
itself for neoliberal restructuring following the entry of global agencies,
such as the World Bank (WB) and the International Monetary Fund (IMF),
in 1991.

Policy analysis literature tends to overlook that NPE 1986 itself
was a preparation for adjustments in the name of edu-reforms that followed economic liberalization after 1991 (ibid.: 125). This was the first
major post-Independence collapse of Indian education policy, the abdication of the constitutional responsibility for direct delivery and the abandonment of policy thrust on establishing a CSS. The phase II policy cycle
coincided with the Congress government coming to office in 1984 with
slogans like 'taking India to the 21st century' in an attempt to introduce
a techno-managerial approach to economic and political life. In keeping
with this economistic trend of the time, NPE 1986 introduced an 'outcome'
orientation (Ayyar 2017: 26) to school education. This new orientation
took the focus away from supply-side variables, such as creating infrastructure like school buildings, teachers' education, the appointment of regular
teachers and teaching-learning processes, to externally observable param-

eters. The most significant of these was the quantification of learning in the name of learning outcomes. The increase in enrolment, fewer dropouts and attenuating disparities were also sought to be assessed in terms of quantitative measures. NPE 1986 introduced the notion of minimum levels of learning (MLL) which trivialized school education to merely literacy and numeracy 'skills' in the name of functional literacy in a behaviouristic approach to learning. The underlying assumption was that education is a linear additive process which can be broken down into measurable competencies. Although POA 1992 aimed at assessing the implementation of NPE 1986, it continued with this emphasis on the outcome by defining the quality of education through MLL. So did later programmes like Sarva Shiksha Abhiyan (SSA), beginning in 2000, based on improving the learning outcome levels as a central objective. The apex body, National Council of Educational Research and Training (NCERT), designed various cycles of National Achievement Surveys for children in grades 5, 5, 7 and 8 to generate time-series data on MLL. It is from here that the quest to develop various 'indicators' aimed at the assessment of learning as reflective of the quality of school education became a major policy referent. This had far-reaching consequences for the next policy cycle (post-2016, phase III), essentially framed around the development of various such indicators of quality school education.

SAP, following the economic liberalization of 1991, nearly coincided with the government signing up for the Jomtien goal of education for all in 1990. The presence of an economistic framework coupled with a neoliberal approach centred on measurable outcomes led to the abandonment of the constitutional agenda of systemic transformation in education, at least as stated in policy texts so far (Raina and Parul 2020). This economistic approach provided a new discursive framework for the altered political economy paradigm of education naturalizing 'this shift within the changing nature of the Indian state, its developmental agenda and class dynamics that have accompanied these changes. The policy priorities in school education, more often than not, have mirrored these shifts' (Mukhopadhyay and Sarangapani 2018: 9). The policy priorities were evident in a downsizing of government spending on elementary education in SAP with minimalistic contribution by the international donor organizations (WB–IMF) in the name of universalization of elementary education (UEE). This was in opposite direction to the phase I policy cycle; even in early phase II, there was some space, or lip service, in policy text for enhanced funding through the state's internal resources to provide for education. SAP-aligned educational reforms lined up with post-Jomtien international forces beginning with the flagship District Primary Education Programme (DPEP) in 1994 and continuing later through SSA in 2000 in 'mission mode', but the external aid came with a changed definition of elementary education. The constitutional guarantee of eight years of elementary education was practically reduced to five or fewer years of primary education with the scope for equality of educational opportunity restricted to the opportunity to attend a learning centre (not necessarily a formal school) and attain MLL in the name of learning. The policy framework for alternatives to regular schooling was already laid by NPE 1986 as DPEP and SSA further buttressed such alternatives. This was the policy demise of constitutionally guaranteed quality equitable education through a neighbourhood CSS. Instead, policy solutions were indifferent to structural distortions operationalized in the form of a multilayered school system including parallel inferior tracks of school education coupled with increased non-state stakeholding. The new layers even included alternative schools, non-formal schooling and initiatives like the Education Guarantee Scheme of Madhya Pradesh in the 1990s. A significant part of educational development (increased enrolment of children in schools) made for celebratory enrolment exclusion accrued from this arena. This outcome approach aligned with tenets of neoliberalization of elementary education: namely, a techno-managerial model in which assessment of education through measurable standards, outcomes and targets was a key aspect.

The narrow posing of school education status via proxy indicators like learning outcomes further created divisions in an already distorted school system. Large-scale assessment and quantification of learning (*Annual Status of Education Report* [*ASER*], various years) tended to create a binary between public and private school systems, which showed public schools as poor centres of learning or even as dysfunctional. As a result of such reports, perceptions of the dysfunctionality of state schooling are commonplace across sections of our society. The resultant 'exit' is reflected in surveys that show that in 2014–15, 30 per cent of children in India attended private schools (NSSO 2016). Data from the District Information Systems for Education (DISE) point out that the proliferation of private schools that began in the 1980s was accentuated over the years. The number of new private schools established from 2010–11 to 2014–15 in comparison to state schools is illuminative. The number of new private schools, as opposed to state schools, was 71,360 and 16,376, respectively. The former is almost four times more. This is a trend that already began in phase II. This trend continued the next year, 2015–16; the number of the former increased to 77,063 while the number of the latter decreased to 12,297. The corresponding increase in enrolment in private schools was 16 million children, and the fall in numbers in government schools was 11 million from 2010–11 to 2014–2015 (NIEPA 2016). The unprecedented further privatization at the current juncture is reflected in recent educational statistics that indicate that out of the 250 million school students in India, 120 million attend 4,50,000 private schools, and 130 million students are going to 1,09,000 state-run government schools (NIEPA 2019). This means that almost half the school students are on the cusp of becoming a part of India's private school system. Even in the avowedly capitalist economies of the Organisation for Economic Co-operation and Development (OECD) countries, the enrolment of children in private schools is below 10 per cent. That India currently has the largest number of children attending private schools in the world is a worrying outcome of neoliberal policy shifts in elementary education. This statistic can be read as a commentary on how the Indian state has fared in elementary education and its progress towards the constitutional goal of creating an equitable, public and quality school system for all our children.

The signpost Right to Education (RTE) Act, 2009, ostensibly aimed at UEE, in fact, restricted the constitutional entitlement (free compulsory elementary education of equitable quality to all children) to much less than that our Constitution already provides (Sadgopal 2010). The Act seeks to universalize schooling not by strengthening government schools but through a distorted market of school education consisting of different types of private schools. The passing of the act provided an escape route for the state and blunted the civil society movement for a CSS. Education activists have read the passing of the act as the death of the idea of CSS even observing 1 April as a black day against the act as it 'siphons off public funds to private operators through reimbursement', 'opens flood gates to thorough commercialization of school education' and 'takes the school system in opposite direction to the long-cherished Common School System' (AIFRTE 2012). The progressive elements in the act such as the specification of input norms and standards in physical infrastructure, academic resources including teachers, etc., were not supported by adequate financial allocation by central or state governments – they are increasingly under dilution in phase III. The EWS provisions for mere symbolic inclusion of children from marginalized social backgrounds in private schools were 'left out entirely to the whims and fancies of the private schools to devise ways and means of selection in arbitrary manner' (AIFRTE 2010). Such an approach does not contribute to equitable elementary education for the vast majority of more than 300 million children in our country.

Phase II of neoliberal policy shifts had two major consequences. First, there was a continuation of the structural distortion of school education into multilayered hierarchies of access. This was coupled with the abandonment of policy solutions to attenuate these distortions. Second, the naturalization of an outcome approach by assessing the status of education largely by proxy indicators of learning that privilege private schools. The future of school education policy got forecasted in this new discursive regime of outcome, performance, managerialism and non-state stakeholding; in which there was a default dismantling of public education, social justice and equity.

Historical Trajectory of the Policy Development Process

There is a trend which has tended to slip under the radar of policy analysis in India. The trend is that educational issues remain invisible in electoral politics, yet regimes take up policymaking with alacrity of forming governments. When the Congress government was elected to office in December 1984, it set a bureaucratic process in motion at the Ministry of Human Resource Development (MHRD) to formulate a new education policy. Policy proposals were ready by August 1985 and were speedily brought to the Parliament in May 1986. Soon after, the NPE 1986 was released in the same month of May 1986.

When the present BJP government first assumed office in 2014, it appointed a committee headed by former cabinet secretary T.S.R. Subramanian to formulate a new education policy for the nation. The Subramanian Committee for Evolution of New Education Policy submitted a 217-page report titled 'National Policy on Education 2016', henceforth NPE 2016, within a few months in May 2016 (GoI 2016). Presumably based on this report, the MHRD released a 43-page document titled 'Some Inputs for Draft National Education Policy 2016', henceforth DNEP 2016, (GoI 2016) in the public sphere. There remained ambiguity about the status of these two policy texts as the government did not make any official pronouncement in this regard. However, the MHRD appointed another nine-member committee in June 2017, headed by eminent space scientist K. Kasturirangan, to prepare a new education policy. The Press Information Bureau released a clarification on 26 June 2017 that the latter committee will draw from both draft policy texts in its policymaking process. The latter committee had formally submitted its 484-page report, DNEP 2019, (GoI 2019) just a day after the new BJP-led government assumed office in May 2019. Both the committees taken together worked for over four years. Finally, the new National Education Policy, henceforth NEP 2020, (GoI 2020) was announced on 29 July 2020, with the pronouncement the next morning that it will be implemented from the forthcoming academic session 2021–22. It is somewhat peculiar to find no names of a drafting committee on the main 66-page NEP 2020 text. The three companion drafts are abbreviated in policy literature as NPE 2016, DNEP 2016 and DNEP 2019. They confirm the ideological basis of the economistic framework that underlines NEP 2020.

The phase II and III policymaking processes contrast with the history of policy development in phase I. The noteworthy IEC was constituted in July 1964 and submitted its detailed report after two years of deliberations in 1968. The seven-and-a-half page NPE 1968 released years later was based on this thorough-going work. There was no room for haste. Experts from the field of education were regarded as indispensable and membership of the commission cut across academics, scientists and public intellectuals from the country and even other countries. This was regarded as essential to policy wisdom which could not emerge from mere bureaucratic exercises.

The era of expert commissions of educationists foregrounding policy development is arguably over since phase I. Phase III is evolving in an altogether altered policy context. The phase III policy texts came with a change of name from the earlier policy parlance of NPE to a new nomenclature NEP as if hinting at a keenness to be a distinct policy cycle (Menon 2020b) to overhaul the education system.

The phase III economistic policy context is also shaded by the neoliberal vision emerging from the state thinktank NITI Aayog's formulations of long-term policy and programme frameworks. The Aayog's 176-page *Three Year Action Agenda* released in 2017 set the ball rolling in this direction. A 153-page document *The Success of Schools: School Education Quality Index* was subsequently released in September 2019. The close alignment of these two significant documents with the current policy of NEP 2020 will be elaborated on in the next section.

Phase III: The Economistic Framework

The post-2016 phase III constitutes a non-linear policy cycle. It breaks away from policy concerns, policy history and policy solutions of the preceding two policy phases. The political economy of the past three decades is dominated by the economistic framework underlying the global wave of market fundamentalism. This further aligns with transnational advocacy networks supporting private schools, essentializing a new discursive regime of thin managerial notions. The new regime is framed around notions of quality, efficiency and accountability with very little reference to 'fundamental aims and purposes of education, the context of a segregated and stratified school institutional system that characterizes the Indian landscape, or the weak institutional structures and outdated frameworks of educational governance that are expected to regulate the relationship between the state and the market in education' (Mukhopadhyay and Sarangapani 2018: 6). This current neoliberal economistic commonsense 'of unprecedented privatization/quasi-privatization of schooling, driven by both the market and the neoliberal state' (Raina 2020b: 83) is reframing new exclusionary policy priorities. The three companion drafts, NPE 2016, DNEP 2016 and NEP 2019, and the two influential NITI Aayog releases mentioned earlier constitute the base work of NEP 2020. This section examines the philosophical and ideological moorings underlying this essentialized economistic discursive framework of school education.

The moorings are reflected at the outset as NEP 2016 accords to education a role that 'will amalgamate globalization with localization' (GoI 2016a: 1), provide a 'new impetus to skill development through vocational education in the context of the emergence of new technologies in a rapidly expanding economy in a globalized environment' and 'encouraging ways of enhancing private investment and funding' (ibid.: 2). The drafting committee's chairman in a summary article reported the state of education in our country to be in disarray and identified 'quality upgradation' and 'inclusivity' as focus areas for rejuvenating the school education system (Subramanian 2016: 30–33). NPE 2016 regards plummeting learning at all levels of school education (GoI 2016a: 3) as a chief policy concern and writes: '. . . the main objective of the school education system, as it has evolved in the last few decades, is to prepare students for the board examinations' (ibid.: 190). This is ironically a policy emphasis that continues in the name of urgency and necessity of foundation literacy and numeracy for 'future schooling and lifelong learning' (GoI 2020: 8). Out of the 56 pages that were dedicated to school education in the 217-page NPE 2016 (GoI 2016a), there was no subheading of the historically key policy concern – CSS. The seminal issue was simply overlooked. The phrase finds mention only twice in the 217-page text:

> The Committee feels that Clause 12(1) (c) Right of Children to Free and Compulsory Education is designed to conform to the spirit of a common curriculum and a common school system.
>
> . . .
>
> Keeping in view judicial pronouncements on the subject and its objectives, the provisions of section 12(1) (c), which deals with the right of children to free and compulsory education will be continued as it is the best way of promoting a common school system and for enhancing social equality. (GoI 2016a: 200)

There is evidently a farcical parallel between the idea of a CSS and the tokenistic provisions in the RTE 2009 for the inclusion of marginalized children in private schools. There is a complete absence of operational details or an analysis of how several other policy initiatives tend to move in a direction opposite to the creation of a CSS. The notions of inclusivity were viewed without contesting the structural inequalities within the social differences, divisions and hierarchies of our society. There is rather a lack of an egalitarian imagination to mitigate inequalities in education. In alignment with the already prevailing discursive regime of new public managerialism school governance, teacher management and Information and Communication Technology (ICT) received considerable space in NPE 2016; an emphasis that continues in DNEP 2019 and NEP 2020.

Its succinct companion document, DNEP 2016, in ideological consonance reiterated a focus on learning outcomes in school education. It emphasized clearly stated prescriptions of curriculum renewal, examination reform, inclusive education and student support through an outcome-based curriculum which provides opportunities to aspire for 'excellence in learning outcomes', 'comparable to student learning outcomes in high performing international education systems', as well as 'designing a common national curriculum for the subjects: science, mathematics and English' (GoI 2016b: 21). The draft does not hesitate to pay lip service to the role of public financing in education for national development when it admits,

> [Education], in Indian context, should be considered a public good and there is a need for greater public investment in the sector. There are evidences to show that countries which have heavily privatized education systems could not economically and socially progress and hence there is a value loss rather than gain. . . . The earlier National Policies of 1968 and 1986/92 had recommended 6% of GDP as the norm for the national outlay on education. However, the actual expenditure on education has remained consistently below this level and in recent years it has hovered around 3.5%. (Ibid.: 40–41)

It recommends a policy initiative of raising the investment in education as a priority. Yet, in the very same document, the term CSS does not appear even once in the text. It can be said that both documents reflected the 'guarded agenda' (Gupta 2016) of regularization of the structural distortion into hierarchies of access in school education, coupled with an outcome orientation that supports the distorted layers.

In NITI Aayog's action agenda 'Education and Skill Development' appear as one of its twenty-four chapters under the section on 'Social Sectors'. 'School Education Action Agenda' seeks to achieve three major goals in three years, that is, 2017–20. First, orient the system towards outcomes; second, provide tools to teachers and students for effective learning; and third, improve governance mechanisms. The document regards the most important goal of the Indian school education system to be that of improving learning outcomes (NITI Aayog 2017: 153) as it proposes: In terms of regulation, states should regulate only based on outcomes and transparency requirements, not through regulating inputs like library, fees and playground. Both private and government schools should be regulated in the same way (ibid.: 137). The agenda pushes market fundamentalism in the wider national context of policymaking. It states:

> Explore the role for private players. A working group should be set up with states' participation to explore and pilot other bolder experiments by interested states. These could include education vouchers and local government led purchasing of schooling services. Public-Private Partnership (PPP) models could also be explored where the private sector adopts government schools while being publicly funded on a per child basis. This latter instrumentality may provide a solution to the problems of schools that have hollowed and are incurring massive expenditures per pupil currently. (Ibid.: 138)

It further argues, 'the hollowing of public schools makes it abundantly clear that the public school system has not achieved the desired outcomes in the country' (ibid.: 155).

In keeping with this outcome orientation, the agenda proposed the new policy construct – School Education Quality Index (SEQI) – as a lever to drive improvements in school quality by tracking outcomes. The agenda in its comprehensive vision to transform India overlooked policy solutions to allay the discriminatory role of multilayered school education as an oppressive instrument that firms up the overlapping social divisions with a differentiated system of schooling for children belonging to different social segments. The term CSS is missing but a mention of hollowing out of public schools finds space in the document text. The agenda does not hesitate to recommend an unapologetic case for private players in school education. Need the state abdicate any more responsibility for the direct delivery of school education?

DNEP 2019 is the actual report of the Kasturirangan Committee submitted on 31 May 2019. It is policy strength that various levels of education are examined in a single continuum from preschool to higher education in an omnibus policy text. The chairman of the committee in his cover letter to the then Minister of Human Resource Development stated that the policy is founded on the guiding goals of access, equity, quality, affordability and accountability. Paradoxically the notions of access, equity and quality have found space in the same sentence with a term like affordability.

The school education policy proposals in DNEP 2019 reiterate a focus on learning outcomes while emphasizing the building of foundational skills like literacy and numeracy, in the name of improving the school education system. It aims at creating a 'solid foundation in reading, writing, speaking, counting, arithmetic, mathematical and logical thinking, problem-solving' (GoI 2019: 56), expressing alarm that 'we are in a severe learning crisis: a large proportion of students in elementary school has not attained foundational literacy and numeracy' (ibid.: 58). It recommends programmes like the National Tutors Programme and Remedial Instructional Aides Programme to enable access, learning and retention. Such recommendations ignore supply-side systemic public provisioning inadequacies, teacher education and classroom teaching and learning processes that are the foundation of student learning in a robust school education system.

It further ignores the concerns of CSS, regional disparities and issues of access to school education. The 'role of schools in dislodging the structural inequality', 'unequal distribution of opportunities of school education' and the 'lack of thrust on strengthening the public provisioning of school education by the state' (Raina 2019: 16) are key policy concerns that are side-stepped. Instead, the concept of 'affordability', a first-in-school education policy parlance was mentioned in the policy text. The term CSS does not appear at all in the lengthy policy text nor does it find mention in NEP 2020. In a marked departure from the quest for a common school system, DNEP 2019 states, 'The nature of education is what economists call a "quasi-public good"' (GoI 2019: 399).

Overlooking the idea of the CSS entrenches further the processes of segregation and differentiation of schooling experiences for different social groups (Maniar 2019: 18). DNEP 2019 ignores the 'single-most important and complex systemic issue plaguing school education in contemporary India' (Raina 2019: 16), which is its divisive stratification into multilayered hierarchies emerging from its class basis.

DNEP 2019 highlighted SEQI as a new referent in policy concerns. On 30 September 2019, just six months after DNEP 2019, NITI Aayog released a publication mainly focused on the new policy construct – SEQI. The policy intent to further operationalize an outcome approach by institutionalizing SEQI is evident. The SEQI will collect, systematize and publicize the measurements in school education, assessing the success of schools by this indicator. The document text details, 'SEQI focuses on indicators that can drive improvements in the quality of education rather than on inputs or specific processes. The index has been developed through the view of an outcome lens rather than a process lens' (NITI Aayog 2019: 119).

The SEQI assessed the states on the basis of learning, access, equity and infrastructure outcomes among thirty other indicators. It uses survey data, self-reported data, from states and third-party verification in a sophisticated scoring methodology replete with quantitative data from all but one state – West Bengal – which did not participate in the evaluation exercise. The process of developing the index frame was in consultation with advocacy networks of liberalization in which de-focus on state schooling emerged as a main influence in policymaking. This new construct in school education policy aimed at 'data-driven decision making, including better targeting of interventions for quality enhancement' (ibid.: 106). The documents together laid the ground for a minimalist vision in an economistic approach.

NEP 2020: Towards a Technocratic Society

The much-awaited NEP 2020 is the third policy in post-independent India released after a gap of thirty-four years. Its promulgation was met with an initial celebratory welcome notwithstanding the campus closure due to the pandemic which blunted possibilities for creative criticism, enabling suggestions and resistance. It is ambitious in its scope as it begins by setting out its aim to reconfigure the 'entire education system' (GoI 2020: 4) with policy proposals for 'the revision and revamping of all aspects of the education structure, including its regulation and governance, to create a new system that is aligned with the aspirational goals of 21st-century education' (ibid.: 4). In its grandiose vision it states that the 'aim must be for India to have an education system by 2040 that is second to none, with equitable access to the highest-quality education for all learners regardless of social or economic background' (ibid.: 3). Its votaries are evident by a plethora of news reports, popular articles and webinars who hailed it as a step forward in transforming the school education system. In re-envisioning the education system, it highlights how the world today is dramatically different from what it used to be, is 'undergoing rapid changes in the knowledge landscape', 'quickly changing employment landscape and global ecosystem', and there is a need to 'address the many growing developmental imperatives of our country' (ibid.: 4). Its policy strength, like that of its predecessor DNEP 2019, is its omnibus nature which is 'very impressive in its breadth of coverage touching every dimension of education' (Govinda 2020: 603). The coverage ranges across all levels of education from pre-primary, primary, secondary and post-secondary to higher education as well as subfields like teacher education, vocational education and technical education.

DNEP 2019 had already spoken of crafting a completely new and farsighted policy. In fact, NEP 2020 is an a historical policy text that lacks policy continuity with the past. Phase III is what analysts term a novel, non-linear and non-sequential policy cycle (Rizvi and Lingard 2009). It makes a cursory reference to 'previous policies' and their unfinished agenda in all but six sentences – possibly for tokenistic textbookish policy continuity – yet steers away from past policy. It drops much of past policy vocabulary, for example, CSS, and adds new phrases like affordability to the policy lexicon.

There is no gainsaying that the India of today is unrecognizable from its past. The attempt to make sense of the pandemic has highlighted that the past may not always be an indication of what the future portends by way of a 'new normal'. NEP 2020 expresses optimism that 'rapid advances in technology present both opportunities and challenges to human well-being', with NEP 2020 aiming to change India by transforming education (Kasturirangan 2020). What is the direction of the quest for transformation? Is it towards the constitutional vision of an equitable schooling system? Are notions of access, equity and equality defined within existing structural stratifications or is a fundamentally egalitarian imagination of education invoked?

NEP 2020 dedicates 25 pages and 8 subsections to school education. Its 6th subsection, 'Equitable and Inclusive Education: Learning for All', sidesteps the structural question altogether. With 'no plan to do away with the discrimination-based multilayered school system' (Sadgopal 2020), and not even a single mention of the CSS in the entire policy text, its reaffirmation 'that bridging the social category gaps in access, participation, and learning outcomes in school education will continue to be one of the major goals of all education sector development programmes' sounds like mere rhetoric (GoI 2020: 25). It is camouflage to proclaim, 'The public education system is the foundation of a vibrant democratic society, and the way it is run must be transformed and invigorated in order to achieve the highest levels of educational outcomes for the nation' (ibid.: 31). It is camouflage because the very next sentence, 'At the same time, the private/philanthropic school sector must also be encouraged and enabled to play a significant and beneficial role' (ibid.: 31), is a policy solution to the contrary. There is the introduction of a new policy vocabulary – public-spirited or philanthropic – words that are frequently hyphenated to the right of private in the policy text. A new acronym Public Philanthropic Partnership (PPP) appears in place of public-private partnership. The contemporary social realities include: economic inequality, domination of private capital, graded social hierarchies, exacerbated multilayers in the educational system, ecological threats jeopardizing our common future, patriarchal barriers to gender justice, caste fault lines and an impending economic crisis for the common people. There are distinct differences between past and present challenges but what ails the school education system for decades now is its stratification into layered hierarchies mirroring social divisions. The policy proposals to establish school complexes/clusters (ibid.: 30) in the name of sharing resources may reverse equity by the closure of small schools in underdeveloped regions.

The spotlight on online education ignores evidence-based policymaking from the most recent reliable indicators of household social consumption on education in India. These indicators reveal the percentage of households with computer and internet facilities from different states. This is a bare 10.7 per cent (4.4 and 23.4 per cent for rural/urban households, respectively) with a computer, and only 23.8 per cent (14.9/42 percent in rural/urban households) for those who enjoy internet facilities (NSS 2019: 47). Personal experience demonstrates the pedagogic limitations of online education which mainly involves no more than uncritical acquisition of inert knowledge (Raina 2020a).

NEP 2020's silences, the ideas it overlooks, its new vocabulary and how it identifies what is wrong with school education make it look factious when it proclaims that 'the aim of the public school education system will be to impart the highest quality education so that it becomes the most attractive option for parents from all walks of life for educating their children' (GoI 2020: 32) because NEP 2020 says so much more, which is aimed at legitimization of privatization in school education. The policy states that school participation is encouraged by 'various successful policies and schemes such as targeted scholarships, conditional cash transfers to incentivize parents to send their children to school', that it will support 'non-governmental philanthropic organizations to build schools, to encourage local variations on account of culture, geography and demographics, and to allow alternative models of education and the requirements will be made less restrictive' (ibid.: 11). This increases the scope of privatization, which is already exponentially rising due to policy support. Such policy solutions are oblivious to growing school differentiation that reinforces existing structural marginalization in a direction opposite to the idea of education as a leveller.

NEP 2020 eschews a social vision for a global knowledge-based economy and society (KBES) in the name of 21st-century skills of critical thinking and problem-solving. The ideas of knowledge are however envisaged as uncritical lifelong learning of skills for the productivity of a national-local citizenry within a globalizing polity. It aims at 'producing engaged, productive, and contributing citizens for building an equitable, inclusive, and plural society' (ibid.: 4). The notion of citizenship is linked with productivity in a neoliberal commonsense rather than with a civic logic common to diversity in a democracy. Citizenship education involves more than capitalist conceptions of productivity beyond bookish knowledge to experience the complex realities, heterogeneity and inequality of our society. It is based on a sensitive recognition of diverse modes of living, ecology and development in tune with the historicity of local culture, geographical environment, language and development model.

In alignment with the proposed KBES ideal, NEP 2020 speaks of a technocratic society which needs 'a skilled workforce, particularly involving mathematics, computer science, and data science' (GoI 2020: 4), also mentioning the 'need for new skilled labour, particularly in biology, chemistry, physics, agriculture, climate science, and social science' (ibid.: 3). The basis of this vision emerges from the 'rise of big data, machine learning, and artificial intelligence' (ibid.) in which 'many unskilled jobs worldwide may be taken over by machines' with a veiled layer of emphasis on 'multidisciplinary abilities across the sciences, social sciences, and humanities' (ibid.). 'Teaching employable skills' was already a paramount concern in phase III companion documents with policy thrust on employable skills (Dhankar 2020: 99) in NPE 2016 and DNEP 2016 in a narrow vision of a technocratic society in which

> [Recommendations] concerning skills dominate every section. It is also understandable that if the society is seen as KBES, then the most important task for education is only to prepare people who can be employed in it. The aims also make it amply clear that the skills are needed to cope in this system, not to challenge or modify it. (Ibid.: 105)

NEP 2020 further entrenches an outcome orientation with a renewed emphasis on centralized examination as early as in grades 3, 5 and 8 in addition to the existing grades 10 and 12 board examinations. This emphasis is supported by proposals like setting up a National Assessment Centre, PARAKH (Performance Assessment, Review and Analysis of Knowledge for Holistic Development), and a new body for setting norms, standards and guidelines for student assessment. A periodic check-up of the overall system through a testing regime is recommended (GoI 2020: 32).

Another significant or rather the most visible recommendation of NEP 2020 is the proposal calling for the radical restructuring of school education, that is, 'the extant 10+2 structure in school education will be modified with a new pedagogical and curricular restructuring of 5+3+3+4, covering ages 3–18' (ibid.: 7). The new school structure of five, three, three and four years of foundational, preparatory, middle and secondary school education is envisaged. The attention to preschool education and foundational stage learning is very welcome. It is a policy strength that detailed qualitative distinctions have been systematically made for proposals at each of these levels. The new system proposes to replace the previous academic structure of 10+2 to which three years of pre-primary level are added for early childhood care and education (ECCE). The assumption is that foundational learning in early childhood education is a prerequisite for school education. The policy aims that 'universal provisioning of quality early childhood development, care and education must be thus achieved by 2030' (ibid.: 6).

In view of the 'country's struggle to provide even eight years of free and compulsory schooling of acceptable quality, it is difficult to take such promises seriously' (Govinda 2020: 604). With public spending priorities shifting away from education to health and defence and the pandemic-exacerbated contracting GDP, the policy's ambiguity on 'where the extra resources are going to come from to support the NEP 2020' (Menon 2020b: 601) is disconcerting. In the very first year of implementation of NEP 2020, the overall allocation for education in the Union Budget for 2021 underwent a major cut. The total education budget was slashed from Rs 99,311 crores in 2020–21 to Rs 93,224 crores with the biggest cut in school education. A standing committee report tabled in Parliament stated that the Department of School Education was allocated only Rs 43,648.66 crores by the finance ministry as against its demand of Rs 82,137.66 crore (Indian Express News Bureau 2021). This begs the question of whether NEP 2020 is a vision document or a policy.

On an educational and philosophical note, the proposal to formalize childhood care and education within the structure of school education comes with the risk of a dystopian homogenization of the very concept of childhood. Childhood is constructed not only through formal school education but located a multitude of sites. Ideas about early childhood care, growth and education are not universal but culture-, home- and community-specific. Every home has a culture with an inherent concept of childhood of its own. A sensitive design of meaningful early childhood education needs to cater to as many diverse childhoods of children as are prevalent in the myriad homes of our plural society. Without adequately designed early childhood teacher education (an already neglected arena in our educational system), children stand the risk of being alienated in a formal school setting which may be disconnected from their home cultures. A homogenization of childhood with all the children of the country attending formal schools at the tender age of three years can alter the natural consciousness that flowers in a home–family–community circle of love. To assume that ECCE would be a powerful equalizer as 'schools providing quality ECCE reap the greatest dividends for children who come from families that are economically disadvantaged' (GoI 2020: 25) sounds like a wishlist.

The post-2016 emergent policy context simply overlooks the basic barriers to an equitable system of schooling: structural distortions, systemic inequalities, decontextualized classroom processes and the development of critical educators (Raina 2020b: 82). The current period is a phase in which school education is cast in a limiting economistic frame ignoring its social aims. This is in alignment with the naturalized transnational trend of 'thinking that the global market has a fundamental role in deciding education policies' (Rizvi 2017; cited in Sharma 2020: 261).

Worrying Outcomes

Recent research explored the impact of neoliberal policies on the municipal school system of Mumbai. It concluded that the educational system stood structurally weakened with macro-level transformations. There was an overall decline in basic provisioning, leading to infrastructure deficits like decrepit buildings, overcrowded classes and multigrade teaching. The RTE 2009 serves 'merely a legitimating function while defusing and depoliticizing the issue of declining provision' (Velaskar 2021: 602) largely impermeable to educational demands from within the system, particularly from the most marginalized. The sections of society who are in an economic position to be fee-paying choose to opt out of government schools diffusing further the movement for CSS. The overall policy shifts since phase II have led to the outcome of reinforcing and further entrenching not simply a binary between the public and the private school education system but also a deeply embedded multilayered graded hierarchy within both of them. The former is widely perceived as embodying dysfunctionality to the extent that its very legitimacy is suspect (Velaskar 2016: 251). In a systemic differentiation, it has been abandoned by any student in a position to attend a fee-paying school. The enrolment in state schools in contemporary India is mainly from disadvantaged social groups like SCs, STs, Dalits and minorities (Sadgopal 2016: 18), which is 'turning state schools into a colony of the underprivileged' (Raina 2020b: 68).

Any student who can afford 'quality' education undertakes an 'exit' from government schools. Also, the socioeconomically marginalized poor who remain left behind are devoid of a 'voice' and therefore fail to have any impact on the dysfunctional government school system. The emaciated government system has thus become 'schools of the last resort' (Mukhopadhyay and Sarangapani 2018: 12). There is a detailed school differentiation in which each type of school system is being attended by children belonging to a certain socioeconomic section of Indian society. Such a highly differentiated schooling system is currently institutionalized in the name of school education. Each of these differential arrangements mirrors the hierarchical socioeconomic divisions of our stratified society. The educational arrangements consist of nine different types of schools, ranging from exclusionary high-fee charging international schools affiliated to overseas certification boards, elite private schools, low-fee private schools, special government schools like Kendriya Vidyalayas, tribal region Ashramshalas for Adivasis to state/local body government schools with intra-access layers (Vasavi 2019: 2) among others. The social differences of class are firming up through this overlap with school education exacerbating not just prevailing social differences of class but leading to further social divisions in our already stratified society. The last two phases of policy changes have, instead of diffusing these differentials, led to the worrying outcome of exacerbating current and inherited inequalities of an unequal school system. The downsizing of state systems, expansion of the private and withdrawal of government from direct delivery of elementary education are global trends in educational policy and practice. The same features are reflected in our current policy context: drastic cuts in state funding of education and rapid creation of education markets (Velaskar 2021: 576) which synchronize seamlessly with the 'outcome' orientation of an economistic discursive framework which is 'sorely suited to a policy convergence in school education between the state and the market' (Raina 2021: 31). When NEP 2020 states that 'education is a great leveller and is the best tool for achieving economic and social mobility, inclusion and equality' (ibid.: 4), without scrutinizing the structural distortion of education in our society, it tacitly awards policy legitimacy to a consensual framework of structural inequalities.

The American educator Horace Mann, euphemistically referred to as the father of the common school movement, coined the term for schools that would be tax-funded for attendance by children cutting across social backgrounds to nurture inclusivity in nineteenth-century United States. He believed that school education in a democratic society must be provided by the state which implied a commitment to the idea of universal, free and non-factional common schools (Cremin 1957: 23–78). Yet racial segregation of blacks and whites in separate schools did not go away. It took a Supreme Court order as late as 1954 to declare such schools illegal (Kluger 2011).

Even though the Indian state passed over the processes of implementation, the idea of CSS was not abandoned till the second phase of policy change. NPE 2020 is silent on the establishment of a CSS as a key policy solution to alleviate inequality in school education. The state did not even require a policy for school education as the Constitution has already shown the way. The Indian state did not seriously attempt to actualize the possibilities of inclusive development through an equitable system of schooling in any of the three phases of school education policy. Social scientists have highlighted the overlapping differences of class, caste, gender, locale and region that lead to social divisions in our deeply stratified society, as school education becomes one more category of social division. A child attending a government school can be read as belonging to the category of poor socioeconomic background. School education has by itself turned into a category of social division in contrast to the constitutional policy wisdom our educational development began with. The contemporary phase III represents 'a gradual consensualisation about the graded schooling hierarchies, consequent social divisions as also the wider underlying educational inequality' (Raina 2020c: 34). Recent research has highlighted that inequality in India is currently at its highest since 1922. We are farthest than ever before to the constitutional vision of equitable elementary education with policy shifts that exacerbate inherited and current inequalities.

References

All India Forum for Right to Education (AIFRTE) (2010), 'AIFRTE Leaflet for Observing 1st April as Black Day Against RTE Act', Hyderabad: AIFRTE, 27 March.

—— (2012), 'Why We Oppose Right to Education Act', Chennai: AIFRTE, 30 June.

Ayyar, R.V. (2017), 'Inclusive Elementary Education in India: The Journey', in M.K. Tiwary, S. Kumar and A.K. Misra, eds, *Dynamics of Inclusive Classroom: Social Diversity, Inequality and School Education in India*, New Delhi: Orient BlackSwan.

Babu, S. (2020), 'New Education Policy 2020: What is Concealed and What is Unveiled', *The New Leam*, available at https://www.thenewleam.com/2020/08/new-education-policy2020-what-is-concealed-and-what-is-unveiled/, accessed 12 August 2020.

Bagade, D.R. (1982), *Ch. Rajarshi Shahu Maharaj Aani Kayadekanu*, Kolhapur: Padm Prakashan Sanstha.

Bhargava, R., H. Reifeld and K.A. Stiftung (2005), *Civil Society, Public Sphere, and Citizenship: Dialogues and Perceptions*, New Delhi: Sage Publications.

Bhatty, K. (2014), 'Review of Elementary Education Policy in India: Has it Upheld the Constitutional Objective of Equality?', *Economic and Political Weekly*, vol. 49, 1 November, pp. 43–44.

Cremin, L.A. (1957), *The Republic and the School Horace Mann on the Education of Free Men*, Columbia University: Teacher's College.

Dasgupta, A.K. (1993), *A History of Indian Economic Thought*, London: Routledge.

Dhankar, R. (2020), 'Draft NEP 2016: Education for "Citizenship" or "Resource Development for a Pliable Workforce"?', in J. Raina, ed., *Elementary Education in India: Policy Shifts, Issues and Challenges*, London and New York: Routledge.

Govinda, R. (2021), 'NEP 2020: A Critical Examination', *Social Change*, vol. 50, no. 4, pp. 603–07.

GoI (Government of India) (1966), *Education and National Development: Report of the Education Commission 1964–66*, New Delhi: Ministry of Education, Government of India.

—— (1968), *National Policy on Education 1968*, New Delhi: Ministry of Education, Government of India.

—— (1986), *National Policy on Education 1986*, New Delhi: Ministry of Human Resource Development, Government of India.

—— (1990), *Report of the Committee for Review of National Policy on Education 1986*, New Delhi: Ministry of Human Resource Development, Government of India.

——— (1992), *Programme of Action 1992: National Policy on Education 1986*, New Delhi: Department of Education, Ministry of Human Resource Development, Government of India.

——— (2016a), *National Policy on Education: Report of the Committee for Evolution of the New Education Policy*, New Delhi: Ministry of Human Resource Development, Government of India, available at http://niepa.ac.in/download/NEP2016/Report NEP.pdf, accessed 10 June 2020.

——— (2016b), *Some Inputs for Draft National Education Policy (Draft NEP)*, New Delhi: Ministry of Human Resource Development, Government of India, available at http://mhrd.gov.in/sites/upload_files/mhrd/files/Inputs_Draft_NEP_2016.pdf, accessed 15 May 2020.

——— (2019), 'Draft National Education Policy 2019', New Delhi: Ministry of Human Resource Development, Government of India.

——— (2020), *National Education Policy 2020*, New Delhi: Ministry of Human Resource Development, Government of India.

Grindle, M. (2004), *Despite the Odds: The Contentious Politics of Education Reform*, Princeton and Oxford: Princeton University Press.

Gupta, V. (2016), 'Politics of the Guarded Agenda of National Education Policy (2015–16)', *Economic and Political Weekly*, vol. 51, no. 42, 15 October.

Indian Express News Bureau (2021), 'The Cut', *The Indian Express*, 10 March.

Kasturirangan, K. (2020), 'NEP will Change India by Transforming Education', *Times of India*, 30 July.

Kluger, R. (2011), *Simple Justice: The History of Brown v Board of Education and Black America's Struggle for Equality*, United States: Vintage.

Kumar, R. (2006), 'Introduction: Equality, Quality and Quantity: Mapping the Challenges before Elementary Education in India', in R. Kumar, ed., *The Crisis of Elementary Education in India*, New Delhi: Sage Publications.

Maniar, V. (2019), 'Overlooking the Idea of Common School in the Education Policy', *Economic and Political Weekly*, vol. 54, no. 17, 14 September.

Menon, S. (2020a), 'NEP 2020: Some Searching Questions', *Social Change*, vol. 50, no. 4, pp. 599–602.

——— (2020b), 'NEP 2020: The New Old', *The Indian Express*, 8 August.

Mukhopadhyay, R. and P. Sarangapani (2018), 'Education in India between the State and Market: Concepts Framing the New Discourse: Quality, Efficiency, Accountability', in M. Jain, A. Mehendale, R. Mukhopadhyay, P. Sarangapani and C. Winch, eds, *School Education in India; Market, State and Quality*, London and New York: Routledge.

Naik, J.P. (1969), *The Main Recommendations of the Report of The Education Commission: A Summary*, New Delhi: NCERT.

National Council of Educational Research and Training (NCERT) (1970), *Education and National Development: Report of the Education Commission 1964–1966 (Kothari Commission)*, New Delhi: NCERT.

National Institute of Educational Planning and Administration (NIEPA) (2016), *Elementary Education in India: Where Do We Stand? District Information System for Education District Report Card, 2016–2017*, vols 1 and 2, New Delhi: DISE, NIEPA.

NITI Aayog (2017), *India: Three Year Action Agenda (2017–18 to 2019–20)*, New Delhi: Government of India.

——— (2019), *The Success of Schools: School Education Quality Index*, New Delhi: Government of India.

NSS (2019), *Key Indicators of Household Social Consumption on Education in India 75th Round July 2017–June 2018*, New Delhi: Ministry of Statistics and Programme Implementation.

NSSO (2016), *National Sample Survey, 71st Round, 2014–15: Social Consumption: Education*, New Delhi: Ministry of Statistics and Programme Implementation.

Prasad, M. (2020), 'A Strategy for Exclusion: How Equality and Social Justice have been Derailed in Indian Elementary Education', in J. Raina, ed., *Elementary Education in India: Policy Shifts, Issues and Challenges*, London and New York: Routledge.

Priyam, M. (2016), 'Policy Reform and Educational Development in a Federal Context', in A.K. Singh, ed., *Education and Empowerment in India: Policies and Practices*, London and New York: Routledge.

Raina, J. (2019), 'What's in it for School Education?: Draft National Education Policy, 2019', *Economic and Political Weekly*, vol. 54, no. 37, 14 September.

—— (2020a), 'A Teacher Discovers What Is Wrong with Online Teaching in Higher education?' *Portside: Material of Interest to People on the Left*, available at https://portside.org/2020-07-04/teacher-discovers-what-wrong-online-teachinghigher-education, accessed 10 August 2020.

—— (2020b), 'Equitable Elementary Education as a Public Good: What is Left of it?', in J. Raina, ed., *Elementary Education in India: Policy Shifts, Issues and Challenges*, London and New York: Routledge.

—— (2020c), 'Indian Society of 2047: What Hope Progress?', *Economic and Political Weekly*, vol. 55, nos 32 and 33, 8 August.

—— (2020d), 'Mapping the Exacerbated Crisis in Elementary Education: Issues and Challenges', in J. Raina, ed., *Elementary Education in India: Policy Shifts, Issues and Challenges*, London and New York: Routledge.

—— (2020e), 'Rediscovering a "New" Reality this Quarantine: The Experiments of a Teacher', *The New Leam*, available at https://www.thenewleam.com/2020/04/rediscovering-a-new-reality-this-quarantine-the-experiments-of-a-teacher/, accessed 10 June 2020.

Raina, J. and Parul (2020), 'Neoliberal Policy Shifts in Elementary Education in India', in J. Raina, ed., *Elementary Education in India: Policy Shifts, Issues and Challenges*, London and New York: Routledge.

Raina, J. (2021), 'School Education in NEP 2020: The Underlying Framework', *Economic and Political Weekly*, vol. 56, no. 8, 20 February.

Rizvi, F. and B. Lingard (2009), *Globalising Education Policy*, New York and London: Routledge.

Sadgopal, A. (1994), 'Report of the Sub-Group on Education (Chair: Prof. Anil Sadgopal)', in National Consultation on Rights of the Child, Ministry of Human Resource Development, Government of India.

—— (2006), 'Dilution, Distortion and Diversion: A Post-Jomtien Reflection on the Education Policy', in R. Kumar, ed., *The Crisis of Elementary Education in India*, New Delhi: Sage Publications.

—— (2009), *Sansad Mein Shiksha ka Adhikar Chhenanewala Bill* (A Bill in the Parliament to Snatch Away the Right to Education), Bhopal: Kishore Bharati.

—— (2010), 'The World Bank in India: Undermining Sovereignty, Distorting Development', in M. Kelley and D. D'Souza, eds, *Independent People's Tribunal on the World Bank in India*, Hyderabad: Orient Blackswan.

—— (2016), 'Common Classrooms, Common Playgrounds', in M. Prasad, ed., *Newsletter* (April), New Delhi: All India Forum for Right to Education.

—— (2020), 'Decoding the Agenda of the New National Education Policy', *Frontline*, 28 August.

—— (2021), 'Post-Independence Political Economy of Education: From Welfarism to Neoliberalism in Alliance with Fascism', in V. Gupta, R.K. Agnihotri and M. Panda, eds, *Education and Inequality: Historical and Contemporary Trajectories*, Hyderabad: Orient Blackswan.

Sharma, G. (2020), 'Book Review: Elementary Education in India: Policy Shifts, Issues and Challenges', *Contemporary Education Dialogue*, vol. 17, no. 2, pp. 261–67.

Subramanian, T.S.R. (2016), 'Education in Disarray: Need for Quality Upgradation and Inclusivity', *Economic and Political Weekly*, vol. 51, no. 35, 27 August.

Unified District Information Systems for Education (2020), *U-DISE Data 2019–20*, New Delhi: National Institute of Educational Planning and Administration, released on 21 January, available at https://www.misinfo.co.in/2020/01/u-dise data-2019-20.html, accessed 2 March 2020.

Vasavi, A.R. (2019), 'School Differentiation in India Reinforces Social Inequalities', *The India Forum*, 3 May.

Velaskar, P. (2010), 'Quality and Inequality in Indian Education: Some Critical Policy Concerns', *Contemporary Education Dialogue*, vol. 7, no. 1.

———— (2016), 'Neo-Liberal Policy and the Crisis of State Schooling', in A.K. Singh, ed., *Education and Empowerment in India: Policies and Practices*, London and New York: Routledge.

———— (2021), 'Destroying Public Education: Neoliberal Policy and Structural Shifts in State Provision in Mumbai', in V. Gupta, R.K. Agnihotri and M. Panda, eds, *Education and Inequality: Historical and Contemporary Trajectories*, Hyderabad: Orient Blackswan.

World Bank (1997), *Primary Education in India, Development in Practice*, Washington DC: International Bank for Reconstruction and Development.

4

Academic Heretic:
A Reflexive Teacher–Educator

Anthony Joseph

Introduction

The National Education Policy 2020 (NEP 2020) pledges new reforms in the Indian education system and recognizes the pivotal role of 9.6 million teachers (2019–20) in the realization of its goals. The policy pledges, in the midst of the raging Covid-19 pandemic, to bring into sharp focus India's social and political context, especially its federal structure, and social characteristics of gender, caste, rural–urban divide and government–private divide. In a complex and diverse sociocultural setting, as in India, a hegemonic pseudo-science of intelligence, drawing on the ambiguous authority of exclusive traditions and narrow cognitivism, glosses over the larger context of social practice and social theory, and forfeits the role of equitable mindsets and practices in educational discourses. Crafted narratives masquerade as academic discourse and serve to reinforce curious and exclusive pedagogical mindsets and practices – rarely conducive to professional development efforts and inimical to scientific engagement. With little or no claims to specialized knowledge, prolonged preparation and professional ethics, teachers' voices for professional autonomy are easily stonewalled by a system that privileges monitoring and accountability. With the need to replace, in fifteen years, about 30 per cent of the current teaching workforce and staring at a deficit of over one million teachers (at current student strength) and the need likely to grow, the purported role of the 'new teacher of a new India with a new history' in the NEP 2020, leaves much to the imagination.

The Vision and Reality

The National Education Policy 2020's goal – ensuring inclusive and equitable quality education and promoting lifelong learning opportunities for all, leading to social inclusion, economic growth and environmental conservation in India – is a task riddled with humongous challenges. In the United Nation's (UN's) World Happiness Report for 2020, India is ranked 144 out of the 153 countries evaluated. The UN's Human Development Index of 2019 ranks India 129th out of 189 countries. The World Inequality Report, 2022, by the World Inequality Lab, declared that India is among the most unequal countries in the world with very high gender inequalities. The Global Hunger Index (2022) places India at the 107th spot among 121 countries. India, the world's most populous democracy, dropped from Free to Partly Free status in Freedom in the World 2021. India is a democracy with multiparty elections, universal suffrage, an independent judiciary and the guarantee of civil liberties; yet, valid observations indicate that this amounts to admiring a form of government for its own sake without concern for the socioeconomic outcomes that are produced. In India, the state's ritualistic attachment to the procedures of democracy has not been matched by an awareness of its implicit goal of a fulfilling life for Indians. The vision of NEP 2020 *to build the foundations of a new India that is a knowledge society* with the objectives of enabling equity, expertise and empowerment to meet the challenges of the future widely awaits implementation to become a reality.

A significant lack of professional skills confronted the teaching workforces' attitudes, behaviours and beliefs about integrating technology in education during the Covid-19 pandemic. Opportunistic efforts to cobble together hybrid modalities to integrate technology in education, an exercise in online adventurism, exposed the vulnerability and insecurity of the teaching workforce. Very poor information and communications technology (ICT) infrastructure and a marked rural–urban disparity served to expose multiple teaching and learning gaps during the Covid-19 pandemic.

The vision of learning for sustainable development highlights the increasing urgency to improve quality, accountability and governance within the sector both at home and abroad. A pervasive global political discontent is manifest in the growing disillusionment with and loss of trust in the governments of the world. There are currently around 44 million people worldwide working in the gig economy. The downsides to this economy include financial instability, decreased loyalty, short-termism, decreased legacy thinking, increased authoritarianism and unrealistic and unsustainable pressure on the education sector to deliver.

True Philanthropic, Private and Community Participation

Globally, the late 1960s and the early 1970s comprised a period of unprecedented economic expansion, and there emerged an ethos of education as development. In the mid-1970s, economic expansion began to wane. In this new climate of economic austerity, the government sought to replace educational innovation with a back-to-basics curriculum. Since the end of the 1970s and now into the twenty-first century, educational institutions the world over have become victims of conservative educational policies that go under the name of neoliberalism. Within the neoliberal mandate, key sectors of health, welfare and education are increasingly being delivered by governments into the hands of market forces and its directives (O'Sullivan, Morrell and O'Connor, eds 2002: xvi). Saddled with a nascent formalized system of vocational training, the inability of the public Indian education and training system to prepare young people for the world of work and the requirements of the employment market, systems of power and privilege – structured around class, race and gender – can easily exploit a leading industrialized nation with a very young population and a high demand for a skilled workforce.

India has one of the youngest populations worldwide. Given its high birth rate, this number is bound to increase. In 2021, about 66 per cent of the population will be between fifteen and 59 years old and thus at an employable age (World Bank 2013); 70 per cent of all Indians will be at an employable age by 2025. The challenges and opportunities are hard to ignore – this 'demographic dividend' could also change quickly into a 'demographic disadvantage' (Mehrotra 2014), related to the huge challenges to qualify potential workers appropriately in order to participate in the nation's growth and to generate prosperity and satisfaction (Hajela 2012; Agrawal 2013).

Educational changes in India over the last few decades have occurred outside the visions and orientations of the NEP – a cause for concern. Political posturing is content to belligerently keep alive the discourse of the colonial plunder and the need to recover India's legacy among other things – its rich education system. The state, drawing from NEP 2020, is increasingly willing to abdicate its role in the development sector to encourage and facilitate true philanthropic, private and community participation. Lending credence to this willingness, the Tripura government in December 2021 announced that it would hand over 100 state-run high and higher secondary schools to private organizations. The gloomy prognosis – pessimism, populism, polarization and collapse – appear to be the horizon of the world's youngest population.

Contemporary educational practice and policy are rife with reforms. The Finnish educator Pasi Sahlberg (2011) describes these globally popular reform strategies as GERM – the Global Education Reform Movement comprising standardization and a focus on core curriculum subjects at the expense of areas such as creative arts, risk-avoidance, corporate management models and test-based accountancy policies. These prevailing strategies as pervasive insidious orthodoxies announce the neoliberal dream of deregulated, compliant, market-responsive knowledge creation. In language that assumes moral and ideological neutrality, market discourse crafted by futurists speaks little of social values and norms which education inherently transmits and yet is instrumental in casting aspersions on the role of the states to rediscover and rearticulate public good in learning and knowledge. Elements of GERM in the contemporary Indian educational practice and policy are a complex set of legislative entanglements signalling new dependency regimes (Brock-Utne 2000; Sadgopal 2003), ushering in privatization (Tilak 1997; Kamat 2002; Mehrotra 2006) and consensus building in support of neoliberalism (Hill and Kumar, eds 2011; Ball 2016). In India, given the absence of large or small movements and public policy responses and strategies that may generate any hope of educational reform to ensure equality and social justice, what alternative strategies can we use to instil within ourselves and our children a sense of global citizenship, healthy intellectual scepticism, respect of India's traditions and appreciation of its diversity?

The Reflexive Teacher–Educator

The language and practices of the market now saturate our technology and modern-day life and continue to usurp systems of power and privilege structured around class, race and gender to reshape human community and environmental values. Caught up in this maelstrom, we are all vulnerable and yet, exploring vulnerabilities is a critical component of reflexivity and the honest critique of ideas, the cornerstones of democracy. In the face of such vulnerabilities, two questions raised about contemporary Indian education policy and practice are *'Is it fair?'* and *'Does it work?'* The importance of these questions is subsumed by *'Who is best positioned to raise these questions?'* Taking such epistemological, emotional and personal risks is not easy for one circumscribed in the vulnerabilities of the teaching–learning profession. This paper positions and explores the possibilities of reflexive teacher–educators to identify and challenge prevailing orthodoxies and voice their potentially 'heretical' views about education in the twenty-first century. We argue that for the reflexive teacher–educator, vulnerability can be an asset in developing understandings of self-cultivation; relating to others and engaging in systems as critiques of contemporary education policy and practice; considering the purpose of the critique (or heresy); and exploring the possibilities that reflexive pedagogy offers for this kind of academic work at a time of uncertainty and change in school and university research and teaching. Reflexive explorations of vulnerability offer a path to building empathy and creating engaged generosity within a community of dissensus. This kind of reflexivity is essential in a society shaped by 'new instrumentalism' or the 'utilitarian turn' in which democratic participation often degenerates into neoliberal silos of discourse and marginalization of others who look, think and believe differently. Where public education enables the development of citizens and not consumers, to engage in social and community-oriented democratic processes, reflexive and equitable teacher–educators are strategically placed to position dialogue, albeit heretical (informed critique), informed by reflexivity, as fundamental to the construction of knowledge and education for survival, critical understanding and integral creativity.

This work is predicated on the conviction that an informed critique (heresy) is a necessary accompaniment to developing and sustaining learning in the larger arena of mind and spirit. The academic project of this paper constitutes a defence of the community and social bonds within which schools and universities have been conceived, legitimated and grown; that which is 'heretical' exists only in claims that are definitively and provocatively anti-social and anti-community.

The Academic Heretic

All intellectual activity can be seen as terrorism against established canons, whether science, culture or sociology.

– Ulitskaya (2011: 178)

Heresy is the dislocation of some complete and self-supporting scheme by the introduction of a novel denial of some essential part therein.

– Belloc ([1938] 2011: 5)

In the twenty-first century, as in the 1950s or 1970s, heresy is somewhat in the eye of the beholder. The words renegade, dissenter and heretic have an archaic or religious sense and a modern-day figurative sense, which is likely to have derived from the religious sense. In modern usage, the word 'heretic' is used either to express extreme distaste for the dissenter's view (they're so wrong that it's as bad as heresy) or to imply opinions quite contrary to the established orthodoxy that the mainstream view from which they dissent is like a religion. From Galileo to today's amateur astronomers, scientists have been heretics and rebels. Academicians, much like artists and poets, in their pursuit of truth as free spirits are guided as much by imagination as by reason. They resist the restrictions their cultures impose on them. Little wonder then that their greatest theories have the uniqueness and beauty of great works of art. The academic project of this paper constitutes a defence of the community and social bonds within which schools and universities have been conceived, legitimated and grown – that which is 'heretical' exists only in claims that are definitively and provocatively anti-social and anti-community.

The continuing social domination of capital, evinced in the capitalization of humanity, persists in the redefining of human capabilities as labour power and poses a threat to the key philosophical bedrock in public and social trust which educators have for centuries been able to engage with decisive responsibilities for the intellectual and practical conditions of such trust. Recognizing the perversion in the form of agency, aimed at the displacement of the human, reflexivity in teacher education argues for the idea of teacher–educators as academic heretics – idols of enlightenment, discovery and resistance – and their place in education to serve as a useful frame to analyse the challenges facing education in recent decades where a global free market determinism is bringing schools and universities to heel. Reflexivity calls on teacher–educators as academic heretics to embark on rediscovering and rearticulating public good in teaching, learning and knowledge.

Systems of power and privilege structured around class, race and gender have served to dislocate learning from the larger arena of mind and spirit, an orthodoxy few venture to engage with. Discourses of exclusion and cultural politics in education are rife in our sociopolitical environment. This paper positions the possibilities of evoking in reflexive teacher–educators essentially radical, provocative and unorthodox views on social, political, economic and cultural issues – to identify and challenge prevailing orthodoxies concerned about their potential to entrench inequality and dampen real curiosity but not without faith in their possibilities and voice their potentially 'heretical' views about education that strive to locate learning in the larger arena of mind and spirit.

Teacher–educators as academic heretics appear to have their work cut out – competence-based education and training (CBET), evidence-based policy (EPB) and group think are some of the epistemologically specious and ideologically unsound shibboleths wrapped in an ethos of economism and purported to foster nation-building. Evidence-based policy (EPB), a major shibboleth of the current era, more often than not precariously hinges on spurious objectivism and unproblematized epistemology, effectively designed to privilege certain forms of research and knowledge over others, in ways redolent with instrumentalism and the utilitarian turn. Simply put, there is no 'scientific method'; there is no single procedure or set of rules that underlies every piece of research and guarantees that it is 'scientific' and, therefore, trustworthy (Feyerabend 1982: 98; see also Feyerabend 2011: 112–13).

As academic heretics, teacher–educators are up against a major transition, an ethos of economism masquerading as nation-building. Critical to the analysis is the technocratic character whereby goals are simply adopted, coopted and implemented in the most efficient manner, without reference to discussions about ends or values; neither the epistemological nor the policy processes support such ambiguous and insidious ambitions. The ubiquity and speed with which philanthropic and private corporates continue to redefine public and social spaces, goods and services spurs the academic heretic to recognize the notion of 'social good' becoming increasingly marginalized: it has become a 'buried discourse' (Pusey 1991: 166) replaced by economistic rhetoric of individual rights, ideologies of 'efficiency' and 'choice'. Pusey pointed to the neutralizing effects of this transition: 'What wins is a kind of "dephenomenalizing" abstraction that tries to neutralize the social contexts of program goals in every area, whether it be education, industry support, public health or water resource management' (ibid.: 11).

The reflexive academic heretics risk their lives by interrogating 'orthodoxy' or neoliberal silos of discourse and marginalization of others who look, think and believe differently. Contemporary reflexive pedagogy shares a surprising historical context – the rich but oftentimes unrecognized literary and philosophical tradition that has existed for nearly two centuries. Arguably, one could trace current reflexive thought through some of the greatest minds of the nineteenth and twentieth centuries – William Blake, Mary Shelley, Charles Dickens, John Ruskin, William Morris, Henry David Thoreau, Ralph Waldo Emerson, Robert Graves, Aldo Leopold and many others – if one were to argue that modern protests against consumptive lifestyles and misgivings about the relentless march of mechanization are part of fascinating hidden history. The reflexive tradition can yield important insights into how we might reshape both technology and modern life so that human, community and environmental values take precedence over the demand of the machine.

Learning or Teaching

> . . . the search for certainty is indeed literally a Kinderkrankheit.
> – Feyerabend, letter to Lakatos, 27 December 1974

The National Education Policy 2020 introduces, among its primary objectives, the promotion of 'lifelong learning opportunities for all'. This is in line with the UN Sustainable Development Goals 2030. In its own words, as per demands emerging in the international market, it is imperative that young Indians *not only learn but, more importantly, learn how to learn.* Even to the casual reader, it is hard to ignore what appears to be a dramatic shift from the learning declared on the very first page to exclusive claims to teaching outlined towards the end of the same document.

'India will be promoted as a global study destination providing premium education at affordable costs thereby helping to restore its role as a Vishwa Guru' reads Section 12.8 on page 39 of the NEP 2020. Notwithstanding the modal associated with place, premium and price, the preordained notion of an amorphous, unitary ideal of a Vishwa Guru ignores the dynamic nature of beliefs, contexts and practices and the evolutionary and differentiated processes of teaching and learning and students and teachers. A science '. . . which insists on possessing the only correct method and the only acceptable results is ideology, and must be separated from the state' (Feyerabend 1978: 308).

The National Education Policy 2020's repeated emphasis on the role of 'tradition' and 'Indian values' in shaping education curriculum and the need to integrate traditional 'knowledge systems' or ways of knowing and learning, with modern curricula matching 'world standards' is mentioned below. The excerpt from NEP 2020 reads:

> The rich heritage of ancient and eternal Indian knowledge and thought has been a guiding light for this Policy. The pursuit of knowledge (gyaan), wisdom (pragyaa), and truth (satya) was always considered in Indian thought and philosophy as the loftiest human goal. The aim of education in ancient India was not just the acquisition of knowledge as preparation for life in this world, or life beyond schooling, but for complete realisation and liberation of the self. (NEP 2020, Introduction)

The emphasis on traditions and values appears to lend an exclusive aura to something that ought to be seen for what they are. Ultimately, traditions are just that: they are neither good nor bad, but simply exist. An inclusive perspective, on the other hand, enables an openness to change, embrace of pluralism and respect for the other's standpoint and replaces the mythical privileges of closed communities of 'experts': '. . . in a free society, intellectuals are just one tradition. They have no special rights. . . . Problems are not solved by specialists (though their advice will not be disregarded) but by the people concerned in accordance with the ideas they value and by procedures they regard as appropriate' (Feyerabend 1982: 9–10, 87).

Every teacher engaging in intellectual activity is essentially an activist, an academic heretic and a terrorist as described by Ulitskaya (2011) and Belloc (1938) above. Yet, the call to intellectual activity and touching hearts and minds is a mindful activity. Removing the blinkers and inviting a panoramic perspective is precisely the purpose of education for transformation as it is being articulated by the likes of Selby (1997; 1998), Miller (1996;

1999) and O'Sullivan (1999). It is the reflexive teacher–educator who can truly engage with the challenging demands of reflexivity.

The concluding part of this paper is devoted to a discussion on reflexivity and its significance in teacher education.

Reflexivity in Teacher Education

Reflexive educators challenge their mindsets and practices with constant interrogation – What is knowledge? Why is it valuable? How much of it do we have (if any at all), and what ways of thinking are good ways to use to get more of it? – enduring attempts perhaps to address what Krishna Kumar describes as 'a whole century has gone by without the instrumentalist character of teacher training being challenged or reformed' (Kumar 2008: 38). The aims of education questions that are asked in epistemology, roughly, the philosophical theory of knowledge, discussed in the foundation courses, never get synchronized with the purpose of teaching chemistry or geography or any other school subject.

Whether teacher education in India is designed to address and engage with mindsets and practices towards enabling the formation of more reflexive educators is a moot question. Teacher education in India has attracted severe criticism from all the major commissions set up to study school education over the last fifty years (Gupta 2020). The instrumentalist character of teacher training fails to include impactful conversations about diversity and identity formation. An important element in reflexive learning is that learning and collaboration are the key mechanisms through which community membership, belonging and identities are gained and engendered. Communities, their representatives and practitioners are thus co-produced. This is positioned as an important element in reflexive teaching, learning and collaborative practice, '[b]ecause learning transforms who we are and what we can do, it is an experience of identity. It is not just an accumulation of skills and information, but a process of becoming—to become a certain person or, conversely to avoid becoming a certain person' (Wenger 1998: 215).

Reflexivity remains hidden, often disguised or at best is taken for granted in social theory. Therefore, what it is and what it does has merited little scientific enquiry necessary for producing clear concepts of reflexivity or a lucid understanding of reflexivity as a social process. The paucity of studies does scant justice to a rich and vibrant concept – a philosophy for and of education.

The reasons for promoting reflexivity to a central position within social theory and teacher education can be outlined in the following premise. The subjective powers of reflexivity mediate the role that objective structural or cultural powers play in influencing social action and are thus indispensable to explaining social outcomes (Archer 2017: 168). The following paragraphs invite teachers and teacher–educators to reclaim and engage reflexively with their pedagogical experiences as central to the human conditions that they serve. Without this, there is no such thing as education.

Much of the literature on reflective learning served to highlight two key elements of reflection: (1) making sense of experience; and (2) reimagining future experience and generally concerned with how, and at what level, learners reflect (Hatton and Smith 1995; Bain *et al.* 2002; Mezirow 2006). Effective choices, however, require a reflexive and lifelong approach to learning whereby the individual engages in a continuous process of questioning and transforming capabilities and motivations in relation to, and as a response to, changing social conditions and expectations of the work or learning environment (Archer 2007). The notion of a reflective practitioner was now enriched by a more comprehensive view of the notion of a reflexive pedagogue who viewed the need for reflexive processes, including reflection.

Gillie Bolton attempts to demystify the difference between reflection and reflexivity in her 2010 book *Reflective Practice, Writing and Professional Development.* Her distinction between reflection and reflexivity is as follows:

> Reflection is learning and developing through examining what we think happened on any occasion, and how we think others perceived the event and us, opening our practice to scrutiny by others . . . it involves reliving and re-rendering: who said and did what, how, when, where and why. It might lead to insight not noticed at the time of the experience.

> Reflexivity is finding strategies to question our own attitudes, thought processes, values, assumptions, prejudices and habitual actions, to strive to understand our complex roles in relation to others . . . it involves thinking from within experiences . . . a questioning process that goes further than the practical reflection of what happened and how can I do better next time. (Bolton 2010: 13–15)

Unlike reflection, reflexivity compels us to engage in critical introspection in the moment, as well as after it, while simultaneously critiquing our sociopolitical contexts (Creswell 2006; Roebuck 2007; Hara 2010; Langer 2016; Zinn *et al.* 2016) while reflection is after and individual reflexivity is ongoing and relational. Reflexive inquiry disrupts normalized assumptions about how we come to knowledge and presents essential questions about our capacities as researchers, to account for an ever-evolving understanding of our experiences (Cunliffe 2003).

Critical reflection, transformative reflection and reflection are terms often used interchangeably with reflexivity (Hatton and Smith 1995; Ryan and Bourke 2013). Reflection in this paper is viewed as a necessary component of reflexivity, the latter characterized by deliberative action following reflective thought. While some forms of reflective learning rely on metacognitive thinking strategies (Dahl 2004) alone, however, these fail to account for social contexts and structures which influence learning, whereas reflexivity is characterized by the reflective interplay between individuals and social structures to understand, maintain or change courses of action chosen by individuals (Archer, ed. 2010). Reflexivity is the acknowledgement of an individual situated within a personal history within the real world.

A reflexive methodology informed by ontological and epistemological considerations requires teachers and teacher–educators to address critical questions about the essence of reality, the construction of knowledge, and the ways in which we engage with each other and society (Cunliffe 2003; Armitage 2012). The dynamic and evolving interrelatedness between the individual and society renews the concept of reflexivity in the literature. Recent additions adopt a view of reflexivity as a conversational, collective and sociopolitically situated practice through which actors question traditional practices and explore new possibilities for joint action (Cunliffe and Easterby-Smith 2004; Cunliffe and Jun 2005).

Our dynamic experiences of life invite us as teachers and teacher–educators, as human beings to develop understandings of self-cultivation and relating to others, and engaging in systems reflexivity, however, serves as a significant framework for critique to reconnect our ways of seeing, being and becoming to what is often taken for granted and concealed by our experiences and theoretical understandings. Such concealing leads human beings to experience the world at a very superficial level. A constant interrogation of our preferred ways of seeing, being and becoming is reflected in the choices we engage with. Table 4.1 illustrates that in reviewing, reflection and reflexivity, we are called to reconnecting to our taken-for-granted ways of seeing, being and becoming.

Despite the growth of several forms of reflexivity – participant reflexivity (Garfinkel 1967); researcher reflexivity (Gouldner 1970); textual reflexivity (Derrida 1978); positional reflexivity (Macbeth 2001); radical reflexivity (Cunliffe 2003); aesthetic reflexivity (Ryan 2014); personal reflexivity (Brand 2015) and transformative reflexivity (Zinn *et al.* 2016) – pedagogic reflexivity or reflexive pedagogy is yet to merit a scientific inquiry. Human reflexivity has come to be viewed as one of the major concerns of the twentieth century. It has been referred to as the most pressing problem of our time. And, yet, as a distinct topic in teacher education, few

TABLE 4.1 Reflexivity: Reconnecting ways of seeing, being and becoming

Ways of seeing	Ways of being	Ways of becoming
Review	Competence	Curiosity
Reflection	Character	Confidence
Reflexivity	Conscience	Choice

philosophers and researchers have either analysed or speculated systematically on so complex a phenomenon as reflexivity.

A scientific inquiry into reflexivity and reflexive pedagogy could help uncover the multiple subjectivities, various contexts and polyvocality of the teacher–educator's enactment of theoretical beliefs about teaching and situating them in their narratives about learning experiences as they relate to praxis development.

As the political terrain continues to change, teacher education – its management and how teacher–educators and students organize, communicate and participate in different ways than they used to – is getting more homogenized. A new strand of imaginative politics is blurring the boundaries between the school and the learner. Reflexivity in teacher pedagogy enables a collaborative exploration between and among a community of learners with how education is pushing the boundaries of the known repertoire of contention and dialogue by not only demonstrating against the status quo but also demonstrating how the world can be different.

> It is in fact a part of the function of education to help us escape, not from our own time – for we are bound by that – but from the intellectual and emotional limitations of our time. – T.S. Eliot

Reflexive pedagogy positions teacher–educators to collaboratively connect the dots from various teaching–learning settings to interrogate how provoked moments of disruption or clarity can fuse various interventions and lead to the mobilization of transformative education for social justice. Reflexive teacher–educators, instead of celebrating institutions that purport to privilege merit to portray new social actors as bearers of better societal alternatives, are open to explore how the said institutions facilitate the cultivation of alternatives to set off the transformation.

As We Journey On

Is reflexive pedagogy an experience of telling our stories or displaying the moral of the story? To open such perspectives for discussion, reflexive educators are directed to three main lines of inquiry: (1) questions (experience) of being (ontology); (2) questions (experience) of knowing (epistemology); and (3) questions (experience) of the telling everyday life (narrative). Although not limited by questions of ontology, epistemology and narrative in dialogue with these critical perspectives, reflexive teacher–educators seek to reflect on the diversity of approaches and methodological modes through which equitable mindsets and practices can and do attend to everyday life.

This exploration of the reflexive teacher–educator as academic heretic attempts to demonstrate the necessity of diverse approaches through which the experience of the knowledge of everyday pedagogical life is produced and articulated. Furthermore, as it problematizes and unsettles non-reflexive notions of everyday life, this chapter provides a space for critical dialogue, questioning and exploring the unique ways in which discourses are related to each other and inform specific cultural narratives. The main assumption driving this chapter is that the many approaches through which we attend to the lived experiences of everyday life often impact on and explicitly relate to the narratives, values and standards that mediate our curriculum, campus and classroom.

The current era of education is inextricably enmeshed in promoting a corporate agenda that privileges the consumer and not citizens, who make up the 'bottom line'. The vitriolic and politically prescribed discourse framing education and teacher education today is ineffective, or worse, harmful. A growing political will to discredit, dehumanize and dismantle liberal and progressive education has led to weaponizing the vulnerabilities of individuals into narratives of fear. Therefore, we fear other nations, we fear the others from within, and we fear change facilitated through ethically bankrupt technocratic management of education that may be used to disperse power to others. In an atmosphere bereft of epistemological, emotional and personal moorings, the corporate elites within a/the society work to exploit these factors and co-opt technologies to consolidate their privilege over teaching and learning. Teacher–educators as academic heretics serving to enhance the humanity of education attempt to reframe teaching and learning as inherently vulnerable undertakings fraught with de-professionalization, alienation and loss of professional autonomy and identity.

Current educational policies particularly in India, have swung so far in the direction of overtly politicized and decontextualized beliefs and practices so much so that clarity becomes impossible and personal freedom and autonomy remain elusive. It is not farfetched to imagine the loss of the imaginative and expressive capacities of a generation of children and adolescents. The reflexive pedagogical imagination – deeply ingrained interior journeys – reflects ways of observing and embracing the world of others, of becoming wise, becoming self and becoming skilled practitioners of meaning-making. Educational narratives in teacher education offer myriad opportunities for the reflexive teacher–educator as an academic heretic to interrogate and engage with wholeness, sustenance and renewal.

Reflexive pedagogy can make a substantial contribution to the current debate about democracy, by emphasizing the central importance of education to political thought and practice; it suggests that only an education system based on liberal democratic principles can offer the possibility of a genuinely free society. Educational contexts are the human arena for interrogating and engaging with values in action and realizing how they frame our cultural ecology and life development. To demand that the systems that administer our lives and the technology that powers them be forced to become more responsive to the needs of individuals than to business and government, with true social liberation as our ultimate goal demands a reflexive imagination of an academic heretic.

Reflexive pedagogy serves to stir teacher–educators to critique (thinking), participate (doing) and realize moral responsibility (relating to others) in exploring values, alterity, dialogue and culture as possible coordinates for a renewed culture of education in the twenty-first century. Informed by a reflexive sensibility, teacher education is uniquely placed to explore avenues for the resurgence of public and social trust, to swing the pendulum of educational practices back to a place of balance and wholeness.

Reflexivity and reflexive pedagogy readily challenge, if not break through, the 'ontological' conceptualization of education in which processes of education are localized in liminality. This paper invites teachers and teacher–educators as heretics, terrorists and activists to reclaim and engage with reflexive pedagogical experiences as central to the human conditions that they serve. Without this engagement, there can be no such thing as education.

References

Agrawal, T. (2013), 'Vocational Education and Training Programs (VET): An Asian Perspective', *Asia-Pacific Journal of Cooperative Education*, vol. 14, no. 1, pp. 15–26.

Altbach, P. and J. Balan (2007), *World Class Worldwide: Transforming Research Universities in Asia and Latin America*, Baltimore: Johns Hopkins University Press.

Apple, M.W. (2012), *Knowledge, Power, and Education: The Selected Works of Michael W. Apple*, New York: Routledge.

Archer, M.S. (2007), *Making Our Way through the World: Human Reflexivity and Social Mobility*, Cambridge: Cambridge University Press.

———, ed. (2010), *Conversations about Reflexivity*, London: Routledge.

——— (2017), 'Reflexivity as the Unacknowledged Condition of Social Life', in T. Brock, M. Carrigan and G. Scambler, eds, *Structure, Culture and Agency*, London: Routledge.

Armitage, A. (2012), 'Silent Voices in Organisations: Conscientization as a Reflexive Research Methodology', available at http://search.proquest.com/docview/1346926394?accountid=142373, accessed 24 January 2018.

Bain, J.D., C. Mills, R. Ballantyne and J. Packer (2002), 'Developing Reflection on Practice through Journal Writing: Impacts of Variations in the Focus and Level of Feedback', *Teachers and Teaching: Theory and Practice*, vol. 8, no. 2, pp. 171–96.

Balagopalan, S. (2011), 'Introduction: Children's Lives and the Indian Context', *Childhood*, vol. 18, no. 3, pp. 291–97.

Ball, S.J. (1994), *Education Reform, A Critical and Post-structural Approach*, Buckingham: Open University Press.

———— (2016), 'Neoliberal Education? Confronting the Slouching Beast', *Policy Futures in Education*, vol. 14, no. 8, pp. 1046–59.

Batra, P. (2005), 'Voice and Agency of Teachers: The Missing Link in the National Curriculum Framework', *Economic and Political Weekly*, vol. 40, no. 40, pp. 4347–56.

Belloc, H. (1938), *The Great Heresies*, Charlotte: TAN Books; digital edition 2011, Seattle: Create Space Independent Publishing Platform.

Beteille, A. (2010), *The University at the Crossroads*, New Delhi: Oxford University Press.

Bolton, G. (2010), *Reflective Practice: Writing and Professional Development*, London: Sage Publications.

Booker, C. (2020), *Groupthink: A Study in Self Delusion*, London: Bloomsbury Continuum.

Brand, G. (2015), 'Through the Looking Glass Space to New Ways of Knowing: A Personal Research Narrative', *The Qualitative Report*, vol. 20, no. 4, pp. 516–25.

Brock-Utne, B. (2000), *Whose Education for All?* New York: Falmer.

Brown, W. (2011), 'Neoliberalized Knowledge', *History of the Present*, vol. 1, no. 1, pp. 113–29.

Creswell, J.W. (2006), *Qualitative Inquiry and Research Design: Choosing among Five Approaches*, Thousand Oaks, CA: Sage.

Cunliffe, A.L. (2003), 'Reflexive Inquiry in Organizational Research: Questions and Possibilities', *Human Relations*, vol. 56, no. 8, pp. 983–1003.

Cunliffe, A.L. and M. Easterby-Smith (2004), 'From Reflection to Practical Reflexivity: Experiential Learning as Lived Experience', in M. Reynolds and R. Vince, eds, *Organizing Reflection*, Aldershot: Ashgate, pp. 30–46.

Cunliffe, A.L. and J.S. Jun (2005), 'The Need for Reflexivity in Public Administration', *Administration and Society*, vol. 37, no. 2, pp. 225–42.

Dahl, O. (2004), *The Growth and Maintenance of Linguistic Complexity*, Studies in Language Companion Series, Amsterdam and Philadelphia: John Benjamins.

Derrida, J. (1978), *Writing and Difference*, London: Routledge and Kegan Paul.

Feyerabend, P. (1978), *Against Method*, London: Verso Books.

———— (1982), *Science in a Free Society*, London: Verso Books.

———— (2011), *The Tyranny of Science*, Cambridge: Polity Press.

Foucault, M. (1988), *Politics, Philosophy, Culture: Interviews and Other Writings, 1977–1984*, New York: Routledge.

Freire, P. (1970), *Pedagogy of the Oppressed*, New York: Seabury Press.

Freire, P. and I. Shor (1987), *Freire for the Classroom: A Sourcebook for Liberators Teaching*, Portsmouth: Heinemann.

Gouldner, A. (1970), *The Coming Crisis of Western Sociology*, New York: Basic Books.

Greene, J.A., W.A. Sandoval and I. Bråten (2016), 'An Introduction to Epistemic Cognition', in J.A. Greene, W.A. Sandoval and I. Bråten, eds, *Handbook of Epistemic Cognition*, New York: Routledge.

Gupta, L. (2020), 'Discourse of teacher education in India', in Krishna Kumar, ed., *The Routledge Handbook of Education in India: Debates, Practices, and Policies*, 2nd edition, New York: Routledge, pp. 175–88.

Hajela, R. (2012), 'Shortage of Skilled Workers: A Paradox of the Indian Economy', *SKOPE,* Research Paper, no. 11.

Hara, B. (2010), 'Reflexive Pedagogy', available at http://www.chronicle.com/blogs/prof hacker/reflexive-pedagogy/22939, accessed 24 January 2018.

Hatton, N. and D. Smith (1995), 'Reflection in Teacher Education: Towards Definition and Implementation', *Teaching and Teacher Education,* vol. 11, no. 1, pp. 33–49.

Hickey, M.G. and M. Stratton (2007), 'Schooling in India: Effects of Gender and Caste', available at http://opus.ipfw.edu/spe/vol2/iss1/6.

Hill, D. and R. Kumar, eds (2011), *Global Neoliberalism and Education and its Consequences,* New York: Routledge.

Hofer, B.K. and P.R. Pintrich (1997), 'The Development of Epistemological Theories: Beliefs about Knowledge and Knowing and Their Relation to Learning', *Review of Educational Research,* vol. 67, pp. 88–140.

Hyland, T. (1994), *Competence, Education and NVQs: Dissenting Perspectives,* London: Cassell.

Kamat, S. (2002), *Development as Hegemony: NGOs and the State in India,* Oxford: Oxford University Press.

Kapur, D. (2011), 'Addressing the Trilemma of Higher Education', *Seminar,* 617, available at https://www.india-seminar.com/2011/617/617_devesh_kapur.htm

Kumar, K. (2008), *A Pedagogue's Romance: Reflections on Schooling,* New Delhi: Oxford University Press.

Kumar, K. and P. Sarangapani (2004), 'History of the Quality Debate', *Contemporary Education Dialogue,* vol. 2, no. 1, pp. 30–52.

Langer, P.C. (2016), 'The Research Vignette: Reflexive Writing as Interpretative Representation of Qualitative Inquiry – A Methodological Proposition', *Qualitative Inquiry,* vol. 22, no. 9, pp. 735–44.

Langeveld, M.J. (1944), 'Beknopte Theoretische Paedagogiek' (Concise Theoretical Pedagogy), Holland: University of Utrecht.

Leaton Gray, S. and G. Whitty (2010), 'Social Trajectories or Disrupted Identities? Changing and Competing Models of Teacher Professionalism under New Labour', *Cambridge Journal of Education,* vol. 40, no. 1, pp. 5–23.

Macbeth, D. (2001), 'On "Reflexivity" in Qualitative Research: Two Readings, and a Third', *Qualitative Inquiry,* vol. 7, no. 1, pp. 35–68.

Martin, R. (2004), 'Turning Pro: Professional Qualifications and the Global University', *Social Text,* vol. 22, no. 2/79, pp. 1–11.

Mehrotra, S. (2006), *The Economics of Elementary Education in India: The Challenge of Public Finance, Private Provision and Household Costs,* New Delhi: Sage.

—— (2014), 'Quantity and Quality: Policies to Meet the Twin Challenges of Employability in Indian Labour Market', *The Indian Journal of Industrial Relations: A Review of Economic and Social Development,* vol. 49, no. 3, pp. 367–77.

Mezirow, J. (2006), 'An Overview of Transformative Learning', in P. Sutherland and J. Crowther, eds, *Lifelong Learning: Concepts and Contexts,* New York: Routledge.

Mulder, M. (2017a), *Competence-based Vocational and Professional Education Bridging the Worlds of Work and Education,* Switzerland: Springer Verlag.

—— (2017b), 'Competence Theory and Research: A Synthesis', in Martin Mulder, ed., *Competence-based Vocational and Professional Education Bridging the Worlds of Work and Education,* Switzerland: Springer Verlag.

Nicolini, D. (2012), *Practice Theory, Work, and Organization,* Oxford: Oxford University Press.

O'Sullivan, E., A. Morrell and M.A. O'Connor, eds (2002), *Expanding the Boundaries of Transformative Learning: Essays on Theory and Praxis,* New York: Palgrave.

PROBE Team (1999), *A Report on Elementary Education in India,* New Delhi: Oxford University Press.

Pusey, M. (1991), *Economic Rationalism in Canberra. A Nation-building State Changes Its Mind*, Cambridge: Cambridge University Press.

Rampal, A. and H. Mander (2013), 'Lessons on Food and Hunger: Pedagogy of Empathy for Democracy', *Economic and Political Weekly*, vol. 48, no. 28, pp. 50–58.

Rea, J. (2013), 'MOOCs, Money and Casual Staff', *Campus Review*, available at http://www.campusreview.com.au/blog/2013/07/moocs-money-and-casual-staff/, accessed 3 November 2020.

Reckwitz, A. (2002), 'Toward a Theory of Social Practices: A Development in Culturalist Theorizing', *European Journal of Social Theory*, vol. 5, no. 2, pp. 243–63.

Rikowski, G. (2002), 'Education, Capital and the Transhuman', in D. Hill, P. McLaren, M. Cole and G. Rikowski, eds, *Marxism against Postmodernism in Educational Theory*, Lanham, MD: Lexington Books.

Roebuck, J. (2007), 'Reflexive Practice: To Enhance Student Learning', *Journal of Learning Design*, vol. 2, no. 1, pp. 77–91.

Ryan, M. (2014), 'Reflexivity and Aesthetic Inquiry: Building Dialogues between the Arts and Literacy', *English Teaching*, vol. 13, no. 2, pp. 5–18.

Ryan, M.E. and T. Bourke (2013), 'The Teacher as Reflexive Professional: Making Visible the Excluded Discourse in Teacher Standards', *Discourse: Studies in the Cultural Politics of Education*', vol. 34, no. 3, available at https://eprints.qut.edu.au/46659/, accessed 24 January 2018.

Sacks, D.O. and P.A. Thiel (1998 [1995]), *The Diversity Myth: Multi-culturalism and Political Intolerance on Campus*, Oakland, CA: The Independent Institute.

Sadgopal, A. (2003), 'Education for Too Few', available at https://frontline.thehindu.com/static/html/fl2024/stories/20031205002809700.htm, accessed 2 May 2019.

Sahlberg, P. (2011), *Finnish Lessons: What Can the World Learn from Educational Change in Finland*, New York: Teachers College Press.

Saul, J.R. (1997), *The Unconscious Civilization*, Toronto: Anansi.

Saxena, S. (2012), 'Is Equality an Outdated Concern in Education?', *Economic and Political Weekly*, vol. 47, no. 49, pp. 61–68.

Sornson, R. (2016), *Over-tested and Under-prepared: Using Competency-based Learning to transform our Schools*, New York, NY: Routledge.

Tapan, M. (2014), *Ethnographies of Schooling in Contemporary India*, Delhi: Sage.

Thomas, S. (2011), 'Teachers and Public Engagement: An Argument for Rethinking Teacher Professionalism to Challenge Deficit Discourses in the Public Sphere', *Discourse: Studies in the Cultural Politics of Education*, vol. 32, no. 3, pp. 371–82.

Tilak, J.B.G. (1997), 'The Dilemma of Reforms in Financing Higher Education in India', *Higher Education Policy*, vol. 10, no. 1, pp. 7–21.

Tukdeo, S. (2015), 'Class Divided: Global Pressures, Domestic Pulls and a Fractured Education Policy in India', *Policy Futures in Education*, vol. 13, no. 2, pp. 205–18.

Ulitskaya, L. (2011), *Daniel Stein, Interpreter*, Melbourne: Scribe.

Vasavi, A.R. (2016), 'The Culture of Government Schools', *Seminar India*, 677, available at http://www.india-seminar.com/2016/677/677_a_r_vasavi.htm, accessed 25 July 2020.

Velaskar, P. (2010), 'Quality and Inequality in Indian Education', *Contemporary Education Dialogue*, vol. 7, no.1, pp. 58–93.

Wenger, E. (1998), *Communities of Practice: Learning, meaning and identity*, New York, NY: Cambridge University Press, p. 215.

World Bank (2013), 'Population Ages 15-64 (% of total population)', available at https://data.worldbank.org/indicator/SP.POP.1564.TO.ZS

Zinn, D., K. Adam, R. Kurup and A. du Plessis (2016), 'Returning to the Source: Reflexivity and Transformation in Understanding a Humanising Pedagogy', *Educational Research for Social Change*, vol. 5, no. 1, pp. 70–93.

5

Progress of Education among the Muslims of Lakshadweep

L.R.S. Lakshmi

This chapter focuses on the educational development among the Muslim community of the Lakshadweep islands. Before we navigate to the core subject, it is important to introduce the reader to the geographical location and the historical background of the region.

Geographically, the Lakshadweep islands are situated about 200 miles west of Kozhikode (also known as Calicut) in Kerala. The group of islands consists of Agatti, Andrott, Kalpeni, Kavaratti and Minicoy. The northern group of the Lakshadweep islands, known as the Amindivi islands, comprises five islands, namely, Amindivi, Chetlat, Kadmat, Kiltan and Bitra, the last being uninhabited till as late as the 1920s (Census of India 1921). As far as the ancient history of the region is concerned, the stone images of a Buddha head in Andrott belonging to the eighth and ninth centuries provide sufficient evidence of the presence of Buddhism in the islands. However, whether Buddhism travelled from Ceylon or Kerala to the islands is not clear. According to tradition, the Hindus of Malabar went in search of the last Chera king, Cheruman Perumal, when he left for Mecca in the ninth century but was shipwrecked on these islands.[1] As these islands were situated on the main Arab trade routes, the islanders seem to have embraced Islam under the influence of an Arab preacher, Ubaidulla (the disciple of the first Khalifa Abu Bakr) from Arabia, around the thirteenth or fourteenth century (Census of India 1891: 278). They adopted Islam under his influence and came to be known as the Mapillas. The similarity between the language and customs of the islands and the mainland shows that these islands, except Minicoy, were originally colonized by the Hindus of Malabar.[2]

There was a significant connection between the islands and the Arakkal (a family name)Ali Rajas of Kannur, the only Muslim royal family in Malabar. Originally a Hindu Nayar, the ancestor of the family was

Ariyan Kulangara Nayar, the hereditary minister of the Kolattiri Raja. Ariyan is said to have embraced Islam at the end of the eleventh or the beginning of the twelfth century. Ali Musa, fifth in the family line, conquered the Maldives for the Kolattiri king, and in the sixteenth century, the king granted him the Lakshadweep (corrupted as Laccadives by the British) islands as an estate in return for a payment of 18,000 *panam*s (cash) (Census of India 1891: 278). He was also granted Kannur and two small *desam*s (sub-division of a revenue division) on the mainland. Thus, the possessions of the Arakkal family consisted of the territory on the Malabar coast and the Lakshadweep islands. They owned large ships that carried pepper, cardamom, coir and other spices to Surat and distant Arab lands.[3] Owing to their Nayar ancestry, the family and its successors followed the *marumakkathayam* (matrilineal) law of succession. The most senior member of the family, male or female, succeeded as the royal head of the family. They called themselves the *arakkal*s and their women were addressed as *beebi*s. The royal family maintained cordial relations with the Ottoman empire, and the Khalifa, in return, acknowledged their traditional custom of matrilineal succession (Kurup 1975: 94).

According to the provisional agreement of 1796 between the Arakkal ruling family and the English East India Company, the family had to bear the administrative responsibility of the islands and carry on its trading monopoly for nearly 60 years for a fixed payment of tribute. But once the tribute fell in arrears, the colonial rulers followed a policy of sequestration. The cession of the islands was officially completed in 1905.

The whole of Minicoy island, which was the largest of the islands, was claimed by the *arrakal* as his own *janmam* (hereditary rights) property. The people of this island were probably of Singhalese origin[4] and were mostly fishermen and sailors. They spoke a language called Mahl, which was the language of the Maldives islands attached to the Ceylon government (Census of India 1921: 37). Minicoy came into the possession of the Ali Raja of Kannur later than the other islands, probably not until the mid-fifteenth century, as a gift from the Sultan of Maldives.[5] The women in Minicoy appeared in public and also took part in public affairs. It is said that they were generally more educated than the ordinary Mappila males of the mainland (Census of India 1891: 278). The Amindivi islands also formed part of the territory of the ruling family for more than two centuries. During Tipu Sultan's conquest of Malabar, these islands were attached to Mysore in 1786. After his defeat at the hands of the British in 1799, South Kanara became British territory, and the islands were attached to the district (Bhatt 1998: 4).

Some authors who have written on Lakshadweep have even

endorsed the British rhetoric that the Lakshadweep islanders were unhappy with the administration of the Arrakal ruling family, and hence the British government had to intervene. That was, however, only an excuse to get control over the islands. Kurup has clearly contended that the interests of the ruling family were suppressed by the imperial policy of expansion and exploitation (Kurup 1975: 6). The author agrees with him because the islands were a major target of British territorial expansion, and the alleged ill treatment of the islanders by the family was only a lame excuse.

The islands became a union territory in 1956 when the Amindivi islands were amalgamated with the Lakshadweep islands, and in 1981, 94 per cent of these Muslims were categorized as Scheduled Tribes. I would argue that this is an anomaly because they do not show any characteristics of a tribe or an Adivasi, and can in no way be compared to any of the tribal communities in India. Tribes have their own distinctive religious practices such as worship of nature in the form of trees, fire, mountains and so on. The Muslims of Lakshadweep socially resemble the Malabar Mapilla Muslims, who are not classified as Scheduled Tribes. In that case, why the central government categorized them as Scheduled Tribes remains an unanswered question. Is it because they were isolated on an island as a different social group, or are they in any way similar to tribal communities like the Gonds, Bhils, Nagas or the Andaman tribes? Similarly, those Mapillas who were transported from Malabar to the Andaman Islands by the British government after the Mappila rebellion of 1921, as a punishment or banishment, have also been categorized as Scheduled Tribes, which is again unjustifiable.

The Transformation of Education from the Colonial to the Post-Independence Period

Education in the islands had taken a backseat for many centuries. Traditional mosque schools founded by the Arakkal rulers did exist, where boys and girls were taught the Koran; there were mosque schools in Agatti where around 60 boys and girls from higher status families learnt the Koran. It was only in the late nineteenth century that the British government began to experiment with the idea of opening schools on the islands. In 1878, the then inspecting officer, Winterbotham, brought three teachers from Madras and started one school each in Kavaratti, Andrott and Agatti. Thirty Muslim boys were enrolled in the school in Agatti, of which only eleven appeared for the examinations in 1880 (Logan 1951: cclxxvii). The school at Kavaratti was closed down in 1880 for lack of students, and a school was opened in Kalpeni instead (ibid.: cclxxxix). Again, in 1884, the schools in Agatti and Andrott were shut down because of slim attendance.[6] Five years later, in 1889, the schools in Andrott, Kavaratti and Agatti were reopened and trained teachers from the mainland were appointed. In Kavaratti and Kalpeni, the local *gumasthas* (agents of the British administration) took on the role of teachers.[7]

The progress in education was very slow in the islands. Out of 10,274 people, only 461 were literate in 1901, and of these, 51 were females.[8] Of the five islands attached to the Malabar district, including Minicoy, only two, namely, Andrott and Kalpeni, maintained a state school each. A school was also opened in Kavaratti in 1904, but in the other two islands, any attempt to start schools was unsuccessful. The schools at Andrott and Kalpeni were each under a trained Muhammadan teacher, and both were inspected and examined for grants. The grants amounted to Rs 60 in Andrott and Rs 86 in Kalpeni. The entire cost of education in these islands was met from the island's funds.[9]

The subjects taught in these schools were Malayalam and Arithmetic. However, there were only six students in the Kalpeni school. In Kavaratti, steps were taken to establish a school by appointing the island schoolmaster. The idea behind the appointment was that as his uncle was a *mukri* (Koran instructor) of one of the principal mosques, there was some prospect of getting students from the mosque schools to join the state school. In Agatti, the new *amin* (judicial administrator) had been directed to persuade Muslim boys to join the state school, while in Andrott, there was a proposal to combine the mosque schools with the secular schools and pay the schoolmaster a small monthly sum. Efforts were also made to hire a Muslim Malayalam teacher on a salary of Rs 15 or Rs 20.[10] A school was founded in Amini in 1904, and a Muhammadan teacher from Kasaragod was appointed (*Lakshadweep Vidyabhyasa Charithram*: 84).[11] In Kalpeni, a bright Mapilla student named Pudiya Illam Koyakidavu Koya was given a monthly scholarship of Rs 5 and sent to study in the Basel German Mission Primary School in Thalasseri, Malabar in 1905.[12] By the 1920s, government schools were established in the Amindivi islands of Kiltan, Kadmat and Chetlat.

In 1945, the sixth standard was introduced in the schools of Kalpeni, Andrott and Agatti, but it was discontinued in 1951 due to lack of funds. A total of 353 students went to school in these islands in 1951.[13] In 1956, when the islands became a union territory, 38 per cent of school-going children attended nine primary schools and the teaching staff was untrained.[14] An assistant educational officer was appointed in 1958 at Kavaratti, and by 1961 four primary schools were opened for girls with 1,299 students. The first high school was started in Amini in 1961, and nursery schools were opened in Kavaratti, Kalpeni, Andrott, Agatti, Amini and Minicoy by 1965.[15]

In Agatti, the Thanveerul Islam *madrassa* was the first religious school for the Mapilla students which held classes up to the fifth standard. On its premises, the Government Junior Basic School (North) was constructed on rent in 1962 for classes up to eighth standard. For high school, the students had to sail to Amini island.[16] It was only in 1985/1986 that a high school was established in Agatti. It was a mixed school for girls and boys, and the medium of instruction was Malayalam.

In Kavaratti, the government school was founded in 1878 and was upgraded to an upper primary school only in 1958.[17] This school later became the Government Senior Basic School with classes up to the eighth standard. It is now called the Government Girls High School, the only girls' school on the island. The Government Senior Secondary School was established in 1962 in Kavaratti. Classes are taught from the eighth to the twelfth standards, and the media of instruction are both English and Malayalam.

Towards the Twenty-first Century

There are no private schools on any of the islands. The number of boys and girls enrolled in 2016 in the Government Senior Secondary School, Kavaratti, were 433 and 146, respectively. There are a total of nineteen teachers in this school on both a permanent and contractual basis. The languages taught here are Malayalam, English, Arabic and Hindi.[18] In the same year, about 500 girls were studying in the Government Girls High School in Kavaratti. The schools in the islands, except for the Kendriya Vidyalayas, follow the Kerala pattern of textbooks.[19] All the government schools in the islands are closed on Fridays for the *juma* prayers and are instead open till noon on Sundays. The students are exempt from wearing their regular school uniforms on Sundays.[20]

Jawaharlal Nehru College was the first junior college founded in Kavaratti in 1972 which offered pre-degree courses. It also introduced a BEd programme for aspiring students and many women candidates enrolled for this course. Ten years later, a second junior college, the Mahatma Gandhi College, was started in Andrott.[21] There were 5,200 students, 232 teachers and twenty-four scholarship holders, that is, eleven for medicine, two each for agriculture and engineering and others for post-matriculate courses (Mukundan 1979: 163). In 1994, Jawaharlal Nehru College was shifted from Kavaratti to Kadmat. The eleventh standard under the Kerala State Board was introduced in both colleges in 2000.[22] The District Institute of Education and Training (DIET) was established in Kavaratti in 2005 and provides a two-year teachers' training course. Although the 2011 census showed that nearly 43 per cent of the Muslim population in India was illiterate,[23] the situation is quite different in Lakshadweep. The islands have a tradition of very high literacy rates. According to the 1981 census, it ranked fourth among all the states and union territories, and by 1991, it overtook Chandigarh to gain the third rank after Kerala and Mizoram. It remained in the same position till 2001. Some of the island representatives claimed that most of the officially declared illiterates were in fact able to read and write Arabic or Mahl (Census of India 1991: 77–78). The gross enrolment ratio in schools was among the highest in the country and higher than the all-India average. According to the 1991 Census, the literacy rate among Scheduled Tribes of Lakshadweep at 80.58 per cent stood second after Mizoram. The island Muslims were in a neck-to-neck literacy race with Kerala (see Table 5.1). Among the islands, literacy levels were the highest in Minicoy and Kavaratti (see Table 5.2). According to the 2011 Census, Kerala was the most literate state at 93.91 per cent, Lakshadweep ranked second at 92.28 per cent and Mizoram held third place at 91.58 per cent.[24] It is significant that Lakshadweep beat Mizoram to take second position after Kerala.

Outstanding performance in science by students of the islands has been widely recognized. Five young scientists from the Government Senior Secondary School, Kavaratti, were selected from the Union Territory in the National Children's Science Congress held at Bengaluru in December 2014.[25] The following year, National Science Day was celebrated in Kalpeni with the participation of students from all the schools in the island.[26] The

TABLE 5.1 Literacy rates in Lakshadweep and Kerala

	1981			1991			2001		
	Males	*Females*	*Total*	*Males*	*Females*	*Total*	*Males*	*Females*	*Total*
Lakshadweep	81.24	55.32	68.42	90.18	72.89	81.78	93.15	81.56	87.52
Kerala	87.73	75.65	81.56	93.62	86.13	89.81	94.20	87.86	90.92

Source: *Lakshadweep Development Report*, 2007, p. 77.

TABLE 5.2 Island-wise literacy rates, 2001

Percentage of literates to total population	
Kavaratti	88.6
Agatti	86.8
Andrott	84.3
Kalpeni	84.4
Minicoy	93.0

Source: Annexure A-22, *Lakshadweep Development Report*, 2007, p. 156.

overall performance of students is commendable, and it is also noteworthy that most schools in the islands can boast of 100 per cent results in the board examinations.[27] In the DIET in Kavaratti, there were twenty-five students enrolled for the BEd course in 2015 and thirty-one in 2016. There are more female students than males registered for the course.[28]

As there are no higher educational institutions in the islands, seats in professional colleges in Kerala and other mainland states have been reserved for them. They have reservation in state engineering colleges, regional engineering colleges, medical colleges and other degree colleges. Scholarships, reimbursement of tuition and hostel fees and return fare once a year are provided to them. Kochi and Calicut, which are the immediate neighbours of the island, are popular destinations for aspiring students.[29]

The Indira Gandhi National Open University (IGNOU) conducted an admission camp in 2018 for the BEd college and the DIET in Kavaratti. It offered free degree courses to the students of Lakshadweep which is a remarkable contribution.[30] In the same year, for the first time in the islands, the Department of Education introduced the Science and Mathematics Olympiad for school children in collaboration with the Science Olympiad Foundation (SOF), Haryana.[31] Every year in December, a Teacher Eligibility Test is conducted simultaneously in Kochi and Kavaratti for candidates interested in pursuing a teaching career in schools in Kerala and the islands.[32]

Lakshadweep also has to its credit many well-educated and talented professionals who have earned an excellent reputation in their professions. For example, B. Amanulla was the first district and sessions judge of Kavaratti District Court. A matriculate from Government High School, Amini, he is an alumnus of Malabar Christian College, Kozhikode, Victoria College, Palakkad and Law College, Thiruvananthapuram. He initially practised as a lawyer in Kerala before moving to Kavaratti.[33] Dr K.K. Anwar Salih, chief medical officer and physician of Government Indira Gandhi Hospital, Kavaratti, was the first islander to become Member of the Royal College of Physicians in the United Kingdom. A native of Andrott, he received his MBBS degree from Kottayam Medical College.[34] In 2015, two teachers from Lakshadweep, Dr M. Mullakoya, Principal, Jawaharlal Nehru Senior Secondary School, Kadmat, and V. Hussain, a primary school teacher in Minicoy, received the meritorious President's Award.[35] Shamina Begum, a native of Kadmat, received her doctorate from the Pusa Indian Agricultural Institute, Delhi, in 2016. A graduate of Kasaragod Agricultural College and a postgraduate in agriculture from Thiruvananthapuram, she cleared the Government Agricultural Service Examinations and has been a scientist at the Kasaragod Agricultural Research Institute.[36]

The Arakkal royal family also had some talented successors like

Yusuf Arakkal, who was a versatile artist, painter and sculptor. His paintings showcased the secular aspects of humanity, and he has won many awards. He was awarded the Lorenzo il Magnifico Silver Medal at the Florence International Biennale of Contemporary Art in 2003. He had wanted to exhibit his paintings on the Jesus series someday at the Vatican, but unfortunately, his dream remained unfulfilled due to his sudden demise on 4 October 2016 (Doctor 2016: 20).

Dr S. Rahmat Beegum is the first woman gynaecologist and represents the first generation of educated people in the islands. That was the time when the odam (wooden boat) was the only mode of transport connecting the mainland. Dr Beegum was the first college-going girl from the islands. She served as director of the medical department for many years and won the Padma Shri Award for her services to the people of Lakshadweep. In her book, written in Malayalam, she has written about her education and also about the health department which now has a helicopter ambulance for patients.[37] Again in the medical field, the first oncologist in Lakshadweep, Dr Muhammad Ali Azher, a native of Amini, studied MD at the Gujarat Cancer Research Institute and did a hands-on certificate course in pain and palliative medicine in Trivandrum.38

Another feather in the cap is Dr Shahida K.P., who won the Gold Medal from MGR Medical University in Tamil Nadu for scoring the highest marks in Diploma in Otorhinolaryngology (ENT). Originally a native of Agatti, she studied there up to the tenth standard and completed her higher secondary at the Al Farook Higher Secondary School, Kozhikode. She pursued her MBBS and house surgery from the Government Medical College, Thrissur, and later did her postgraduation from the Government Medical College, Thanjavur, in Tamil Nadu.[39]

Recently, doctorate degrees have also been awarded to one or two islanders as in the case of P.V. Ahmed Amirsha in geography at Madurai Kamaraj University. He completed high school in Andrott and later moved to Manjeri in Kerala for his higher studies.[40]

Conclusion
Amartya Sen has argued that Bengali Muslims constitute 27.01 per cent of the population of West Bengal, but are poorer and more deprived in literacy, health, economic conditions and gender (Bagchi and Singh 2016: 8). So is the case in Telangana: the four-member enquiry commission headed by G. Sudhir has argued that 85 per cent of the Muslims in the state are backward and that effective measures should be taken to improve their lives.[41] The panel report on the socio-economic and educational conditions of Muslims has recommended 9 to 12 per cent reservation for the commu-

nity in social and educational sectors. It has recommended the introduction of Urdu as the second official language in the state, filling the posts of Urdu language teachers, start-up funds for small traders among Muslims, scholarships for students, land distribution to landless Muslims in rural areas, new high schools and junior colleges for Muslim girls, and increasing the share of government posts for Muslim women.[42]

The *Justice Sachar Committee Report* published in 2006 has highlighted the backwardness of the Muslim community in education and livelihoods. The report records that good-quality government schools in Muslim areas are scarce and that Muslims are poorly represented in government services and other employment avenues.[43]

How education from its humble beginnings in mosque schools to government schools reached its peak in Lakshadweep in the twenty-first century might not be general knowledge, but for a modern social historian, it is an important historical event. The islands being fully literate is a major achievement by the islanders in the Indian context. Belonging to a special category of Scheduled Tribes, they have been given full government support in their educational endeavours. The close affinity of the island Muslims with Kerala Mapillas is reflected in their achievement of the country's high literacy rates. Whether it is correct to compare these island Muslims with the rest of India is a question because they are a particular seafaring community confined to the Lakshadweep islands where the sea is very rough, and the weather conditions are unpredictable. Under hard living conditions, where travelling to the neighbouring islands or the mainland is conditioned by the rough seas, achieving full literacy is a remarkable historical achievement. Lately, in the pandemic situation that had arisen due to Covid-19, students of the islands had to switch to online classes in colleges and universities in Kerala. For this, they are provided with high-speed bandwidth connectivity by BSNL and the Department of Art and Culture in Lakshadweep.[44]

Notes

1. The stone images of the Buddha head are preserved in the Government Golden Jubilee Museum, Agatti, which was established in 2000. The author personally visited the museum in November 2016.
2. *Imperial Gazetteer of India*, 1908, vols 16, 19, Oxford: Clarendon Press, p. 361.
3. 'Letters from Tellicherry, 1736–7', *Records of Fort St. George*, vol. 5, Madras: Government Press, 1934.
4. *Imperial Gazetteer*, 1908, vol. 9, Oxford: Clarendon Press, p. 360.
5. Ibid., p. 361.
6. *Lakshadweep Vidyabhyasa Charithram*, 2001–02, p. 84.
7. Ibid.
8. *Imperial Gazetteer*, 1908, vol. 16, p. 88.
9. *Report on the Administration of the Madras Presidency, 1904–5*, Madras: Government Press, 1905, p. 106.

10 Proceedings/Nos. 80–83, Foreign Department, National Archives of India (NAI), September 1907, p. 80.

11 *Lakshadweep Vidyabhyasa Charithram*, p. 84.

12 Ibid.

13 Ibid.

14 Ibid.

15 Ibid.

16 Interview with the Principal, Government Junior Basic School (North), Agatti, 12 November 2016.

17 *Lakshadweep Vidyabhyasa Charithram*, p. 1.

18 Interview with the Principal, Government Senior Secondary School, Kavaratti, 14 November 2016.

19 'DRG Training on Revised Textbooks of Kerala', *The Lakshadweep Times,* 11 May 2015, p. 2.

20 Information was provided by the teachers about the system when the author visited the schools in Agatti on a Sunday.

21 *Lakshadweep Vidyabhyasa Charithram*, p. 84.

22 Ibid.

23 'Muslims least, Jains most literate: Census', *The Hindu*, 1 September 2016.

24 'International Literacy Day 2016: All You Need to Know about India's Literacy Rate', *The Indian Express*, 8 September 2016.

25 'National Children's Young Scientist of Lakshadweep', *The Lakshadweep Times*, 16 January 2015, p. 1.

26 'National Science Day Celebrated', *The Lakshadweep Times*, 17 March 2015, p. 3.

27 'Excellent Performances of Kendriya Vidyalayas in Class XII CBSE Exams', *The Lakshadweep Times*, 27 May 2015, p. 2.

28 Interview with the Principal, DIET, Kavaratti, 15 November 2016.

29 *Lakshadweep Development Report, Planning Commission, Government of India,* New Delhi: Academia Foundation, 2007, p. 79.

30 'IGNOU Camp in Sangadipichu', *The Lakshadweep Times*, XXXIII, 26 March 2018, p. 6.

31 SOF is an educational organization popularizing academic competition for school-children for over two decades. 'Orientation Programme on National Science and International Mathematics Olympiad', *The Lakshadweep Times*, XXXII (31), 25 October 2018, p. 3.

32 'Teacher Eligibility Test December 30, 31 Teithigalil', *The Lakshadweep Times,* 13 December 2018, p. 6.

33 'B. Amanulla, First District and Sessions Judge Has Passed Away', *The Lakshadweep Times*, 27 April 2015, p. 2.

34 'Dr. K.K. Anwar Salih the First Islander Bagging MRCP UK', *The Lakshadweep Times*, 27 April 2015, p. 2.

35 'Two Teachers of Lakshadweep Received Meritorious National Award', *The Lakshadweep Times*, 16 September 2015, p. 1.

36 'Shamina Begumth in Doctorate', *The Lakshadweep Times*, 3 June 2016, p. 4.

37 'The Fragrance of Literature of the Island', *The Lakshadweep Times*, 5 February 2019, p. 5.

38 'Dr. Muhammad Ali Azher, the First Oncologist in Lakshadweep', *The Lakshadweep Times*, 2 October 2020, p. 2.

39 'Dr. Shahida bagged Gold Medal in Otorhinolaryngology (ENT)', *The Lakshadweep Times*, 18 May 2020, p. 2.

40 'PhD Awarded to Ahmed Amirsha', *The Lakshadweep Times*, 1 November 2020, p. 3.

[41] 'Sudhir Panel for 9–12 p.c. Quota for Muslims', *The Hindu*, 11 December 2016.

[42] Ibid.

[43] See the concluding chapter in Lakshmi (2012), where the educational levels of Muslim communities in different states are discussed at length.

[44] 'High Speed Bandwidth Connectivity for Students', *The Lakshadweep Times*, 9 October 2020, p. 1.

References
Primary Sources
A.J. Platt Papers (1922–44), Nehru Memorial and Museum Library, Delhi; also available at India Office Library, London.

Billam: Kavaratti Senior Basic School Smaranika (Malayalam), 2001–02, Kavaratti Senior Basic School.

Census of British India of 1871–72 (1875), London: George Edward Eyre and William Spottiswoode (Printers of the Crown).

Census of India (1891, 1901, 1911, 1921 and 1931), Madras: Superintendent, Government Press.

——— (1991), Delhi: Registrar General and Census Commissioner, Government of India.

Imperial Gazetteer of India (1908), vols 16, 19, Oxford: Clarendon Press.

Records of Fort St. George (1934), Letters from Tellicherry, 1736–37, vol. 5, Madras: Government Press.

Report on the Administration of the Madras Presidency, 1904–05 (1905), Madras: Government Press, 1905.

Lakshadweep Development Report, Planning Commission, Government of India (2007), New Delhi: Academia Foundation.

Lakshadweep Vidyabhyasa Charithram (2001–02).

The Hindu, various issues.

The Indian Express, various issues.

The Lakshadweep Times, various issues.

Secondary Sources
Bagchi, S. and S.S. Singh (2016), 'Muslims in West Bengal More Deprived, Disproportionately Poorer: Amartya Sen', *The Hindu*, 15 February.

Bhatt, S. (1998), *South Kanara (1799–1860): A Study in Colonial Administration and Regional Response*, Delhi: Mittal Publications.

Doctor, G. (2016), 'Versatile Artist and Sculptor Yusuf Arakkal Dies at 71', *The Hindu*, 5 October.

Ellis, R.H. (1924), *A Short Account of Laccadive Islands and Minicoy*, Madras: Government Press.

Kurup, K.K.N. (1975), *The Ali Rajas of Cannanore*, Trivandrum: College Book House.

Lakshmi, L.R.S. (2012), *The Malabar Muslims: A Different Perspective*, Delhi: Cambridge University Press.

Logan, W. (1951), *Malabar*, Vol. 1, reprint, New Delhi: Government Press.

Mukundan, T.K. (1979), *Lakshadweep: A Hundred Thousand Islands*, Haryana: The Academic Press.

Interviews
Principal, Government Junior Basic School (North), Agatti, 12 November 2016.

Principal, Government High School, Agatti, 12 November 2016.

Principal, Government Girls High School, Kavaratti, 14 November 2016.

Principal, Government Senior Secondary School, Kavaratti, 14 November 2016.

Principal, District Institute of Education and Training (DIET), Kavaratti, 15 November 2016.

6

Reclaiming Education Policy for Equality and Social Justice

Madhu Prasad

The National Education Policy (NEP) 2020 has prominently claimed that it is breaking new ground and is poised to achieve what no previous education policy has been able to achieve in more than 70 years, that is, providing quality education for all India's children. However, the policy process itself shows inadequacies of procedure and fails entirely to analyse the obstacles facing such a claim or to consider the achievements and failures of previous policies.

This essay focuses on the entrenched nature of discrimination, oppression and exclusion in Indian society. A brief historical survey highlights the impact of the caste system and colonial rule (neither of which is even mentioned in the NEP 2020) on the country and states how the more-than-a-century-long struggle for independence from imperialist domination (which again doesn't find a place or consideration in the policy) finally raised the call for liberty, equality and fraternity in a meaningful way. Consequently, the idea of education as a crucial component of an egalitarian social transformation of India emerged and found expression in the earlier education policies. The reasons for its failure to be realized are indicated and the descent of the education system into a crisis-ridden state is examined.

The influence and intervention of the World Bank and International Monetary Fund (IMF) began to be exerted from the 1980s onwards. Once the Government of India adopted the Economic Reforms Programme in 1991, the intrusions in education policy became more direct, which altered the very course and purpose of the education system as a whole. The state began to withdraw from its constitutional responsibility, and the expanding privatization, commercialization and corporatization of education promoted the conception that knowledge was a commodity to be traded in the marketplace and made accessible only to those sections who could afford to pay for it.

NEP 2020 reveals itself as a deliberate market-oriented education policy which is a manifest carrier of both historically entrenched exclusions and contemporary neoliberal inequalities. It betrays the promise of the egalitarian alternative elaborated in the conception of independent India as a *modern* republic and hence stands out as diverging from the constitutional guarantee of the right to education as a fundamental right.

Education and the Social Order

A system of education and a policy for its implementation form an integral part of a social order. Therefore, the policy decision to make school education universal is not merely a question of reaching statistical targets even when these are articulated in the form of apparently laudable slogans such as 'no child left behind' and the like. Such a decision must be identified as a fundamental component of an approach to society in which all sections of the population, including children, have equal rights and claims on the state, not merely to protect those rights but also to ensure that they are realized in ways complying with constitutional principles of equality and justice.

The progress towards the formation of the *modern* state, one that could be held accountable for performing this role, was an outcome of the primacy of the market under ascendant capitalism more than 200 years ago. This necessitated the 'secularizing' of the economic, social and political functions that had previously been hegemonized by religious institutions. In Europe, the dominance of the church, already confronted with the pre-eminence of reason associated with Enlightenment thought, declined as the growth of scientific knowledge accelerated productivity and greatly enhanced trade. The division of labour with the rise of capitalism united the dispossessed small peasantry and rural workers into a potentially productive working class for growing industry. Freed from the bondage of landlord–serf relations, this expanding population was exploited by the capitalists as a 'reserve army of labour'.

However, social reformers and workers' movements saw in it the future of modern society. That work, the productive activity of humankind in society, deserved to be recognized as the repository of knowledge and the means to acquire and expand it was a revolutionary break with the historically feudal past in which 'skill' was downgraded and the 'culture' of the leisured classes alone was valued as learning and true knowledge. The earliest expression of this essentially modern theory of learning was found in the writing and endeavours of the seventeenth-century Quaker, John Bellers. 'I have often thought,' Bellers writes, of the 'misery of the Poor of this Nation, and at the same time have reckoned them the Treasure of it . . . and many thoughts have run through me how then it comes that the Poor should be such a Burden . . .'.

In 1817, a well-known radical, Francis Place, came across his booklet, *Proposals for Raising a College of Industry of All Useful Trades and Husbandry* (1696), and enthusiastically sent it to Robert Owen, who copied and distributed a thousand copies acknowledging in his autobiography that it predated his work.

Bellers attached great value to education. Karl Marx recognized Bellers as 'a phenomenon in the history of political economy, who saw clearly, at the end of the 17th century, the necessity for abolishing the present system of education and division of labour, which begets hypertrophy and atrophy at the two opposite extremities of society'. Amongst other things, he says, 'An idle learning being little better than the learning of idleness. . . . A childish silly employ leaves their minds silly' (Marx 1887: 483–84, 488).

Learning through work combined action and theory, practice and experience so that the desire for rote learning did not arise. But the work must follow a definite plan and not be a mere tiring out of the body.

In his critique of the eighteenth-century materialist writings, *Third Theses on Feuerbach,* Karl Marx pointed out:

> The materialist doctrine that men are products of circumstances and upbringing, and that, therefore, changed men are products of other circumstances and changed upbringing, forgets that *it is men who change circumstances* and that it is essential to *educate the educator himself.* . . . The coincidence of the changing of circumstances and human activity can be conceived and rationally understood only as *revolutionizing practice.* (Marx [1845] 1976, vol. 5: 7)

This was how the modern approach to education was determined and how its goals were identified. It was for the masses, for the children of workers and peasants. The utilitarians, including Jeremy Bentham who moved the Great Reform Bill in the British Parliament in 1832, demanded that the state provide universal education for this section in the interest of capital. The socialists/communists focused on educating them as self-conscious workers with a deep sense of their historical role and agency. Thus, the prospect of achieving the democratic individual freedoms articulated during the Enlightenment became a distinct possibility and the secular state was conceived of as obligated to be the provider and defender of the rights of its citizens.

From the nineteenth century onwards, industrializing nations placed the responsibility for providing education on the modern state. However, it was recognized that the concepts of right, equality and justice were problematized due to the exploitative inequality inherent in the contradictory economic interests of the capitalist class and the working people.

In 1845, Fredrick Engels made this very clear while upholding the rationale of a modern rights-based perspective. According to him, the

> [general] education of all children without exception at the expense of the state–an education which is equal for all and continues until the individual is capable of emerging as an independent member of society . . . would be only *an act of justice . . .* for clearly, *every man has the right to the fullest development of his abilities and society wrongs individuals twice over when it makes ignorance a necessary consequence of poverty.* (Engels 1845)

Almost 175 years later, this idea appears to have lost none of its force. That every child has a *right* to receive an education provides the impetus for universalizing education.

In the 1990s, when the strategies of neoliberal capitalism that commoditized even social services like health and education were fast becoming 'commonsense', not only in the developed world but even in developing countries under pressure from the World Bank and the World Trade Organization (WTO), the American political scientist Myron Weiner noted that 'development' itself was founded on treating every child's right to education as a legal duty of the state: 'parents are required to send their children to school, children are required to attend school and the state is required to enforce compulsory education.' The state as the provider of education becomes the barrier protecting children from the economic compulsions of impoverished parents and would-be exploiters (Weiner 1994: 83–86). Compulsory and free formal education, Weiner argued, was the only way to make the exploitation of child labour socially unacceptable and bring this repugnant practice to an end.

The Caste System

In India, the early emergence of a deeply hierarchical division of castes and status under dominant Brahmanism denied any opportunity for the productive 'lowered castes', as B.R. Ambedkar so perceptively referred to them, to educate themselves or even live a life of social acceptance and dignity. The continuity of this inhuman system for centuries was not due to any inherent occupational or social values that it has been claimed to possess but because it allowed the economic surplus to be easily extracted from the semi-enslaved labouring and industrious sections of the village community (Habib 2009).

Within this system, the 'guru-shishya' tradition, so carelessly referred to as an 'ideal' relationship between teacher and student – particularly now when anything harking back to the fiction of an 'ancient golden age of Vedic India' is treated as sacrosanct – was, in fact, imminently suited to indoctrination in dominant caste orientation and practices. However, it is completely out-of-place and even detrimental within a democratic conception of society and education. Within this tradition, knowledge is regarded as being 'received', like water poured into an empty vessel, by the subordinated student. The teacher, the possessor of wisdom and truth, is not only beyond critical questioning but also empowered to deny this knowledge at will. The guru demands only the 'discipline' of complete adherence from the shishya. That this relation should be idealized even today signals the persistent failure to break with unequal and rigidly discriminatory stratifications.

It is unfortunate that the NEP 2020 chooses to uncritically eulogize 'Sanskrit knowledge systems', which are deeply entrenched within the caste ideology, as the sole basis for evolving a contemporary system of education steeped in the 'Indian ethos' (GoI 2020: Introduction). Extolling the virtues of the early universities of Nalanda and Takshashila, NEP 2020 astonishingly fails to even mention that these famed institutions were centres of Buddhist learning which rejected caste exclusion, welcomed scholars from Afghanistan, China and Southeast Asia and were renowned for delving deep into the rich and diverse literatures of the Pali and Prakrit traditions.

Colonial Subjugation

At the other end of the pendulum, British colonialism is often lauded as the engine of modernization of education and society. This shows little understanding of the predatory nature of imperialism and its impact on Indian society.

> It is a startling but too notorious a fact, that, though loaded with a vastly greater absolute amount of taxation, and harassed by various severe acts of tyranny and oppression, yet the country was in a state of prosperity under the native rule, when compared with that into which it has fallen under the avowedly mild sway of British administration . . . almost everything forces the conviction that we have before us a narrowing progress to utter pauperism. . . . Most of the evils of our rule in India arise directly from, or maybe traced to, the *heavy tribute which that country pays to England*. (Marriott 1846: 11)[1]

Under such circumstances, even the technological modernity required by colonial economic interests did not encourage modern consciousness and practices in society. For example, the introduction of the railways in April 1853 was undoubtedly a major step towards the technological 'modernization' of the country, but we cannot ignore the fact that lowered castes were prohibited from drinking water from the supposedly 'common' facilities provided at railway stations.

The East India Company's (EIC's) early educational initiatives followed both caste strictures and religious divisions. The Calcutta Madrassa (1781) and Benaras Sanskrit College for Brahmins (1791) followed traditional Persian/Islamic and Vedic curricula, respectively. It was only in 1823–24 that the government colleges at Delhi and Agra were started with 'open' admissions and Oriental literature, science, history and jurisprudence being taught along with mathematics and modern science. These features, in fact, continued a practice prevalent in the madrassas of the region which was still under the cultural influence of the Mughal court. A large number of Khatris and Kayasthas, who had been denied higher education reserved only for Brahmins, attended these schools of Persian literature, science and jurisprudence and went onto serve the Mughals and other Indian courts with distinction. 'The Persian schools are the most genuine educational institutions in the country. They are attended largely by the Khatris, the Hindus forming a greater proportion than the Muhammadans' (Arnold 1922: 290).

The exclusionary colonial policy for education, advocated in Macaulay's infamous 'Minute on Indian Education' of 1835, was already contained in a Despatch (29 September 1830) of the EIC's Court of Directors. Promoting English as the medium of instruction, it aimed at creating 'an elite class of learned natives' trained in European science and literature, who would 'communicate *a portion* of this improved learning to the Asiatic wider classes'. The government in India was instructed to use 'every assistance and encouragement, pecuniary or otherwise', including a declared preference in government employment, to further this goal. '*We wish you to consider this as our deliberate view of the scope and end to which all your endeavours with respect to the education of the Natives should refer*' (Howell 1872: 20–21).

However, the promise of jobs in the government succeeded primarily in promoting 'baboo', that is, clerical, culture. The term, a derogatory distortion of the word 'baboon', reveals the attitude of EIC officials towards the education and opportunities provided for Indians as these lowly positions were the only jobs open to the 'natives'. It compared mimicking monkeys with these native 'imitators' of their colonial masters; '[that] the baboo should be created and then ridiculed is of a piece with the ideology of the cultural subjugation of colonial rule' (Chaudhary 2002: 86).

Not surprisingly, one of the principal 'weaknesses of the native student' was soon identified as 'the strong temptation to lay aside his studies as soon as employment supplies his moderate necessities; the scanty inducement to fit himself for higher duties, – all help to dwarf the moral and intellectual growth. . . . His ambition waits upon his daily wants'.[2] The EIC's decision to abolish the common madrassa practice of providing stipends for non-elite students who could not afford private education at home and to impose fees undoubtedly aggravated this tendency.

The dismissive attitude of the traditional cultured classes, particularly in Delhi where the learning, aesthetic and tastes of the Mughal court remained vibrant well into the twentieth century, was evident in the comment of Urdu poet and writer Altaf Hussain Hali:[3] '. . . in the society in which I was raised . . . English education was not seriously regarded as learning . . . we regarded English as a means of getting a job, not an education' (Gupta 1981: 7).

The situation altered little after the direct rule of the British Crown was established following the defeat of the rebellion of 1857. The gap in years of schooling between India and early leaders, such as the US and Germany, which was less than two years in 1870 increased to 7.8 years by 1950 (Lee and Lee 2016). As late as 1921, only 11 per cent of India's population was even literate.[4] British India had the lowest public expenditure in the world between 1860 and 1912 (Davis and Huttenback 1986).

In stark contrast, during the latter half of the nineteenth century and in the early twentieth century, rulers of Indian states spent twice as much per capita on education. In 1848, while individuals like Savitribai Phule and Fatima Sheikh were engaged in radical endeavours to open up education for all, including lower castes and girls, the maharajas of Kolhapur and Baroda and the begums of Bhopal, among others, provided free primary education for all. Greatly influenced by social reformer Jyotiba Phule, Shahuji Maharaj of Kolhapur was associated with many progressive and path-breaking activities during his rule (1894–1922). Primary education for all regardless of caste and creed was one of his most significant priorities.

While introducing a bill on compulsory primary education on 16 March 1911, which would be defeated in the Imperial Legislative Council, Gopal Krishna Gokhale pointed out that

> His Highness [of Baroda] began his first experiment in the matter of introducing compulsory and free education into his State eighteen years ago in ten villages at the Amreli Taluka. After watching the experiment for eight years, it was extended to the whole taluka in 1901, and finally, in 1906, primary education was made compulsory and free throughout the State

for boys between the ages of 6 and 12, and for girls between the ages of 6 and 10. (Natesan 1916: 725–26)

A great reformer in the tradition of her mother and grandmother, Sultan Jahan of Bhopal founded several important educational institutions in Bhopal, establishing free and compulsory primary education in 1918. During her reign, she had a particular focus on public instruction, especially female education. She built many technical institutes and schools and increased the number of qualified teachers.

Education for All and the Struggle for Independence

The demand that the government accept its responsibility for providing education for all had already been powerfully raised with the Education Commission in 1881 by nationalist economist Dadabhai Naoroji and social reformer Jyotiba Phule. The former drew support from the analysis of Frederick John Shore, judge of the civil court and criminal sessions, District Farrukhabad, who left the following account on the condition of the people:

> But the halcyon days of India are over; she has been drained of a large proportion of the wealth she once possessed, and her energies have been cramped by a *sordid system of misrule to which the interests of millions have been sacrificed for the benefit of the few*. The grinding extortions of the English Government have effected the impoverishment of the country and people to an extent almost unparalleled. (Shore 1837: 28)

In his appeal to the Education Commission (1884),[5] Naoroji demanded that having pauperized the people with its policies, the government must open the path to recovery by providing free and compulsory education to all children for four years. Phule argued in his deposition to the commission that although the government extracted its surplus from the ryots, it expended it on higher education which benefitted only the Brahmins and the wealthy; the masses were left to wallow in ignorance. Unfortunately, little came of their appeals which went largely unheard.

As the freedom movement gained in spread and intensity, drawing in more and more sections of the population, the demand for education for all became an important expression of the people's rising consciousness. The Nagpur session of the Indian National Congress (INC) in 1920 directly addressed the students and youth calling upon them to withdraw from existing colonial schools and colleges, which only taught empire worship, and join the struggle for freedom. It demanded that nationalist educational institutions be set up. The Jamia Millia Islamia in New Delhi was the first such well-known institution to be established in 1920. It showed that the idea of a system of education – providing equal opportunity and propagating values of national independence and which could become an instrument of social transformation – had become an integral part of nationalist thinking.

The proceedings of the Wardha Conference (1937) on 'Nai Talim' (New Education) were formulated as proposals in the Zakir Husain Committee Report. It recommended a system of free and compulsory education in the mother tongue based on practical work as the pedagogical means to enhancing comprehension and generating knowledge. Accessible to *all* children for eight years, that is, up to fourteen years of age, it was defined as 'equivalent to matriculation *minus* English *plus* craft' (Naik 1975). Breaking the elitist mould of colonial education, 'through craft, (Gandhi) wanted to impart knowledge on all important branches of knowledge' (Biswas and Aggarwal 1994: 90).

Emphasizing that modern educational thought was 'practically unanimous in commending the idea of educating children through some suitable form of productive work', the Zakir Husain Committee Report observes that this psychologically 'relieves the child from the tyranny of a purely academic and theoretical *instruction* against which its active nature is always making a healthy protest' (Hindustani Talimi Sangh 1938: 12). The social impact of productive work

> to be participated in by all the children of the nation will tend to break down the existing barriers of prejudice between manual and intellectual workers, harmful alike for both. It will also cultivate in the only possible way a true sense of the dignity of labour and of human solidarity – an ethical and moral gain of incalculable significance. (Ibid.: 13)

However,

> to secure these advantages it is essential that two conditions should be carefully observed. First, the craft or productive work chosen should be rich in educative possibilities. It should find natural points of correlation with important human activities and interests, and should extend into the whole content of the school curriculum. . . . The object of this new educational scheme is NOT primarily the production of craftsmen able to practise some craft *mechanically* but rather the exploitation for educative purposes of the resources implicit in craft work. This demands that productive work should not only form a part of the curriculum – its craft side – but should also inspire the *method* of teaching all other subjects. (Ibid.: 14)

Gandhi himself clarified that this meant that 'handicraft has not to be taught merely mechanically as it is done today, but scientifically. That is to say the child should learn the why and wherefore of every process' (ibid.: 15).

The productivity-based teaching-learning methodology inculcated, as a vital part of the curriculum, the social values of equality and justice which would become the core values of the Indian Constitution. At the Haripura session of the INC in 1938, it was resolved that the national system of education would be built on a 'wholly new foundation'.

Far from analysing and learning from the 'Nai Talim' approach of letting knowledge flow from practice, NEP 2020 does not even refer to it. It adopts a conservative, feudal and prejudicial approach to so-called 'vocationalization'. Skilling is treated as a lesser alternative for the children of lower castes and classes, who it presumes, must start earning as quickly as possible to contribute to their pitifully low family incomes. Formal book learning remains appropriately reserved for the privileged. NEP 2020 locating three 'exit' stages in elementary education itself – at classes 3, 5 and 8 – can only be comprehended in this context. Each stage envisages a possible transition to vocational training for the vast majority of India's children who are drawn from the oppressed and marginalized sections of society. A co-related initiative aims at *selectively* making the elementary curriculum vocational for targeted educationally backward and tribal areas.

For students from the more privileged sections of society, exposure to productive labour is eulogized as a 'fun course', a 'ten-day bagless period sometimes during Grades 6–8 where [the students]intern with local vocational experts such as carpenters, gardeners, potters, artists, etc.'. The underlying agenda is revealed when this 'hands-on experience' is to be 'decided by . . . local communities and as mapped by local skilling needs' (GoI 2020: 4.26). Given the prevalence of caste prejudices, dominant castes and administrators will exercise their choices for students from oppressed and marginalized castes/classes or for those from upper castes/classes accordingly.

This is especially challenging since a recent amendment (2016) to the Child Labour (Prohibition and Regulation) Act, 1986, now permits even ten-year-olds to participate in labour in 'family enterprises'. This will reinforce caste-based occupations as children will be 'pushed out' of academic courses and denied the opportunity to acquire access to other professional openings. Unfortunately, NEP 2020 thereby retreats even from the Right of Children to Free and Compulsory Education (RTE) Act, 2009, which stipulates through its no-detention policy that, as per their constitutional fundamental right, children be retained in school till the age of fourteen years. The emphasis on vocational education in the NEP 2020 and the restructured 5+3+3+4 with three 'exits' at the elementary stage are directed at facilitating 'exclusion from Class III onwards. . . . NEP 2020 would be the first policy since independence to deny classroom-based education at school level . . . to more than 75–80% of the children and youth!' (AIFRTE 2021: 16–17).

How does one account for this complete reversal of policy from its constitutional moorings? The failure of successive governments to achieve constitutional commitments has undoubtedly been the cause of the crisis-ridden state of India's education system, but even this failure needs to be distinguished from the present policy's complete volte-face. For it has totally withdrawn from the constitutional goals, values and responsibilities which the freedom movement placed before the evolving Indian republic. And it has done this without a democratic national debate among the people, by riding roughshod over the federal rights of the states and by using its brute parliamentary majority to push through legislation without any discussion or meaningful consideration in the House committees which a crucial policy for education deserved.

The fact is that NEP 2020 has a huge gaping void in its history of the subcontinent. Over 1,200 years that have played an enormous role in the technological, sociocultural, linguistic and politico-ideological growth of the country and its civilizational evolution are completely absent from its viewpoint. As a result, it shows an inability to sensitively comprehend the experiences of British colonial domination or adequately grasp the implications of the damage it inflicted on the living conditions of the working people. Therefore, it also fails to comprehend the significance of the freedom struggle and the Constitution which reflected its range and values in constituting our society into a nation. They add nothing to the narrative of the NEP 2020. Its perspective remains obsessed with the supposed purity of what has thereby become an almost mythical 'ancient' past.

NEP 2020 claims that the rich heritage of ancient and eternal Indian knowledge and thought has been a guiding light for this policy. The pursuit of knowledge (*jnan*), wisdom (*pragyaa*) and truth (*satya*) was always considered in Indian thought and philosophy as the highest human goal. The aim of education in ancient India was not just the acquisition of knowledge as preparation for life in this world, or life beyond schooling, but for the complete realization and liberation of the self.

This ancient heritage 'must not only be nurtured and preserved for posterity, but also researched, enhanced and put to new uses through our education system' (GoI 2020: Introduction). 'Ultimately knowledge is a deep-seated treasure and education helps in its manifestation as the perfection which is already within an individual' (ibid.: 4.4). This hegemonic ideological posturing creates the fiction of a closed and unchanging tradition in which all that is novel must be dubbed 'alien' until it is stamped with the seal of its approval.

A National System of Education

However, history unavoidably alters evolving nations and the growing militancy of the working class and the peasantry through the 1920s;
the 1930s and 1940s expanded the foundations of the freedom movement.
The October Revolution in Russia in 1917 had an important political and
intellectual influence on India. The Communist Party of India (CPI) was
established in 1920 and trade unionism grew rapidly; at Lucknow in 1936,
following the general session of the All-India Kisan Congress, a *Kisan
Manifesto* was released demanding the abolition of *zamindari* and cancel-
lation of all usurious debts to bring an impatient peasantry firmly within
the ranks of the movement. The student and youth movements also exerted
an important influence – the Bharat Naujawan Sabha (a left-wing movement to arouse worker and peasant youth in rebellion against the British
Raj) was founded by Bhagat Singh and his comrades in March 1926 and
the CPI's All India Students Federation (AISF) was established ten years
later. Growing anti-fascist and pro-democracy ideologies gained in stature
and strength through the 1930s and 1940s.

By the 1940s, even the colonial administration had been compelled
to respond to the increasing radicalization of the freedom movement. The
report of the Central Advisory Board of Education (CABE), *Post-War Plan
of Educational Development in India*, withdrew from the earlier colonial
position and declared that 'the minimum provision which could be accepted
as constituting a national system postulates that all children must receive
enough education to prepare them to earn a living as well as to fulfill themselves as individuals and discharge their duties as citizens'. Further, it was
argued that

> if there is to be anything like equality of opportunity, it is impossible to
> justify providing facilities for some of the nation's children and not for
> others. A national system can hardly be other than universal. Secondly, it
> must be compulsory, if the grave wastage which exists today under a vol-
> untary system is not to be perpetrated and even aggravated. And thirdly, if
> education is to be universal and compulsory, *equity requires that it should
> be free and commonsense demands that it should last long enough to
> secure its fundamental objective.* (GoI 1944: 3)

The recommendations of the report of the B.G. Kher Committee on the
Ways and Means of Financing Educational Development in India (1950)
shaped Article 45 of the Directive Principles of the Constitution mandating
that the 'State shall endeavour to provide within a period of ten years from
the commencement of this Constitution for free and compulsory education
for all children until they complete the age of 14 years'.

The demand for universalizing free and compulsory education was taken up as an essential component of the Indian people's right to constitute themselves as an independent nation by repudiating traditional and colonial hierarchies of caste/class and race. Incorporating the notions of both *selfhood* and *nationhood*, it brought to the forefront the idea of the democratic rights of all citizens. The Constitution of the newly independent republic was itself the culmination of the struggle and set the standard for evaluating policies, distinguishing between those that would strengthen and *advance* the freedoms promised in the Constitution and those that undermined its potential by compromise, infringement or direct violation.

It is important to emphasize that the very idea of a national system of education was a matter of great significance and a major democratic advance.

Policy for an Independent Citizenry

Independent India's first Education Commission (1964–66) was headed by D.S. Kothari and dealt with the education system as a whole including both school and higher education. For the latter, it emphasized the democratization of the structure of institutions of higher education (IHE) on the one hand, and non-interference from politico-ideological, bureaucratic and market forces on the other. For IHE, the commission argued, academic autonomy could not be viewed as a 'privilege' but as the necessary 'enabling condition' for the academic community of teachers and students to achieve their intellectual and social goals.

NEP 2020 has made a mockery of this crucial recommendation. It has centralized and concentrated all power of decision-making in so-called 'independent bodies' that are in fact subordinated to the central government which constitutes them but are indeed 'independent' from academia. Accreditation, eligibility and evaluation, the right to award degrees and even to continue to function are made over to these bodies which have minimal disciplinary representation from academia. Within IHEs, all democratic functioning and representation are to be ended. The institutions which will perforce have to become 'autonomous', even as their academic communities lose all autonomy, will be autocratically administered by self-perpetuating boards of governors with a preponderance of investors and financial experts to ensure their 'efficiency'.

For school education, the Kothari Commission had advocated far-reaching structural changes for setting up a *national system of free and compulsory education*. This, it was argued, could not be modelled on elite private schools 'transplanted in India by British administrators and we have clung to it so long because it happened to be in tune with the traditional hierarchical structure of our society. Whatever its place in past history maybe, such a system has no valid place in the new democratic and socialistic society we desire to create'(Kothari 1966: 1.38).

It recommended the establishment of state-funded common neighbourhood schools with a socially, culturally and economically diverse student body as authentic institutions of a pedagogically sound and egalitarian national system of education which would 'provide "good" education to all children because sharing life with the common people is, in our opinion, an essential ingredient of good education' (ibid.: 10.19).

The Report of the Committee of Members of Parliament on Education (1967) endorsed the Kothari Commission's view:

> the unhealthy social segregation that now takes place between the schools for the rich and those for the poor should be ended; and the primary schools should be the common schools of the nation by making it obligatory on all children, irrespective of caste, creed, community, religion, economic conditions or social status, to attend the primary school in their neighbourhood. This *sharing of life among the children of all social strata will strengthen the sense of being one nation* which is an essential ingredient of good education. (Sen 1967: 2)

This principle was reiterated in a recent landmark ruling of the Allahabad High Court (18 August 2015) which stated that the failure to establish common neighbourhood schools fulfilling the constitutional obligation to provide education for all has created an unhealthy division of schools solely on the basis of privilege and wealth. Lacking educational or social value, the so-called good schools are in fact enclaves of the rich and powerful which exclude 'almost 90% children'. If government schools were strengthened and properly run (as Kendriya and Navodaya Vidyalayas and other special government schools show), private schools would become irrelevant.

NEP 2020 claims to have drawn its concept of the 'school complex' as the basic unit of the education system from the Kothari Commission Report and lauds itself for implementing what earlier policies had failed to do. However, the commission's *basic unit* was the common neighbourhood school and only small groups of such nearby schools were recommended for meaningfully interacting with each other. NEP 2020's school complex on the other hand extends over an area of ten to fifteen kilometres. This is a formidable distance for elementary school children to be covering on a daily basis and will increase the number of 'drop-outs'. It will almost certainly be used to further advance the 'rationalization' scheme of NEP 2020 which seeks the merger and closure of government neighbourhood schools. Already well over one lakh schools have been merged/closed over the past few years and the policy is to be rapidly implemented in the name of greater efficiency only to 'cut costs'.

Subversion of the Radical Goals of the Freedom Movement: Bourgeois–Landlord Alliance

As the struggle for independence advanced in a more radical direction, the Indian capitalist class began to align itself with sections of the feudal land-owning elite. The alliance with the landlord classes meant that the Indian bourgeoisie was 'open' – as we find it currently 'opening up' to the interests of international finance capital and crony capitalism – to compromising on the egalitarian goals of the freedom movement. In particular, two major areas of 'under-achievement' were blatantly obvious.

Land reforms were not implemented effectively across the country and hence accommodation with Brahmanical ideology (despite powerful social justice movements in southern and western India), which sanctioned harshly exploitative caste divisions among the toiling masses, was a foregone conclusion.

The democratic goal of universalizing school education which was at the core of the freedom movement's conception of a *modern* republican nation could never be achieved by India's bourgeois-landlord ruling elite. The egalitarian socialist ideals and powerful principles of social justice gradually evaporated into mere slogans. Caste and class prejudices remained intractable. The linkage of 'privilege' with 'quality' inherited from the past could not be broken.

As the desire to enter the education system spread among the broad masses of people, it was not merely the failure of governments to adequately finance and expand the system but also the insensitivity to the life experiences of the oppressed and the marginalized that brought about the veritable collapse of public schools. The attempt at the elementary level 'to extend to the poor people an education system basically meant for the well-to-do middle classes did not succeed and the rates of stagnation and wastage became disturbingly high' (Naik 1975: 47). The poor and the marginalized lacked not only the economic but also the sociocultural resources to take advantage of such a system.

Not only does NEP 2020 fail to address this problem, but it also adopts a 'solution' which will harshly aggravate its impact. It has rejected the conditions laid down in RTE 2009 for providing adequate infrastructure and permanent faculty for improving government schools and claims that its attention is centred not on 'inputs' but on 'outcomes'. This approach seeks to homogenize all learning into predetermined 'proficiencies' and all students are required to attain *uniform* patterns of proficiency in specified *units of knowledge* within a prescribed time. The offline and now increasingly eulogized online 'classrooms' become merely the physical or digital 'space' in which instruction is transmitted.

All meaningful references to an individual's personal experience as well as to historical manifestations of privilege and discrimination are removed from the classroom context. NEP 2020 repeatedly uses the expression 'merit alone' as the basis on which its accreditation, eligibility and assessment mechanisms operate. What will, or will not, count as knowledge or achievement is thereby *predetermined* and *standardized* irrespective of who comes to, or what happens in, the classroom.

Thus, SC/ST/OBC students, minorities, women and persons with disability (PWD), who have direct experience of oppression and are influenced by culturally imbibed histories of deprivation and discrimination, are expected to achieve the *same* 'learning outcomes' as those coming from backgrounds of privilege. How is that either desirable or even possible?

'Merit alone' cannot appreciate the diversity of experience or enhance the potential that the deprived sections, in particular, contribute to learning. It therefore significantly denies *agency* to the socially and educationally marginalized to effect social transformation and emancipation. Such a competitive and market-oriented concept of merit can only reinforce the hold of the privileged, thereby strengthening existing inequalities and injustices. Not surprisingly, NEP 2020 undermines and challenges the principle of reservation that the Constitution provides for those who for centuries have been, and still are, systematically discriminated against.

NEP 2020 provides a policy-based acceleration to the process of exclusion as it rejects the need for a creative pedagogical curriculum and adequate public funding to revitalize the education system. It exploits the multi-track discriminatory streams that exclude larger and larger sections of children from what had once been envisaged as a national system of quality education. Privatization will continue through enhancing public–private partnership (PPP) schemes, and it will merely be a matter of time before the so-called 'best practices' of fee imposition for every activity will be introduced in government schools and salaries of teachers will be pegged according to management decisions to 'incentivize' appointments and promotions. The creation of an administrative and financial 'cadre' to head institutions rather than selecting principals from among senior academicians will further downgrade faculty.

NEP 2020 has talked of the importance of teacher training, but it welcomes volunteers, social workers, counsellors, locally eminent persons, school alumni, active and healthy senior citizens and local public-spirited community members to intervene and become part of the school system from early childhood care and education (ECCE) to class 12 in undefined roles and without meeting any academic eligibility requirements (GoI 2020: 2.7 and 3.7). Opening the floodgates for such volunteer cadres from 'like-minded' organizations, which will invariably be patronized by the parent organization of the present ruling party, makes a mockery of the very idea of a scientific and evidence-based system of knowledge.

NEP 2020 also adopts the discredited idea of 'alternate schools' with 'special emphasis on socio-economically disadvantaged groups (SEDGs) . . . to facilitate multiple pathways to learning involving both formal and non-formal modes of education. Open and Distance Learning (ODL) Pro-grammes . . . will be expanded and strengthened to meet the learning needs of young people in India who are not able to attend a physical school' (ibid.: 3.5). The 'requirements of schools will be made less restrictive . . . less emphasis on input and greater emphasis on output' in order to create space for a variety of non-governmental organizations (NGOs) and religious bod-ies to set up 'alternate' schools and even boards as well (ibid.: 3.6).

Finally, NEP 2020 has discovered a technological 'cherry' on the top of the cake of 'alternate schooling' – online education. ODL is of course not new to the process of covering up the failure to provide access to for-mal education for a large majority of India's children from, what the policy refers to as, the SEDGs. What is absolutely new, however, is the introduc-tion of online learning at the school level and the graduate and postgradu-ate levels as a crucial component of the mainstream system of education. 'Blended learning' is the current buzzword in governmental and hence administrative circles when discussing NEP.

NEP 2020 has utilized the Covid-19 pandemic crisis to eagerly embrace and promote this option. Starting with the idea of about 20 per cent of all curricula to be covered through this format, as the union govern-ment is proceeding with its imposition of NEP 2020 across the country, almost 50 per cent is now likely to be covered in this mode. In keeping with the Prime Minister's call for 'atmanirbharta', this mode will gradually push the entire financial burden on the individual and family, as the Government of India retreats from the education sector to make room for the entry of IT corporates.[6]

The tendency to grasp online teaching-learning as an effective means for homogenizing knowledge into digitally consumable units on the one hand, and a convenient low-cost option for governments to cope with problems of access on the other, has been vigorously advocated by the World Bank's 'Strengthening Teaching-Learning and Results for States' (STARS) programme which was finalized and incorporated barely two months before the cabinet cleared NEP 2020's Samagra Shiksha Abhiyan.

However, Government of India's ready adoption of this 'solution' shows no concern for its pedagogical limitations. Still, less does it reveal any apprehension about the enormous exclusion that would result because in India only 8 per cent of households with children aged between five and twenty-four years have access to both a digital device and internet connectivity and 37 per cent of households have only a single dwelling room.

Neoliberal Reforms Policy and the Crisis in Education

The 1993 judgement (*Unnikrishnan vs the State of Andhra Pradesh*) of the Supreme Court was the last significant attempt to defend the right of India's children to receive quality education through a state-funded system of formal education by linking Article 45 of the Directive Principles with Article 21, the fundamental right to life, making the right to education a fundamental and justiciable right.

However, in 1991 the Government of India had embarked on the neoliberal economic reforms programme. After this, the impact of neoliberal dictates and the direct intervention of the World Bank, IMF and WTO's General Agreement on Trade in Services (WTO-GATS) became a recurrent feature of the Indian education system as GoI gradually began financially starving, disparaging and dismantling state-run schools and public universities (as per WTO-GATS dictates). The National Policy on Education (NPE) 1986, its Programme of Action and their modified versions (1992) put into operation a series of 'missions' and *abhiyan*s imparting 'skills', with the lowestone being 'functional literacy'. By 1994, the WB's first direct intervention through the District Primary Education Programme (DPEP), introduced 'low-cost' infrastructure and recruitment practices as well as multigrade teaching in government schools. NGOs, the preferred delivery mechanism of the World Bank, were inducted to 'improve' the quality. Although this virtually brought the primary school system to the verge of collapse, the World Bank's second intervention was invited through the Sarva Shiksha Abhiyan in 2002. Non-formal education programmes were renamed and the Education Guarantee Scheme (EGS) and Alternative and Innovative Education (AIE) were incorporated into the Sarva Shiksha Abhiyan.

The 86th Amendment to the Constitution, introduced in 2002, was designed to coincide with WB's pressure to reduce public spending on education. Instead of covering all children 'up to 14 years', the fundamental right was now restricted only to children between six and fourteen years of age. NEP 2020 has been lauded for bringing three- to six-year-olds into the foundation stage of its altered 5+3+3+4 format, by including anganwadis, which already cover their health and nutritional needs. However, there are many apprehensions on this account as the NEP 2020 policy document makes no mention of 'extending' RTE 2009 from three to eighteen years, that is, extending the *fundamental right to education* for all from pre-nursery to class 12.

The RTE 2009, framed within the parameters laid down by the 86th Amendment, legalized the discriminatory streams of 'education' that had mushroomed over the decades and signalled that the very idea of a national system of state-funded education for which the union and state governments would be held responsible and accountable had been given up. Private unaided schools and government-run 'good' special schools were placed outside the purview of the act. The PPP schemes promoted under World Bank pressure required at least a 25 per cent quota for admitting students from the economically weaker sections (EWSs) which were to be reimbursed by central and state governments. Years after the 2013 deadline for meeting the beneficial infrastructural requirements stipulated by RTE 2009, fewer than 12 per cent of schools are RTE-compliant on 'inputs', but the aspiration for 'private' schooling has been fuelled at public expense by the PPP quota leading to a proliferation of low-budget private schools.

Keeping children out of school or 'pushing' them out of the formal system of education is the result of a range of *socially negative attitudes and priorities that have come to dominate education policy*. To segregate the poor and the disadvantaged in institutions catering only to them, while 'privilege' uncritically masquerades as 'merit', is a form of exclusion that reproduces entrenched social inequalities, ensures that the vast majority of children are denied their fundamental right to education, are condemned to a childhood of labour[7] and a 'future' as lowly paid daily wage workers.

This anti-constitutional and unjust view has gained credibility because not only labour, goods and services but all human activities including culture, social relationships and institutions are treated as appropriately merchandised under neoliberal principles. Learning, a 'private good', knowledge, a 'commodity', and education, a marketable 'service', can be bought and sold and traded in the marketplace not merely by investors/providers but ultimately also by 'consumers' in search of employment. Those who pay more can expect higher returns.

However, neoliberal policies have resulted in a declining standard of living for the working classes. The Arjun Sengupta Committee's *Report on the Conditions of Work and Promotion of Livelihood in the Unorganized Sector*, based on government data for the period between 1993–94 and 2004–05, a decade of neoliberal reforms, showed that an overwhelming 78 per cent, that is, 836 million people in India were found to be living on a per capita consumption of less than Rs 20 a day. The per capita consumption of the extremely poor was Rs 12 per day.

The present situation has only further deteriorated. The adoption of the contemporary phase of neoliberal 'jobless growth' with privatization and corporatization of all essential services based on user-pays principles of market 'efficiency' has resulted in a massive 'exclusion' of those who *simply cannot afford to pay*. Following the economic shock of demonetization on small and medium enterprises which employed almost 93 per cent of the workforce, the numbers of the impoverished have grown rapidly as wealth is concentrated in fewer and fewer hands.

The Covid-19 pandemic has certainly not caused or been responsible for this situation, but it has starkly exposed, through the effects of the sudden, unplanned nationwide 'lockdowns' leading to an unprecedented migration of lakhs of contract workers, daily-wagers and low-income self-employed, the precarious condition of the vast majority of India's working people.

NEP 2020 and World Bank's Third Intervention in the Samagra Shiksha Abhiyan

The STARS programme is the World Bank's third intervention in school education. It covers the entire period from pre-nursery up to class 12 and includes teacher training, promotion and accountability, institutional governance and community interaction as well. Like NEP 2020, it claims to ensure access to quality education for all.

The National Achievement Survey (NAS) 2017 (covering classes 3, 5 and 8) has shown that nineteen of thirty states performed below the national average. At the secondary level, NAS 2015 findings showed that as many as 85 per cent of class 10 students couldn't answer more than half the questions in English and mathematics. Formal education, the STARS document concludes, has benefitted only a small percentage of students.

The solutions of the STARS programme and NEP 2020 to the earlier mentioned long-standing indicators of the crisis of education do not show an allegedly 'path-breaking' direction as the latter has claimed. The well-worn World Bank-inspired concepts of the 1990s are once more being promoted to increase the scope of school learning by restricting formal education to a minority and excluding the deprived and marginalized through recourse to (1) 'multiple avenues of learning' including the introduction of different levels of syllabus complexity in the same classes, diverting students to ODL in national and state-level open schooling and online learning (GoI 2020: 3.5); (2) targeted vocationalization of syllabi and vocational training; (3) 'less restrictive' infrastructural input requirements for schools in order to facilitate entry of 'non-state actors' in low-budget private education and encouraging its spread through reimbursement and voucher system schemes; and finally, (4) the involvement of community, alumni and 'volunteers' for 'one-on-one tutoring', 'extra help sessions', 'support and guidance for educators', career guidance and mentoring of students. 'Databases of literate volunteers, retired scientists/government/semi-government employees, alumni and educators will be created for this purpose' (ibid.: 3.7).

In fact, NEP 2020 has taken giant strides in 'synergizing' the role of private and government players. In its proposed school complexes and mega-universities across the country, there is to be a twinning/pairing of private and government institutions so that they can collaborate, share assets and introduce 'the best practices of private institutions' in the government ones (ibid.: 7.10).

However, the PPP strategy has so far not provided quality education. In fact, it has increased exclusion by commercializing education and placing education beyond the grasp of most children. NEP 2020 has merely renamed public–private partnership as 'public-philanthropic partnership' but made no attempt to regulate their flaws.

The STARS programme is designed to promote greater involvement of 'non-state actors' instead of holding the union and state governments responsible and accountable. The effects of such a strategy will be disastrous. The National Sample Survey Organization's (NSSO's) most recent survey on education (71st Round) already reveals a *pattern* in the exclusion that is affected in education. Only 6 per cent of young people from the bottom fifth of the population attend educational levels above higher secondary. Less than 10 per cent of SC/ST/OBC, minorities especially Muslims, complete class 12 and become eligible for reservation quotas.

The World Bank has consistently advocated a market-oriented *model of knowledge*, with greater emphasis on 'learning outcomes' than on 'inputs', and a merchandised *model of education delivery* that involves centralizing decisions to arrive at policies for the privatization, commercialization and corporatization of education.

NEP 2020 shares the World Bank's model of knowledge. To make knowledge market-friendly it has to be reduced to 'competencies' and 'outcomes'. NEP 2020 is firmly committed to shifting classroom transactions 'towards competency-based learning and education. The assessment tools (including assessment 'as', 'of', and 'for' learning) will also be aligned with the learning outcomes' (ibid.: 4.6). The proposed multiple exit and entry points are also based on the identification of skill levels. 'Specific sets of skills and values across domains will be identified for integration and incorporation at each stage of learning, from pre-school to higher education' (ibid.: 4.4). This makes it clear that the strategy is primarily one of facilitating exits from the formal system of education. Any re-entry is dependent on possessing a specified set of skills and does not allow for choice from a wider range of options.

Knowledge as a resource for critically comprehending the contemporary world, society and value systems is now treated as being 'too heavy' for current teaching-learning methodologies and curricula to handle. A functional assembly of performance-oriented qualities defines the basic unit, module and topic of learning. These skill units can be easily monitored, measured, graded and readied for the market. The 'learning outcome' too is predetermined. Developing 'standardized' assessment mechanisms to monitor the achievement levels reached for predetermined sets of 'outcomes' further degrades the teaching-learning process from being a diverse and complex interactive relationship to merely functioning as a conveyor transmitting pre-set modules of 'information' from teacher-facilitators to student-recipients.

This process of depriving students of the 'content' of learning, which develops fundamental disciplines, critical thinking and creativity to oppose social injustices and to innovate and overcome forms of discrimination, makes a mockery of all learning as it cultivates conformism in thought and produces persons fitted only for being cogs in the economic and technological machine.

Education for Equality Is a Social Responsibility

Once the democratic space for rights has been *delegitimized*, the existing sites and modes of peaceful democratic debate, dissent and resistance are turned into 'anti-national' acts of sedition. The autonomy and self-governing capacity of the people shrink as corporate/technological 'expertise' claims precedence in the marketplace. The *democratic unity* that actually constitutes the nation is thereby severely threatened.

This is already being seen at campuses across the country and wherever people, whether women, minorities or farmers and workers, question and protest against policies imposed without their consent or consultation. A brute parliamentary majority alone cannot ensure the survival of the republic when every other democratic institution and practice is either pushed aside or made subservient through bribery and corrupt inducements on the one hand or sought to be suppressed through authoritarian modes of arrests without trial or state-instigated and protected fascist acts of violence on the other. Showing no concern for people's welfare and in the absence of appropriate policies to address their extreme deprivation, the present government's approach, favouring only a select group of capitalists to 'revive' the economy, harshly portrays the *social irrationality of bare market transactions*.

A vibrant national system of education has to be transformational and emancipatory; it cannot reproduce and strengthen existing hierarchies and disparities. The real challenge for the education system lies in transforming a heterogeneous and diverse population into a rich learning source for the development of sensibilities that are not marked by conformism and prejudice but are open to critical self-questioning. This cannot be left to the vagaries of the market where profit rules and private players respond accordingly.

Still, less can be left to a policy that seeks to homogenize people and knowledge through authoritarian governmental dictation. NEP 2020's repeated declarations in favour of 'one nation, one tradition/one pedagogical methodology/and one digital platform' run counter to the diversity of India's peoples, languages and socio-cultural histories. Respecting, celebrating and engaging with this *diversity* has led to India's unity as a nation through the struggle against British colonialism and in overcoming the tragedy of the partition. In a democratic environment, such as that provided for in India's Constitution, liberties and rights are *enabling conditions* in the ongoing politics of *democratically negotiated nationalism*.

In the continuing struggle for creating a modern society and nation in which every citizen's right to a life of dignity must not only be protected but advanced, the education system from the pre-primary stage up to higher education has an especially significant role to play.

Notes

[1] Marriot Saville, Commissioner of Revenue in the Deccan and later Member of Council, Government of Bombay, in a letter to Sir R. Grant, 16 January 1836.

[2] *Report of the Indian Education Commission: Appointed by the Resolution of the Government of India*, Calcutta: Superintendent of Government Printing, 1882, pp. 300–04.

[3] Hali (1837–1914) wrote one of the earliest works of literary criticism in Urdu, *Muqaddamah-i-Shay'r-o-Sha'iri*. Its critical preface, 'Muqaddima-i-Sher-o-Shairi', led the way to literary criticism in Urdu literature.

[4] A uniform definition of literacy for British India was adopted beginning with the 1911 Census – an individual was recorded as literate if he or she could read and write a short letter to a friend. Although officials point to certain problems with the post-1911 enumeration such as enumerators on occasion adopting school standards, they do indicate that 'the simple criterion laid down was easily understood and sensibly interpreted' (Census of India 1921).

[5] *Report of Indian Education Commission, Bombay, Volume 2*, Calcutta, 1884.

[6] 'Prime Minister Narendra Modi deliberated on the reforms required in the education sector, including the National Education Policy (NEP). Special emphasis was given to the use of technology in the education sector and enhancing learning and adapting by the use of technology such as online classes, education portals and class-wise broadcast on dedicated education channels.' *Hindustan Times*, 2 May 2020.

[7] A 2015 report of the International Labour Organization (ILO) puts the number of child workers in India aged between five and seventeen at 5.7 million, out of 168

million globally. More than half of India's child workers labour in agriculture and over a quarter in manufacturing. Children also work in restaurants and hotels and as domestic workers. Child labour rates are highest among tribal and lower caste communities.

References

All India Forum for Right to Education (AIFRTE) (2021), *Reclaim Constitution, Social Justice and Education*, Delhi.

Arnold, W.D. (1922), 'First Report, 1857', in J.A. Richey, ed., *Selections from Educational Records (Part II)*, Calcutta: Superintendent of Government Printing.

Biswas, A. and S.P. Aggarwal (1994), *Development of Education in India: A Historical Survey of Educational Documents Before and After Independence*, Delhi: Concept Publishing.

Census of India (1921), Volume 1, chapter VIII.

Chaudhary, S.I. (2002), *Middle Class and the Social Revolution in Bengal: An Incomplete Agenda*, Dhaka.

Davis, L.E. and R.A. Huttenback (1986), *Mammon and the Pursuit of Empire: The Political Economy of British Imperialism, 1860–1912*, New York: Cambridge University Press.

Engels, F. (1975 [1845]), 'Speeches in Elberfeld: February 8, 1845', *Marx–Engels Collected Works* (MECW), Volume 4, Moscow: Progress Publishers.

Government of India (GoI) (1944), *Post-War Plan of Educational Development in India*, Central Advisory Board of Education, New Delhi: Manager of Publications.

——— (2020), *National Education Policy 2020*, Ministry of Human Resource Development, New Delhi, available at https://www.education.gov.in/sites/upload_files/mhrd/files/NEP_Final_English_0.pdf, accessed 8 November 2020.

Gupta, N. (1981), *Delhi Between Two Empires (1803–1931): Society, Government and Urban Growth*, New Delhi: Oxford University Press.

Habib, I. (2009), 'Economics and the Historians', Krishna Bharadwaj Memorial Lecture, Jawaharlal Nehru University, New Delhi.

Hindustani Talimi Sangh (1938), *Basic National Education: Report of the Zakir Husain Committee*, Khandwa: Subodh Sindhu Press.

Howell, A. (1872), *Education in British India: Prior to 1854 and in 1870–1871*, Calcutta: Superintendent of Government Printing.

Kothari, D.S. (1966), *Education and National Development: Report of the Education Commission*, New Delhi: Ministry of Education, Government of India.

Lee, J.W. and H. Lee (2016), 'Human Capital in the Long Run', *Journal of Development Economics*, vol. 122, pp. 147–69.

Marriott, S. (1846), *India: The Duty and Interest of England to Inquire into its State*, London: Longman & Co.

Marx, K. (1965 [1887]), *Capital*, vol. 1, Moscow: Progress Publishers.

Marx, K. and F. Engels (1976), 'Theses on Feuerbach', *Marx–Engels Collected Works* (MECW), vol. 5, Moscow: Progress Publishers.

Naik, J.P. (1975), *Equality, Quality and Quantity: The Elusive Triangle in Indian Education*, Tagore Memorial Lectures, Poona University, New Delhi: Allied Publishers.

Natesan, G.A. (1916), *Speeches of Gopal Krishna Gokhale*, Madras.

Sen, T. (1967), *Report of the Committee of Members of Parliament on Education*, New Delhi: Ministry of Education, Government of India.

Shore, F.J. (1837), *Notes on Indian Affairs*, vol. 2, no. 37, London: John W. Parker.

Weiner, M. (1994), 'India's Case Against Compulsory Education', *Seminar*, vol. 413, January, pp. 83–86.

7

Continuity amidst Changes

Longue Durée of Educational Apartheid in India

Mohd. Bilal

The decision of the union government to finally approve the National Education Policy (NEP), 2020, came amid the Covid-19 pandemic, that is, when the Parliament was not in session. It was approved surreptitiously at a time when all the educational institutions in the country were shut, owing to which the protests against its retrograde measures were minimal. Sensing the opportune time for finally giving it a nod, the Bhartiya Janta Party (BJP)-led government at the centre proceeded with its agenda to finally abdicate its responsibility of providing quality publicly funded education to the masses. The draft policy was already in the public domain, and it was vehemently criticized by students, teachers, academics and activists, among others. A powerful, sustained movement against its enforcement was not seen due to the generalized phenomenon of lockdown/unlock restrictions and the long-term normalization of the general populace towards inequality in education.

The NEP 2020, in simple words, will set to worsen the already pathetic situation of education in the country. The policy has incorporated the interests of the Rashtriya Swayamsevak Sangh (RSS), the industry-cum-corporate sector and the dominant classes. It correspondingly seems to subordinate the interests of the people. Instead of tackling the real issues aimed at bringing inside a vast section of those hitherto outside mainstream education, with measures such as increasing the number of formal educational institutions, the NEP also seeks to provide a policy framework to the existing ad-hoc measures and practices that are rampant in the education sector and have been reproducing social and economic inequalities. It seems that NEP 2020 simply intends to formally announce and facilitate the state's renunciation of its role.

The policy has led social activists and the teaching fraternity to denounce what can easily be viewed as conservative measures. However, the ruling political party has so far remained immune to the sharp criticisms of activists and the teaching community. Even the opposition parties have not been too vehement in their criticism of the policy which is going to drastically transform the education scene in the country. Such inuring to the well-placed criticism of the policy has been possible because of the absence of outrage among the people. Indeed, the sharp critiques of the policy can easily be contrasted with the largely apathetic response of the general public to it. This is worrisome but understandable, given the long history of the exclusion in education, which has over the years become so normalized that a large section of the masses is trapped by the dominant view that there is bound to be inequality in education as the state cannot provide for the education of all. In this way, even the measures being brought in by the policy are not easily registered. Considering these points, one needs to look at not just the policy to understand the various regressive measures but also the antecedents of the new policy, which too, are far from being progressive.

It will be argued in the essay that the education policies in India have largely remained exclusionary despite the pronouncements of political leaders and educationists to the contrary. The argument also highlights the various conservative tendencies which permeated the leadership in the anti-colonial movement that imbibed the hegemony of the elites. The aspirations of the common masses failed to materialize in the post-colonial period, reflecting the failures of the left and national-popular movements to erode the hegemony of the elites (Joshi and Josh 2011). The hegemony of elites and the historic failure of the nation to come to its own (Guha 1982) found manifestation in the educational schemes which were launched in the post-colonial period and policy measures. In this regard, I also trace the historical process through which inequality in education has come to be viewed as normal.

Education in the Colonial Period

It is well known that education in the pre-colonial times was exclusive as only the upper classes were able to pursue it to a large extent (Crook 1996: Introduction; Veeraraghavan 2020: 76). The actual education systems might have differed across the subcontinent, but this was the prevalent motif. Prior to the colonial conquest and subsequent rule over the Indian subcontinent, there existed a traditional system of education which was highly decentralized. For example, in Bengal, there was a system of higher learning which consisted of Persian and Arabic schools called *madrasah*s and Sanskrit schools called *tol*s. The pupils were generally from the upper castes and leisured classes, who had sufficient time and resources to devote to educational pursuits. It was a highly decentralized system in the sense that there was no set curricula, system of examination, etc., which was followed by the traditional higher learning institutions. The mode of functioning of *madrasah*s and *tol*s was largely determined by the teachers, and these centres of higher learning were patronized by wealthy benefactors and *zamindar*s. The course of study at *tol*s was Hindu logic, law and literature, while at *madrasah*s it comprised Muslim law and Islamic religious science (Acharya 1978).

Apart from these schools of higher learning that were chiefly attended by the leisured classes, there were *pathshala*s or village schools, which were patronized by the trading and agricultural classes. Here, the curriculum largely consisted of three Rs, that is, reading, writing and rudimentary arithmetic. Though these schools were also dominated by traders and agricultural castes, a significant proportion of the students in these schools was from the 'lower' castes. It is significant that in Burdwan in the early nineteenth century, more than 50 per cent of the scholars in *pathshala*s were from lower castes (ibid.).

However, in colonial times, changes were made in the education sector which informed the later developments and crystallization of ideas about education in the colonial period. One of the earliest debates in the early colonial period arose on the issues concerning education between the Orientalists and Anglicists. The grounds of debate between them were related to the importance to be accorded to indigenous education or English education. However, even this ground was premised on the real aims of governing a 'different' people. The Orientalists and Anglicists both held a certain view of Indian society concerning which they suggested education policies that, according to each, best helped govern it. The Orientalists called for understanding and promoting the study of Indian texts for people were best governed according to their own rules which were contained in their texts. For the Anglicists, the obverse was true. They wanted to introduce English language education in India, for it entailed the creation of a class which would appreciate the 'richness' of English culture, and this in turn would create grounds for British rule being strengthened in the country (Upadhyay 2012).

These formulations of the Orientalists and Anglicists were to lay grounds for the developments in education in the succeeding decades. However, it needs to be emphatically remembered that the policies of the colonial rulers were geared towards what they regarded as the leisured classes, that is, the upper castes and classes, who were seen as harbouring the necessary will and intellect to be accorded an education. For the rest, especially for the lower classes, education would have to be filtered down through the literate classes. The education policy of the colonial state was based on downward filtration theory, and efforts were only made to provide education to a minuscule minority, comprising the sons of *raja*s and *nawab*s and those belonging to the upper classes (Veeraraghavan 2020: 77). No effort was made to provide mass education. Despite the differences in their thought and advocacy of policies related to education, the Orientalists and Anglicists had a common ground inasmuch as mass education was deemed an impossible and unworthy task.

Thus, as early as 1823, Holt Mackenzie, an Orientalist and the Secretary to the Bengal government, wrote that 'to provide for the education of the great body of the people seems to be impossible'. He further thought that 'the natural course of things in all countries seems to be that knowledge introduced from abroad should descend from the higher or educated classes and gradually spread through their example' (Upadhyay 2012).

The sense of educating a section of Indian society while denying education to the rest was informed by a class attitude. It can be observed in the dispatches of John Stuart Mill which reinforced the approach of his father. He explained:

> As we strive for an equal degree of justice, an equal degree of temperance, an equal degree of veracity, in the poor as in the rich, so ought we to strive for an equal degree of intelligence. . . . It is absolutely necessary for the existence of the human race, that labour should be performed, that food should be produced, and other things provided, which human welfare requires. A large proportion of mankind, that labours, only such a portion of time can by them be given to the acquisition of intelligence as can be abstracted from labour. . . . There are degrees, therefore, of intelligence, which must be reserved for those who are not obliged to labour. (Vishwanathan 1989: 149)

The ruling idea, therefore, was to give a smattering of education to the Dalits and the oppressed, which only enabled them to keep to their stations in society. In line with such a policy came Macaulay's Minute in 1835; in it Macaulay, as Law Member of the Governor-General's Council and President of the Committee of Public Instruction, denigrated the 'vernaculars' and called for promoting 'English education alone' (Ramachandran and Ramkumar 2005). Thereafter there were some lukewarm attempts to spread school education (ibid.), with efforts being chiefly directed towards spreading English education through higher learning institutions. In the process, the British destroyed whatever indigenous system of education the masses had accessed, without of course replacing it with anything meaningful (Acharya 1995).

While the emphasis was on the education of the upper classes (which primarily meant upper castes and those in positions of power and status), the colonial rulers exhibited a drifting concern with the education of Dalits and lower castes. The Caste Disabilities Removal Act of 1850 and Wood's Despatch of 1854 can be seen as non-committal utterances that half-heartedly aimed at overcoming the inordinate dependence on upper castes, and the opposition to the education of the Dalits by the upper castes. However, these were cautionary approaches which can be evinced by the restraint advised by the Hunter Commission in going ahead with the policy of opening government schools to all classes. While emphasizing that 'no boy be refused admission to a Government college or school merely on the ground of caste', it added that 'even in the case of government or board schools, the principle must be applied with due caution' (Nambissan 2002: 81).

The consequence of such a lopsided policy was that a large section of the population remained outside the sphere of education, chiefly those from the exploited and oppressed sections.

The education policy of the colonial rulers, therefore, only served to excessively broaden the educational difference between the upper classes and those from oppressed sections. Indeed, in studies such as that of Philip Constable (2000), it has been amply shown that even the few Dalits who enrolled in schools were discriminated against, and for lower-caste students, education continued to remain a discriminatory experience due to the active connivance of British officials who looked for the support of the local dominant castes. In this context, the blame can be put squarely on the nature of colonial rule over the Indian people. Since colonial education was geared towards its own agenda – that of ruling over the masses – it devised policies catering to such an aim. However, nationalist politicians despite

TABLE 7.1 Disparity in the level of education among different strata of population, c. 1923

Classes of population	Primary education, students per 1,000 of the population of the class	Secondary education, students per 100,000 of the population	College education, students per 200,000 of the population
Advanced Hindus	119	3,000	1,000
Mahomedans	92	500	52
Intermediate classes	38	140	24
Backward classes	18	14	Nil (or nearly 1 if at all)

Source: Upadhyay (2012).

their anti-colonial stance were not very different from the colonial ruling elite in this regard.

Attitude of the Anti-Colonial Leadership

Historical evidence amply highlights the evolving attitudes towards mass education among Indian politicians in the nineteenth and early twentieth centuries. Gopal Krishna Gokhale was one of the early anti-colonial leaders who spoke about the need and feasibility of educating the masses. In his Free and Compulsory Education Bill presented before the Imperial Legislative Council in 1911, he argued that free and compulsory primary education was a possibility, citing a modest earmarking of the colonial government's resources for the purpose. Though the Bill was rejected, it highlighted the feasibility of the provision of compulsory education, which even in independent India was to be delayed till as late as 2009.

However, Gokhale's was a largely lonely voice among the nationalist leaders when it came to the question of mass education. Even among the early social reformers, mass education was not counted as a possible cause. Ishwar Chandra Vidyasagar's pronouncements in this regard serve as examples of elitist tendencies even among the Indian social reformers, which are not wholly different from those of colonial administrators. Talking about the education policies of the colonial government, Vidyasagar remarked:

> . . . it seems almost impracticable in the present circumstances of the country . . . the government should, in my humble opinion, confine itself to the education . . . on a comprehensive scale . . . mere reading and writing and a little of arithmetic, should not comprise the whole of this education. Geography, History, Biography, Arithmetic, Geometry, Natural Philosophy, Moral Philosophy, Political Economy and Physiology should be taught to render it complete. . . . *By educating one boy in a proper style the government does more towards the real education of the people, than by teaching a hundred children mere reading, writing and a little arithmetic.* (Quoted in Ghosh 2012: 44, emphasis added)

Moreover, when confronted with the possibility of upper castes refraining from sending their children to Sanskrit College – if castes other than Brahmans and Vaidyas were admitted – Vidyasagar expressed his opinion thus, 'I see no objection to the admission of other castes than the Brahmans and Vaidyas, or in other words, different orders of Sudras in the Sanskrit College. But as a measure of expediency, I would suggest that at present Kayasthas only be admitted' (ibid.: 45). On the issue of mass education, Vidyasagar remarked:

An impression appears to have gained ground both here and in England, that enough has been done for the education of the higher classes and that attention should now be directed towards the education of the masses. . . . An enquiry into the matter will however show a very different state of things. *As the best, if not the only practicable means of promoting education in Bengal, the government should, in my humble opinion, confine to the education of the higher classes on a comprehensive scale.* . . . (Quoted in Acharya 1995: 671, emphasis added)

Though attempts have been made to celebrate the legacy of Vidyasagar as a stalwart of the Bengal Renaissance, his stance on mass education reflects the bias against lower castes and classes which pervaded the psyche of elites or *bhadraloks* in Bengal.

Even among nationalist leaders who were Gokhale's contemporaries, Bal Gangadhar Tilak was vehemently opposed to any policy advocating mass education. Though regarded as one of the tallest leaders of the pre-Gandhian era, the leader's take on mass education was far from salutary and exhibited caste, class and gender biases – all of which underline the elitist tendencies of an entire generation of leaders.

The overriding concern for this group of nationalists was to defend the system of caste; they viewed reforms as a loss of nationality or *rashtriyata*. The group around Tilak included Vishnushastri Chiplunkar and V.N. Mandalik. They declared that 'the institution of caste had been the basis of the Hindu society and undermining the caste would undermine the Hindu society'. Claiming themselves to represent Hindus, they termed Lokhitwadi and Phule as 'traitors to the nation-*rashtra*', who advocated the abolition of caste-based inequalities (Rao 2009).

The campaigns for compulsory primary education by Gokhale and non-Brahman leaders such as Phule were vociferously challenged by Tilak. He devised various arguments against compulsory primary education and argued that teaching Kunbi (peasant) children to read, write and learn the rudiments of history, geography and mathematics, would actually harm them. Rather, for him, the peasant's children were better taught traditional occupations, for the curriculum meant for the children of upper castes and classes was unsuitable for them. According to him, if:

You take away a farmer's boy from the plough, the blacksmith's boy from the bellows and the cobbler's boy from his awl with the object of giving him liberal education . . . and the boy learns to condemn the profession of his father, not to speak of the loss to which the latter is put by being deprived of the son's assistance at the old trade.[1]

Tilak was also opposed to any augmentation of the educational infrastructure and viewed any expenditure on the same as a waste of resources. He wrote:

> Whatever the eloquence of the facts and figures of Mr. Gokhale, we stick to our view and say that the leaders of public movement are committing serious blunder in insisting upon [the] government to continue to maintain and manage institutions, the utility of which is disproportionately too small compared to the cost they entail and in which hardly any scope for development.[2]

He criticized the effort of the colonial government to bring education to the villages and encouraging the peasants' children to take up education. He argued that by supporting the extension of 'liberal education for the masses the reformers were committing a grave error' as 'English education encouraged the people to defy the caste restrictions and the spread of English education among the natives will bring down their caste system'.[3]

Nai Talim or Basic Education Scheme of Gandhi

Post the First World War, with the promulgation of the Montagu-Chelmsford Reforms of 1919, the Government of India Act 1919, was enacted. In the provinces of British India, the portfolio for education was entrusted to Indian ministers. Following this, different provinces enacted legislation for compulsory elementary education in selected cities and towns. After the Karachi Congress in 1931 and the formation of Congress Ministries in eight provinces in the 1937 provincial elections, the programme of primary education received some attention (Veeraraghavan 2020: 79). It was in this context that Gandhi came out with his 'basic education' programme (*Nai Talim*), which was largely envisaged by him in the 1930s and came to be formulated in the Zakir Husain Committee Report (1938).

Based on Gandhi's socioeconomic policies of the self-sufficient village community, his basic education scheme was premised on free and compulsory education along with craft-based learning which was to be taught in the native tongue of the students. The curriculum was to be so devised that it was related to the craft in every aspect. *Nai Talim* as per Gandhi's formulation was:

> . . . whatever is taught to children, all of it should be taught necessarily through the medium of a trade or a handicraft . . . instead of merely teaching a trade or a handicraft, we may as well educate the children entirely through them. Look at *takli* [spindle] itself, for instance. The lesson of this *takli* will be the first lesson of our students through which they would

be able to learn a substantial part of the history of cotton, Lancashire and the British empire. . . . How does this *takli* work? What is its utility? And what are the strengths that lie within it? Thus the child learns all this in the midst of play. Through this he also acquires some knowledge of mathematics. When he is asked to count the number of cotton threads on *takli* and he is asked to report how many did he spin, it becomes possible to acquaint him step by step with good deal of mathematical knowledge through this process. And the beauty is that none of this becomes even a slight burden on his mind. . . . While playing around and singing, he keeps on turning his *takli* and from this itself he learns a great deal. (Gandhi's address at the Wardha Education Conference, 22 October 1937)

The Gandhian formulation of *Nai Talim* can be seen as propagating a new kind of learning based on practical education or what can be called in latter-day terminology 'vocational education'. Emphasis on holistic learning based on the dignity of labour has led to support for this scheme in the present day, when we are confronted with an education system which lays undue stress on performance, rather than learning. Instead of talking about its perceived merits, which, if implemented, would bring about a revolution in pedagogy and education, based as it is on a holistic approach, that is, of integrating head, heart and hand, emphasizes the essentiality of the mother tongue and the principle of self-support (Sadgopal 2014), one needs to look at the way in which the question itself is wrongly posed.

The schools in the colonial period were themselves based on a deeply hierarchical model. The masses, especially a majority among the untouchable community and the lower classes, were without resources and thus were condemned to learn skills without any opportunity whatsoever for entering formal or higher education which would lead them to better-paid occupations in the labour market. What was envisaged as holistic education based on crafts, was already a bleak reality for the masses, for without any means of gaining formal education, they were left to reproduce their labour generationally, and this often meant that they remained tied to stigmatized occupations.

Of a remarkably similar scheme of vocational education for African Americans in the southern states of the United States of America, noted African American educationist and social activist, W.E.B. Du Bois remarked (1973):

There comes a distinct philosophy of education which makes the earning of a living the centre and norm of human training and which moreover dogmatically asserts that the subject matter and methods peculiar to technical schools are the best fit for all education. This doctrine is fundamentally false. . . . We must give to our youth a training designed above all to make them men of power, of thought, of trained and cultivated taste; men who know whither civilization is tending and what it means.

Thus, the insistence of the *Nai Talim* on learning crafts and basing it as the foundation for a self-sufficient village community can be juxtaposed with the vehement criticism of a similar policy received by one of the most noted African American activists of Gandhi's time. In India, the *Nai Talim* scheme was put to work in the Modified Scheme of Elementary Education or Rajaji scheme which was brought in the erstwhile Madras state in 1953 by the government of C. Rajagopalachari.

The Stance of Non-Brahman and Dalit Leadership on Mass Education

While a section among nationalist leaders was opposed to the general education of the masses, efforts were made for mass education by non-Brahman and Dalit leaders as well. Phule in his memorandum to the Hunter Commission argued for the need for the expansion of government-funded primary and higher education for the lower classes and women (Phule 2002). The leaders of the non-Brahman movement, especially in the Madras and Bombay presidencies, led movements for educational opportunities for the oppressed and exploited sections and pressed for the creation of schools. Indeed, even in certain princely states like Travancore, organized resistance of Dalits on questions of access to educational opportunities was visible. It is said that the first-ever strike of 'untouchable' agricultural labourers of the Pulayar caste, led by the radical social reformer Ayyankali, was triggered around 1907 when a Pulayar girl was denied enrolment in a government school (Ramachandran 2000: 103–06).[4] This strike soon galvanized the Pulayar community on other issues of livelihood and dignity, forcing the Travancore state to remove discriminatory provisions in its schooling system.

Despite the gradual expansion of the government-funded schooling system in certain parts of the country, the overall number of schools remained minuscule, and the masses remained excluded from education. Even till the late 1920s, the small section of Dalits and other so-called lower-caste students who acquired access to education was largely confined to primary education and industrial schools. The concentration of the Dalits and lower-caste students in industrial schools is particularly telling, as instruction in such schools only fed them into a hierarchical labour market, where there was intense competition for premium jobs. Moreover, even entry into such institutions was highly competitive and aspirants from lower castes and the untouchable community were made to compete for the very limited number of seats available (John 2018: 16).

The non-Brahman and Dalit leadership, while pressing for the need of making education accessible to the majority, envisaged measures which catered to a minuscule minority, thereby reimposing the notions of merits and competition within the untouchable community and subordinate castes. Consequently, just a small section of Dalits and lower classes was able to enter formal education. For example, in a report prepared by the officiating secretary to the Government of Bombay, dated 23 July 1928, it is noted that a recurring provision of Rs 9,000 was made in the budget of 1928 for grants-in-aid to hostels for Depressed Class students under private management. The largest part of this provision was to be used to launch a scheme envisaged by B.R. Ambedkar and another non-official member of the Bombay Legislative Council for the establishment of hostels in different parts of the Presidency proper for boys of the Depressed Classes who were attending secondary schools. The scheme was based on *competitive* examinations and promoted education for a select group of students from within the untouchable community. Such schemes, it should be noted, were also based on the notion of *proportionality* wherein seats were reserved in institutions as per the proportion of Depressed Classes in the population. Due to a meagre number of seats in these institutions reserved for them, a large section of the masses and lower classes was excluded and remained trapped in circumstances wherein they continued to perform stigmatized labour in agrarian and other traditional occupations (John 2016).

This can be contrasted with the opening of factory schools in many provinces where a large section of children from the marginalized and Depressed Classes was employed as child labour. In provinces such as Bombay, there was a stark convergence between the reformers who called for educating children who worked in factories, the employers and the colonial governments. Various legislations were enacted in the course of the late nineteenth and early twentieth centuries which called for the reduction of work hours of child labour in factories, which was vehemently contested by the employers' lobby. However, among both the critics and supporters of child labour, the idea remained intact that the child was a future worker. For both the social reformers and employers' lobbies, the befitting education that could be imparted to the child workers was vocational or technical education. Such education, it was believed, would inculcate industriousness and 'dignity of labour' in them. Such arguments were used as an expedient to set up factory schools in order to impart training to the child workers that was, more often than not, a mere ploy to keep children within the factory, easily accessible for factory work (John 2018).

At a time when the larger untouchable community had scant resources for education, such schemes only served the interests of a very small section of Dalits who had resources for investing in education and had the required wherewithal to corner a section of skilled jobs in the labour market and the government sector. The memoirs of Ramchandra Babaji More (More 2019), a communist leader from the Dalit community and the principal organizer of the historic Mahad Satyagraha, are especially telling in this regard. The memoirs very forcefully describe the experience of financial and social difficulties for a majority of lower castes and Dalits, which made it especially difficult for them to invest in education. More's account of his struggle of gaining admission to the local school at Mahad highlights the socioeconomic conditions that the wider section of lower castes faced. In this context, the schemes of Dalit and non-Brahman leadership – wherein education was envisioned for only a section of the children from lower castes – clearly appear problematic as it paved the way for the larger body of children from these communities to remain out of school and trapped in exploitative working conditions, such as in factories in Bombay as child labour (John 2018).

In this context, it becomes obvious as to why in post-colonial India, the ruling elite failed to incorporate the right to education in the Constitution. The Constituent Assembly – brought into power by an election based on property franchise – framed the Constitution of India whilst failing to incorporate the aspirations of the masses regarding education, despite Ambedkar playing a major role in it. Despite the popular yearning for equality exemplified by the Satyashodhak current in the Bombay presidency, the Namasudra movement in Bengal, lower-caste movements in Bihar and elsewhere, anti-feudal struggles in the Andhra region and Kerala, etc., the right to education was not consecrated as a fundamental right. Instead, it was inserted in the Directive Principles that are not mandatory for the state to follow, and which noted commentators on the framing of the Constitution have termed 'a veritable dustbin of sentiment' (Dhawan 2008). It is significant that an advisory body – the Central Advisory Board of Education (CABE)[5] – in its report *Post-War Plan of Educational Development in India* (CABE 1944: 3), also known as the Sargent Plan, declared that:

> If there is to be anything like equality of opportunity, it is impossible to justify providing facilities for some of the nation's children and not for others. In the first place, therefore, a national system can hardly be other than universal. Secondly, it must be compulsory, if the grave wastage which exists today under a voluntary system is not to be perpetrated and even aggravated. And thirdly, if education is to be universal and compulsory,

equity requires that it should be free and common sense demands that it should last long enough to secure its fundamental objective.

However, instead of making education a fundamental right in line with the interest of the masses, it was relegated to the non-mandatory part of the Constitution. This exposes the pretensions of the elite who only paid lip service to the aspirations of the masses. Unfortunately, the motives of the early post-colonial state have not been aggressively questioned in this regard, and many uncritically hail the initial efforts of the early post-colonial period.

Basic Education Scheme in Action: Madras, 1953

After Independence, while there was no formal education policy regarding school education, one of the most important controversies erupted in Madras state on the nature and content of school education. The controversy revolved around the Modified Scheme of Elementary Education which was sought to be implemented by the government of C. Rajagopalachari in 1953. The principal features of the scheme were: (1) a reduction in the number of study hours in elementary schools in the panchayat villages of the State, from five to three per session, (2) the introduction of two three-hour shifts in schools, one in the morning and the other in the afternoon, and (3) enabling children to learn a craft or trade at home or in a workshop in the village during leisure hours. The second session in which the students would be out of school was to be utilized for obtaining the objectives of the basic education system – learning through living and training in self-reliance (Veeraraghavan 2020: 85).

The scheme was devised to ostensibly provide education to the students on the basis of *Nai Talim*. Though some of the critics of the scheme were Gandhian educationists such as J.C. Kumarappa, it was largely supported by Dr Zakir Hussain and G. Ramachandran (ibid.: 91). However, non-Brahman political leaders and the communists raised serious objections about the kind of education it envisaged, based as it was on the notion of learning *hereditary* crafts and occupations. Thus, instead of providing avenues for the students to get out of exploitative caste-based occupations, the scheme was seen as a move aimed at strengthening caste hierarchies.

Various state-level campaigns against the scheme ultimately made the Madras government back down, and the scheme was eventually withdrawn in 1954 by the government of K. Kamaraj. However, while the contentions of the leaders condemning the scheme were taken as valid, the experiment itself was seen to be a well-intentioned, though abortive, example of the *Nai Talim* scheme. The Gandhian *Nai Talim* has been seen as a radical departure from the Brahmanical-cum-colonial paradigm, but the Modified Scheme of Elementary Education based on it was rightly perceived as promoting *kula kalvi* (casteist education) (National Focus Group 2007). A conundrum, therefore, arises as to the reason for the dichotomy between the lofty ideals of an education policy and the disastrous consequences of its being implemented. The reason can be gauged in the absence of policy measures aimed at creating equality in independent India.

Post-colonial Education Policy

The early decades of educational development in post-colonial India ignored an *actual* policy thrust on elementary education (Bhatty 2014). The University Education Commission and the Secondary Education Commission were constituted in 1948–49 and 1952–53 respectively for looking into the scene of higher education and secondary education. The Education Commission under D.S. Kothari constituted in 1964 was the first to provide a comprehensive review of the education scene in the country.

It has been noted that the anti-colonial leaders envisaged an education policy which did not question the link of education with the labour market. In this vein, the call for vocationalization in secondary and higher secondary education dates back to the Indian Education Commission/Kothari Commission (1964–66) whose recommendations were readily absorbed in the Fifth Five-Year Plan (1974–79). The Commission recommended vocationalization of education for laying the ground for a meaningful, purposive and practical school-level education. On close reading of the Kothari Commission, one can find that common schooling is only given as a gesture at incorporating the aspirations of the masses, while it is mainly silent on the concrete measures to be taken for its implementation (ibid.: 102). The result is the reproduction of existing inequalities between the elite and the masses. While vocationalization became a norm for educating the masses, the academic stream remained reserved for the elites.

The implementation of this recommendation has only served to reproduce the prevailing inequalities between the rich and the poor. It has been argued that this has been possible for two reasons. The primary reason is that the vocational stream is mainly pursued by students coming from a working-class background, or they are rather pushed into it, while the rich students hegemonize high-level professional jobs by opting for the academic stream. While students from lower classes 'opt' for formal vocational education, the upper-class youth (studying in expensive private schools) engage with vocational studies merely in the form of industrial art classes and socially useful productive work (SUPW) camps. The second reason for the reproduction of inequality through vocationalization is 'the lack of cross-migration and cross-fertilization between the academic and vocational streams' (John 2013: 51).

The National Policy on Education (NPE) 1986 criticized the earlier National Policy on Education 1968, which was based on the recommendations of the Kothari Commission. In its review of NPE 1968, NPE 1986 criticized the lack of financial outlay for implementing the measures envisaged in it. It was argued that it resulted 'in compounding the problems of "access, quality and utility of education" to "massive proportions"' (Bhatty 2014: 102). However, NPE 1986 itself remained tied to the presumption that there was a lack of demand for education among the poor and marginalized. Consequently, though a boost was given to access in the government schools, the overall paradigm remained that of providing poor-quality education for the poor and marginalized. The policy also talked about excluded groups such as Scheduled Caste (SC), Scheduled Tribe (ST), minority, women and 'handicapped' students and came up with various measures to ostensibly bring the excluded groups into mainstream education. These measures included incentives for the SC, ST and other educationally backward students, emphasis on recruitment of women and SC teachers, and reservation for SC and ST students in Navodaya Vidyalaya, among others.

The policy measures facilitated by the NPE 1986 continued to perpetuate inequality by only catering to a handful of children from socio-economically disadvantaged sections to pursue quality education through 'model schools' such as Kendriya Vidyalayas and Navodaya Vidyalayas.[6] The students from well-resourced Kendriya Vidyalayas (KVs), Sainik Schools and Jawahar Navodaya Vidyalayas (JNVs) across the country receive an education, which is way beyond the means of the labouring masses. The people sending their wards to these elite government schools are typically wealthier sections of the peasantry in the case of the Navodayas and middle-class professionals in government service in the case of KVs and Sainik schools. These model schools provide quality public-funded education to a minuscule section of students while the general education scene remains pathetic. Such model schools have left unresolved the challenge of educating the masses through the network of regular neighbourhood government schools 'where most of India's children and almost all of its children from socially and economically weaker sections were being sent' (ibid.). Typically, model government schools have been based on the premise that they would enable those with greater 'merit' to pursue quality education and tap their potential that would otherwise be unrealized in regular government schools. The expenditure per student in these schools is way above that expended on regular government school students. 'In government schools the average per child expenditures was Rs 4,269 (2011–12);

whereas in the Sarvodaya Vidyalayas it is in the range of Rs 8,000 to Rs 10,000, and in Kendriya Vidyalayas as high as Rs 13,000 – three times the amount spent in a regular government school' (ibid.).

For the masses, the NPE 1986, especially its modified version in 1992, only succeeded in providing poor-quality education. Instead of prioritizing financial boost to schools, the cost-cutting measures implemented under the policy, such as the setting-up of education guarantee centres (EGCs) and the recruitment of para-teachers that were not required to conform to the established standards of educational quality and teaching, served to alienate the masses from the ostensible plan of the policy to achieve 'education for equality'.

Coupled with the phenomenon of hierarchy in the public schooling system, private schools have progressively increased in the country. The earliest recommendations made for the common school system by the Kothari Commission did not lay down any concrete measures for the creation of such a system, which resulted in cementing of a dual system of education, that is, 'government-run free schools for the subordinated people and an elite private system for the powerful' (Saxena 2012). Studies have highlighted the differentiated educational regimes which exist in the country from elite residential schools to resource-poor government schools. Such differentiation, it has been argued, 'further disadvantages the already underprivileged by reinforcing, instead of reducing, existing social and economic inequalities, as the pupils of these widely disparate institutions are endowed with very uneven qualities and quantities of economic and social wherewithal' (Majumdar and Mooij 2012).

The phenomenon of private schools co-existing with government schools has served to make way for the rich to corner seats in premier higher educational institutions and thereby monopolize higher segment jobs, while the majority of school-going children simply find themselves locked into the lower segment and exploitative jobs due to the poor quality of instruction rampant in government schools. However, the government school system contains deep divisions within itself. This division within the public school system has perpetuated hierarchies of access to public-funded education.

In this context, it is appropriate to look at the Right to Education (RTE) Act passed in 2009, which made it mandatory for the governments to provide compulsory primary education from ages six to fourteen. The RTE 2009 had a catch inasmuch as it did not contest the existence of inequality in education. In fact, it instituted a 25 per cent quota for admissions in private schools for the students from the economically weaker sections (EWS), thereby making way for a minuscule fraction of students from marginalized backgrounds to enter private schools; this in turn obliterated the issue of the unequal dual system of education existing in the country. This measure has provided a fillip to the normalization of inequality in the school education sector.

The growing phenomenon of tuition and coaching centres further widens the gap between the masses and the elite by fuelling the 'successes' of students of elite private and government schools. There has been an absence of government policy regarding the tuition and coaching centres which mushroomed in the country, especially since the 1980s and 1990s. Becoming an important component of the market with the coming of big-scale formal coaching establishments in various metropolitan cities and the development of some cities as hubs of coaching centres for various competitive examinations, the coaching industry was worth 40 billion dollars in 2015. Also, the annual money spent on coaching for premier institutions such as Indian Institutes of Technology (IITs) and National Institutes of Technology (NITs) was 1.5 lakh crores which is way above the annual budget for all IITs and NITs put together (Moudgalya 2015). These coaching institutes serve as conduits to premier universities and plush jobs in the government and private sectors and serve to keep the youth from lower classes at a disadvantage so that they are in no position to compete with students from private schools who have had access to the best coaching institutes due to their higher financial status.

Contrast this picture with that of common government schools in the country which have none of the facilities which the private and elite government schools enjoy. The students in regular government schools are fortunate if the government ever employs the required number of teachers. Needless to say, the government actively ignores the needs of these students. Even if these students try to fill the gap by studying harder, their efforts can never amount to much in the entrance examinations of various higher educational institutions, which favour elite students who have had access to quality education and the best coaching institutes. This effectively mars the efforts of the majority of students from deprived backgrounds to enter premier higher educational institutions.

The NEP 2020 can be seen as forming a logical continuum which is in line with the developments in the education policy of successive regimes post-Independence.

National Education Policy (NEP) 2020 and School Education
Early Childhood Education (ECE)

The NEP 2020 envisages early childhood education with no plan to implement it. In place of any concrete plan to achieve the objective, the policy simply relies on the frontline *anganwadi* workers who are responsible for implementing government schemes aimed at immunization, food provision, primary healthcare, pre-schooling and other such services to children below six and their mothers through the Integrated Child Development Services (ICDS). The NEP 2020 does not call for employing elementary teachers for the purpose of providing preschool education to children. Instead, it only advocates the expansion of the network of ill-trained *anganwadi* workers. According to the policy, the existing *anganwadi* workers with 10+2 qualifications would be given a tokenistic six-month training to enable them for the purpose. Moreover, those with lower educational qualifications shall be given a one-year diploma programme covering early literacy, numeracy and other relevant aspects of ECE. The training of *anganwadi* workers at present is ad-hoc, and it is unwisely expected by the government that the existing workers would receive adequate training through online mode while running the *anganwadi* centres.

Moreover, across the country, private playschools and preschools have proliferated which cater to the needs of the middle and upper classes. While private ventures in education are being promoted, the policy clearly eschews the need to bring in more sufficiently trained elementary teachers to cater to the needs of the vast majority of the children of the country who are currently dependent on pathetic *anganwadi* centres and ill-trained, ill-paid contractual *anganwadi* workers. Thus, the policy measure on this point is mere hogwash which amounts to a deft evasion of the issue.

Informalization of Education at the School Level

The policy talks at various places about the students from socially and economically disadvantaged sections (SEDGs). It mentions gross enrolment ratio (GER) for various grades since the RTE 2009. GER for grades 6–8 was 90.9 per cent, while for grades 9–10 and 11–12, it was only 79.3 per cent and 56.5 per cent respectively. Though these GERs are themselves inflated, the policy aims to achieve 100 per cent GER by 2030. However, such lofty motives stand betrayed when one peruses the measures sought to bring about such GER. One of the most important reasons for the decrease in GER after grade 8 is the widespread tendency of government schools to push students into an informal mode of education such as the National Institute of Open Schooling (NIOS) or simply refuse to take them in. A telling example of such tendencies is the Delhi government schools, much celebrated over the country for being so-called model of good education, which have seen a drastic reduction in student enrolment over the years. A total of 9.96 lakh students were enrolled in state government schools in 2011–12, the enrolment fell to 8.97 lakhs in 2014–15, 8.77 lakhs in 2015–16 and 7.41 lakhs in 2018–19 which amounts to a 17 per cent drop.[7]

The Draft National Education Policy 2019 (GoI 2019) had suggested that RTE would be extended to cover the age group 3–18 (ibid.: 72). While this was a positive measure, it has been removed in the final version, and the final version slyly absolves the government of expanding the RTE by simply stating that the goal is to achieve 100 per cent enrolment from preschool to secondary level by 2030. This measure also frees the government of its bounden duty to increase the public educational infrastructure by advocating the informalization of education. It simply aims at shoving students into open schooling systems such as the National Institute of Open Schooling (NIOS), where the facilities and infrastructure are dismal and which had a mere 31 per cent passing rate for grade 12 in 2018. The NIOS and state open schools would be expanded to have a greater number of students enrolled in them after the formal-mode schools are closed and merged. Instead of massively increasing the infrastructure so that the majority of the students who are dependent on public-funded education have access to the formal education system, emphasis is laid on the provision of education through the open and distance learning (ODL) mode. The buzzwords used in the policy such as 'technology-enabled', 'online', etc., are aimed at freeing the government of its commitment towards the goal of providing formal-mode education to all since such ODL and online-mode education cannot be a substitute for proper schooling. Clearly, the emphasis on online and ODL modes only paves the way for massive informalization at the school level.

Entry Door to NGOs and Private Bodies

One of the main causes of inequality in the country is the lack of access to public-funded quality education. While there is an urgent need to open more schools and establish a common school system, the government has declared its intention to promote the opening of private schools in a massive way. Moreover, to pave way for private investment in public education, the public–private partnership (PPP) model is to be promoted. Likewise, non-governmental organizations (NGOs), which thrive on government funds and serve to make education a commodity which is to be doled out according to their whims, are being promoted. This would usher in privatization in a big way and would serve to debar a majority of Dalits, tribals, minorities, women and those from lower classes from formal-mode education.

An excessive reliance is placed on private bodies and crowd-funding to even provide the learning resources such as textbook materials to the students in schools. Such a stance serves to abdicate the government of its responsibility to provide education to the masses, and instead ropes in private players to mint profits. Further, private bodies are to be encouraged to set up schools, and thus leave the government free from its task to ensure equality and education for all.

Preparing Grounds for Entry of School Students into the Informal Labour Market

There is much emphasis on vocational education in the NEP 2020. It has been the declared aim of the government to bring in vocational education from early school grades. What in effect would be just a superfluous subject for those studying in private schools would serve as a trap for students from deprived sections in so far as it would impart skills which would ensure their early entry into the informal labour market and thereby preclude a majority from entering higher education. Moreover, the policy envisages massive entry of students into the informal labour market by citing its intent to expose at least 50 per cent of the students to vocational education by 2025, that is, in the next five years.

According to the statistics given by Ramesh Pokhriyal 'Nishank', the MHRD Minister in February 2020 in Parliament, the dropout rates of students in classes 9 and 10 had crossed almost a fifth of the total enrolment rate in 2017–18. He also specified that in as many as eleven states, the dropout rate in secondary school was over 20 per cent. In Assam, about a third of the students dropped out and in Bihar, it was 32 per cent despite an improvement from the previous years. The dropout rate in Bihar was 39.7 per cent in 2016–17 (Radhika 2020). The students who drop out of classes after class 9 invariably belong to the most deprived and marginalized sections of society and are forced to enter the informal labour market as child labourers. The policy states: 'The students will be given increased flexibility and choice of subjects to study, particularly in secondary school – including subjects in physical education, the arts, and vocational crafts – so that they may be free to design their own paths of study and life plans.'

Thus, instead of ensuring measures to retain the students in the formal education system, the overarching emphasis on vocational education is only meant to provide cheap and skilled labour to the highly exploitative informal sector in the country.

Opportunities and Encouragement to Only a Few

The policy has also laid down a lofty need to encourage 'talents' in government schools under the section 'Support for Gifted Students'. It is a well-known fact that the government schools which provide education to the vast majority of school-going students in the country are in a pathetic condition. Consequently, there is an urgent need to provide more and more resources to these schools. Instead, the government is openly abdicating its duty by only providing for the selection of a few 'talented' students in schools who will be encouraged, while leaving the majority to fend for themselves. The policy aims to encourage students who show particularly high-performing strong interests and capacities in a given realm. Moreover, it has been enjoined upon the teachers to 'encourage students with singular interests and/or talents in the classroom by giving them supplementary enrichment material and guidance and encouragement . . . through specific funding allocated for this purpose'. Furthermore, even the National Council for Educational Research and Training (NCERT) and the National Curriculum Framework for Teacher Education (NCFTE) will develop guidelines for the education of 'gifted' children. Furthermore, such 'talents' would be promoted through 'rigorous merit-based residential summer camps', implying that only a selective few would be fostered while the commitment to the majority remains dispensable.

In all, such measures would encourage a handful of students to go for higher studies, who in conjunction with vocational education for the majority would end up perpetuating a hierarchy of employment and thereby increase inequality in society.

Closure of Schools and Decline in Standards for the Setting Up of Schools

There is a growing phenomenon of the government 'rationalizing' school education in recent years through the closure of schools that are deemed to be less attended. State-government-run schools have been closed in massive numbers in various states across the country, Delhi and Haryana being the most notable examples. As such, the policy reinforces such measures by providing for such rationalization by integrating schools in school complexes and clusters. What in effect such a measure would mean is the closing of schools and the degradation of the existing ones. The policy further envisages lowering of specifications for setting up of schools and openly advocates for the physical and infrastructural requirements to be made 'more responsive' to realities on the ground, e.g. regarding land areas and room sizes, practicalities of playgrounds in urban areas, etc. (GoI 2020: 32). It allows for 'these mandates to be adjusted and loosened, leaving flexibility for each school to make its own decisions based on local needs and constraints'. This relaxation of specifications for setting up of schools will only expedite the process of compromise on ensuring quality educational infrastructure to cater to the needs of the vast majority of the students of the country.

Needs of Persons with Disabilities (PwD) and Students from Socioeconomically Deprived Backgrounds Forsaken

The policy expresses at various points its concern for the students of the socioeconomically deprived sections. However, the measures only amount to providing opportunities for the handful, while denying them to others. Point 6.16 (GoI 2020: 27–28)[8] provides for fee waivers and scholarships for 'talented' and 'meritorious' students, thus creating a category of students for whom there would be no fee waivers. The policy skillfully evades the need of creating and expanding the educational infrastructure so as to enable access to quality education for all.

Further, the need to develop infrastructure is de-emphasized in point 6.19 which stresses the need for a change in school culture (ibid.: 29).[9] The purported aim is to produce empowered individuals by sensitizing the school staff and students towards the notions of 'equity, inclusion, and the respect, dignity and privacy of all persons'. How the lofty notions of 'equity' are to be ingrained without even ensuring equal access to quality education for all remains unstated.

Likewise, for persons with disabilities (PwD), among whom a large majority belong to socioeconomically deprived sections, no concrete measures have been proposed. The quality of education for the PwD requires dedicated funds for their special needs and it is very likely that the government will transfer all the responsibilities to the NGOs or will simply make no efforts to put up basic infrastructure to ensure access to education as the policy does not set a timeline. Also, PwD students and their parents need to be active participants in the execution of any policy aimed at them. But there is no mechanism in the policy for consultation with the stakeholders at the level of the school to ensure the specific concerns and interests of PwD students.

The teachers and fellow students play an important role in empowering PwD students throughout their academic life. By advocating distance learning and schooling through NIOS, the policy contradicts the Rights of Persons with Disabilities (RPwD) Act that recommends disabled students to be educated along with students without disabilities.

Importantly, while NEP 2020 will enhance unequal access to quality school education and efface completely the imprint of common schooling from the country's educational policy framework, it will also further consolidate the rampant inequality in access to quality higher education. Let us turn to the existing realities of hierarchy and unequal access in higher education.

The Issue of Inequality in School Education and Access to Quality Public-Funded Higher Education

It has long been a liberal assumption that one of the primary purposes of university courses is to train students into becoming broad-minded, tolerant and self-reliant citizens. While this assumption continues to prevail, the vast majority of students and parents seek higher education as it is seen to enhance employability. The same is observed by the Committee to Advise on Renovation and Rejuvenation of Higher Education (2009), chaired by Professor Yashpal:

> As more youngsters from different segments of society enter the universities, they look at higher education as a means to transcend the class barriers. Consequently, university education is no longer viewed as a good in itself, but also as the stepping stone into a higher orbit of the job market, where the student expects a concrete monetary return. (GoI 2009)

Nevertheless, the existing dual system of education, that is, private schools coexisting with public schools, has led to the strengthening of the hold of privileged students even in elite higher education institutions such as central universities and technology and management institutes like IITs and IIMs. Meanwhile, the majority of students from lower classes are pushed into second-grade and poorly funded regional universities and colleges, B-grade private institutes and open and distance learning (ODL) institutions run by public-funded universities. It also needs to be remembered that the majority of youth is pushed out of formal higher education altogether. The premier public-funded institutions which are liberally funded by the government stand in contrast to the run-down second-tier regional universities and fund-starved ODL institutions. The premier institutions nurture a culture of exclusivity by maintaining a limited number of seats that are easily monopolized by privileged sections of the country's youth. While these students gain quality, subsidized higher education, scores of students who are products of the government school system are compelled to pay full tuition fees in ODL institutions and skyrocketing fees of B-grade private institutes (John 2020).

How exactly premier public-funded institutions exclude marginalized students can be gauged by admission policies of universities such as Delhi University (DU) and Jawaharlal Nehru University (JNU). At DU, every year, about 3 lakh students apply for admission. However, with seats in regular colleges being around 70,000, almost 2.5 lakh students are denied admission. A majority of the students who are denied admission to the regular colleges of DU comprise students who have passed out of regular government schools. These students are compelled to take admission to DU's

School of Open Learning which is an ODL institution or the Indira Gandhi National Open University (IGNOU), the largest open university in India.

A university like JNU has of course often been showcased as a model for a more inclusive admission policy. It has long been seen as following a progressive policy of awarding deprivation points to students coming from backward districts, wards of Kashmiri migrants, female and transgender candidates. The said policy has apparently led to the diversification of the composition of university students. According to the 49th Annual Report 2018–19,[10] of the total 7,821 students in JNU, 1,147, 600 and 2,565 are from Scheduled Caste (SC), Scheduled Tribe (ST) and Other Backward Classes (OBC) categories, respectively. This trend has been hailed by some commentators as a positive development which has brought the hitherto marginalized into the mainstream and has changed the political discourse in JNU (Ranjan 2016; A. Kumar 2014a). However, despite the achievement of diversity in student intake, the JNU admission policy remains ridden by class blindness – a crucial blind spot in its envisioning and defining of 'deprivation'.

According to the JNU Admission Policy and Procedure, 2020–21,[11] Deprivation Points are awarded to candidates residing in Quartile 1 and Quartile 2 districts of the country;[12] the districts have been categorized based on their literacy status, productivity per hectare and proportion of workers engaged in non-agricultural work. These points are also awarded to wards of Kashmiri migrants, female and transgender candidates. These points are awarded to the candidates in addition to the reservation quota earmarked for them by the central government. This policy compensates a candidate for her/his deprived conditions, so that s/he may be able to attend the university. However, the policy remains oblivious to certain basic structural class-based factors behind unequal access to quality school education.

Looking closely at the categorization of districts into Quartile 1 and Quartile 2, we can find that the conditions in these backward districts are far from the same for everyone. For example, Darbhanga, which is included in the list of Quartile 1 districts, has some well-equipped private schools, which charge exorbitant fees to their students. These schools have facilities not only for different sports but boast of providing their students with an 'all-round development', which include music and swimming classes. Now, the students from these schools, though studying in backward areas do not share any of the deprivations that students from government schools have to suffer from in these same areas. Even, the students from state-run Kendriya Vidyalayas (KVs), Sainik Schools and Jawahar Navodaya Vidyalayas (JNVs) in these areas receive an education, which is way beyond the means of labouring masses of these areas. The people sending their wards to these private schools and elite government schools are the elites of these areas, and the majority among them are lawyers, government officers, clerks, big shopkeepers, rich farmers, contractors, etc.

The students residing in forward areas and excluded from the deprivation points list have to face far worse conditions in the government schools, in contrast to private school students of backward areas. Let us take as an example a Government Senior Secondary School in Badarpur in Delhi, which can be taken as a paradigm for the situation in government schools in forward areas (which obviously do not include KVs, JNVs and Sainik schools). Now, this school in Badarpur has none of the facilities that a private school student in a backward area enjoys. The students here are fortunate if ever the government employs the required number of teachers. Needless to say, the government actively ignores the needs of these students. Even if these students try to fill the gap by studying harder, their efforts can never amount to much in the JNU entrance examinations, where elite candidates from backward areas easily outperform them. However, sadly, this is not counted as a deprivation which is to be compensated for with deprivation points in the JNU entrance examinations. Thus, the model of deprivation points has allowed the urban and rural elites of various regions to monopolize the seats in the institution which is otherwise celebrated for 'fuse[ing] excellence with non-elitist character' (Joshi and Srinivas 2019).

Complementing such skewed admission policies in premier institutions is the glaring phenomenon of informalization of education through the ODL institutions, which is related to the existing policies and which the NEP 2020 seeks to nurture. It is known that a large section of the population in metropolitan cities comprises the labouring masses. The students from deprived working-class and lower-middle-class families do not get admission to the premier seats of learning that are located in these cities, such as Delhi University, Mumbai University, Calcutta University, etc. Most of the students passing out of class 12 from regular government schools in these metropolitan cities have to necessarily get admitted in ODL institutions of the dual-mode premier universities or the open universities, as they are denied seats in regular courses due to very high cut-offs and a limited number of seats.

The idea of private study/self-study through radio talk shows and correspondence courses was first mooted in the First Five-Year Plan. Though it was not immediately implemented, the Kothari Committee recommended that distance education be imparted to the large section of students who could not avail of a regular college education. The recommendation was first implemented by Delhi University, where the Bachelor of Arts course began to be offered in the correspondence mode in the School of Correspondence Courses and Continuing Education. Subsequently, the Kothari Commission (1964–66) drew attention to the pilot experiment in DU and recommended that by 1986, at least a third of all students could be enrolled in a non-formal alternative system of higher education offered through correspondence courses and evening colleges (John 2020). The establishment of open universities and the correspondence department in the regular mode universities over the years had provided a boost to the informalization of education on an unprecedented level. According to the Distance Education Council (now District Education Bureau), by 2005, the percentage of students in distance education was approximately 20 per cent of the total students enrolled in higher education. It has increased even further in the last decade. IGNOU, in fact, has seen an increase of 248 per cent in the enrolment of SC students and 172 per cent in the enrolment of ST students (Gohain 2020). With the NEP 2020, which is building on the actual policies of successive governments of promoting informalization in higher education, it will be the future of these students more than anyone else that will be in jeopardy.

Looking at the skewed admission policies of the premier public-funded higher education institutions, one can easily surmise the bitter irony in that the less privileged who are products of up to twelve years of government schooling are precisely the ones excluded from quality higher education imparted in the regular mode of public-funded universities. The educational inequality that the mass of students inherit from regular government schools paves the way for the denial of education to them in the premier public-funded higher education institutions. On the other hand, wealthy students passing out of elite private schools and armed with privilege and 'good marks' end up outpacing government school students in securing seats in premier universities such as DU and JNU; thereby easily transitioning from top-quality education in private schools to affordable, quality education offered in the premium public-funded universities (John 2020).

Conclusion

The educational apartheid which has been bred by the policies of successive post-colonial governments in India has drawn little criticism from the critics who vociferously denounce the current education policy and who have been critical of the privatization of education. It is ironic that the issue of privatization of education institutions at the school and higher levels has garnered criticism, but the pervading inequality in school education which paves the way for differential access to higher education institutions has been largely ignored. Such a dubious stance on the issue of inequality has only served to give root to the impression that the early post-colonial ruling elite, who were thought of carrying forward the legacy of the anti-colonial struggle, were largely benign in their motivations, and the rot has only set in post the neoliberal policies which were brought in the 1990s.

Indeed, in this vein, it has been argued by some that the current unequal structure of the education systems in the country has been a result of neoliberal reforms which were ushered in India in the early 1990s. Scholars published in the edited volume *Education, State, and Market: Anatomy of Neoliberal Impact* (R. Kumar 2014b) provide a backdrop of changes which contextualizes the neoliberal assault on education. The editor of the volume emphasizes the boost that the neoliberal policies of the self-regulated market and the diminished role of the state have given to the dismantling of the public education system in India. This has been achieved by eliminating the notions of social justice and of education being a public good. It has been followed by the commodification of education and the closing of 'debates on a Common School System' and even the 'possibility of equality in elementary education or higher education' (ibid.).

Such analyses ignore the intimate *historical* connection of education policies with the segmented labour market which has perpetuated the elitist bias against quality mass education and has been a factor in denying the masses equality in education since the colonial era. The education system in the country has evolved hierarchically even prior to the so-called neoliberal phase and contributes to the reproduction of labour for a deeply segmented job market. While a large section of society equipped with primary education remains tied to the basic subsistence labour and extraction work, a minority with secondary (including vocational) education pursues simple processing, and a minuscule section armed with elite education in private schools and premier universities lands well-paying jobs in research-intensive industries with a large science and technology components, and management and the highly specialized education sectors (John 2013). Thus, the hierarchical system only reproduces the class structure and inequality which prevails in society (Bowles and Gintis 2011).

Moreover, glossing over the fact that the anti-colonial leadership and post-colonial ruling elite were largely dismissive of quality mass education only serves to obfuscate why the response of the general public towards the new education policy has been muted. The faint response can only be comprehended by locating the issue of normalization towards inequality in education that has been achieved over the decades by education policies, and the fleeting criticism that these policies have garnered from so-called critics. So-called critics from the mainstream left or the Dalit-Bahujan movement conveniently ignore the inequality at the school level which has been instrumental in creating a hierarchy of 'merits' that pits the disadvantaged against the privileged few – a process that has simply allowed the privileged to easily monopolize access to higher education. One can understand the blind spot in their criticisms as the majority of these 'critics' are themselves largely products of elite private schools. However, critics and intellectuals from even marginalized backgrounds who denounce inequality have no qualms about sending their children to private schools (Hunt 2014: 135), now that the aim of establishing the 'common school system' has been endlessly deferred. In this respect, the Bengali Dalit writer, Manoranjan Byapari, has rightly observed an emerging gap between *dalitta* (Dalit-ness) and *daridrata* (poverty), due to the creation of a new class of privileged out of the creamy layers of the backward castes, who are oblivious of the real conditions and needs of the majority of their brethren (Byapari 2018; Chakrabarti 2019).

In the bid to criticize the new NEP 2020, it then becomes imperative that the intimate link that education policies have had with the prevailing structure of hierarchy in society and their role in perpetuating such hierarchy, be emphasized. The elitist class bias of the anti-colonial leadership and post-colonial regimes also needs to be unmasked so as to dismantle the dubious criticisms which spring from blind spots, and to surmount the challenges posed by the new policy.

Notes

[1] *Mahratta*, 22 March 1891, Editorial.
[2] *Mahratta*, 16 March 1890, p. 2
[3] *Mahratta*, 15 May 1881, p. 3
[4] There are varied opinions on the date of the said strike, with some dating it to 1915.
[5] CABE was first established in the year 1920 but was dissolved later. It again came into existence in the year 1935. It is the highest and the oldest advisory board for governments in the educational domain, available at https://www.icbse.com.
[6] Kendriya Vidyalayas were set up in 1963 to provide education to the well-paid employees of central government and armed forces. Navodaya Vidyalayas were set up in 1986 to provide education to the rural students with facilities at par with the best residential schools. Both of these have gone on to exclude the students from urban and agrarian poor backgrounds and have thus become examples of centres of exclusion and facilities for the elite.
[7] 'Enrollment In Delhi Government Schools Declining', available at https://www.ndtv.com/education/delhi-government-schools-enrolment-declining2082698, accessed on 24 October 2020.
[8] The point states: 'Within SEDGs, and with respect to all the above policy points, special attention will be given to reduce the disparities in the educational development of Scheduled Castes and Scheduled Tribes. As a part of the efforts to enhance participation in school education, special hostels in dedicated regions, bridge courses, and financial assistance through fee waivers and scholarships will be offered to talented and meritorious students from all SEDGs on a larger scale, especially at the secondary stage of education, to facilitate their entry into higher education.'

9 The point states: 'What is also required is a change in school culture. All participants in the school education system, including teachers, principals, administrators,
counsellors, and students, will be sensitized to the requirements of all students, the
notions of inclusion and equity, and the respect, dignity, and privacy of all persons.
Such an educational culture will provide the best pathway to help students become
empowered individuals who, in turn, will enable society to transform into one
that is responsible towards its most vulnerable citizens. Inclusion and equity will
become a key aspect of teacher education (and training for all leadership, administrative, and other positions in schools); efforts will be made to recruit more high-
quality teachers and leaders from SEDGs in order to bring in excellent role models
for all students.'

10 The JNU 49th Annual Report 2018–19, available at https://www.jnu.ac.in/sites/
default/files/annual_report/49AnnualReport_Eng_0.pdf.

11 The JNU Admission Policy and Procedure 2020–21, available at https://jnu.ac.in/
admission/Admission%20Policy%20Final-2020-21.pdf.

12 The quartile list of districts is available at https://www.jnu.ac.in/adm/Quartile%20
Districts.pdf.

References

Acharya, P. (1978), 'Indigenous Vernacular Education in Pre-British Era: Traditions And
Problems', *Economic and Political Weekly,* vol. 13, no. 48, p. 1981, pp. 1983–88.

——— (1995), 'Bengali "Bhadralok" and Educational Development in 19th Century Bengal',
Economic and Political Weekly, vol. 30, no. 13, pp. 670–73.

Bhatty, K. (2014), 'Review of Elementary Education Policy in India: Has It Upheld the
Constitutional Objective of Equality?', *Economic and Political Weekly,* vol. 49,
nos 43–44, pp. 100–07.

Bowles, S. and H. Gintis (2011), *Schooling in Capitalist America: Educational Reform and
the Contradictions of Economic Life*, Chicago: Haymarket Books.

Byapari, M. (2018), *Interrogating My Chandal Life: An Autobiography of a Dalit*, translated
by Sipra Mukherjee, New Delhi: Sage Publications.

Central Advisory Board of Education (CABE) (1944), *Post-War Plan of Educational Development in India*, Allahabad: The Indian Press.

Chakrabarti, P. (2019), 'Rage Becomes Him: The Author Who Writes About Those with
Nothing More to Lose', available at https://https://indianexpress.com/article/
express-sunday-eye/rage-becomes-him-manoranjan-byapari-5780602/, accessed 19
October 2020.

Constable, P. (2000), 'Sitting on the School Verandah: The Ideology and Practice of
"Untouchable" Educational Protest in Late Nineteenth-Century Western India',
The Indian Economic and Social History Review, vol. 37, no. 4, pp. 383–422.

Crook, N. (1996), 'Introduction', in N. Crook, ed., *Transmission of Knowledge in South
Asia: Essays on Education, Religion, History and Politics*, Delhi: Oxford University
Press.

Dhawan, R. (2008), 'Review of Sarbani Sen, Popular Sovereignty and Democratic Transformations: The Constitution of India', *Indian Journal of Constitutional Law,* vol.
204, no. 2, pp. 204–20.

Du Bois, W.E.B. (1973), *The Education of Black People*, New York: Monthly Review Press.

Ghosh, P. (2012), *The Pioneer of Indian Renaissance, Iswar Chandra Vidyasagar: A Marxist
Evaluation*, Kolkata: Gandabi Printers and Publishers.

Gohain, M.P. (2019), 'In 9 yrs, Number of SC students at Ignou Rose by 248%, STs by
172%', available at https://timesofindia.indiatimes.com/home/education/in-9-yrs-
number-of-sc-students-at-ignou-rose-by-248-sts-by-172/articleshow/71572573.
cms, accessed 26 October 2020.

Government of India (GoI) (2009), 'Report of "The Committee to Advise on Renovation and Rejuvenation of Higher Education"' (Yashpal Committee Report), Ministry of Human Resource Development, Government of India, New Delhi, available at https://www.aicteindia.org/downloads/Yashpal-committee-report.pdf, accessed 26 October 2020.

—— (2019), 'Draft National Education Policy 2019', Ministry of Human Resource Development, Government of India, New Delhi, available at https://www.mhrd.gov.in/sites/upload_files/mhrd/files/Draft_NEP_2019_EN_Revise.pdf, accessed 23 October 2020.

—— (2020), *National Education Policy 2020*, Ministry of Human Resource Development, Government of India, New Delhi, available at https://www.mhrd.gov.in/sites/upload_files/mhrd/files/NEP_Final_English_0.pdf, accessed 23 October 2020.

Guha, R. (1982), 'On Some Aspects of the Historiography of Colonial India', in R. Guha, ed., *Subaltern Studies I: Writings on South Asian History and Society*, Delhi: Oxford University Press.

Hunt, S.B. (2014), *Hindi Dalit Literature and the Politics of Representation*, New Delhi: Routledge.

John, M. (2013), 'Critiquing Reforms in Higher Education: Understanding the 'Education Question in India', *Social Scientist*, vol. 41, nos 7–8, pp. 49–67.

—— (2016), '(De)skilling Caste: Exploring the Relationship between Caste, State Regulations and the Labour Market in Late Colonial India', in R.P. Behal and S. Bhattacharya, eds, *The Vernacularization of Labour Politics*, New Delhi: Tulika Books.

—— (2018), 'Regulating the "Half-timer" in Colonial India: Factory Legislation, Its Anomalies and Resistance', in S. Beynon-Jones and E. Grabham, eds, *Law and Time*, New Delhi: Routledge.

—— (2020), 'Online Education, The Latest Stage of Educational Apartheid', *Mainstream Weekly*, vol. 58, no. 26, available at http://mainstreamweekly.net/article9480.html, accessed 20 October 2020.

Joshi, P. and A. Srinivas (2019), 'Does JNU Combine Success and Access?', available at https://www.thehindubusinessline.com/specials/india-file/does-jnu-combine-success-and-access/article30149011.ece, accessed 20 October 2020.

Joshi, S. and B. Josh (2011), *Struggle for Hegemony in India*, New Delhi: Sage Publications.

Kumar, A. (2014a), 'Dalitbahujan Assertion on "Red Soil"', available at https://www.forwardpress.in/2014/11/dalitbahujan-assertion-on-red-soil/, accessed 23 October 2020.

Kumar, R. (2014b), 'Education, State, and Market: Anatomy of Neoliberal Impact: An Introduction', in R. Kumar, ed, *Education, State, and Market: Anatomy of Neoliberal Impact*, New Delhi: Aakar Books.

Majumdar, M. and J. Mooij (2012), 'The Marks Race: India's Dominant Education Regime and New Segmentation', in C. Sleeter, S.B. Upadhyay, A.K. Mishra and S. Kumar, eds, *School Education, Pluralism and Margnality: Comparative Perspectives*, New Delhi: Orient Blackswan.

More, S. (2019), *Memoirs of a Dalit Communist: The Many Worlds of R.B. More*, edited by Anupama Rao, New Delhi: LeftWord Books.

Moudgalya, K.M. (2015), 'Growing Influence of Coaching Classes: "Change in JEE Criteria Has Failed to Achieve the Desired Objective"', available at https://indianexpress.com/article/india/india-news-india/growing-influence-of-coachingclasses-change-in-jee-criteria-has-failed-to-achieve-the-desired-objective/#sthash.M3X3GOJm.dpuf, accessed 23 October 2020.

Nambissan, G. (2002), 'Equity in Education? The Schooling of Dalit Children in India', in G. Shah, ed., *Dalits and the State*, New Delhi: Concept Publishing Co.

National Focus Group (2007), 'Position Paper 3.7: Work and Education', New Delhi: National Council of Educational Research and Training (NCERT).

Phule, J. (2002), *Selected Writings of Jotirao Phule*, edited by G.P. Deshpande, New Delhi: LeftWord Books.

Radhika (2020), 'Dropout Rates Increasing in Classes 9 and 10 in Some States: MHRD', available at https://news.careers360.com/dropout-rates-increasing-in-classes-9-and-10-in-some-states-mhrd, accessed 24 October 2020.

Ramachandran, P. and V. Ramkumar, 2005, *Education in India*, New Delhi: National Book Trust.

Ramachandran, V.K. (2000), 'Kerala's Development Achievement and their Replicability', in G. Parayil, ed., *Kerala: The Development Experience: Reflections on Sustainability and Replicability*, London: Zed Books.

Ranjan, P. (2016), 'Bahujan Discourse Puts JNU in the Crosshairs', available at https://www.forwardpress.in/2016/02/bahujan-discourse-puts-jnu-in-the-crosshairs/, accessed 22 October 2020.

Rao, P.V. (2009), *Educating Women and Non-Brahmins as 'Loss of Nationality': Bal Gangadhar Tilak and the Nationalist Agenda in Maharashtra*, available at https://www.cwds.ac.in/wp-content/uploads/2016/09/EducatingWomen.pdf, accessed 26 October 2020.

Sadgopal, A. (2014), 'Countering Neoliberal Conception of Knowledge, Building Emancipatory Discourse: A Historical Overview of Phule–Ambedkar's Critique and Gandhian Nai Taleem', in R. Kumar, ed., *Education, State, and Market: Anatomy of Neoliberal Impact*, New Delhi: Aakar Books.

Saxena, S. (2012), 'Is Equality an Outdated Concern in Education?', *Economic and Political Weekly*, vol. 47, no. 49, pp. 61–68.

Upadhyay, S.B. (2012), 'Dalits and the Modern Education in Colonial India', in C. Sleeter, S.B. Upadhyay, A.K. Mishra and S. Kumar, eds, *School Education, Pluralism and Margnality: Comparative Perspectives*, New Delhi: Orient Blackswan.

Veeraraghavan, D. (2020), *Half a Day for Caste?: Education and Politics in Tamil Nadu, 1952–1955*, edited by A.R. Venkatachalapathy, New Delhi: LeftWord Books.

Viswanathan, G. (1989), *Masks of Conquests: Literary Study and British Rule in India*, New Delhi: Oxford University Press.

8

Construction of a State-regulated Market for Indian Higher Education Reform
A Reflection on NEP 2020

Saumen Chattopadhyay

Introduction

The policy recommendations mooted in the National Education Policy (NEP) (GoI 2020a) seek to usher in a major structural transformation in the Indian higher education sector to cater to the economic needs of the country in the context of the emerging challenges in a globalizing world. Though the Indian higher education sector is now the second largest in the world, the quality of higher education has continued to remain a source of major concern. While the implementation of the NEP poses major challenges in a federal set-up with a sub-optimal level of institutional functioning with limited resources and deeply embedded inequities, it is important to unravel the basic approach to higher education reform as encapsulated in the NEP for the purpose of understanding and appraisal.

The basic approach to higher education reform has mainly been informed by the neoliberal logic of market-based reform in major parts of the world. This involves university governance reform based on corporate principles in the form of new public management (NPM) and the construction of a regulated higher education market. This chapter seeks to understand and assess the NEP against the backdrop of this typical neoliberal approach to higher-education reform.

We begin with an appraisal of the challenges being faced in Indian higher education as identified by the NEP to understand how the proposed policy framework seeks to deal with these identified challenges.[1] We follow it up with an overview of the major policy recommendations of the NEP to understand how the accountability mechanisms have been proposed to be fixed up and what are its possible implications for academic autonomy. In the end, we attempt to trace the possible implications for the public good character of the NEP.

Challenges Facing Indian Higher Education

The Indian higher education sector has witnessed rapid growth, fuelled particularly by the increasing participation of the private sector in recent years to respond to the rising demand as indicated by the rising gross enrolment ratio (GER). In absence of rising budgetary support and unscrupulous private participation, there has not been much of an improvement in the quality of higher education.[2] However, there are a few pockets of excellence both in the set of publicly funded and privately funded higher education institutions (HEIs).

Inefficient resource utilization at the institutional level, the suboptimal scale of operation and the suffocation of academic activities due to compartmentalization and regulatory restrictions have made the higher education sector inflexible and constrained, devoid of life and energy, the Draft National Education Policy (DNEP) (GoI 2019) indicates. Universities are not vibrant as they suffer from poor governance and weak leadership. The DNEP points out that the regulatory policies have failed to be efficacious because 'Too much has been attempted to be regulated with too little effect' (GoI 2019: 205).

It is possible that the faculty might have felt demotivated due to poor infrastructure, temporary and ad hoc appointments, unfilled vacancies, heavy and unequal distribution of teaching load mostly at the undergraduate level coupled with a lack of autonomy in teaching and curriculum design. Micromanagement in the backdrop of structural deficiencies has suppressed the faculty's inherent propensity to innovate, resulting in demotivation and eventual dissipation of energy, the DNEP (GoI 2019) argues. As a way of illustration, the DNEP points out unhesitatingly that setting the target of academic output for faculty as required by the UGC regulations has in fact resulted in substandard research publications, particularly in fake journals.[3] The performance-based appraisal system (PBAS) template which amounts to standardization involves straitjacketing of regulatory intervention because it ignores diversity in the faculty community, differences across disciplines and the university mandates (Das and Chattopadhyay 2014). An analysis of the API (academic performance indicators) can throw some light on why there has been a proliferation of fake journals. The computation of the API allows for several possible ways to score the requisite number of points. Each path involves different levels of costs in terms of the time teachers can allocate and the uncertainty they face. Constrained by time and capability, a teacher chooses a particular combination of academic activities to maximize scores even well beyond the minimum number of points required by the API template. Publication in good and reputed journals takes time with high rates of rejection, comparatively speaking.[4] The instrumental rationality manifests in terms of a high propensity to choose the path with minimum time costs, given capabilities which are generally associated with poor-quality publications.

The process of appointment of the faculty and their career progression has been subverted by vested interests and unwarranted interventions from external agencies. Seniority rather than performance has unfortunately been invoked in case of deciding faculty promotion (GoI 2019: 258). At the same time, doing justice to the ground reality in Indian higher education, the DNEP takes note of the fact that political interference has rendered a serious blow to the autonomy of the university. The prevalence of corrupt practices, particularly in financial matters, has raised doubts about the way the institutions are governed, and, in particular, the manner in which core activities of teaching and research are carried out.

Since regulation is an imperative to ensure uniformity and achieve certain policy objectives, the important policy question is the nature and extent of such regulatory interventions.

Higher Education Reform Policy Shifts

Let us look at the basic approach of the NEP to reform the higher education sector. To deal with this issue, we need to have a closer look at the policy shift the neoliberals advocate. The policy shift in higher education can be viewed and explained from an economic perspective in terms of two concepts of efficiencies: technical and allocative. The former pertains to the reform of university governance, while the latter refers to the construction of a quasi-market for higher education to operate under the supervision of a regulatory authority (Chattopadhyay 2009). This policy shift entails a transition from internal accountability to the various forms of external accountability with concomitant transformation in the scope and forms of academic freedom. This shift is based on the assumption that academic freedom is generally abused by self-interest-driven teachers, resulting in suboptimal performance of faculty, and consequently the poor performance of universities (Olssen, Codd and O'Neill 2004). Kehm (2014) points out two very important factors which are also responsible for policy shifts, one is the standardization of research output, and two, an absence of a well-defined educational production function which seeks to describe and relate the input in the form of the teachers, students and output of the universities. This weak relationship between input and output which is essentially indicative of technical inefficiency is primarily attributable to the suboptimal performance of the teachers who are central to the functioning of a university. This is tantamount to the abuse of academic freedom. If the teachers, the main inputs are self-optimizing agents, the fixing of teachers' accountability requires quantification and standardization of teachers' output and incentivization of teachers' delivery in the spheres of teaching and research. This approach is typically akin to new public management (NPM), a form of governance reform which has gained currency the world over. There are mainly two components of NPM: quantification of output without which accountability measures cannot be installed, and the introduction of an audit culture which seeks to evaluate faculty performance (Marginson 2008) other than incentivization.

In a way, the realization of technical efficiency requires that the universities are made to function within a quasi-market which is a regulated one. The neoliberals, therefore, focus on market construction to achieve both the efficiencies that entail the construction of a regulated quasi-higher education market to achieve allocative efficiency and realize technical efficiency to be supported by NPM-type governance reform for two reasons. It is claimed that a market-like ambience fosters competition, which becomes compelling for universities and faculty to deliver their best and achieve efficiency in the use of resources and deliver quality in the process. At the same time, the market gives choices to the participants and upholds the principle of sovereignty, both for the students as well as the HEIs.

Though the neoliberal approach to higher education reform identifies the poor performance of public-funded universities as the core issue, they offer a different solution. They argue that this 'government failure' can be overcome without there being any need for market construction which has adverse implications for equity and excellence, suitably defined keeping in mind the public good character of higher education. The crux of university governance reform relies on the assumption that the teachers are trustworthy and not typical self-interest-driven individuals. Whether this assumption about human behaviour violates reality is a very big question. Reposing faith in the teachers to be intrinsically motivated and deliver their best independent of monitoring and provision of incentives to restore optimal university functioning is contested by the neoliberals.

The other contention is that the market construction is a hindrance to a public good character for higher education. It is inimical to the attainment of quality too. In India, poor governance of publicly funded HEIs is indeed true for the majority (Chandra 2017). Hence, the focus should be on repairing and improving the functioning of the publicly funded colleges and universities to overcome government failure which is claimed to be intrinsic to government-funded institutions. However, this requires increased public funding to ensure a 'level playing field' for the HEIs, institutional autonomy and a shared governance structure based on trust and cooperation. The opponents of the neoliberals believe that teachers are essentially trustworthy and motivated if they are so empowered and liberated from their work-place constraints. Market failure is a serious problem because it results in suboptimal funding and an uncertain impact on quality, as exemplified by the Indian higher education scenario. Most importantly, the market makes education inaccessible to the socioeconomically disadvantaged in society. Further, in the neoliberal world, as a university is run more as a factory and education gets commodified, the very purpose of education is undermined and devalued.

Despite this contention, policymakers the world over have shown a clear preference for the neoliberal approach because overcoming government failure is projected to be more daunting than facilitating market construction and privatization. While fiscal constraint is ubiquitous, there do exist good publicly funded HEIs where teachers are driven by high self-esteem and zeal, irrespective of competition and incentives which is the traditional and liberal conceptualization of academia.

Against this background, we now look at the factors behind the policy shifts witnessed the world over and examine to what extent this is reflected in the NEP.

NEP Proposal for Reconfiguration of the Regulatory Structure

We look at the institutions and participants, that is, the HEIs and the students and how they collectively conjure up a market to analyse the higher education system. We begin with the regulatory policy instruments and the institutions, followed by an analysis of the two sides of the market, the education providers and the students. As expected of the market participants, the two sides are analysed in terms of the extent and the nature of freedom that they are bestowed with.

Based on the diagnosis of the deficiencies in the Indian higher education system, the central theme of the entire policy framework hinges, as expected, on the issue of autonomy of teachers and universities, and the institutionalization of accountability within the university and across universities in the higher education system as a whole.[5]

The Higher Education Commission of India (HECI) (NEP 18.3) will be the overarching institution to coordinate the functioning of a set of four institutions for four important dimensions of policy interventions for the HEIs, blurring the divide between public and private, general and professional, and the centre and the states. These are the National Higher Education Regulatory Council (NHERC), the National Accreditation Council (NAC), the Higher Education Grants Council (HEGC) and the General Education Council (GEC).[6]

In view of the inefficacy of the erstwhile regulatory intervention, the NHERC will regulate in a 'light but tight' manner with a focus on good governance and transparency to ensure financial probity (NEP 18.3). The National Assessment Accreditation Council (NAAC) will be renamed as NAC, the National Accreditation Council, which will be a 'meta-accrediting body' to be entrusted with the responsibility of developing an eco-system of accreditation agencies in view of the large size of the Indian higher education system (NEP 18.4). The HEGC (NEP 18.5) will assume the onerous responsibility of allocation of grants based on the requirements of the HEIs based on their institutional development plans (IDPs). To ensure fair and equitable distribution, a set of indicators may have to be developed later by the HEGC. The fourth institution is the GEC, whose responsibility will lie with the learning outcomes and quality of education (NEP 18.6) to set academic standards. Professional bodies, such as the Indian Council of Agricultural Research (ICAR) and the National Council of Teacher Education (NCTE) will operate like Professional Standard Setting Bodies (PSSBs) as members of the GEC. The task of the GEC will be to formulate a National Higher Education Qualification Framework (NHEQF) to synchronize with the NSQE for seamless integration of vocational education into higher education. This would require setting up a framework to facilitate credit transfer and equivalences through NHEQF.

Institutional Autonomy

One major policy recommendation of the NEP is to give the HEIs the freedom to offer multidisciplinary courses. Autonomy is viewed as essential to rejuvenate higher education, foster creativity and innovations and achieve excellence. The system of affiliation of colleges should be discontinued which makes all the institutions independent. If this is implemented, it would constitute a serious step because it would involve a major restructuring of the system as a whole. In a federal set-up, with so many HEIs, this will virtually be a shaking change.

Students' Sovereignty

The proposal to set up the Academic Bank of Credits (ABC) (NEP 11.9) (GoI 2021) and promotion of online courses (which was raised from 20 per cent to 40 per cent of the credits per semester), which can be opted for from the platform Study Webs of Active-Learning for Young Aspiring Minds (SWAYAM), was notified a couple of days after the NEP was unveiled (GoI 2020b). Online courses such as Massive Open Online Courses (MOOCs) give students more freedom to choose courses from e-learning platforms with the additional flexibility of earning credits over an extended period. This has the potential to infuse competition in the market by expanding students' choices, which will surely impact the autonomy of teachers and institutions. This may lead to a compromise with the rigour of courses and scholarships as students may choose easier options to earn credits and increase grades. This can restrict the scope for realizing the vision of a university department. The issue is not one of denial of freedom to students. Instead, the issue is whether courses will be chosen with the purpose of maximization of grades and/or minimization of efforts at the expense of learning and scholarship, and how much freedom the students can be bestowed with. Nixon, Scullion and Molesworth (2011) observe this in the context of the UK. If universities are funded directly by the HEGC based on the IDP, the impact on teachers' autonomy will remain comparatively limited.

The ABC and Rising Dependence on Online Education

The institutionalization of the ABC seeks to help in the consolidation of credits earned and store them digitally in an account by the students who are argued to be inclined to learn from 'anywhere and anytime'. This will be made feasible because the UGC circulars have given clear signals to continue with online education which was initially thought to be only a panacea to tide over the disruption caused by the pandemic in the operation of the HEIs with policy support from the NEP 2020. This, in fact, will serve two major purposes – one to nurture and promote the culture of multi-disciplinarity as advocated in the NEP as students can now opt for courses they desire to pursue from other institutions and government-promoted e-learning platforms, and two, to enable the students respond to the changing demand for skill in the job market by choosing relevant courses to enhance their employability. Some private universities have already begun to allow their students to opt for courses which are offered by globally recognized e-platforms such as Coursera and Udemy. As ABC gains prominence in the Indian landscape, the possible implications will manifest in the weakening of teacher-student relations and therefore undermining the emotional connection between the university and the students. Informed decision-making is difficult given the students' tendency to maximize grades by choosing softer options and uncertainty over course content and the efficacy of online instructions. However, the most important fallout on the higher education system would be the eventual discontinuation of many of the courses due to the fall in the number of students leading to even closure of some departments/centres in some colleges and universities over time.

Besides giving freedom to the participants and setting up a regulator structure to regulate, continuation with online education, change in the funding and the function envisaged for the GEC are going to foster the creation of the higher education market.

Online Education Facilitates the Construction of an Education Market

Online education redefines the concept of space and time associated with university functioning, essentially by converting teaching which is in the nature of a service to a digital product which can be reproduced at a minimal cost, stored digitally and shared through the virtual medium with those who are interested in opting for these courses. The four walls of the classroom are transcended with ease, and teaching becomes asynchronous as students can join the lecture from the world over. Policymakers promote online teaching because it saves costs while increasing enrolment and improving quality. It fosters internationalization at both home and abroad.

These structural changes in the university system in the wake of rising digitalization are being assisted by the exercise of freedom the students are bestowed with by the policymakers. The ABC as proposed by the NEP 2020 is an example. The ABC will create conditions for marketization. This is expected to facilitate the choice of the students who constitute the consumer side of the market. The students can now opt for courses across various streams and universities, and in the future, it may be possible to exercise this choice at the international level. The students can now enter and exit academic institutions to study at their convenience to respond to the job market opportunities. All these changes facilitate the construction of a higher education market. Segmentation in the market and differentiation in the quality of teaching which are typical of a higher education market get reduced as online education spreads and quality is reproduced digitally. Arguably, there is a compromise with quality in online teaching due to limited interaction in the classroom. The latest advances in technology are recreating the classroom to give a feel of real-time experience. Campus life is affected which, in turn, can affect the self-formation of the students and their consequent contribution to society and weaken the role the teacher and students' unions play. The producers are also keen to broaden their operations in a market where regulatory interventions will become increasingly less but be tightly enforced as indicated by the NEP 2020. The courses offered in the teaching programmes are being unbundled, and in the process, it infuses competition in the market. The universities are tying up with the global e-platforms like Udemy and Coursera to expose to their students the latest developments in the field of technology which is in demand.

Proposed System of University Governance and University Accountability

The HEIs will be made accountable on the basis of their IDPs, which will be made public for transparency and public accountability (GoI

2022d). The IDPs would reveal the university's plan to achieve educational and research outcomes, the quality of those outcomes, financial and human resource development plans, designing of course curriculum and adoption of innovative practices (NEP 12.3, 13.6). The HEIs will have to compete for funds for research with the National Research Foundation (NRF) (GoI 2019: 269–70) and the HEGC. A fast-track tenure system will be instituted to reward select faculty for achieving excellence in their academic engagements, which will be based on predetermined criteria to incentivize and encourage the faculty to achieve more.[7] The DNEP lamented the absence of incentives for faculty who demonstrated outstanding performance. This will be a clear deviation from the existing system. This would require the HEIs to have the liberty to deviate from the recommended payscale as approved by the UGC.[8] It will create divisions within the faculty and erode collegiality because faculty will be differently treated depending on their 'high impact research' which is not really applicable to the humanities and social sciences.

The question is how these policy recommendations would affect the conduct of teaching and research by the faculty or their academic freedom, which is considered to be the hallmark of academia.

Proposed Reform in Higher Education Funding

There are three main issues in the debate on university funding in the international context which are relevant for India too: to decide both the quantum of public funding and the mode of funding along with the issue of the purpose of funding, primarily teaching and/or research. The NEP 2020 has classified higher education as a quasi-public good which means both the public and private sectors have a legitimate role to play, and in connection with this, it is heartening to note that the NEP proposes to raise the total budget for the education sector to 6 per cent of GDP over a period of ten years. In all likelihood, this long-standing demand is unlikely to materialize as the concern for fiscal crunch will continue to pose a challenge for the centre and the states and more so in the post-Covid era.

There are two sources of public funding from the union government, the HEGC as mentioned above and the National Research Foundation (NRF) as the sole body for funding research. Allocation of funds among the HEIs would be made based on their institutional development plan (IDP) duly approved by the Board of Governors (BoGs). Though the fund allocation is to be based on certain criteria presumably to ensure uniformity among the HEIs, there is likely to be a gradual shift from input-based funding to output/performance-based funding as well. Over time, delivery by the HEI as per the submitted IDP will come into play in the future for the allocation of funds. While this is likely to avoid the adverse effects of a typical new public management (NPM)-based university governance, the implementation of this proposal would require reconstitution of the university governance structure which is a daunting exercise. Given the paucity of funds for higher education, which is a perennial feature for almost every government across the globe, competition among the institutions for maximizing their share in public funding will intensify.

The NEP has suggested three categories of HEIs: the research university, the teaching university and the degree-granting autonomous colleges (ACs). Since funds for research are to be allocated mostly on a competitive basis, the best of the universities are likely to appropriate a chunk of the research funds. While this categorization may be indicative, the NEP desires that the teaching universities and ACs strive to acquire the status of the research university. However, given the scarcity of time in view of the institutional mandates for doing research and research funds, achieving this progression in practice will be very difficult. In the process, this will also impede the career progression of a majority of the faculty employed in the teaching universities and ACs. The overall impact would be the accentuation of the existing hierarchy in the higher education sector. This would partially nullify the benefits accruing to the socioeconomically disadvantaged groups arising out of the massification of Indian higher education as the students from the top-ranking HEIs stand to gain in the job market as higher education credentials become 'positional goods'.

The Scope for Academic Autonomy and the Role of External Accountability

While academic autonomy will be given albeit at the basic level of faculty engagement as indicated by the NEP 2020, the actual scope and nature of institutional autonomy have to be understood to fathom the scope and extent of faculty autonomy. The institutional autonomy will manifest in terms of the offering of courses and establishing collaboration with academic partners across the universities. Institutional autonomy is granted under the assumption that it would be followed by institutional reorganization (Kehm 2014). We need to look deeper into the issues of IDP (GoI 2022d).

The concept of teacher and institutional autonomy as defined and envisaged in the NEP appears to be a chimaera. What is so distinguishing about the IDPs is that faculty would collectively decide to deliver within a period of time a certain quantum and quality of output (ibid.). In a way, this is an example of self-determination not only by the faculty but by the entire university community including students and staff, as opposed to the typical neoliberal managerial practices where the faculty are required to conform to the template designed by the regulatory authority in their academic activities. But once decided, the IDPs would become binding for the faculty in particular and the university leadership. The release of funds by the HEGC in subsequent periods would be made contingent upon the IDPs and their realization. If this proposal is accepted, it would mark a departure from the existing system of university governance and fund allocation among the HEIs. This is a bottom-up approach at the formative stage, and once it is approved, it will be imperative on the part of faculty to deliver as per their assurances as incorporated in the IDPs formulated.

The faculty perforce will take into account while planning their future activities and deliverables that financial support from the HEGC will be ultimately determined in a highly competitive situation, as all the HEIs compete for funds given the perennial budget constraint. The faculty will not, therefore, have the necessary freedom in a broader sense. Teacher autonomy will remain restricted to what they want to do rather than in terms of the quantification of their academic output.

The university community and the university leader, the vice-chancellor, will be reporting to the Board of Governors (BoG). The assessment of university performance will remain vested with the NAC. There are two kinds of grading: the binary accreditation (BA) and the graded accreditation (GA) will be implemented over time after the HEIs acquire the capability to function like a self-governing institution (ibid.). As alerted in the DNEP 2019, if an institution fails to live up to the promises made in the IDP by 2030, the institution will be shut down (GoI 2019: 328; NEP 18.4).

In addition, the HEIs have to compete for research grants to the NRF. This is crucial as research output determines the performance of a university.[9]

As stressed by Bhushan (2019), building the capabilities of faculty should be a prerequisite for exercising 'agency freedom'. Exercise of academic freedom defined in terms of independence of thoughts and utterances requires a culture, tolerance of the state, and a healthy and vibrant ambience. As Sundar (2018) and Apoorvanand, ed. (2018) have pointed out, this is sadly missing in the case of India.

As Bruneau (2015) argued, merely asking faculty to furnish details of their performance is not to constrict their academic freedom. The neoliberal attack to erode academic freedom begins with an emphasis on the issue of efficiency, effectivity and the imposition of the concept of what quality is. Conceptualization of quality by the NAC and the influence of ranking parameters adopted by the Quacquarelli Symonds (QS) and Times Higher Education (THE) will affect faculty behaviour in their conduct of research and its dissemination.

The institutions will be given freedom in academic, administrative and financial matters to pursue their mandates in an unfettered manner. Although the institutions will be subject to compliance requirements of the regulatory interventions by the institutions as proposed, the salience of freedom remains important and vital in the proposed system.

In research, academic autonomy will remain limited due to both the inadequacy and mode of funding.

In teaching, there will be options to diversify in terms of the offering of courses, but the market forces to be unleashed by the ABC will also acquire the potential to interfere with the faculty. It may be noted that faculty autonomy in the true sense of the term can only be exercised under input-based public funding which is adequate. As new sources of funding are explored, academic autonomy will be interfered with and this is expected to percolate down to the faculty.

The Role of Leadership

The emphasis on leadership in the NEP is an admission of the fact that the HEIs will be operating in a competitive scenario, nationally and globally, where universities are to be led by the vice-chancellor. The 'executivization' of university administration implies strengthening the hierarchical structure and concomitant dilution of faculty autonomy at the horizontal level. Stress on leadership is understandable as the HEIs are made accountable to the NAC and other institutions like the HEGC in a highly competitive situation where even the exercise of 'agency freedom' would remain circumscribed. Kehm (2014) has described this tendency of involving many actors to fix accountability as multi-level governance in the European context.

As mentioned earlier, the NEP recommends that the nature of regulatory intervention would be 'light but tight'. The basic approach is to focus on only a few aspects of a university's functioning, including transparency in financial probity and various university processes involved. This approach to regulation has to be analysed in the context of the prevalent scheme of Graded Autonomy (GoI 2018) which seeks to categorize HEIs into three categories depending on their NAAC score and/or world ranking. Category-I institutions, being the top-performing ones, are being assured a considerable amount of autonomy, whereas Category-III HEIs have been placed under the strict enforcement of regulations ostensibly to ensure the best utilization of their resources, human and financial, and to curb abuse of freedom to do better.[10] Category-II represents a blend of regulation and autonomy. It remains to be seen to what extent Category-I HEIs capitalize on the freedom assured in the scheme of graded autonomy.

The Envisaged Role of the Private in the Restructuring of Higher Education Reform

Curbing of Commercial Practices

There is a clear message to the private sector that commercial practices are best avoided as they are detrimental to the attainment of quality and what education and universities stand for (NEP 18.2). The NEP (GoI 2019: 404–05) urges enhancing private funding through corporate social responsibility and philanthropic contributions. This is indicative of the apprehension towards unleashing the forces of market commercial in nature to drive the higher education system towards the realization of the mythical concepts of efficiency and quality. The big question is whether transparency in financial probity and monitoring by regulatory institutions will effectively curb commercial practices. Manipulation of accounts is often resorted to with impunity in the privately funded higher education system to siphon out profits (Chattopadhyay 2009).

In contrast, the NEP 2020 seeks to construct a state-regulated market for higher education which appears to be different from a typical neoliberal market-based reform in at least three respects. One, the NEP does not approve of commercialization and instead, it argues for responsible private sector participation funded by philanthropy and CSR which are driven by non-profit motives along with the urge to increase budgetary allocation for education; two, reform of university governance is not typically akin to NPM which is based on corporate principles with adverse effects on faculty autonomy and quality and three, channeling of public funds based on university performances rather than providing financial assistance to the students to help them pay high fees which are fixed near to the recovery levels. However, the approach of NEP remains one of market construction as evident from three policy initiatives which support market construction: setting up an overarching regulatory framework and giving freedom to two sides of the market in their decision-making, the students through the ABC and the HEIs to evolve as autonomous institutions. To conclude, if public funding is not adequately augmented, fostering competition among the HEIs based on ABC and competitive funding for teaching and research, it will be unfair to expect the HEIs to compete and survive under the system of binary accreditation in the absence of a level playing field. This is, however, not to deny that there is no need for consolidation, particularly in view of a large number of small HEIs as indicated in the Draft NEP 2019 and giving autonomy to the students and institutions.

The recommendations made by the NEP for the reform of university governance are largely in line with the neoliberal vision. The neoliberal elements appear in the form of two major recommendations. We have argued above that while IDP is not a typical NPM, it is close to it in terms of intent and impact on the autonomy of teachers and institutions. The rationale for setting up a regulatory framework is similar to the construction of a higher education market advocated by the neoliberals. However, this market construction is a state-engineered market with two important qualifications. One, there is an assurance to augment the budget for higher education, and two, there is the encouragement of private participation, preferably with a philanthropic motive with the admonishment of commercial practices.

The proposed system will be a state-engineered competitive one where the HEIs will have to compete for funds, including for research. Although private and public-funded HEIs will be regulated at par, there will be no provision of public funding for the private. Enhancing students' choices and increasing reliance on online education – both within the country and outside – will add to the competitiveness of the market. The accountability mechanisms proposed in the form of IDPs are very strong. The system of accreditation led by NAC will eliminate the under-performers because of the possible adoption of binary accreditation (NEP: 18.4).

Strategizing Internationalization for Globalizing Indian Higher Education

The elements of internationalization and implications for globalization are to develop a comprehensive understanding of the NEP. As Knight (2014) has pointed out, internationalization and globalization are linked but are two different things. Internationalization is based on the principle of cooperation, primarily to achieve excellence in teaching and research, but globalization seeks to commodify education in the global arena. *The Economic Survey 2021* (GoI 2022a: 360) lists globalization as one of the objectives of higher education reform. The Union Budget 2022–23 has extended substantial financial support to world-class universities or Institutions of Eminence as per the policy document (GoI 2017). The proposal to set up a digital university is expected to encourage scholars to cooperate across the border. The possibility of a foreign university setting up campuses here is a distinct possibility. While there are gains to be reaped from internationalization, there lurks the possibility of commercialization of higher education in the process of achieving globalization.

Augmenting Public Funding Is Critical

The proposal is to enhance government budgetary support for education as a whole by one percentage point every year, from the prevailing allocation of 10 per cent of government expenditure to 20 per cent in a span of ten years (GoI 2019: 406–07). As per the Budget estimate for 2021–22, the centre and the states spend 3.1 per cent of GDP on the education sector as a whole (GoI 2022a: 352). The NEP reiterates the importance of realizing the target of 6 per cent of GDP for the education sector (NEP 26.2). There are indications that only the select IoEs will get additional financial support from the government, and for the rest, budgetary support may remain unchanged as Category-I HEIs are being pushed to be financially independent and explore other sources of financing. The HEIs are also being encouraged to approach HEFA to borrow for investment which would require only the capital amount to be repaid. As noted, the concept of financial autonomy in relation to the larger issue of university autonomy is misleading because of the inevitable clash between compulsions of the cost recovery and the compulsions of free and quality academic engagement. It is unlikely that public funding for higher education will witness a rise in the near future given the Covid-19 pandemic and its impact on the economy and fiscal health of the country.

Concluding Remarks

This essay has examined how academic freedom and university autonomy have been conceptualized to play a critical role in the NEP to rejuvenate the Indian higher education system. We have argued that the policy shifts as suggested by the NEP have neoliberal elements in the form of target-setting for universities and the construction of a regulated quasi-market for higher education. However, the NEP has strongly favoured increased public funding, phasing out of commercial practices, and granting autonomy to faculty only at their base level of academic engagement. The advocacy for autonomy for faculty and the HEIs has to be understood within the overall state–university governance system as proposed. This will restrict the scope for autonomy for both teachers and institutions as envisaged by the NEP. The envisioning of higher education restructuring has to be assessed in the context of ineffective regulatory interventions in university affairs, low faculty motivation, inadequate funding and political interference. This article has shown why the neoliberal form of governance reform need not necessarily guarantee quality unless faculty are empowered to realize their goals and their constraints are removed or even substantially mitigated. It is equally true that academic freedom comes with professional responsibilities which need collective reflection by academia to do justice to the freedom that faculty long for. The proposed increase in public funding is crucial to ensure a 'level playing field' for the public HEIs before they embark on their journey in the new system. With a growing reliance on online education, post-Covid-19 in the country and across the border, and with permission for foreign direct investment and external commercial borrowing in higher education as announced in the union budget for 2020–21, the Indian higher education sector is geared for greater private participation. The digitization of Indian higher education is policy-induced as indicated both in the NEP and its implementation. One rationale could be to accelerate the process of massification at a much lower cost. The technology will further help the government to internationalize. Setting up a digital university (GoI 2022b) as proposed in the union budget is a step in that direction. It appears very clearly that there is an attempt to repurpose education with an increasing orientation towards skill formation. This requires free mobility of the students between general and vocational education as the proposed Skill Qualification Framework is expected to achieve.

I am grateful to the referee (anonymous) for her/his suggestions and comments. I must also thank Dr Binay Kumar Pathak and Dr Emon Nandi for their comments and suggestions on an earlier version of the paper. However, I remain solely responsible for any errors that may remain.

Notes

[1] In the diagnosis of the challenges facing the Indian higher education system and envisioning of the policy, the NEP is broadly similar to the Draft National Education Policy (DNEP) (2019). One major addition in the NEP is the proposal to invite the top 100 universities of the world.

[2] Kapur and Mehta (2017) argue that the three objectives of containment of cost or budgetary support for higher education, achieving quality and ensuring expansion of the sector, what they call 'trilemma', cannot be fulfilled simultaneously. However, governance reform is the only way out of this impossibility which ensures the best possible utilization of resources given the cost to deliver quality.

[3] Though Indian universities do not feature in the global list of the top 100 universities in world ranking, in 2019, with 1,87,432 scientific papers published by the higher education institutes and research institutes, India stood fourth in the ranking after China, the USA and the UK (*International Facts and Figures 2020*). Given that there are 1.5 million teachers teaching in 1,043 universities, 42,343 colleges and 11,779 stand-alone institutions, per capita productivity is low, assuming that around 30 per cent of the papers are contributed by the research institutions. In terms of citation index, however, India stands twelfth. Featuring in the list of the top 100 universities in the world ranking has now been made the mandate of the select Institutions of Eminence (IoEs) and also one of the targets for Category-I institutions classified under the scheme of Graded Autonomy.

[4] Rejection rates range between 80 to 90 per cent in leading journals in the sciences and social sciences because of the rigorous review process (Bok 2013: 330).

[5] This is echoed in Chandra (2017: 291) who writes, '. . . universities in India are unable to demand accountability because they do not provide autonomy'.

[6] The proposed four institutions under the HECI are supposed to be independent verticals to avoid conflict of interest and concentration of power. But since all the aspects are non-separable in the case of education, the scope for negotiation by the HEIs will remain limited, and pursuit of goals may be hindered if all the four dimensions are at cross purposes for an HEI. It is also not clear in what manner the HECI will intervene and coordinate.

[7] This would be an element of a neoliberal approach to higher education, and it can be construed as a major departure from the existing system. The present system of remunerating the faculty is based on the assumption that the teachers are trustworthy, and they remain intrinsically motivated in their academic activities.

[8] Under the policy of Graded Autonomy, there is an indication that Category-I institutions will have the necessary freedom to introduce incentives in the pay packages of faculty.

[9] The NEP has argued for three types of HEIs: research-intensive, teaching-intensive and autonomous degree-granting colleges. While doing research is of crucial importance for research-intensive universities, it can be important for the other two as well, depending on their future plans to transit to the first type.

[10] The universities are categorized mainly as follows. Category I: NAAC score of 3.5 and above or in the top 500 of world-ranking universities as per the QS and THE; Category II: NAAC score between 3.01 and 3.49; Category III: Neither I nor II as mentioned. Featuring in the National Institutional Ranking Framework (NIRF) as a criterion for classification has been discontinued with the revised policy (GoI 2018).

References

Apoorvanand, ed. (2018), *The Idea of a University*, Delhi: Context, an imprint of Westland Publications.

Austin, I. and G.A. Jones (2016), *Governance of Higher Education: Global Perspectives, Theories, and Practices*, New York: Routledge.

Berdahl, R. (1990), 'Academic Freedom, Autonomy, and Accountability in British Universities', *Studies in Higher Education*, vol. 15, no. 2, pp. 169–81.

Berg, M. and B.K. Seeber (2016), *The Slow Professor: Challenging the Culture of Speed in the Academy*, Toronto: University of Toronto Press.

Bhushan, S. (2019), 'Contesting the Present in the Evolution of Public Higher Education', in Sudhanshu Bhushan, ed., *The Future of Higher Education in India*, New Delhi: Springer.

Bok, D. (2013), *Higher Education in America*, Princeton: Princeton University Press.

Bruneau, W. (2015), 'Five Defences of Academic Freedom in North American Higher Education', in P. Zgag, U. Teichler, H.G. Schuetze and A. Wolter, eds, *Higher Education Reform: Looking Back-Looking Forward*, Frankfurt am Main: Peter Lang.

Chandra, P. (2017), *Building Universities that Matter: Where Are Indian Institutions Going Wrong?*, Hyderabad: Orient BlackSwan.

Chattopadhyay, S. (2009) 'The Market in Higher Education: Concern for Equity and Quality', *Economic and Political Weekly*, vol. 44, no. 29, 18 July, pp. 53–61.

——— (2016), 'Neoliberal Approach to Governance Reform in the Universities: A Critique and a Possible Alternative', in Ravi Kumar, ed., *Neoliberalism and Educational Crisis in South Asia: Alternatives and Possibilities*, New Delhi: Routledge.

——— (2019), 'World Ranking of Universities: What Does it Entail for the Future', in Sudhanshu Bhushan, ed., *The Future of Higher Education in India*, New Delhi: Springer.

Clark, B.R. (1983), *The Higher Education System: Academic Organization in Cross-national Perspective*, Berkeley, CA: University of California Press.

Das, D.N. and S. Chattopadhyay (2014), 'Academic Performance Indicator: Straitjacketing Higher Education Reform', *Economic and Political Weekly*, vol. 49, no. 50, pp. 68–71.

Donoghue, F. (2008), *The Last Professors: The Corporate University and the Fate of the Humanities*, New York: Fordham University Press.

GoI (Government of India) (2016), 'UGC (Minimum Qualifications for Appointment of Teachers and other Academic Staff in Universities and Colleges and Measures for the Maintenance of Standards in Higher Education) (3rd Amendment), Regulations', *The Gazette of India*, 10 June 2016, Part III, Section 4.

——— (2017), 'University Grants Commission (Declaration of Government Educational Institutions as Institutions of Eminence) Guidelines 2017', available at https://www.ugc.ac.in/pdfnews/2170800_Guidelines-for-Educational-lnstitutions-as-lnstitutions-of-Eminence-2017.pdf, accessed 12 August 2020.

——— (2018), 'Ministry of Human Resource Development UGC (Categorisation of Universities [only] for Grant of Graded Autonomy) Regulations 2018', *The Gazette of India*, Part III, Section 4, 12 February, available at https://www.ugc.ac.in/pdfnews/1435338_182728.pdf, accessed 13 August 2020.

——— (2019), 'Draft National Education Policy', Ministry of Human Resource Development, New Delhi, available at https://www.mhrd.gov.in/sites/upload_files/mhrd/files/Draft_NEP_2019_EN_Revised.pdf, accessed 9 August 2020.

——— (2020a), *The National Education Policy 2020*, Ministry of Human Resource Development, New Delhi, available at https://www.mhrd.gov.in/sites/upload_files/mhrd/files/NEP_Final_English.pdf, accessed 9 August 2020.

——— (2020b), 'Public Notice: Expression of Interest (UG Course Mapping/SWAYAM), dated 31.07.2020', New Delhi: University Grants Commisson, available at https://www.ugc.ac.in/pdfnews/4981711_Public-Notice-EOI.pdf, accessed 11 Aiugust 2020.

——— (2021), 'UGC (Establishment and Operationalization of Academic Bank of Credits (ABC) Scheme in Higher education) Regulations', available at https://www.ugc.ac.in/pdfnews/5266217_Draft-version-ABC-Regulations-2021-SPT-02-01-2021.pdf

——— (2022a), *The Economic Survey 2021–22*, Ministry of Finance, Government of India, available at https://www.indiabudget.gov.in/economicsurvey/

——— (2022b), 'Budget 2022–23 Speech of Ms Nirmala Sitharaman, Minister of Finance', Government of India, available at https://www.indiabudget.gov.in/doc/Budget_Speech.pdf

——— (2022c), 'Draft Guidelines for Transforming Higher Education Institutions into Multidisciplinary Institutions', New Delhi: University Grants Commission, available at https://www.ugc.ac.in/pdfnews/4885262_Draft-Guidelines-for-Transforming-HEIs-multidisciplinary-Institutions.pdf, accessed 17 March 2022.

——— (2022d), 'Draft Institutional Development Plan for HEIs', University Grants Commission, Government of India, available at https://rgu.ac.in/wp-content/uploads/2022/02/IDP_Part-1.pdf

Kapur, D. and P.B. Mehta (2017), *Navigating the Labyrinth: Perspectives on India's Higher Education*, Hyderabad: Orient BlackSwan.

Kehm, B.M. (2014), 'Beyond Neo-liberalism: Higher Education in Europe and the Global Public Good', in P. Gibbs and R. Barnett, eds, *Thinking about Higher Education*, Springer.

Knight. J. (2014), 'Is Internationalization of Higher Education Having an Identity Crisis?' in A. Maldonado-Maldonado and R.M. Bassett, eds, *The Forefront of International Higher Education*, Higher Education Dynamics, Springer, pp. 75–88.

Marginson, S. (2008), 'Academic Creativity under New Public Management: Foundation for an Investigation', *Educational Theory*, vol. 58, no. 3, pp. 269–87.

Nixon, E., R. Scullion and M. Molesworth (2011) 'How Choice in Higher Education Can Create Conservative Learners', in E. Nixon, R. Scullion and M. Molesworth, eds, *The Marketization of Higher Education and the Student as Consumer*, Oxon, UK: Routledge.

Olssen, M., J. Codd and A.M. O'Neill (2004), *Education Policy, Globalization, Citizenship and Democracy*, London: Sage Publications.

Pritchard, R.M.O. (2015), 'Academic Values and English Higher Education', in P. Zgag, U. Teichler, H.G. Schuetze and A. Wolter, eds, *Higher Education Reform: Looking Back-Looking Forward*, Frankfurt am Main: Peter Lang Edition.

Sharma, A. (2018), 'Accountability and Academic Freedom of Faculty: A Study of Select Public Universities in India', PhD thesis submitted to Jawaharlal Nehru University, New Delhi.

Sundar, N. (2018), 'Academic Freedom and Indian Universities', *Economic and Political Weekly*, vol. 53, no. 24, 16 June, pp. 48–57.

Trow, M. (1996), *Trust Markets and Accountability in Higher Education: A Comparative Perspective*, Research and Occasional Paper Series, Berkeley: Centre for Studies in Higher Education, University of California.

9

'Blending' the Futures of Higher Education
Digital Capital and the Indian University

Debaditya Bhattacharya

To work today is to be asked, more and more, to do without thinking, to feel without emotion, to move without friction, to adapt without question, to translate without pause, to desire without purpose, to connect without interruption. . . . Of course this fantasy of what Marx called the automatic subject, this fantasy that capital could exist without labor, is nothing new but is continually explored at the nexus of finance capital, logistics and the terror of state-sponsored personhood which is instantiated in various pageants of conferral and withholding. It is marked today by the term human capital.

(Harney and Moten 2013: 87, 90)

The scourge of the pandemic in India has proved that the 'pageants of conferral and withholding' – the substance of state welfarism and regulation – are foisted on what Harney and Moten call 'state-sponsored' fictions of 'personhood'. There are two ways of looking at this: one logistical and the other juridical. In either case, it becomes apparent that 'conferral' and 'withholding'– the two dominant state functions of guaranteeing rights and controlling excesses – are not linked by the logic of contiguity, but practically seem to coincide with each other.

Of Sacrificial Men and Rightless Citizens

Within a neoliberal harnessing of human capital as the fuel for national 'growth', to confer is to potentially withhold and vice-versa. In classic labour market jargon, what has long been peddled as an 'entrepreneurial' ethic[1] now evolved into a new euphemistic shibboleth: 'self-reliance'.[2] The Finance Minister's laboured announcements for a relief package to tide over the current economic crisis were calculated to this end, insofar

as they opened up major sectors of government activity for private investment.[3] Such emergency-conjuring of a 'self-reliant India' (Aatma Nirbhar
Bharat) thus follows on a time-worn moral fable of individual enterprise
and sacrificial labour, while only lengthening the receding shadow of the
state and eugenically consigning populations to their differing degrees of
survivability.

When relief is viewed as reliance on the state – and a call to redistributive welfare – the 'nation' is nominally materialized in its 'publics'.
This runs counter to the ideological manifesto of human resource accounting, where every trace of life is, in the final instance, an extractive source
of capital accumulation. The moment at which such life is ejected from
systems of production is also the moment when it must be left to fend for
itself or reinsert itself into alternative circuits of circulation.[4] The nation,
within this order of economic rationalization of wealth as always-already
potential in life, must parasitically live off its publics, rather than provide
for the latter's claim to livelihood *as such*.

It was this truth that one saw played out in these past few months
– where 'to do without thinking, to feel without emotion, to move without
friction, to adapt without question, to translate without pause, to desire
without purpose, to connect without interruption' was the injunction
passed down to the world's largest democratic hoax. The middle classes
were asked to clang plates and light candles,[5] the public press ordered to
act as conduits for government data (Singh 2020; Panneerselvan 2020), the
informalized migrant workforce threatened with punitive action even while
they were belched out by factories and cityscapes,[6] and educational institutions were overnight reinvented as smartphone data (Bhattacharya 2020;
Kundu 2020).

This was a wholesale transition into the originary dream of modernity – the non-mathematical calculus that equates labour with logistics.
Historically, the spectre of the nation-state had emerged out of this trans-
latability. To turn people into logistics is to evacuate their subjectivity, and
thus render the variability of labour-power into the *form* of a commodity. It
is how labour is made invisible; unsuspecting of its own disappearance into
capital. The corollary of this is the resulting perception of capital becoming
self-generative. This is the first sense in which an interpellation into 'self-
reliance' works.

The second dimension, as I noted above, is juridical. It implodes
the state's 'gift' of citizenship as no longer productive of guaranteed
rights and consequently subjects an order of infinite circulation (of labour
power) to the random sovereignty of numbers. This is the rule of body
count, fancifully hailed as 'demographic dividend' – aggregated not in the

legal members of a national community but as exchangeable entities in the marketplace. Majoritarianism emanates from infirmities in the market, and not from some underlying clash of civilizations.

Every living body in such a polity – whether culturally marked as normative or deviant – is predestined as disposable and yet potentially capable of a surplus. It must survive on its own and through a wage hunt, but not be preserved. Across annals of history, the securitization of a nation-state has been coincident with the global auctioning of its labour power. And, just as the raking up of citizenship claims (in the Citizenship Amendment Act 2019 and a promised National Register of Citizens) occurred in the context of a flailing economy (Das 2018; Chatterjee and Sengupta 2019; Unnikrishnan 2019), so will the neoliberal route of a post-pandemic recovery spend itself in cultural angst and aggression. To make citizenship redundant for economic survival, while at the same time dematerializing labour as logistical transport, will only make the shipment of bodies inseparable from the territorialism of borders. Every act of moving, underwritten into the globality of capital and evicted from the materiality of being, is automatized as the terror of the unknown.

Shipping and Skilling Labour

Having set out a staggeringly large terrain, the question that this essay will attempt to answer is: how will the higher education sector in India bear the brunt of a nationalistic narcissism disguised as 'self-reliance'? Using terms from the foregoing discussion, how will this 'human capital' – disowned by the state and marked as permanent surplusage – be reintegrated into annual reports of national growth?

On the face of it, human capital – viewed as self-reliant and self-generative – must be successively upgraded for it to retain 'value' despite depreciation or falling demand. In other words, there must be an exponential increase in the scramble for higher-order cognitive skills at significantly lower costs.

The entire workforce that in its logistical transformation is alienated from its labour power and hollowed of its subjective character will seek to substitute/supplement its erstwhile skills with new ones. In most cases, unmoored from the protections of the state and left at the mercy of ruthless competition in a free market, existing/erstwhile wage labour in the private sector will try to boost its productivity through part-time stints at acquiring new skills. Understandably, these will be skills that promise alternative professions of dignity or serve as additional benchmarks for the quality of renewed labour power to be pawned in the market. Since most of these new entrants into college education – aspiring to achieve the status of knowledge workers from mere skilled wage labour – will be required to balance work commitments outside of their academic careers, there will result a massive demand for online courses from reputed universities at minimal costs.[7]

The process is already underway.[8] The final tranche of relief announcements, while in the throes of the pandemic, launched a scheme under which the 'top 100 universities' in the country were empowered to offer online degrees without any regulatory approval or legislative control (Mohanty 2020). Since none of this necessitates investment in physical infrastructures or the costs of their upkeep, the revenue requirements of such courses are expected to be low and predictably shared by a far wider enrolment base than the traditional classroom initiates. On what is popularly termed as a cost-sharing basis among end clients, the nation's online transitioning of higher education is touted as imminently cheaper and yet a greenfield investment opening for private ed-tech capital.

But why is this to be rolled out as a sop for the 'top 100' alone? The answer to this is two-pronged. While university branding is calculated to attract both private investors (in the hope for greater enrolments) and enrolments (in the hope for better services or knowledge outcomes), the deliberate policy linkage of ranking with 'autonomy' is to function as an incentive for other non-'performing' institutions to follow suit. More and more institutions will competitively digitize knowledge content without much need for coercive scaremongering, in seeking the nod of accreditation agencies and their push for graded deregulation.

Private Aid and National Debt

In May 2021, when a deadly second wave of the pandemic was raging through the country with thousands going up in numbers and smoke every day for lack of basic medical infrastructure,[9] the University Grants Commission (UGC) shot off a missive to the executive heads of all higher educational institutions (HEIs) proposing a futurist manifesto. In the fear that this futurism might seem too ill-timed for public sympathy, a 'concept note' was simultaneously published on the commission's website[10] – in order to be able to sell the outrageous fantasy now propped up as the Indian academy's compulsory destiny. It urged that a return to better times meant that the classroom must stage a theatre of its own disappearance for all times hereafter, by effectively teleporting between 40 to 70 per cent of every regular 'taught' course onto digital platforms.[11] This 'blended learning' (BL) model was to be adopted by the entire college sector, with 'clusters' of a minimum of ten neighbourhood institutions serving as one operation unit for content production and transmission.[12] The arithmetic in these numbers might seem all fortuitous cursorily, but will bear out a prophecy when connected to what immediately went before.

A university-level implementation committee for the National Education Policy (NEP) 2020 (which I shall take up for lengthier analysis soon hereafter) had already been convened by the Delhi University administration, and in the course of fourteen meetings conducted between October 2020 and February 2021, the committee drafted a new structure for undergraduate courses in all disciplines.[13] Given how Delhi University's massive undergraduate system has historically become the opportune site for experimenting with top–down curricular 'reforms' before they are exported *in toto* to radically non-identical institutional settings in every other part of the country, it is a truth foretold that the new template was but a portal into national educational futures.[14] Resurrecting a once-discarded four-year undergraduate programme (FYUP) model from 2013, this proposed framework divided a total of forty credits between papers that may be commonly applicable to all streams of study. This was to be the compulsory 'multidisciplinary' initiation into liberal education – evidenced in 'value addition' papers such as social and emotional learning, ethics and culture, IT skills, data analysis and mathematics, science and society or innovation and entrepreneurship. Barring this, the remaining non-specific 'elective' component – to be also commonly shared between disciplines – was an average of thirty-six more credits.[15] Together, the total common mean of subject choices that could easily be cross-streamed and digitally pooled for mass subscriptions was exactly about 40 per cent of the cumulative credit worth of any course.

To continue with the sinister subtexts underwritten into the euphoria for BL, one needs to persist a little longer with the same NEP outline. A pre-pandemic version of its draft had already argued for a dramatic downsizing of the number of higher educational institutions from the then 52,000 to 12,300 – which translates into more than a 70 per cent contraction of the sector.[16] I will return to this point again, later in this essay. But, in light of these numerical projections, it appears that the UGC's 2021 commandment about digitally 'blending' 40 to 70 per cent of teaching content was not exactly an outlandish fantasy. It was calculated with precise intention and rolled out with unobtrusive prior planning, insofar as scaled-and-weighed proportions of the public-funded university were now to be handed out to private learning management software companies on indefinite contracts. This 'blend' was the accurate apotheosis of the public–private partnership (PPP) model of university governance and financing, which the Finance Minister touted as 'relief-package'.

One of the most prescient 'concepts' forwarded by the UGC's

BL-concept note – and under the discursive tutelage of the NEP – is what it called the 'Academic Bank of Credit (ABC)'.[17] The evil irony of acronymic play aside, the 'ABC' of Indian higher education was to be a national fund of acceptable and tradable debt-currency – measured in certification and saleable as skill. Public-funded institutions, now moulded as 'credit'-disbursal agencies, could only make the student into a permanent debtor of the state. The teacher on the other hand, as the note announces without making any bones about it, will have to 'shift his/her role from "teach" [sic] to "facilitator"' (31). Bonded for life into a repayment clause that requires oblation to the global market, we are finally transitioned into a 'World Bank'-ethic of higher education. The structural adjustments demanded of the sector are only a passage into what Thomas Friedman had, nearly a decade ago in 2013, eulogized in strikingly reminiscent terms as a 'budding revolution in global online higher education':

> Imagine how this might change *U.S. foreign aid*. For relatively little money, the U.S. could rent space in an Egyptian village, install two dozen computers and high-speed satellite Internet access, hire a local *teacher as a facilitator*, and invite in any Egyptian who wanted to take online courses with the *best professors in the world*, subtitled in Arabic. (Emphases mine)

Is Access Infrastructural?

By all appearances, we are headed for the cherished dream of mass democratization of higher education. The university sector is finally to be opened to people of all ages and places and professions, the hierarchies of value between on-campus courses and open-distance learning are to be dismantled, and the structural exclusions perpetrated by centuries of intellectual apartheid are to be remedied. The trilemma that governed the misfortunes of Indian higher education – identified by Devesh Kapur and Pratap Bhanu Mehta as the non-contiguous welding of 'quality-access-financing'[18] – is to be ironed out by the online university, in as far as it promises the best possible education to the largest possible audience at the lowest possible cost. If online teaching is to achieve the maximum amplitude of 'publicness' within structures of higher education, isn't it a just replacement for the public university?

I would emphatically argue that, quite to the contrary, the virtualization of pedagogy performs an accurate inversion of the raison d'etre of public education. And, the plain arithmetic of access – as encoded in the statistical fetish for enrolment ratios – is grossly ill-equipped to grapple with this scandal.

Access is neither a measure of social opportunity nor a humanist resilience against odds; it is, in the final instance, a question of the responsiveness of infrastructures to histories of disprivilege and dispossession. A public education system begins from the premise that the state must assume this burden of historical guilt and therefore make the inaugural move towards redressal. Formal access to infrastructural provisioning must therefore be the commitment of the state and not the onus of the private individual. While the brick-and-mortar public university exists in order to correct inequities of access to infrastructures of knowledge production and reception, the spectre of online education consists in privatizing these access costs entirely. Not only is private entitlement to technological gadgets/devices/resources the key to one's ease of access to education but the quality and substantive content of such education are also made incumbent on the quantum of technological capital that may be afforded (nature of the device, size of the mobile screen, configuration of software, speed and bandwidth of internet connection, memory space on the device, etc.). Despite the avowed 'low cost' of 'good' online education, it eventually turns out that the quality, access and financing of such offerings devolve differentially on the individual's capacity for buying them. And it is here that the state finds a most opportune exit route from its constitutional responsibility towards the education sector.

Having said this, it needs to be maintained that political resistance to the ploy for privatizing higher education (through online means) cannot be articulated in terms of the reality of its unequal access. Though the overwhelming majority of public critiques has resorted to highlighting data around the 'digital divide' – and how it plays out along lines of caste, class, gender, community, religion and region[19] – this would not prove a sufficient counterargument on specific grounds.

First, the question of individual access understands the state's withdrawal from social-sector provisioning as dependent on context, and not as a larger structural adjustment. Consequently, it argues for alternative arrangements to even out disparities across contexts – for example, the state provisioning of internet services or the nationalization of broadband data. Given the quantum of resources that the state is likely to save by pulling out of the physical infrastructures of education (and its recurring costs of reproduction), it is not impossible for doles of monthly data to be made freely available as incentive to students who opt for substitutive online means. Against the backdrop of the Indian state's intimate partnerships with the telecom sector, such a reform model for revamping higher education – and, in the process, instituting mechanisms of cyber-surveillance[20] – is in fact entirely believable.

Second, there is no denying that a large-scale transition of higher education to digital platforms – through massive open online courses

(MOOCs) and the like – will initially enlarge enrolments to an unprecedented extent. This is because a large section of adult working male populations will log into the fabled adventure of university education without having to physically attend the university, till the myth of its promised enlightenment wears off in unanticipated ways. It is true that many of the new entrants into tertiary education will also represent communities that have been millennially deprived of the right to higher intellectual pursuits and forced into situations of semi-manual or mechanical labour. Access is precisely the arithmetic that the government too will be trumpeting in its attempts at advertising the relative merits of a digital university (McKenzie 2020). Couching reform in terms of its possible critique is something that the state bureaucracy has learnt exceedingly well. This was best demonstrated by the rhetorical self-projections of the Draft NEP (DNEP) 2019 that made liberal education seem the sole ideological instrument of a fascist regime,[21] which had faced the stiffest resistance from university communities for suppression of liberal voices.[22]

The third and final reason why access parameters might not be the best defence is the fact that what we are defending has not been innocent either. Ranged against an online onslaught is the hubris contained within the history of the traditional university itself – and its prolonged complicity with forms of systemic discrimination, suspicion of first-generation learners, disavowal of contingent knowledge practices and non-secular life-worlds. Despite having generated myths about its penchant for intellectual emancipation as well as a means for social-economic mobility, the public university has veritably failed its public vocation for decades (Bhattacharya 2019a). It has neither been as substantively transformative nor as democratically self-oriented as its hallowed vision documents claimed. Over time, the government has carefully sculpted an image of the colossal betrayal of democracy and social justice within traditional higher educational institutions – and therefore mooted the need for a thorough overhaul through reorientation of policy. Part of this imagination of the 'failed project' of Indian higher education was manufactured by successive drafts and the final Cabinet-approved version of the new NEP 2020.

The University as a Sick Asset

To en-frame an alternative in policy terms is not merely about positing imaginary benefits; it demands a prior debunking of existing systems and an aggravation of the apparent chasms between what they professed as opposed to what was achieved. To have successfully done the latter is to already strengthen an alternative as imperative.

Spanning nearly four years of stock-taking and two separate committees,[23] the draft of the new education policy begins by ruing the minimal penetration of higher education among the bulk of India's population of college-going age. With a gross enrolment ratio (GER) of only 26.3 pitched against a massively unwieldy spread of nearly 52,000 institutions (GoI 2019: I–II), the university sector is flagged off at the very outset as limping under its own weight. The bloated obesity of the institutional architecture is lamented as the cause of a regulatory malfunction.

Add to this an apparent failure of social justice policies in effectively redistributing public resources and enhancing formal inclusion of 'under-represented groups' (URGs), later re-acronymized as 'socio-economically disadvantaged groups' (SEDGs), such that there is need for a clear bifurcation of educational goals. While 'employability' is still cited as the limit of intellectual labour for the socially marginalized,[24] liberal education becomes the opiate of the mainstream. The vocational and the liberal are self-separated by pedagogical difference but welded together in the cause of an ill-fitted commitment to equality. In the process, social mobility and democratic citizenship are mapped out as mutually exclusive pursuits within the liberal university – the bulk of populations coming out of which is destined to near-indefinite un(der)employment.

This damning policy portrait of the public university is then given the aura of a providential truth by years of spectacular prophesying that went before. The absurd fee hikes and tuition increases across government-funded institutions had already made the sector appear like an unsustainable investment.[25] The significantly lower returns – portended by accurately stage-managed theatres of 'anti-national' sloganeering by slothful scavengers of university students, living off public resources unto eternity – had further discounted higher education as an immoral economy of consumption and debauchery.[26] References to an overpaid, underworked and ill-prepared teaching force – marching out into the streets on the slightest caution of reform – confirmed the wasteful expenditure on higher education, insofar as these 'urban naxals'[27] were made to represent a 'Harvard' of lethargic privilege against the 'hard work' of active nation-building (Verma 2017). Their old-fashioned teaching methods, it had been repeated *ad nauseam,* were at the heart of every debacle that the nation fathomed itself going through – from employment crisis to breakdown of the family, from a bohemian punk-rebellion to internal security threats.

Digitality as Reform Antidote

The effigy of the public university had already been erected for nationwide public consternation and censure before a new NEP draft came up and proposed a magical formula for ridding the system of its rot: a wholesale merger of physical institutional campuses to a quarter of its current size, while at the same time doubling student enrolments.[28] Till the pandemic provided the fuel in which to douse the public university in its entirety, we hardly noticed that the 'magic' in the policy draft was simply the spark of an online sleight. A plan for mass deportation of classroom populations onto digital platforms was afoot, and the global alarm around 'physical distancing' merely draped policy intention with the force of fatalism. To that extent, the pandemic has just been cleverly used to foreshutter the gates of a sector that had long been scripted into such a destiny. An analogy with how online education swelled within American and European college contexts in the backdrop of austerity cuts, mandated by the 2008 recession in international finance, is instructive here (Newfield 2016a). A spectre of an immediate crisis external to the sector must always be called upon to necessitate 'reform' as the only condition of possibility of survival.

It has been severally remarked that a long-term solution to the threat of similar disruptions and future pandemics will have to be devised, and a compulsory streaming of college courses on digital platforms might be the only way out. While an existing set of regulations – published by the UGC in 2016 – allowed a maximum of 20 per cent of an institution's academic offerings to be made available online,[29] a committee appointed to debate the future of digital higher education in the context of the pandemic is reported to have doubled the limit as a basic minimum for the running of courses.[30] A separate committee revising academic calendars owing to lockdown closures issued a fiat for one-fourth of every department's teaching to be made virtually transmissible.[31] Coupled with the NEP's proposal for merging institutions and drastically curtailing their numbers, digital evangelism within higher education is assumed to be a one-step reform antidote to all the lineaments of crisis surrounding the public university. From boosting enrolments to effectively deregulating the market for educational services, widening the drive for social mobility through an absolute diversification of consumer bases, lowering the financial liability of states as well as beneficiaries, curbing the menace of the lazy 'anti-national' greying eloquently on university campuses, revamping teaching methodology beyond its lecture-theatre tedium – an online adaptation was all it needed for the university system to start paying off and paying back its debts to both the state and global finance capital.

The most recent survey data on higher education trends holds that nearly 74 out of every 100 potential enrolments in the college-going age bracket have no access to a college degree.[32] For the year 2018–19, this would amount to a 105 million-strong youth left out of the nation's university cartographies. If this proportion of the 'demographic dividend' could be tapped into, alongside the expansion of demand within working populations, private vendors offering online knowledge solutions are expected to flock wholesale into educational shareholding. It is with such promise of returns that the government illegally rolled out a public–private partnership scheme in the National Educational Alliance for Technology (NEAT) – a body first named in the draft NEP[33] and made operational much before the final policy was unveiled. Through tie-ups with private tech-providers, free to charge for courses and services at market rates, this platform is designed to enable a leveraging of public universities for competitive bids.

Ushering in a private equity model within higher education – or what Christopher Newfield describes as a 'leveraged buy-out' of the university system (Newfield 2016a: 177) – technological start-ups could effectively make use of public resources and institutional reputation to sell their products to prospective buyers of online education. In the course of such venture-capitalist invasion into the sector, the public university is successively disintegrated into smaller service-assets and pawned off to multiple shareholders. According to Newfield, the MOOC years in the United States (2011 to 2016) were witness to identical developments that – in his prescient discerning of a cautionary tale – make for a fairly advanced 'Stage 6' of the 'unmaking of public universities' (ibid.).

Who Are the Surplus Peoples?

The caution in the tale extends further, inasmuch as the bubble of enhanced enrolments in online courses is fated to a dramatic implosion. While American universities, riding on the post-recessionary MOOC wave, have had an average of 60 per cent of their initial course subscriptions drop out by the third year, fully online academic programmes have registered the highest-ever attrition rates in the history of global higher education. The latter variety saw its graduation rates in the US dip to an abysmal one-eighth of regular public university classroom courses, and almost a quarter of community college completion statistics (ibid.: 191–92). Significantly enough, the social profile of dropouts from online programmes accurately coincides with those who were supposed to benefit from it – to be more precise, first-generation college-goers and working adults who neither have the academic motivation nor the necessary social capital to survive the demands of intellectual rigour.[34]

When transposed into an Indian context, the 'social justice' claims enunciated by a digital reinvention of the public university will only end up in a consummate perversion – by making collaterals out of minority, Dalit–Adivasi and women enrolments. The policy prescription for such a scenario is to inordinately dilute content and relax testing mechanisms, which would only go on to compromise the credibility of such courses for potential employers and provide no 'value-addition' to the skill sets that an incumbent already comes with. Structures of discrimination are thus to be incrementally reified through a social credentialing of unfit/undeserved labour power and bad debts doubled by a plan that professes to democratize higher education.

On the other hand, what a digital proselytism within the university sector achieves in the long term is a complete dispensability and precariatization of multiple forms of academic and non-academic labour that keep the brick-and-mortar university running. Learning from the American example, even a partial onlining of university curricula leads to a major outsourcing of teaching labour – not only to underpaid adjuncts or non-tenured contingent faculty but also to teachers who are contractually engaged by tech companies.[35] Faculty positions cease to be the exclusive preserve of educational institutions, and knowledge consulting within a corporate service sector emerges as the largest (but also the most tenuous) recruiter of intellectual capital. Teachers are hired on variable course contracts and wages clocked against specific hours of online content creation, thus forcing a near-total disappearance of the idea of tenured or permanent employment.[36]

This wholesale casualization of teaching work plays into the branding strategies for online coursework, insofar as specific programmes are run in the names of celebrity professors, while the hard labour of content designing is passed on to underpaid teaching assistants or relatively younger temporary recruits. The 2016 UGC Regulations, in hailing the MOOC turn in Indian higher education, urges a replacement of faculty vacancies within institutions through online course imports.[37] In this lies an implicit policy nod for cutting down teaching positions within departments where digital resources are available. In the same vein, the Regulations empower colleges to offer elective papers in the remote online mode, even if they lack the immediate infrastructural requirements and faculty strength to run them.[38] Needless to say, the UGC's ploy for enabling digital cross-streaming of courses across institutions not only made economic sense – in that a course could now be physically run at one college but offered at many others at no extra cost to the state – but it also entrenched the concept of 'credit transfer' in the garb of which a 'one-size-fits-all' common national syllabus was imposed on the nation's colleges the year before (Sharma 2015; *Newsclick* 2015; Tewary 2015; Kumar 2015).

This new curriculum – rammed in through classic executive unilateralism – was advertised as retaining a greater amplitude of student 'choice' and therefore more attuned to personalized 'learning outcomes', while assuming that student populations who enter the country's higher education sector are but mirror reflections of homogeneity. It occasions no wonder that a uniform syllabus preceded the move towards online learning since it only makes an effective cost-cutting mechanism seem so much more like a push for standardization of knowledge output (or, in governance terms, 'streamlining'). In truth, the choice based credit system – by virtue of its insistence on mass mechanical reproduction of syllabi across contexts – makes it infinitely more possible to convert courses with inter-departmental and cross-university student enrolments into online teaching modules.

The digital transitioning could, for example, begin with papers that call for larger classroom sizes, better material infrastructures, greater teaching workload, more maintenance staff salaries, that is, the ability enhancement compulsory courses (AECC) and skill enhancement courses (SEC). As an illustration, it might be worth pointing out that if a single AECC paper is wholly digitized, every undergraduate college with a relatively conservative annual intake of 1,000 students will lose an average of two sanctioned teaching posts in the relevant discipline. Multiply this by the number of public-funded undergraduate colleges in the country (which, in 2018–19, was in the range of 8,500),[39] and that is the size of the labour abscess dug up in one discipline alone. I am leaving private unaided institutions out of the equation, though the faculty attached to such spaces are likely to bear as much of the brunt of this resource shedding, if not more.

The Teaching Industry and *Varna*-labour

From the discussion thus far, it is evident that any critique of the forced online transformation in higher education needs to urgently move beyond access data and ethnographic field notes on the 'digital divide'. The magnitude of this structural reconfiguration of the university may, in my understanding, assume full proportions when viewed in the context of policy and historical precedent – though the latter might be borrowed as lessons from a context not too far from our own policy infatuations.

Although I have already touched on the impact of a digitally outsourced college education on faculty numbers and recruitment patterns, what is it about online teaching that devalues teaching labour at the same time as it promises to massify or globalize its reach? How are the moral economies of merit (and caste-based rights of professional access) reified into unbreachable hierarchies via forms of 'digital idealism'[40] now in evidence? The former had historically conjured the figure of the 'teacher' as a subject of prophetic intervention – most often, through a careful epistemological separation between what Gopal Guru calls the 'theoretical Brahmins' and 'empirical Shudras' (Guru and Sarukkai 2012: 10).[41] In what ways will the 'teaching industry' be recalibrated in the model of a factory ethic of

eliminationism,[42] where more and more people can enter a life of undigni-
fied drudgery while fewer attain heights of unimpeachable authority? In
effect, the university system will continue to enable vertical mobility for an
even more restricted coterie of the caste elite, while at the same time widening horizontal access to the toiling multitudes of a casualized bottom-end
cognitariat[43] – a perfect example of re-packaging what Ambedkar called the
principle of 'graded inequality' within the *varnashrama* ideal.

I have already gestured at this division of interests within the intellectual community, festered by separating a privileged minority of tenured
professors (who also double up as the managerial class within university
governance) from a large floating population of 'ad hoc' and part-time/
guest lecturers who are usually tasked with keeping the departments running. The marketing of online courses not only exploits but also feeds into
this feudalism of productive relations through strategic investments in
celebrity capital.

While the Supreme Court of India contended that teachers are not
'workmen' but part of a 'noble vocation' – and therefore exempted from
the mundane pettiness of 'industrial disputes'[44] – how would state bureau-
cracies under the shadow of the NEP 2020 use this hallowed feudality of
the teacher's professional rank and position to re-institute socially differentiated sectors of intellectual labour? In other words, how would the current moment in history widen the deep institutional chasms between the
enlightened moral guardianship of the upper-caste professoriate and the
'life of the Dalit mind'? (Guru 2013: 39). Considered in similar terms, how
might the Gramscian imagination of 'traditional intellectuals'– who 'experience through an "esprit de corps" their uninterrupted historical continuity and their special qualification' (Gramsci 1971: 7) – reinstate its power
and privilege against the 'moving moral menace' (Guru 2013: 41) of the
Dalit-Bahujan organic intellectuals entering the digital university as low-
skilled informal teacher–workers?

The studied (and sinister) silence of the NEP 2020 on state-
mandated policies of caste-based reservation, while at the same time
bundling all forms of historical disprivilege under the vacuous rhetorical
elasticity of an acronym like 'SEDG',[45] goes hand in hand with its meritocratic lament about failing 'quality' standards of a rapidly expanding higher
education sector. This casteist bias within the policy is accentuated through
repeated references to 'merit-appointments and career progression', concerns about 'quality and engagement of faculty', stocking of statutory bodies with 'persons having high expertise . . . and a demonstrated track record
of public service' or 'eminent public-spirited experts' or 'highly qualified,
competent and dedicated individuals'.[46] This hankering for a moral creden-

tialing of 'eminence', however infamous by precedent,[47] runs parallel to a conscious inattentiveness to any kind of structural representation of caste or religious minorities on policy-making platforms as envisioned by the framework. The NEP advocates the cause of making 'tenure-track' faculty appointments in the same section where it ironically champions the furtherance of faculty autonomy and academic freedom.[48] Damningly, such tenure-track entrants into the teaching profession will have to depend on 'peer reviews' for their annual appraisals and renewal of contracts. It does not beg explanation that this culture of 'peer review' as a precondition for the career progression of casualized teaching labour will only reproduce the university as a site of feudal kinship relations, based on existing caste distinctions. The 'theoretical Brahmins' will command (and own) the slave labour of the workmen–teachers, who must necessarily do the former's bidding at online content creation as teaching assistants/apprentices. A system of moral character certification – another variant of the patronage economy of 'recommendations' on the basis of merit assumptions – will now be built into the map of professional success within academia. However, the nature of labour demanded from such claimants to certification will largely be informal care work, in as far as the latter must provide consulting and mentoring support to student consumers of knowledge data.

The summary scrapping of the MPhil programme by the new policy[49] also contributes to the emboldening of the caste-Hindu stronghold in terms of research access and routines of advanced intellectual training. It is a rarely debated and historically corroborated fact that the sheer duration of a PhD course – a minimum of four to six years – discourages women scholars and those from marginalized communities from committing to it for lack of financial resources, social capital and chances of cultural survivability. In such a scenario, most of them seek a rite of passage into the research sector through the MPhil degree, secure jobs and then look for doctoral opportunities while in service. With the *All India Survey on Higher Education (AISHE) Report* pegging the rate of research enrolments at 'less than 0.5 percent' of total GER in higher education,[50] the exact institutional census would resemble something like this: if out of a sample of 1,000 adults only 263 can minimally access higher education, it is only one among these 263 college-educated youth that dares to enter the portals of research. The identity permutations that facilitate such research 'ambitions' are not difficult to guess, and it is still less difficult to fathom how universities systemically exclude the 'empirical Shudras' in order to become fit spaces for a 'noble vocation'.

Of course, none of this is a new development, since the neoliberal turn in educational policymaking consisted precisely in a remodelling of the non-profit public good of knowledge along principles of the market. For nearly three decades now, economic prospects of 'revenue generation' have structured administrative behaviours as well as the approach of the funding state towards the university intellectual. Forms of punitive performance audit, charges of irrelevant research, repressive codes of professional conduct, threats to fundamental academic freedoms have gone hand in hand with an unchecked contractualization of teaching jobs, as the surest means of keeping a class of potentially 'enlightened' citizens perpetually at risk and therefore in control.

The Classroom Is a Missed Call!

Apart from the crippling changes in the conditions of work and pay, how does the ceremony of a digital shift alter the *idea* of the university?

In referring back to Harney and Moten and returning to a strand of argument I began with, it begs being reiterated that methods of digital delivery reduce academic labour to a set of logistical arrangements. Stretched along a fortuitous coincidence of time and place – and their distensions over speed and connectivity – the practice of 'online learning' is voided of the subject and her situatedness. The alchemy of contact and the possible violence of collisions, between the necessarily disconnected life-worlds of those occupying a classroom is where academic practice becomes an act of labour. It is the labour of trying and failing to connect with *an other* without miraculous aid, technological assistance or digital conversion. And, it is in such failure that labour is recognized *as such*. To succeed is to connect without an investment of the body, an effort of the imagination, a plunge into the materiality of time and space.

The classroom is where one struggles not to reconcile, but to surrender to the in(de)finite disjunction of subject-positions – the unrelenting difference that distracts sense from senselessness, the sensate from the sensible. It is the space where an ethics of labour is both postulated and elaborated, in the naïve conviction that *our* world too may be the habitat of many others.

Counterposed against such naivete is the labour of rejection (by the student–subject), the refusal to inhabit or to acknowledge the *charity* of hospitality. Such refusal is a resolute investment in the history of one's *own* situation – or, perhaps a difficult escape from a history one had not chosen into a space of hostile desire. In terms borrowed from Harney and Moten's powerful manifesto, the classroom is also the site of fugitivity (Harney and Moten 2013: 23–43), the space of the undercommons. It allows one to steal what should have been one's own, to dream in spite of the historical weight of injustice, to defy despite the order to obey.

There is no instant connect, no mute button, no volume control here, and yet there is all of that in the permanent possibility of slipping out of one world while staying in another. The classroom is a zone of chronic connectivity failure; and in as far as it thrusts the radicality of otherness in our faces (in someone's choosing to look out of the window, giggle away, doze off or whisper in muted syllables), it replicates the default injustice of production. It is the site of working *at* a world, once at a time, in wonder and frustration, feeling and guessing. In its rootedness within the incompletion of world-making, academic labour is not global and it can neither be transmitted as data nor coded as an algorithm. Online classrooms do not build commons – because, as the Edu-factory Collective poignantly maintains, the commons is not universal.[51] To build it is to stake a claim on it; in the digital classroom, capital predates (on) the labour of building a commons.

Mortgaged Labour, Hidden Debts and Credit Points

Time is *lived* in the translation of embodied labour into abstract labour power, imagined as 'socially necessary' when contributing to systems of production. But there is always a time outside of this cycle of crude economic approximation, which is either productive yet unwaged or immaterial and determinedly unproductive. The latter order, classically speaking, is informal immediate labour, not tied to the expropriative interests of capital. In this, it is the most subjective and heterogeneous component of time – one that claims a recuperation from productive work or reproductive housework. Such socially unnecessary appropriation of time by living labour, always-already outside the surveillance of capital, is spent in activities like planning disobedience, imagining insurrection, wishing away law or perhaps forgetting the trauma of abjectness. Absolutely indispensable to radically transformative politics, this order of immaterial temporality is constantly at the risk of being preyed on and abstracted by capital, and then subsequently criminalized in the cause of governance.

The physical classroom provides a collaborative site for multiplying these informalities of living, while the online class achieves just the opposite. The latter assumes a commonality between all these disjunctive times and forces immaterial labour into the synchrony of a choreographed appearance on-screen, on-device, on-your-mark. Till all are ready and cued in.

An online charade of knowledge networking first blurs the distinction between productive and social reproductive labour and then slouches towards eliminating the irreducibility of unproductive unwageable labour. Insofar as the student must log in at the same time as look after an ailing parent, keep an eye on the kitchen stove, calm a restless toddler, shut out a boisterous neighbour, run an errand, answer a command, swallow a father's jibe or ignore the noise of the radio in the other room – all the while listening to a teacher's narcissistic baritone – the business of online education is both about doing 'business-as-usual' and making business out of the unusual. It allows no consciousness of the difference between earning course credits and doing unpaid care work at home. All labour is commodified irrespective of wage value and consequently 'credited' by the university as capital to be invested in future and reaped profits of. Seen differently, all forms of labour are rendered into debt, attracting credit, only to compound the debt for reinvestment at higher rates of future productivity. In terms borrowed from a 'knowledge management' discourse, the online student–learner must learn to 'multi-task' because that's the only key to maximizing labour productivity and wage credit.

The Everyday Reproduction of the University

Just as the digital university makes social reproductive labour at home indistinguishable from and coeval with routines of cognitive production, it also issues a death warrant against all sectors of lower order (read: blue-collar) non-academic work that reproduces the institution on a daily basis (Caffentzis and Federici 2009). With the increasing delegitimization of the brick-and-mortar infrastructures of a university campus, the kinds of labour that create a conducive setting for the 'disinterested' surplus of teaching and research are now dispensed with. The cleaner, the mess worker, the canteen waiter, the groundkeeper, the janitor, the caretaker, the gardener, the newspaper vendor, the campus grocer, the photocopy machine-operator, the barber – and several such forms of daily wage labour – are, in one fell stroke, declared excessive to the *systems* university.

It was this lifeworld that allowed the university to confront a history of its own injustices and exclusions; it was here that the university realized its potential for a self-critique as the inaugural condition for social justice. The class–caste–gender and civic solidarities that soiled the insides of higher education – and its meritocratic rites of access as the sole formal right of entry – were only to be questioned in the everyday encounters with an ever-swelling precariat propping up the haloed quest for emancipation. The liberal university's 'original sin' was at the same time its only claim to a redemptive self-interrogation – but often, outside the centres for post-colonial studies, social exclusion or gender studies. In the online transitioning of cognitive capital, the physical institution blows up its salvatory prospects by becoming a 'systems-management' unit. What swells at the cost of this mass-precariatization is the administrative–technical bureaucracy, the class of data-miners and knowledge consultants. For example, Annexure IV (Human Resource and Infrastructural Requirements) of the recently published UGC (Open and Distance Learning Programmes and Online Programmes) Regulations 2020 does not mandate any 'physical infrastructure' for the opening of a 'Centre for Online Education', thus eliminating the need for secondary amenities and consequent staffing requirements altogether. Even while academic personnel are to be roped in from existing 'Departments or Schools of Studies', technical recruitments are differentiated across eight new grades.[52]

Intersectionality is the name of alliance building, a claim to sharing a commons. It is an imaginative exercise and begins with a forsaking of the economy of intellectual rights. Imagination is preconditionally equal, the intellect is historically its obverse. For the university to become the site of a knowledge-commons, its non-intellectual communities are a potential window to the outsides of theoretical reason – the realm of know-how and tactical contingency. It is here that the imagination meets development practice, distinct from state-sponsored sample-sized wellness therapy, manoeuvring as governance theory.

The hurried move towards online education – in the name of compensating for 'academic loss' caused by the pandemic – decisively pronounces the sovereignty of the intellect as the only province of higher education. It champions the unimpeachable right to cognitive labour over the costs borne by social reproductive labour within the university. The nagging regrets monotoned by university administrations (and the online–academic ilk) – about 'depletion of teaching time', 'impossibility of laboratory-based practicals', 'unviability of field-work' – seem to me to echo a Brahminical nostalgia for an unquestioned continuum of intellectual privilege. In its fetishization of that same privilege, it argues for the globalization of knowledge as data, whereas what is foreclosed in the process are the forced encounters with difference.

The Digital University and the Organic Intellectual

The adventure of equality through 'little acts' of the imagination could only be provoked by the encounters I detailed above.

In fact, many of these 'little acts' were already in sight during the recent lockdown. The doors to chemical labs in colleges were indeed bolted open by students coming together to make gallons of sanitizers and package them or to stitch together face masks for free distribution to the poor[53] while the government was trading in export profits on protective equipment (Gunasekar and Sanyal 2020). How are these not practicals enough? Why can't the field of the university-affiliated ethnographer be shifted to relief camps in cyclone-affected south Bengal or colonies of migrant labour? How is running a community kitchen for the stranded poor not worthy of term-paper credit? Is sheltering a Muslim family displaced by a state-backed pogrom in northeast Delhi not adequate learning for a lost semester? Is opening a community radio station to relay our collective (but divergent) experiences of the pandemic – or simply writing a song to mourn the death of a neighbour whose ambulance arrived a little too late – too little for an examination's worth of teaching? If so, the public university had become a relic even before we shoved and shelved it online.

For months before the outbreak of the pandemic, students at Indian universities moulted into the primary apprentices of a political revolution – a 'democracy from below' (Beg 2020; Ara 2020a). They streamed into the streets, occupied alleys, sat on highways, marched towards Parliament, thronged the gates of ministers' residences and blocked police headquarters against a 'chronology' of citizenship legislations that sought to disenfranchise, detain and deport the Muslim poor as 'illegal migrants'.[54] The spring in their slogans thundered against the darkness of state terror till the 'imaginative work' made possible by a public university demanded a republic of commons. There was intimacy and laughter, dread and defiance in this festival of political vagrancy; the physical space of the university was beginning to transform itself by exceeding its body and borders. It was as if the country became a university of outsiders and immigrants, learning to love and live with every other.

The pandemic's online swoop on these teeming multitudes has helped policy architects of public education imagine a not-too-far-away future, where universities may be swept clean of student bodies altogether. Not a stray loiterer, not a voice out of choir, not a poster out of place, not a protestor out on the prowl – a 'Swachh Bharat' dream come true! Such is a university logisticized; a prison-house of self-quarantined dissent and data-pack(aged) labour.

Sitting in Mussolini's prison, Gramsci wrote about the need for a new class of 'organic intellectuals' whose 'mode of being . . . can no longer consist in eloquence, which is an exterior and momentary mover of feelings and passions, but in active participation in practical life, as constructor, organiser, "permanent persuader" and not just a simple orator' (Gramsci 1971: 10). Since the digital university is about 'connecting' away from 'practical life', it can only log in to the national(ist) organization of a future *sans* organic intellectuals.

Postscript: A Pan(aca)demic Excursus

George K. Varghese recounted his field experiences from colleges in Karnataka and Kerala to point at a deep sense of 'alienation', structurally reproduced by humanistic pedagogy and curricula across institutions

(Varghese 2011: 91–98). He went on to chart a history of the disciplinarization of social and human sciences in the west, finally contending that the power of the digital invasion into 'matters' of academic inquiry has only led to an era of baffling 'super-specialisation'. In a Deleuzean sense, he regards these 'territorialisations, deterritorializations and rhizomic interconnections between far-end disciplines' (ibid.: 98) as postulating a new and necessary order of default 'multidisciplinarity' – something that he accuses the post-Independence Indian encounter with humanities and social science teaching as incapable of meeting the challenge of. On that note, he complains: '[w]ith a few outdated governmental institutions given the mandate for the overall nurture of knowledge what we have witnessed [in India] is tenacious immobility, distortion and degeneration of these non-science disciplines' (ibid.). This is a familiar lament couched in terms of a moral inadequacy and normative idealism, even if one were to un-hear Varghese's stealthy suggestion for de-regulating social science teaching (from being the 'mandate' of 'outdated governmental institutions') towards a new crop of elite private liberal arts universities of the kind that he himself taught in. This was 2011, and the age of Shiv Nadars and Ashokas and Jindal Globals had already begun,[55] often with the tacit and not-so-tacit enlisting of innovation enthusiasts from the ilk of social scientists and humanists. Turning Varghese's lament into a prophecy, the new NEP 2020 champions a wholesale move towards broad-based 'multidisciplinary' liberal education and argues for a phasing out of single-stream institutions or their mergers into 'multidisciplinary education and research universities' (MERUs).[56]

So, are we finally 'delivered' into global relevance, as Varghese would have imagined close to a decade ago? The answer however stands at an immeasurable distance from the desired ideal, insofar as the NEP's imaginative glossary for 'multidisciplinarity' only consists in the structural mechanics of optional course offerings; for example, a student of physics taking a semester's course in Sanskrit or a student of sociology dabbling in a paper's worth of accountancy. Alongside this order of cognitive skill-training in multidisciplinarity, what does not find a single mention in the government's new policy manifesto are the *actual* instances of interdisciplinary social science practice that emerged from those same 'outdated governmental institutions' that Varghese talks so disparagingly of – namely, women's studies, studies in social exclusion or social and economic planning, human rights studies, minority studies. Quite the contrary, such centres have been at the receiving end of the government's threats for closure and defunding since 2013 (Bhattacharya 2019b: 194–96); the latest of such targets being Jamia Millia Islamia's Sarojini Naidu Centre for Women's Studies (SNCWS) (Ara 2020b). What Varghese misses in his elaborate 'global tour' of the institutional lives of the social sciences is precisely this epistemological dichotomy: between the substance of the 'interdisciplinary' and the shadow of the 'multidisciplinary'. The latter is aimed at reproducing the conditions of survival of a recessionary economy – that is, an order of multi-tasking labour that thrives on cheap, semi-skilled, informal job contracts. For it, a cursory flirtation with accountancy and sociology is quite enough, as well as effective in forestalling any penchant for critical inquiry. The interdisciplinary social sciences on the other hand begin by questioning the limits of disciplinary methods and conventions and are therefore potentially committed to teasing the imaginative contours of democracy.

The chronicle of the post-pandemic Indian university, as foretold by NEP 2020, is unsurprisingly both hydra-headed in its multidisciplinary proliferations as well as minimalistic in its reliance on 'faceless' interactions.[57] It recalls the triumphalism of a virtual multiplicity. The economics and arithmetic of this 'multiplicity' bear out the truth in the paradox. It resounds through policy diktats and regulatory circulars:[58] minimization of physical teaching routines and yet an increase in the number of workdays and working hours, fewer face-to-face classes and yet longer daily shifts, blended teaching methods and yet biometric attendance scans, work-from-home schedules that consist in turning your home into the scientist's laboratory or the ethnographer's field at will. Time will walk us into classrooms that resemble airport lounges; each of us sitting at feet-measures of 'social distance' but permanently logged into our devices, never meeting till a message pops up on our screens.

This is no dystopian science fiction. It is the little workshop of a 'brave new world', where there is little work worth its name and little play that does not worsen the rules of the game.

Acknowledgement: A word of gratitude is owed to the anonymous reviewer, for the provocative comments and suggestions that followed an earlier version of the essay.

Notes
1 Jan Breman, in his deep ethnographic account of informalization of labour in southern Gujarat and large-scale migration of a rural proletariat into the non-agricultural urban economy, presciently notes how governments and state-appointed committees have repeatedly given in to a 'dominant tendency to see the informal sector as a reservoir of self-employed'. Conducting his fieldwork through the period that saw the Indian economy transition from 'national capitalism' to a free market regime, he points at a poignant irony within state-led policy planning: 'According to this stereotype, the heterogeneous mass of energetic and inventive mini-entrepreneurs inhabiting the lower echelons of the economy are quite able to look after themselves and are in fact better off without state intervention' (Breman 1996: 197).
2 In the midst of a Covid-induced national lockdown which saw thousands of migrant labourers and daily wage workers stuck without work or food, and away

from home for months, the Prime Minister announced the unveiling of a 'stimulus' package as the route to economic recovery. The package, called Aatma Nirbhar Bharat Abhiyaan ('Self-Reliant India Mission') promised a total of Rs 20 lakh crore of relief, which was to devolve into a series of sector-wise 'structural reforms' to be subsequently elaborated by the Finance Minister. For details of the PM's televised speech, see Misra (2020).

³ As part of the Rs 20 trillion 'fiscal stimulus', the key public sectors marked out for 'structural reforms' – in the form of enhanced foreign direct investment (FDI) and entry of private capital – include defence, coal, minerals, civil aviation, power distribution, social infrastructure and space–atomic energy. For a summary of the package, see Government of India (2020). For a break-up of the package details, see Institute of Policy Research Studies (2020). For an analysis of announcements, see Roychoudhury (2020); Abrol and Franco (2020); 'Centre's economic package: Centre raises FDI in defence to 74 per cent, allows commercial coal mining', *Scroll.in,* 16 May 2020, available at https://scroll.in/latest/962130/centres-economic-package-centre-raises-fdi-in-defence-to-74-allows-commercial-coal-mining; 'Modi's Rs 20 Lakh Crore Package Will Likely Have Fiscal Cost of Less Than Rs 2.5 Lakh Crore', *The Wire,* 17 May 2020, available at https://thewire.in/economy/modi-rs-20-lakh-crore-package-actual-spend

⁴ Jan Breman prefers to call such forms of 'labour nomadism', 'circulation instead of migration' (Breman 2013: 6).

⁵ While infection rates in the country were steadily on the rise and the government's lack of preparedness with public health infrastructures became apparent, the Prime Minister made periodic appearances on national television to urge citizens to perform symbolic charades in their 'fight' against the virus. On 19 March 2020, days before the world's longest-ever lockdown was to be announced at four hours' notice, the PM urged people to thank the 'Corona warriors' – essential service workers – by clapping from their balconies or banging steel plates or blowing conch shells (Panwar 2020). With the situation getting grimmer by the day and with masses of migrant working populations forced to walk back home with no recourse to public transport, the Prime Minister made another televised appeal on 3 April for people to fight the 'darkness' of a pandemic by switching off lights and flashing candles or mobile torches (Narendra Modi, 'Let us switch off lights at home & light a lamp for 9 minutes at 9 PM on 5ᵗʰ April', 3 April 2020, available at https://www.narendramodi.in/text-of-prime-minister-narendra-modi-s-address-to-the-nation--549108). Millions of people across the country mimed the Prime Minister's call for theatrical symbolism with unquestioned devotion, sometimes by dancing to drumbeats with plates in their hands or by bursting firecrackers in festive revelry – a testimony to how fascist commandeering works by holding people's minds hostage. For more, see 'Social Distancing Forgotten, Country Raises a Racket at 5 pm', *The Wire,* 22 March 2020, available at https://thewire.in/society/coronavirus-janata-curfew-racket; 'Modi Harnesses "Power of Light", Questions Remain on Strategy to Combat COVID-19', *The Wire,* 5 April 2020, available at https://thewire.in/politics/narendra-modi-coronavirus-diwali

⁶ An order issued by the Government of Haryana (ADGP/Law and Order), Ref. No. 5264-5304/L&O-3 dated 29 March 2020 – captioned 'COVID-19 Instructions Regarding Flow of Migrant Labour Across Haryana' – cited the Union Home Ministry's 'alarm and unhappiness at the large-scale movement of migrant labour on roads by foot' and issued 'clear directions from the Central Government' to ensure that 'there is no movement of people on roads'. Section 4 of the order empowers the 'State Home Department to declare big indoor stadiums or other similar facilities as Temporary Jails, so that people who refuse to obey the lawful

directions of district administration can be arrested and placed in custody for the offence committed by them under the Disaster Management Act'. See also Yadav (2020); Suffian (2020).

[7] Sections 20.5.3 and 20.5.4 of the Draft National Education Policy (DNEP) 2019 (New Delhi: Ministry of Human Resource Development, 2019) observe that the 'projected requirement for upskilling and reskilling youth is several times larger than that of training fresh candidates. HEIs [Higher Educational Institutions] can consider ways to address this requirement, through evening courses, online courses and so on that can bring in additional revenue for them. . . . This task will also require projections of the need for such skilling in various sectors (e.g. skills gap analysis). . . . A large percentage of India's workforce is in the unorganized sector and in small businesses. They must have the option of moving from being hired as unskilled or semi-skilled labour to becoming skilled labour instead and being paid correspondingly higher wages. Many of them would also benefit greatly from receiving training in areas like entrepreneurship, financial and digital literacy. HEIs must be incentivized to look for models to address this need. The infrastructure for adult education as well as online education must also be used to provide opportunities for them to get trained during off work hours' (pp. 370–71).

[8] As a demonstrative example of recent developments towards this goal, see 'University Grants Commission (Open and Distance Learning Programmes and Online Programmes) Regulations 2020', *The Gazette of India: Extraordinary*, New Delhi: University Grants Commission, 4 September 2020.

[9] For detailed coverage on the tragic mishandling of the second wave of the pandemic by the Indian government in April–May 2021, see Dutt (2021); Gettleman *et al.* (2021); Pandey and Nazmi (2021); Bhowmick (2021); 'We are Burning Bodies as They Arrive: India's Crematoriums Overwhelmed as Covid Crisis Spirals', *Independent*, 25 April 2021, available at https://www.independent.co.uk/news/india-covid-crematoriums-graveyards-b1837109.html

[10] Refer to 'Blended Mode of Teaching and Learning: Concept Note', New Delhi: University Grants Commission, May 2021, available at https://www.ugc.ac.in/pdfnews/6100340_Concept-Note-Blended-Mode-of-Teaching-and-Learning.pdf

[11] See 'Public Notice Ref. No. D.O. No. 1-9/2020 (CPP-II) dated 20 May 2021', New Delhi: University Grants Commission, available at https://www.ugc.ac.in/pdfnews/7782448_Public-Notice.pdf, in consonance with Section 6.5.1 of 'Blended Mode', p. 36.

[12] Refer to Section 8 of Table 6.1, 'Blended Mode of Teaching and Learning: Concept Note', p. 34.

[13] See 'Recommendations of the National Education Policy 2020 Implementation Committee, University of Delhi (NIC) on structure of Undergraduate Programs of the University of Delhi', available at https://u.pcloud.link/publink/show?code=XZmE4uXZvU2WTYu6BXjl2Xb5utrY0zDAgK67

[14] Agrawal (2021), while documenting the fortunes of a four-year undergraduate programme (FYUP) in Delhi University from 2013 to its current reincarnation post-NEP, reports: 'DU is now collaborating with 40 other universities across the country under the "Vidya Vistar Scheme" to provide assistance and working knowledge to other universities across the country.'

[15] 'Recommendations of the National Education Policy 2020 Implementation Committee', pp. 5–8.

[16] Addendum 1, Section 4.7 of DNEP 2019. See note 28 below, for a more exact index of numbers.

[17] See Section 1.2, 'Blended Mode of Teaching and Learning: Concept Note', pp. 1–3.

[18] See Kapur and Mehta, eds (2017). In the 'Introduction' to the volume, the editors

identify the 'trilemma' of Indian higher-education policy as consisting in the cross-cutting challenges of access, quality and financing.

19 See Nagarajan (2020); Goradia (2020); Bhaskaran (2020); and 'Digital Divide May Turn Shift to Online Classes Operational Nightmare, Warn Experts', *The Week,* 8 June 2020, available at https://www.theweek.in/news/sci-tech/2020/06/08/Digital-divide-may-turn-shift-to-online-classes-operational-nightmare-warn-experts.html

20 For an understanding of how, in the context of the pandemic, concerns about privacy and data protection have re-surfaced, see Kapur (2020). The Internet Freedom Foundation, vide its letter Ref. No. IFF/2020/131 dated May 02, 2020 addressed to the Prime Minister, flagged these concerns (available at https://drive.google.com/file/d/1RR3tBnJCSkQvSDp0uVcMQr6C2RILgqg4/view). A comprehensive report on the question of data privacy and India's tryst with forms of cybersurveillance has been published by the Centre for Internet and Society, *The State of Privacy in India,* available at https://privacyinternational.org/state-privacy/1002/state-privacy-india#policiessectoral.

21 Part II, Chapter 11 ('Towards a More Liberal Education') of the original DNEP 2019 (New Delhi: Ministry of Human Resource Development), notes: 'A comprehensive liberal arts education develops all capacities of human beings – intellectual, aesthetic, social, physical, emotional and moral – in an integrated manner. Such education, which develops the fundamental capacities of individuals on all aspects of being human, is by its very nature liberal education, and is aimed at developing good and complete human beings' (p. 224).

22 'Editorial: University as Battleground', *Economic and Political Weekly,* vol. 52, no. 8, February 2017, p. 25, available at https://www.epw.in/journal/2017/8/editorials/university-battleground.html. See also Thapar (2016); Kumar (2016).

23 Refer to '9-member panel to prepare final draft of National Education Policy', *Business Standard,* 26 June 2017, available at https://www.business-standard.com/article/news-ians/9-member-panel-to-prepare-final-draft-of-national-education-policy-117062600537_1.html. See also Sharma (2018).

24 Refer to Section 14.4 (p. 33) of the final National Education Policy 2019 – revised from the Kasturirangan Committee report by the MHRD, and leaked to press. Titled 'Equity and Inclusion in Higher Education', this section aims at 'increasing economic and employability potential of higher education programmes' in order to set 'targets for higher GER for URGs'. However, Section 11.7 of the same document names 'employability' as only a 'by-product' for the overwhelming majority of students enlisted for a 'liberal education' curriculum across all 'types' of institutions (p. 29).

25 See 'Digital Divide May Turn Shift to Online Classes Operational Nightmare, Warn Experts', *India Today,* 19 December 2019, available at https://www.indiatoday.in/india/story/education-for-all-universities-across-india-fight-fee-hikes-1629501-2019-12-19; see also Shankar, Nagpaul and Dwivedi Johri (2019); Kaushal (2019); Sharma (2019).

26 For references to how public universities across the country have been systematically branded by the Hindu right in power as a cauldron of sedition and 'anti-national' sentiment, see Yamunan (2015); 'Rohith Vemula Didn't Get Fellowship for Past 7 Months, Says Letter', *The Economic Times,* 19 January 2016, available at https://economictimes.indiatimes.com/news/politics-and-nation/rohit-vemula-didnt-get-fellowship-for-past-7-months-says-letter/articleshow/50638216.cms?from=mdr; 'My Birth is My Fatal Accident: Rohith Vemula's Searing Letter is an Indictment of Social Prejudices', *The Wire,* 17 January 2019, available at https://thewire.in/caste/rohith-vemula-letter-a-powerful-indictment-of-social-prejudices; 'Police Crack Down at JNU, Arrest Student Leader for Sedition', *The*

Hindu Business Line, 12 February 2016, available at https://www.thehindubusi-nessline.com/news/education/police-crack-down-at-jnu-arrest-student-leader-for-sedition/article8229344.ece; Pandey (2018); Sethi (2016); Hebbar (2016); 'After National Flag, Smriti Irani Ropes in Army to Teach Nationalism on Campus', *India Today,* 15 March 2016, available at https://www.indiatoday.in/india/story/after-national-flag-smriti-irani-ropes-in-army-to-teach-nationalism-on-cam-pus-313367-2016-03-15.

27 'Who is an Urban Naxal, asks Romila Thapar', *The Hindu,* 30 September 2018, available at https://www.thehindu.com/news/national/who-is-an-urban-naxal-asks-romila-thapar/article25088465.ece.

28 Addendum 1, Section 4.7 of the DNEP 2019, indicates a reduction of the total num-ber of higher educational institutions across all 'Types' to a maximum of 12,300 – from its current size of 51,649, as recorded in the *All India Survey on Higher Education (AISHE) Report 2018–19,* New Delhi: Ministry of Human Resource Development, 2019. Section 2.3 of the *AISHE Report 2018–19* needs to be read in consonance with Chapter 9 of DNEP 2019 in order to understand the doubling of enrolments proposed by the latter.

29 Clause 4.3 of University Grants Commission, 'UGC (Credit Framework for Online Learning Courses through SWAYAM) Regulation 2016', *The Gazette of India Extraordinary,* Part III – Section 4, 20 July 2016, New Delhi: Government of India.

30 See 'Online Teaching Limit in University Courses Needs to be Doubled: UGC Panel', *ABP Education,* 27 April 2020, available at https://www.abpeducation.com/news/online-teaching-limit-in-university-courses-needs-to-be-doubled-ugc-panel-1.1142437

31 See University Grants Commission, 'UGC Guidelines on Examinations and Academic Calendar for the Universities in View of COVID-19 Pandemic and Subsequent Lockdown', New Delhi: Ministry of Human Resource Development, appended to Letter D.O. No. F.1-1/2020 (Secy), dated 29 April 2020, p. 7.

32 As per Section 2.3 of the *AISHE Report 2018–19,* p. 18, the GER for higher edu-cation in the age bracket 18 to 23 years is estimated at 26.3 per cent. This figure implies that 73.7 per cent of the relevant age cohort does not even enrol for a col-lege or university degree.

33 See Section 23.3 of the final National Education Policy 2019, by the Ministry of Human Resource Development (revised from the Kasturirangan Committee report and leaked to press). It says: 'An autonomous body, the National Educational Alliance for Technology (NEAT), *will be* created to provide a platform for the free exchange of ideas on the use of technology to enhance learning, assessment, plan-ning, administration, and so on' (p. 49; emphasis mine). Much before the policy was approved by the Cabinet, the said body was announced as functional by a press release from the Ministry of Human Resource Development in September 2019. The original Press Information Bureau (PIB) release has recently been removed from the official website, but a copy of the announcement is archived and available at https://www.phdcci.in/wp-content/uploads/2019/09/Ministry-of-Human-Resource-Development-announces-National-Educational-Alliance-for-Technology-NEAT-Scheme.pdf. See also 'Government Portal to Offer Education Technologies Using Artificial Intelligence for Personalised Learning', *The Hindu,* 19 September 2019, available at https://www.thehindu.com/sci-tech/government-portal-to-offer-education-technologies-using-artificial-intelligence-for-personal-ised-learning/article29460680.ece

34 Newfield's essay (2016b) cites from a 2013 study, *Adaptability to Online Learning: Differences across Types of Students and Academic Subject Areas,* conducted by D. Xu and S.S. Jaggars, researchers at Columbia University: 'Overall, the online

format had a significantly negative relationship with both course persistence and course grade, indicating that the typical student had difficulty adapting to online courses. While this negative sign remained consistent across all subgroups, the size of the negative coefficient varied significantly across subgroups. Specifically, we found that males, Black students, and students with lower levels of academic preparation experienced significantly stronger negative coefficients for online learning compared with their counterparts, in terms of both course persistence and course grade. These results provide support for the notion that students are not homogeneous in their adaptability to the online delivery format and may therefore have substantially different outcomes for online learning. . . . These patterns also suggest that performance gaps between key demographic groups already observed in face-to-face classrooms (e.g., gaps between male and female students, and gaps between White and ethnic minority students) are exacerbated in online courses. This is troubling from an equity perspective.'

[35] Ibid.: 26, where the author registers findings from an early 2013 survey on the relationship between MOOCs and educational resource allocation in the US: 'Our first question was, how do online programme personnel compare to those of face-to-face programmes? Our hypothesis was that they would have reduced teaching staff compared to traditional colleges and universities. We first noted that virtually all of the higher education companies that used online as their primary teaching mode were for-profit companies. Even including the not-for-profit firms, distance-only [online degree] institutions have one third as many full-time faculty as community colleges, and about one eighth as many as public research universities. Student–faculty ratios were the highest (worst) in the business – worse even than community colleges, and three times higher than the gold standard of liberal arts college.'

[36] See Schell (2009: 114–18). The author notes: 'The US has been a major incubator of for-profit universities. Perhaps best known of them all, the University of Phoenix models what these universities are all about – profit. Students meet in empty office buildings or rented spaces at night to attend classes or log-on to virtual campuses. Approximately 95% of all teachers at the University of Phoenix are contingent faculty working off the tenure-track. . . . For-profit educational institutions are profitable because they do not carry real estate and labor costs in the same way that traditional universities do. They make money because they don't keep up expensive grounds and expensive libraries and student centers – all things associated with traditional universities. They also do not make commitments to expensive, tenure-line faculty. They quite literally and quite nakedly make their money off of contingent faculty's backs. They "outsource" their entire faculty operation to contingent faculty or they employ a few big name professors to design online courses (course ware) that are then facilitated by online contingent faculty. . . . Contingency is to be accepted, capitalized upon, and celebrated. This entrepreneurial rhetoric of the happy adjunct plays right into the entrepreneurial rhetoric of outsourcing and online education.'

[37] Clause 4.4(a) of the University Grants Commission, 'UGC (Credit Framework for Online Learning Courses through SWAYAM) Regulation 2016', *The Gazette of India Extraordinary*, Part III – Section 4, 20 July 2016 (New Delhi: Government of India), explicitly empowers the academic council of a university to 'allow' online courses if 'there is non-availability of suitable teaching staff for running a course in the Institution'.

[38] Clause 4.4(b) (ibid.) extends provisions for online enrolments if 'the facilities for offering the elective papers (courses), sought for by the students are not on offer in the Institution, but are available on the SWAYAM platform'.

[39] Table 5, *AISHE Report 2018–19*, p. 18

40 I borrow this term from the severally scattered allusions by Gayatri Chakravorty Spivak, in her accounts of an 'epistemological performance' with the children of subalterns in rural Bengal, to the moral entrepreneurialism of corporate-funded NGOs armed with digital doles of skill-relief packages. This model of knowledge management, Spivak repeatedly maintains in her lectures, is only aimed at reproducing feudal behaviours in the subaltern – the 'social responsibility' logic of globalised finance capital.

41 Structured as an internal debate between the two authors, this book is fundamentally hinged on Guru's diagnosis of the epistemic hierarchies that condition the rite of passage into social science practice in India. Guru observes how, in advanced social scientific research, the right to abstract theoretical thinking has continued to be the historical preserve of the caste elite while raw 'lived experience' remains the only repository of Dalits and Bahujans.

42 Bourdieu and Passeron (1979: 27) explain this principle of 'eliminationism' based on cultural capital thus: '. . . the potency of the social factors of inequality is such that even if the equalization of economic resources could be achieved, the university system would not cease to consecrate inequalities by transforming social privilege into individual gifts or merits. Rather, if formal equality of opportunity were achieved, the school system would be able to employ all the appearances of legitimacy in its work of legitimating privileges.'

43 Christopher Newfield (2010) incisively invokes the scourge of 'knowledge management' within what is understood as the American knowledge economy. Though specifically rooted in the US higher education context, the discussion is of prescient use in contemporary settings across the world. In the piece, Newfield refers to the triadic tiering of university education – where the lowest order is 'focused on regional needs and vocational training' and confers 'mass degrees that offer their possessor no special advantage in the job market'. He continues: 'Though their graduates have acquired meaningful cognitive skills and some focused credentials, they have obtained no social advantage. These institutions are about basic employability, but not about social mobility. They are increasingly seen as the only destination for knowledge training that the society's leaders are willing to pay for. They are the training grounds of the true "cognitariat", knowledge workers and rarely knowledge managers, and in fact heavily managed starting with curricula oriented towards immediate job skills from their first year in college.' They, in Newfield's analogy from pre-revolutionary France, eject their beneficiaries into a 'Third Estate' which includes 'the vast majority of brainworkers whose jobs require college degrees, additional specialised knowledge, and complicated experiential "know-how" – nurses, social workers, accountants, urban planners, architects, and college professors with doctorates in anthropology or the history of art'.

44 Supreme Court of India, *Miss A. Sundarambal vs Government of Goa, Daman and Diu*, 5 September 1983. The bench, comprising Justices G. Couto and R. Jahagirdar, debated about 'whether a teacher is a workman as defined in Section 2(s) of the Industrial Disputes Act' (para 16). It finally came to the conclusion that teaching work, by virtue of involving higher-order intellectual skills, does not fall within the scope of the said Act and cannot claim relief to disputes under its provisions.

45 Section 6.2 (appearing under the section title 'Equitable and Inclusive Education: Learning for All') of the Cabinet-approved *National Education Policy 2020* (New Delhi: Ministry of Human Resource Development, published on the MHRD website on 30 July 2020, p. 24) announces: 'Socio-Economically Disadvantaged Groups (SEDGs) can be broadly categorized based on gender identities (particularly female and transgender individuals), socio-cultural identities (such as Scheduled Castes, Scheduled Tribes, OBCs, and minorities), geographical identities (such as students

from villages, small towns and aspirational districts), disabilities (including learning disabilities), and socio-economic conditions (such as migrant communities, low income households, children in vulnerable situations, victims of or children of victims of trafficking, orphans including child beggars in urban areas, and the urban poor).' The 'breadth' of the 'categorization' is so expansive that it effectively reduces 'disadvantage' to ahistorical generality.

[46] Ibid., Sections 9.3(e), 13.1, 18.10, 19.2.

[47] Refer to the government's anointing of a yet-unestablished Jio University – a private university project piloted by the Reliance Foundation – as an 'Institute of Eminence' (IoE) in 2018, while its academic operations were reported to begin in 2021. See 'Jio Institute, Still on Paper, Gets "Eminence" Tag, Sparks Row', *Hindustan Times,* 10 July 2018, available at https://www.hindustantimes.com/india-news/still-on-paper-jio-institute-gets-institution-of-eminence-tag-draws-criticism/story-w45LROLHvX95uUB4eKdfXO.html

[48] Section 13.6 of *National Education Policy 2020*, p. 40.

[49] Ibid., Section 11.10, p. 38.

[50] See 'Key Results of the *AISHE Report 2018–19*', p. II.

[51] Edu-factory Collective, 'Introduction: All Power to Self-Education!', in *Toward a Global Autonomous University: Cognitive Labor, The Production of Knowledge, and Exodus from the Education Factory,* New York: Autonomedia, 2009, p. 5.

[52] 'University Grants Commission (Open and Distance Learning Programmes and Online Programmes) Regulations 2020', *The Gazette of India: Extraordinary,* New Delhi: University Grants Commission, 4 September 2020, p. 91.

[53] For example, see 'Coronavirus: Jadavpur University, Kolkata College Make Low-cost Hand Sanitisers', *The New Indian Express,* 21 March 2020, available at https://www.newindianexpress.com/nation/2020/mar/21/coronavirus-jadavpur-university-kolkata-college-make-low-cost-hand-sanitisers-2119471.html; Rumi (2020); Mullick (2020).

[54] See '"Aap chronology samajh lijiye": Amit Shah's phrase on NRC-CAA is the internet's favourite meme', *The Free Press Journal,* 30 December 2019, available at https://www.freepressjournal.in/india/aap-chronology-samajh-lijiye-amit-shahs-phrase-on-nrc-caa-is-the-internets-favourite-meme; Ramakrishnan (2020); Johri (2020); 'Resistance, revolution and resolve: How Indian students led the anti-CAA protests', *Sabrang,* 23 December 2019, available at https://sabrangindia.in/article/resistance-revolution-and-resolve-how-indian-students-led-anti-caa-protest

[55] For a discerning account of the political developments and legislative plans that enabled the sprouting of a private 'hub of higher education' (in Haryana) through the first decade of this century, see Roy Chowdhury (2018).

[56] See Sections 10.11 and 11.11 of *National Education Policy 2020*, pp. 35, 38.

[57] Section 18.10 of *National Education Policy 2020* insists on 'a faceless and transparent regulatory intervention' and unflinchingly advocates 'use [of] technology extensively to reduce human interface to ensure efficiency and transparency' (p. 48).

[58] For example, see 'UGC Guidelines on Academic Calendar for the First Year of Under-Graduate and Post-Graduate Students of the Universities for the Session 2020–21 in View of COVID-19 Pandemic', New Delhi: University Grants Commission, September 2020, available at https://www.ugc.ac.in/pdfnews/1019576_Guideline.pdf

References

Abrol, D. and T. Franco (2020), 'Time to Revitalise the Public Sector', *Frontline,* 17 July 2020, available at https://frontline.thehindu.com/cover-story/article31954249.ece

Agrawal, S. (2021), 'DU's New FYUP Won't be Like Failed 2013 Attempt, Will be Student-Centric, Says Acting VC', *The Print,* 28 August, available at https://theprint.in/

india/education/dus-new-fyup-wont-be-like-failed-2013-attempt-will-be-student-centric-says-acting-vc/723361/

Ara, I. (2020a), '"Walls Are the Publishers of the Poor": How Women Sketch the Language of Resistance', *The Wire*, 15 February, available at https://thewire.in/women/walls-are-the-publishers-of-the-poor-how-women-sketch-the-language-of-resistance

———— (2020b), 'As Students and Teachers Panic, Jamia Withdraws Notice Disbanding Two Departments', *The Wire*, 7 April, available at https://thewire.in/education/as-students-and-teachers-panic-jamia-withdraws-notice-disbanding-two-departments

Beg, S.M. (2020), 'The Colourful Dissent: When Shaheen Bagh, Jamia Become a Canvas for Protest', *The Indian Express*, 19 January, available at https://indianexpress.com/article/cities/delhi/the-colourful-dissent-when-shaheen-bagh-jamia-become-a-canvas-for-protest-6223028/

Bhaskaran, R. (2020), 'Great Lockdown: Online Classes, Remote Working Widen India's Digital Divide', *Policy Circle*, 15 April, available at https://www.policycircle.org/economy/online-classes-remote-working-widen-indias-digital-divide/

Bhattacharya, D. (2019a), 'What "Use" is the Liberal Ruse? Debating the "Idea" of the University', in D. Bhattacharya, ed., *The University Unthought: Notes for a Future*, London and New York: Routledge.

———— (2019b), 'Between Disciplines and Interdisciplines: The University of In-Discipline', in D. Bhattacharya, ed., *The University Unthought: Notes for a Future*, London and New York: Routledge.

———— (2020), 'A Viral Education? Into the Future of Our Locked Classrooms and Shut Campuses', *The Wire*, 31 March, available at https://thewire.in/education/covid-19-online-teaching-future-classrooms.

Bhowmick, N. (2021), 'How India's Second Wave Became the Worst COVID-19 Surge in the World', *National Geographic*, 23 April, available at https://www.nationalgeographic.com/science/article/how-indias-second-wave-became-the-worst-covid-19-surge-in-the-world

Bourdieu, P. and Jean-Claude Passeron (1979), *The Inheritors: French Students and their Relation to Culture*, translated by Richard Nice, Chicago and London: The University of Chicago Press.

Breman, J. (1996), *Footloose Labour: Working in India's Informal Economy*, Cambridge: Cambridge University Press.

———— (2013), 'Introduction', in *At Work in the Informal Economy of India: A Perspective from the Bottom Up*, New Delhi: Oxford University Press.

Caffentzis, G. and S. Federici (2009), 'Notes on the Edu-factory and Cognitive Capitalism', in Edu-factory Collective, ed., *Toward a Global Autonomous University: Cognitive Labor, The Production of Knowledge, and Exodus from the Education Factory*, New York: Autonomedia, pp. 125–31.

Chatterjee, H. and A. Sengupta (2019), *Ei Banglar Udbastu: Smriti, Sangkhya, Bhabishyat*, Kolkata: People's Study Circle.

Das, D. (2018), *Assam-e Nagarikpanjir Satkahan*, Kolkata: People's Study Circle.

Dutt, B. (2021), 'India's Health System Has Collapsed', *Hindustan Times*, 17 April, available at https://www.hindustantimes.com/opinion/indias-health-system-has-collapsed-101618558934636.html

Friedman, T.L. (2013), 'Revolution Hits the Universities', *The New York Times*, 26 January, available at https://www.nytimes.com/2013/01/27/opinion/sunday/friedman-revolution-hits-the-universities.html

Gettleman, J., S. Yasir, H. Kumar, S. Raj and A. Loke (2021), 'As Covid-19 Devastates India, Deaths Go Undercounted', *The New York Times*, 24 April, available at https://www.nytimes.com/2021/04/24/world/asia/india-coronavirus-deaths.html

Goradia, A. (2020), 'As Schools Switch to Online Classes, Students from Weaker Sections

Get Cut Off from Learning', *The Indian Express*, 28 April, available at https://indianexpress.com/article/cities/mumbai/as-schools-switch-to-online-classes-students-from-weaker-sections-get-cut-off-from-learning-6347739/

Government of India (GoI) (2019), *All India Survey on Higher Education Report 2018–19*, New Delhi: Ministry of Human Resource Development.

—— (2020), 'Press Information Bureau (PIB) Release: Finance Minister Announces Government Reforms and Enablers across Seven Sectors under Aatma Nirbhar Bharat Abhiyaan', New Delhi: Ministry of Finance, 17 May, available at https://pib.gov.in/PressReleasePage.aspx?PRID=1624661

Gramsci, A. (1971), 'The Formation of the Intellectuals', in Q. Hoare and G.N. Smith, eds and trans., *Selections from the Prison Notebooks*, New York: International Publishers.

Gunasekar, A. and A. Sanyal (2020), 'India Sends COVID-19 Protective Gear To Serbia Amid Huge Shortage At Home', *NDTV*, 2 April, available at https://www.ndtv.com/india-news/india-sends-covid-19-protective-gear-to-serbia-amid-huge-shortage-at-home-2203900

Guru, G. (2012), 'Egalitarianism and the Social Sciences in India', in G. Guru and S. Sarukkai, eds, *The Cracked Mirror: An Indian Debate on Experience and Theory*, New Delhi: Oxford University Press.

—— (2013), 'Freedom of Expression and the Life of the Dalit Mind', *Economic and Political Weekly*, vol. 48, no. 10, 9 March.

Harney, S. and F. Moten (2013), *The Undercommons: Fugitive Planning and Black Study*, Wivenhoe, New York, Port Watson: Minor Compositions.

Hebbar, P. (2016), 'Haryana Professors Reprimanded For Staging Play Based on Mahasweta Devi Story', *Huffpost*, 9 November, available at https://www.huffingtonpost.in/2016/11/09/haryana-professors-reprimanded-for-staging-play-based-on-mahaswe_a_21601996/

Institute of Policy Research Studies (2020), PRS Legislative Research, 'Summary of Announcements: Aatma Nirbhar Bharat Abhiyaan', New Delhi: Institute of Policy Research Studies, 20 May, available at https://www.prsindia.org/sites/default/files/parliament_or_policy_pdfs/Summary%20of%20Aatma%20Nirbhar%20Bharat%20Abhiyaan.pdf.

Johri, A.D. (2020), 'From Anti-CAA Protests, to JNU and Jamia, Why Women are Leading the Fight', *The Indian Express*, 19 January, available at https://indianexpress.com/article/express-sunday-eye/women-resistance-caa-protests-jamia-millia-islamia-jnu-aishe-ghosh-6219828/

Kapur, D. and P.B. Mehta, eds (2017), *Navigating the Labyrinth: Perspectives on India's Higher Education*, Hyderabad: Orient BlackSwan.

Kapur, M. (2020), 'The Indian Government's Tech Initiatives Keep Failing Privacy Benchmarks', *Quartz India*, 13 May, available at https://qz.com/india/1853583/indias-aarogya-setu-aadhaar-other-tech-keep-failing-on-privacy/

Kaushal, R. (2019), 'Dream of Higher Education Moves Farther with Fee Hikes', *Newsclick*, 2 December, available at https://www.newsclick.in/Higher-Education-Fee-Hike-IIMC-NLU-IIT

Kumar, P. (2015), 'FYUP to CBCS, Game of Choices', *Deccan Herald*, 9 August, available at https://www.deccanherald.com/content/494228/fyup-cbcs-game-choices.html

Kumar, U. (2016), 'The University and its Outside', *Economic and Political Weekly*, vol. 51, no. 11, 12 March, available at https://www.epw.in/journal/2016/11/university-under-siege/university-and-its-outside.html

Kundu, P. (2020), 'Indian Education Can't Go Online – only 8% of Homes with Young Members Have Computer with Net Link', *Scroll. in*, 5 May, available at https://scroll.in/article/960939/indian-education-cant-go-online-only-8-of-homes-with-school-children-have-computer-with-net-link

McKenzie, L. (2020), 'India Opens the Door Wide for Online Learning', *Inside Higher Ed.*, 17 February, available at https://www.insidehighered.com/news/2020/02/17/indian-government-opens-market-online-higher-education

Misra, U. (2020), 'PM Modi's Atmanirbhar Bharat Abhiyan Economic Package: Here is the Fine Print', *The Indian Express*, 14 May, available at https://indianexpress.com/article/explained/narendra-modi-coronavirus-economic-package-india-self-reliance-6406939/

Mohanty, B.K. (2020), '100 Varsities to Go Online Amid Covid-19 Lockdown', *The Telegraph*, 17 May, available at https://www.telegraphindia.com/india/100-varsities-to-go-online-amid-coronavirus-lockdown/cid/1773781

Mullick, R. (2020), 'IIT Kanpur Community Kitchen Feeding 800 Street Kids', *Hindustan Times*, 6 April, available at https://www.hindustantimes.com/education/iit-kanpur-community-kitchen-feeding-800-street-kids/story-YlsC8PMTCE1U9rihLVcoiK.html

Nagarajan, A. (2020), 'Online Illusion: E-Learning and the Digital Divide', *Frontline*, 19 June, available at https://frontline.thehindu.com/cover-story/article31739849.ece

Newfield, C. (2010), 'The Structure and Silence of the Cognitariat', *Eurozine*, 5 February, available at https://www.eurozine.com/the-structure-and-silence-of-the-cognitariat/

———— (2016a), 'Private Vendors Leverage Public Funds: The Case of the MOOCs', in *The Great Mistake: How We Wrecked Public Universities and How We Can Fix Them*, Baltimore: John Hopkins University Press.

———— (2016b), 'Aftermath of the MOOC Wars: Can Commercial Vendors Support Creative Higher Education', *Learning and Teaching*, vol. 9, no. 2, pp. 12–41.

Pandey, M.C. (2018), 'JNU Student Najeeb Ahmed's Disappearance to Remain Mystery, CBI Ends Search', *India Today*, 16 October, available at https://www.indiatoday.in/india/story/jnu-student-najeeb-ahmed-disappearance-to-remain-mystery-cbi-ends-search-1368745-2018-10-16

Pandey, V. and S. Nazmi (2021), 'India Covid-19: Deadly Second Wave Spreads from Cities to Small Towns', *BBC News*, 29 April, available at https://www.bbc.com/news/world-asia-india-56913047

Panneerselvan, A.S. (2020), 'Shooting the Messenger', *The Hindu*, 6 April, available at https://www.thehindu.com/opinion/columns/shooting-the-messenger/article31263931.ece

Panwar, T.S. (2020), 'COVID-19: Plate's Noise to Drown Govt's Failure in Protecting Health Workers?', *Newsclick*, 22 March, available at https://www.newsclick.in/Plates-Noise-to-Drown-Govt-Failure-in-Protecting-Health-Workers

Ramakrishnan, V. (2020), 'What is the BJP Up To?', *Frontline*, 17 January, available at https://frontline.thehindu.com/cover-story/article30431432.ece

Roy Chowdhury, S. (2018), '"World Class" in Sonipat: How Privileged Private Universities are Settling Down in Rural Haryana', *Scroll.in*, 5 September, available at https://scroll.in/article/890578/world-class-in-sonipat-how-privileged-private-universities-are-settling-down-in-rural-haryana

Roychoudhury, A. (2020), 'FM gives Reforms Pill for Ailing Economy with Privatisation, Policy Tweaks', *Business Standard*, 17 May, available at https://www.business-standard.com/article/economy-policy/fm-gives-reforms-pill-for-ailing-economy-with-privatisation-policy-tweaks-120051700026_1.html

Rumi, F. (2020), 'Patna: AN College Students Make Masks', *The Times of India*, 22 April, available at https://timesofindia.indiatimes.com/city/patna/a-n-college-students-make-masks/articleshow/75279625.cms

Schell, E. (2009), 'Online Education, Contingent Faculty and Open Source Unionism', in Edu-factory Collective, ed., *Toward a Global Autonomous University: Cognitive Labor, The Production of Knowledge, and Exodus from the Education Factory*, New York: Autonomedia.

Sethi, A. (2016), 'Reading Foucault in Mahendragarh, or Why We Need a Public University System', *The Wire*, 10 May, available at https://thewire.in/education/reading-foucault-in-mahendragarh-or-why-we-need-a-public-university-system

Shankar, A., D. Nagpaul and A. Dwivedi Johri (2019), 'Not Just JNU: How India's Public Universities Becoming Costlier Hurts the Most Vulnerable', *The Indian Express*, 1 December, available at https://indianexpress.com/article/express-sunday-eye/jnu-fee-hike-protest-students-underprivileged-sections-tiss-presidency-college-jamia-millia-islamia-hostel-fee-6141302/

Sharma, K. (2018), '4 Years On, India's Still Waiting For New Education Policy – Modi Govt's Big 2014 Promise', *The Print*, 14 September, available at https://theprint.in/india/governance/4-years-on-indias-still-waiting-for-new-education-policy-modi-govts-big-2014-promise/117022/

Sharma, N. (2019), 'The JNU Uprising has Profound Implications for India's Student Community', *Quartz India*, 4 December, available at https://qz.com/india/1752775/jnu-fee-hike-protest-affects-iits-nlu-other-india-universities/

Sharma, S. (2015), 'Choice-Based Credit System: Standard of Education Will Suffer, Says Teachers', *The Indian Express*, 15 May, available at https://indianexpress.com/article/cities/delhi/choice-based-credit-system-standard-of-education-will-suffer-says-teachers/

Singh, B. (2020), 'Media in the Time of COVID-19', *Economic and Political Weekly Engage*, vol. 55, no. 16, 18 April, available at https://www.epw.in/engage/article/media-time-covid-19

Suffian, M. (2020), 'Odisha's Migrant Worker Brutally Beaten to Death by Surat Police', *India Today*, 16 May, available at https://www.indiatoday.in/india/story/odisha-migrant-worker-beaten-to-death-surat-police-gujarat-coronavirus-lockdown-1678682-2020-05-16

Tewari, R. (2015), 'Explained: Neither Clarity nor Credit, C is for Confusion in New UGC System', *The Indian Express*, 26 May, available at https://indianexpress.com/article/explained/explained-neither-clarity-nor-credit-c-is-for-confusion-in-new-ugc-system/

Thapar, R. (2016), 'Fear of the Intellectual: Targeting Institutions of Higher Education', *Economic and Political Weekly*, vol. 51, no. 10, 5 March, available at https://www.epw.in/journal/2016/10/commentary/targeting-institutions-higher-education.html;

Unnikrishnan, D. (2019), 'Citizenship Mayhem is Perfect Smokescreen for Government to Hide Real Economic Issues, But the Clock is Ticking', *Firstpost*, 18 December, available at https://www.firstpost.com/business/citizenship-mayhem-is-perfect-smokescreen-for-government-to-hide-real-economic-issues-but-the-clock-is-ticking-7797461.html

Varghese, G.K. (2011), 'Rethinking Social Sciences and Humanities in the Contemporary World', *Economic and Political Weekly*, vol. 46, no. 31, 30 July, pp. 91–98.

Verma, L. (2017), 'Harvard vs Hard Work: With GDP Data, PM Narendra Modi Snubs Note Ban Critics', *The Indian Express*, 2 March, available at http://indianexpress.com/elections/uttar-pradesh-assembly-elections-2017/harvard-vs-hard-work-with-gdp-data-pm-modi-snubs-noteban-critics-4550000/

Yadav, U.R. (2020), 'Coronavirus Lockdown: Police "Punish" 80 Migrants, Make Them Walk Back 17 km Under Tight Escort', *Deccan Herald*, 7 May, available at https://www.deccanherald.com/city/top-bengaluru-stories/coronavirus-lockdown-police-punish-80-migrants-make-them-walk-back-17-km-under-tight-escort-834480.html

Yamunan, S. (2015), 'IIT-Madras Derecognises Student Group', *The Hindu*, 28 May, available at https://www.thehindu.com/news/national/tamil-nadu/iitmadras-derecognises-student-group/article7256712.ece

10

Citizen, Consumer, User

Covid-19, the Platform University and Higher Education in India

Rohan D'Souza

The World Health Organization (WHO) officially declared Covid-19 as a global pandemic on 11 March 2020. Many governments in what seemed like a race against time sought to snap off human-to-human contact with lockdowns and implemented various types of curfews. Amidst this crisis-driven and evolving pandemic response, universities and schools were amongst the first to be closed.[1]

Two years onwards from the WHO's pandemic declaration, an acceptable normal remains elusive. While vaccination drives and other initiatives to contain infections have borne results, the Covid-19 virus and its variants such as the Delta and Omicron are expected to continue to haunt and trouble global health efforts. Similarly, restoring in-person teaching in universities and schools has also proved to be complicated and troubled. Classrooms and corridors are difficult spaces to sanitize, and teaching calls for levels of interactions that make strict social distancing norms near impossible to implement. Small wonder then that the case for the 'online' remains compelling, even as its overall implications for education continue to be debated (Kakkar 2020; Pednekar 2020; Rapanta *et al.* 2021: 715–42).

The push for online education in India, as in many other countries, actually pre-dated the pandemic. In May 2017, the marketing and consultancy group KPMG (Klynveld Peat Marwick Goerdeler) and the digital technology company Google teamed up to publish a study on the potential for online education (OE) in India.[2] Their report was unabashedly enthusiastic. India's online education, they calculated, was poised to grow steeply – from a customer base of 1.6 million in 2016 with a market size of $247 million to becoming, at the very least, 9.6 million customer-strong by 2021 and a $1.96 billion market. The report also talked up the need for a shift from the current OE focus on primary and secondary education by visualizing an even bigger role in higher education. A strong caveat was added nonetheless. Appropriate changes in the existing regulatory framework, it was pointed out, would be an absolute must if take-off conditions for OE were to be created within India's existing university and college ecosystem.[3]

In February 2020, Nirmala Sitharaman, Finance Minister, Government of India, in a budget speech, hinted that the then working draft of the National Education Policy (NEP) 2020 would allow universities to offer 'fully online degrees' in higher education (McKenzie 2020). Following the approval of the NEP (2020) by the Union Cabinet of India on 29 July 2020, the online push was inaugurated as one of the defining features of the new education strategy itself.[4]

In the first half of 2020, the Government of India, in fact, had already allowed the 'top 100 universities' to offer online degree courses.[5] The following year in 2021, the University Grants Commission, the premier higher education regulatory body in India, allowed colleges to conduct up to 40 per cent of their courses through SWAYAM (Study Webs of Active Learning for Young Aspiring Minds) – which is India's national massive open online course (MOOC) platform.[6]

India with its much-talked-about demographic dividend has, unsurprisingly, also emerged as a hot destination for educational technology (ed-tech) companies – defined as learning platforms that can combine information technology (IT) tools with educational practices. The chief calling card of ed-tech companies is the claim that they can curate individual or customized learning by deploying artificial intelligence, teaching analytics, cloud computing and learning apps. India, in fact, witnessed a 'Covid-19 ed-tech bonanza' of sorts by attracting close to $1.4 billion in investments by October 2020. Several industry trackers even foresaw a near tripling within the next five years: with ed-techin India growing from a $2.8 billion (2020) to a $10.4 billion (2025) market (Singh 2020). Reportedly, from January 2020 to barely halfway through 2021 itself, three Indian ed-tech startups – Unacademy, Eruditus and UpGrad – became unicorns, with Byju's soon turning into a decacorn (Bhalla 2021). In startup parlance, a company that is valued above $1 billion is a unicorn, while a company valued above $10 billion is a decacorn (D'Souza 2021).

The significance of this hard push towards the online, however, draws deeply upon context – in particular, by recalling the rupture that was initiated in the 1990s, which saw higher education in India being radically re-envisioned. The shift from producing political citizens through the public university system to becoming instead a profit-oriented private-university-led service for the student-consumer. In the emerging Covid-19 scenario, the embrace of OE appears to have generated new and unprecedented pressures on the consumer-student complex.

Online education, in fact, as I aim to suggest in this essay, is not only about the introduction of digital infrastructures and other technical logistics but, more profoundly, requires the very notion of the student to be re-jigged as a 'user' – a term that has been compellingly theorized by the social psychologist and philosopher Shoshana Zuboff in her path-breaking *The Age of Surveillance Capitalism* (2019). According to Zuboff, the notion of the user within the architecture of digital capitalism is no longer a customer nor a product of the commercial process. Rather, the user, by producing 'data-exhaust' or 'behavioural surplus' – the inevitable by-products of digital interactions – provides data that can be harvested by digital platforms. For online education, the user-student, in effect, becomes the primary 'sources of raw-material' (Zuboff 2019).

Higher Education in Independent India

Following India's independence in 1947, higher education was considered a public-funded endeavour. Government-funded universities steadily increased from twenty-seven (1951–52) to forty-six (1960–61). The number of intermediate colleges similarly witnessed a jump from 772 (1955–56) to 1,050 (1960–61) (Thorat 2017: 17). While infrastructural expansion drew attention in the early decades, demands for putting higher education on a systematic policy pathway soon grew louder. The Education Commission of 1964–65 was subsequently tasked with the exercise and carried out elaborate consultations before finally issuing the first significant resolution in 1968, titled the 'National Policy on Education' (NPE). While the NPE spelt out the urgency for developing a robust higher education capacity in India, it also underlined that education needed to be principally aimed at achieving a 'socialist pattern of society' through 'national integration': 'The educational system must produce men and women of character and ability committed to national service and development. Only then will education be able to play its vital role in promoting progress, creating a sense of common citizenship and culture and strengthening national integration' (ibid.: 19).

In effect, higher education was meant to attain the broader goals of nation-building, national culture and for producing responsible citizenship.

In the 1990s, however, there began a distinct mood shift.[7] For starters, the Dr Swaminathan Panel (1992) and the Punnayya Committee (1992–93), in rapid succession, recommended that higher education institutions had to take steps to increase their cost recoveries (higher fees) from students, and the government too was urged to begin the process for tapering off its subsidies in the education sector. The implication, in essence, was a call to dilute public funding and enable the 'privatization' of higher education. Interestingly enough, in the 1980s, self-financing (or profit-driven) colleges were already allowed in engineering, management and medicine. Under the generic moniker of 'capitation fee colleges', these self-financing colleges quickly proliferated in the southern Indian states of Andhra Pradesh (now Telangana and Andhra), Tamil Nadu, Karnataka and the western state of Maharashtra. These private colleges, however, did not have the authority to design or offer their own courses, and their curriculum remained governed by the rules laid out by public universities, which the former were, moreover, perforce required to be affiliated with (Varghese and Malik, eds 2015: 6).

While efforts to reduce public funding for higher education were timid efforts throughout the 1990s, by the opening decade of the twenty-first century, for-profit education witnessed a huge mood shift. In 2000, the then Prime Minister's Council on Trade and Industry (PMCTI) set up a special subject group to deliberate on possibilities for 'private investment in education, health and rural development' (V. Sharma 2001: 25). The committee, interestingly enough, was headed and stewarded by two of India's then-wealthiest industrialists: Mukesh Ambani (convenor) and Kumarmangalam Birla (member). In the Ambani-Birla submission, titled the 'Report on a Policy Frame Work for Reforms in Education' or what came to be more widely and popularly referred to as the Ambani-Birla Report (ABR), the overall purpose and direction for higher education in India was profoundly re-envisioned. Unlike the earlier NPE of 1968 which put citizen training and nation-building at the heart of the urgency for education, the ABR framed the main challenge as being chiefly aimed at realizing economic outcomes:

> Education is universally recognised as an important *investment in building human capital*. Human capital affects growth in two ways. First, human capital levels act as a driver of technological innovation. Second, human capital stocks determine the speed of technology. It is now widely accepted that human capital, and not physical capital, holds the key to persistent high growth in per capita income. . . . Knowledge has become the new asset. . . . About two thirds of the future growth of world GDP is expected to come from *knowledge led business*. (Ambani and Birla 2000: 840; emphases mine)

That is, for the ABR, education needed to be integrated into an economic narrative – defined by a cycle of investment, human capital and business. Only through such a profound shift, it was felt, could India be decisively reoriented towards becoming a 'competitive knowledge economy' in which education could meaningfully tap the next technological high wave by being integrated with information and communication technologies (ICTs). And the main vehicle to carry out this turn to an ICT-oriented education, in the opinion of the ABR, was to be private universities that could be established through a 'Private University Bill'. Despite the overwhelmingly economic tone, the ABR rounded off its recommendations by demanding that all political parties be kept away from educational institutions and that 'any form' of political activity be comprehensively banned within university campuses (ibid.: 845). In sum, the idea of the political citizen for a national culture was to be entirely abandoned and instead replaced by a notion of the consumer-student seeking education as a commodity that was, in turn, shaped within a competitive market.

It is probable that the Ambani-Birla Report provided the road map for the subsequent chain of decisions that tried to transform/reform education in India. Between 2002 and 2011, around 178 private universities were established and the share of unaided (not public-funded) private higher education institutions in India grew from 42.6 per cent in 2001 to 63.9 per cent in 2012 (Gupta 2017: 360). From 2009 onwards, in fact, several corporate houses and private investors in India began to fund and start universities even in the social sciences and the humanities – notably, the O.P. Jindal Global University, the Azim Premji University, the Shiv Nadar University and the Ashoka University. There have also been instances where universities have even been founded by modest small-town family business concerns such as Lovely Professional University, which was started by a successful sweet shop chain (Lovely Sweets) in the state of Punjab (Dogra 2010).

This steady shift from public-funded to private higher education via privatization in India, nonetheless, it must be emphasized, was not unique nor against the changing current in the higher education trajectory at the global level. A transformation, however, that must be understood for being far more profound and ideologically driven than simply heralding a change in the pattern of funding or the loss of government control.

Humboldt Makes Way for the Consumer-Oriented Corporation

According to Bill Readings in his masterful *The University in Ruins* (1996), the 'animating principles' that established the 'modern university' was put forward sometime in the early decades of the nineteenth century in Europe and, in the main, by the intellectual efforts of the Prussian philosopher, linguist and diplomat Wilhelm von Humboldt (1767–1835). For Humboldt, the primary role of the modern university was to produce the national subject whose task was to nurture and elaborate upon a national culture for the nation-state. Readings, moreover, saw in the intense debates within the German Idealist tradition (the writings, for example, of Schiller

[1759–1805], Fichte [1762–1814], Kant [1724–1804] and others) the ambitions to also consolidate the modern university around pursuits such as reason, research, teaching and the cultivation of thought and action (Readings 1996: 54–70). Put differently, the modern university arose in the nineteenth century essentially as a political project that was aimed at sustaining citizenship for a republic – education, in essence, that was meant to expand upon constitutional rights, duties and obligations for a citizen rather than for buttressing the authority and power of an emperor or king.[8]

From the latter half of the 1980s, however, Readings notes, the Humboldtian University ideal was steadily transformed 'from an ideological arm of the state into a bureaucratically organized and relatively autonomous consumer oriented corporation' (Reading 1996: 11). Economic globalization primarily drove this shift and also set about metamorphosing the student into a consumer. The impacts of the corporate university on higher education have been substantially critiqued and reviewed in innumerable studies (Collini 2012; Cote and Buller 2010; Donoghue 2008; Gindsberg 2011; Giroux 2007; Nussbaum 2011). The limitations of space in this essay, however, allow us to touch on only a few aspects.

The alarming rise in student debt has been one of the most striking features of the corporate university education model (Chamie 2017). In the United States, student debts have climbed to more than $1.86 trillion in 2021 with close to 44.3 million Americans having federal student loans as part of their financial burdens, and in all likelihood, they will take years, if not decades, to pay off both the principal amount and the interests on the principal loan (Sainato 2021).

In India too, there has been a noticeable spike in how education loans for both institutions and students have grown. In the opening year of 2000, loans amounting to roughly Rs 3000 million were disbursed for higher education; by 2016, higher-education loans had turned into the runaway sum of Rs 720,000 million. Much of this huge demand for loans was, in fact, intended to fund private colleges (Pushkar 2018). Paralleling this growth in loans for higher education has been the equally stunning rise in what has begun to be declared as non-performing assets (NPAs) within the education sector in India, referring to loans that could not be realized or paid back by the borrowers who took it primarily for educational purposes.

While in March 2013, Rs 26,150 million worth of student loans were declared to fall under the NPA category, the latter jumped to Rs 63,360 million by December 2016 (ibid.). The NPA in the education sector further jumped to 8.97 per cent at the end of March 2018 as compared with 7.29 per cent in March 2016. Covid-19, however, brought about a dramatic disruption with a steep plunge in job availability; banks in India turned extra cautious about student loans (Unnikrishnan 2020). For Nandini Chandra, student debt is described as the 'GATS-ification of higher education'. More pointedly, as the phenomenon where students are compelled to 'confront the university as an academic market' that, in turn, is increasingly run on a 'micro-finance model' – a 'combination of self-financing and high interest rates' N. Chandra (2019).[9]

Besides disciplining the student through loans, debt and fee hikes and transforming them into customers of education services, the second significant corporate-inspired shift has been to rewire the internal design of the university. At the University of California in the United States, for example, despite a sharp spike in student fees, faculty employment actually fell by 2.3 per cent between 2009 and 2011, even as student enrolment increased by 3.6 per cent. Several studies also show that in both the UK and the US, actual instructional costs are being steadily hammered downwards by universities, who prefer to rely more heavily on ad-hoc, part-time and adjunct faculty. That is, teaching is expected to be carried out by part-time and temporary, rather than tenured faculty.

The revenue bump from increased student fees, on the other hand, tended to be directed mostly at enhancing administration costs and student facilities. The University of Essex typified this newfound priority:

> ... at the University of Essex academic staff numbers increased [by] 27 per cent between 2005 and 2015 while administrative staff numbers increased by 81 per cent. In the US during the same two year period in which faculty employment fell by over 2 per cent at the University of California, jobs for managers increased by 4.2 per cent. The other major money pit has been the extraordinarily zealous investment in luxurious student housing, recreation and sports facilities. For example one luxury dorm at the University of North Florida cost $86 million to build and includes a Lazy River – essentially a theme park water ride where students float on rafts. (Ford 2015: 145–46)

A third equally telling fallout has been the systematic marginalization of the traditional humanities and liberal arts. In part, the claim here is that universities today are compelled to emphasize technical, instrumental and vocational courses (STEM: science, technology, engineering and mathematics) because of the urgency for employability, given how precariously placed most students are with high fees and loan repayment schedules. The contemplative and reflexive mood for higher education, consequently, has begun to lose traction. Though, in recent years, several efforts have begun to develop a version of 'corporate humanities' that, ironically enough, instead of questioning the status quo is intended to orient the liberal arts towards sharpening the neoliberal profit-maximizing individual (Di Leo 2013; D'Souza 2015).

Another recent source for concern within academia relates to the detrimental effects of corporate-style competition on teaching and research. The 'winner takes all' cultures of 'publish or perish' and the seemingly endless validation and credentialization (or branding) exercises that academics find themselves in have, in fact, been meticulously detailed in Maggie Berg and Barbara Seeber's critically acclaimed monograph, *The Slow Professor*. The authors describe how a vast number of academics in western universities chronically suffer from low self-esteem and the constant undermining of their emotional well-being. These debilitating and sometimes fatal stress levels were traceable to the 'time poverty' strategies foisted upon them by the corporate university (Berg and Seeber 2016). The creation of time poverty – whereby the academic always runs short of creative time to reflect and write – can be linked to the ruthless regime for the measurement, assessment and control of academic performance through audit cultures[10] or what Jerry Muller refers to as the 'tyranny of metrics' (Muller 2018). Notably, how ranking, benchmarking, ratings and standard-setting exercises have compelled faculty members to furiously compete and produce unsustainable research outputs. For Muller, more pointedly, the distinctive histories and missions of different universities are erased and through the 'ranking arms race' become instead homogenous commodities that are set up for unrelenting competition over 'academic output' (ibid.: 67–88).

Despite the intense contradictions brought on by student debt, competitive pressures on faculty, the marginalization of the liberal arts and the rise of audit cultures, the corporate university continues to gain ground over that of the Humboldtian University ideal. How has education as a commodity defeated the idea of the student as a political citizen? Was triumphant neoliberalism the real game changer?

Can Economics Defeat Politics?

By the latter half of the 1970s, several astute commentators began to track a discernible qualitative shift within industrialized capitalist countries. Daniel Bell in a provocative thesis spelt out in *The Coming of Post Industrial Society* argued that developed countries, in this period, were beginning to radically restructure in which a sudden decline in manufacturing (especially in the US) was accompanied by a steep rise in service sector employment (Bell 1999: 121–64). That is, developed economies saw a shift from blue-collar to white-collar occupations.

In such 'post-industrial' societies, in Bell's reckoning, universities and college degrees increasingly became critical to enabling social mobility (ibid.: 242–50).[11] The sociologist and philosopher Zygmunt Bauman also conceptualized this period of change as being marked by a shift from a 'society of producers' to that of a 'society of consumers' or as the transition from 'hard modernity' to liquid modernity'.[12] That is, the consumer and consumption become the defining force in such societies.

Arguing within the same stride of such reasoning was Daniel T. Rodgers' critically acclaimed *Age of Fracture*, which convincingly mapped out how the Reagan (1981–89) and Thatcher (1979–90) eras actually heralded the systematic jettisoning and replacement of the post-Second World War 'vocabularies of social thought' – Keynesian economics and social planning – with notions about the social and economic virtues of the competitive self-regulating market. Throughout the course of the 1980s, in fact, Rodger explains, 'free markets' and 'possessive individualism' were naturalized and legitimized as being the most authentic realms for exercising freedom, choice and reason. The government or 'big government', on the other hand, was not only the source of coercion but was so mired in the politics of concession and compromise that it inevitably distorted market efficiencies (Rodgers 2012: 41–76).

In a similar vein, the Marxist scholar and geographer David Harvey argued that the ascendency of the competitive market throughout the 1980s, in fact, ended up laying the foundation for defining and elaborating the notion of neoliberalism, which as an ideological project he described as, '. . . a theory of political economic practices that proposes that human wellbeing can best be advanced by liberating individual entrepreneurial freedoms and skills within an institutional framework characterized by strong private property rights, free markets and free trade' (Harvey 2007: 2).

Harvey was also keen to underline that neoliberalism as an 'ism' for free market enthusiasts afforded a muscular policy strategy for shaping interventions such as (1) deregulation (of the economy); (2) liberalization (trade and industry); and (3) privatization (state-owned enterprises) (Steger and Roy 2010: 11–14).

While the notion of neoliberalism is often defined as a 'winner takes all' competitive ethos, for William Davies, the operative logic is 'the disenchantment of politics by economics'. That is, at the heart of the neoliberal turn, is the effort to undermine deliberative democracy with the rule of the expert and professional elites, who are freed of political pressures. In other words, for the neoliberal imagination only the presumed 'laws of the market' can define freedoms and help individuals make aspirational choices. Instead of nurturing the political citizen for the nation-state, neoliberalism, therefore, chiefly desires the commoditized-customer student, who is primed for competing in market conditions (Rider 2009: 83–104).

The ideals of political democracy, social justice and meaningful collective living, in effect, are not expected to find any significant place within the design of corporate universities.[13]

In India, the shift away from the political citizen of the public university to the indebted consumer student of the private university begins to become palpable from the late 1990s onwards. The decade in which the Indian government had, in fact, begun to initiate a troubled but decisive economic turn towards embracing the logic of globalization, free market completion and what was widely referred to as 'economic liberalization'.[14] While the public university system still retained its dominance throughout the opening decades of liberalization, it was, nonetheless, as pointed out by Devesh Kapur and Elizabeth Perry, mired in a crisis. A decline in educational quality and a loss of institutional vitality that, in the estimate of the authors, had been chiefly brought about as being a result of the 'collateral damage of Indian politics':

> The vast majority of government colleges in small towns offer dismal educational outcomes. For politicians, the benefits of the license-control raj extend beyond old-fashioned rent seeking by manipulating contracts, appointments, admissions and grades in government run colleges and universities, to the use of higher education admissions for vote-banks and partisan politics and a source of new entrepreneurial activities (in private higher education).[15] (Kapur and Perry 2015)

Despite their careful enumeration of the political ills that afflict Indian higher education, Devesh and Perry seem to dodge the equally burning question over whether private universities in India – with their in-built proclivities for financial and social exclusion – could end up achieving anything other than further buttressing existing privilege. That is, could the replacement of public universities by a dominantly private university eco-system meaningfully address caste-based discrimination and enable the social mobility of disempowered groups? Privately funded educational institutions, for instance, as they currently stand, are not legally mandated to carry out any kind of affirmative policies either in the recruitment of students or in the hiring of faculty.

Nandini Chandra, in fact, provides a telling analysis of how private universities as neoliberal initiatives, the world over, were essentially expressions of invested capital in the search for profits and therefore de-linked higher education from the pursuit of social mobility (N. Chandra 2019: 63–91). This pay-as-you-go neoliberal higher education, thus, sustained existing privilege rather than upset the status quo.[16] Small wonder that public higher education, despite all its ills, continues to evoke considerable enthusiasm amongst India's marginalized and disempowered social groups. Rawat and Satyanarayana, in a recent edited collection, for example, acknowledge the role of public university education in enabling several generations of Dalits (socially discriminated untouchable castes) to break into the ranks of the urban middle class, oppose social discrimination and even for abetting the rise of a 'dalit intelligentsia' (Rawat and Satyanarayana, ed. 2016).[17]

It is quite probable that such social and economic gains made by previously excluded and marginalized caste groups grew into a source of alarm and anxiety for many amongst India's urban and privileged upper castes. Ravinder Kaur's path-breaking *Brand New Nation,* in fact, suggests such a plausibility. In a study of the voluble and popular India Against Corruption (IAC) campaign that swept through several major cities between 2009 and 2011, Kaur ably reveals a clear upper-caste messaging bias. The IAC, she shows, repeatedly wedged a contrast between a morally corrupt government and a meritorious and industrious private sector. In effect, the government – the source of public goods and for being constitutionally mandated to recruit from deprived social groups was ruthlessly targeted, while the upper-caste-dominated private sector was held to be the domain of efficiency and virtue (Kaur 2020: 195–242).

In the Indian general election of 2014, the Bharatiya Janata Party (BJP) – the dominant constituent of the National Democratic Alliance – under the leadership of Narendra Modi swept to power with a clear majority. The BJP occupies the extreme right of the Indian political spectrum with deep ideological roots in the Rashtriya Swayamsevak Sangh (RSS)– an organization committed to propagating Hindutva, which advocates an exclusivist interpretation of Hinduism.[18] Not unexpectedly, the radical ideological shift and the political convulsion of 2014, in several profound and forceful ways, impacted the Indian public university system. Not only in the manner in which the Modi-led government aggressively carried on with the broad momentum for privatizing higher education but, significantly, in re-framing the public university as a national security threat and a site for ideological confrontation.

Finding the 'Anti-National' in Jawaharlal Nehru University

On 9 February 2016, a protest meeting against capital punishment was organized at the Jawaharlal Nehru University (JNU). Such post-dinner meetings were a regular feature of the predominantly residential campus' famed cultural life that was marked by intense debates and politically charged discussions.[19] Organized by members of the Democratic Students Organization (DSO), the meeting was to debate the hangings of Afzal Guru (found guilty of masterminding an attack on the Indian parliament) and the

Kashmiri 'separatist' Maqbool Butt. In ordinary times, what would have simply passed off as a loud and engaged disagreement at best, turned instead into a near physical and ugly clash between students, which several later accounts suggest that the aggression was chiefly initiated by members of the Akhil Bharatiya Vidyarthi Parishad (ABVP) – the student wing of the RSS.[20]

By the morning of 10 February, the Zee News a pro-BJP Hindi channel was agog with claims that a celebration event of Afzal Guru had been held within the JNU campus and that 'anti-India' slogans were uninhibitedly chanted by left-wing radicals.[21] By late evening, several other channels picked up the allegations and turned them into incontrovertible facts by repeatedly playing unverified video clips (later proved to be doctored) of sloganeering masked men. Troll armies then burst forward and swamped Twitter, Facebook and other social media sites with wild claims about JNU being a haven for training terrorists and mostly populated by students fattening on taxpayers' subsidies. According to the political scientists Singh and Dasgupta, this ferocious assault on JNU showed all indications of being deliberate and planned. In their estimate, there seemed to have been a larger plot in which a strategically directed 'spin' was aimed at generating a 'politics of emotions', the main focus being to 'de-contextualize' JNU from its otherwise known 'representational function' as a university to one now linked to a series of 'alarming associations' such as 'anti-national', 'India-breaking', *'tukde-tukde-gang'* and the 'urban-naxal' (Singh and Dasgupta 2019: 59–78).

Small wonder that instead of immediately instituting an impartial enquiry to sort out the many allegations and conflicting media claims, more fuel was poured on the fire: on short notice, the ABVP assembled a march of its members in Delhi and demanded the complete shutdown of JNU. Home Minister Rajnath Singh soon followed with the astounding claim (later proved false) that Hafiz Saeed from the *Lashkar-e-Taiba* was behind the JNU events. The then Education Minister Smriti Irani (earlier a small-screen actress) exploded in tears before cameras over what she now held to be true (without enquiry) that 'anti-India' slogans were chanted on campus. Meanwhile, waves of policemen raided JNU, carried out room-to-room searches of the dormitories and began questioning students at will. And amidst this almost apoplectic mayhem of scare and alarm, slogan-shouting mobs suddenly turned up outside the main gate of the university and laid siege to the campus for several days.

One evening, a large group of aggressive BJP and ABVP party workers assembled unchecked in JNU and overran the lawns of the faculty residential complex (Paschimabad apartment block) and through a blow-horn openly issued threats and warnings to teachers and their families. Throughout this planned assault, the newly appointed Vice-Chancellor maintained a curious, if not clearly complicit, silence (Chakraborty 2017; Swain 2017).

On 12 February, the police once again swooped into the campus and this time around arrested Kanhaiya Kumar – the then president of the Jawaharlal Nehru University Student's Union (JNUSU) – under the charge of sedition.[22] The notion of sedition, it must be noted, has its origins in the colonial period, where it provided the British government with the legal means for suppressing opposition. In independent India, however, as Atul Dev is keen to remind us, 'a person charged with sedition must live without their passport, barred from government jobs, and must produce themselves in the court on a loop. All this, while bearing the legal fee' (Dev 2016; Gabriel and Vijayan 2016). More arrests followed, with the 'organizers' of the meeting Umar Khalid and Anirban Bhattacharya being charged under the Indian Penal Code (IPC) Section 120B, which deals with criminal conspiracy against the state, and 124A, which arguably also responds to the charge of sedition. The subsequent outcry by democratic groups and especially a stubborn campaign by students across India, however, did much to challenge the BJP's narrative on the 'JNU sedition row' (as it came to be popularly referred to).[23] Questions and debates focused on the rights for dissent, the legitimacy of student politics and, importantly as well, what constituted 'anti-nationalism' in the first place.[24]

For many, however, the JNU incident of 9 February was a product of a larger plot line that should be traced to the tragic suicide of a bright and promising scholar Rohith Vemula – an activist of the Ambedkar Students Association (ASA) at the University of Hyderabad (Minhaz 2017; Shanta 2018). According to a fact-finding investigation carried out by faculty members from the Tata Institute of Fundamental Research and the Indian Institute of Astrophysics, Vemula had run afoul of the local unit of the ABVP, essentially over political and ideological differences. The ABVP, as it turns out, then chose to leverage central government ministers (Union Minister of Labour Bandaru Dattatreya and also the controversial Education Minister Smriti Irani) to force a series of disciplinary actions on the ASA members. In a telling letter that was sent out by the local members of the BJP unit to the Union Minister there are, in fact, several ominous elements of the script that subsequently played out in JNU:

> Why is it made to perceive on campus that it is shameful to be a Hindu and Indian in Indian Universities. . . [The minister Dattatreya is requested to] direct [the] University of Hyderabad to enquire into all activities of ASA and other radical groups on campus . . . set up committees to moni-

tor activities of radical and anti-national students and faculties at the University of Hyderabad. (Raju, Shastri and Banyal 2017)

The very same fact-finding team was also keen to underline that Vemula's fatal decision to end his life could not entirely be reduced only to the political machinations of the ABVP and the central government. Caste discrimination and psychological violence against historically discriminated communities are quite rife in most Indian universities, and suicides by Dalit students continue to remain a shocking reality, caused and abetted by what should and is often described as a form of 'institutional murder'.[25]

On the other hand, despite the overall hostile learning environment, the academic and civil rights activist Anand Teltumbde opines that public universities still provide relatively greater intellectual and political possibilities for challenging the ferocity of caste violence within Indian society.[26] Public institutions, unlike private universities, Teltumbde argues are, at the very least, constitutionally required to meaningfully address the challenges of caste-based discrimination and other forms of social injustices. Unsurprisingly, therefore, radical Dalit ideologies and groupings that have aimed to confront social discrimination in India have been able to mostly proliferate within public university environs: notably, for example, the emergence of the Ambedkar-Periyar Study Circle (APSC) at the Indian Institute of Technology (Madras); the Birsa Ambedkar Phule Students Association (BAPSA) at Jawaharlal Nehru University; and the Ambedkar Student Association (ASA) at Hyderabad Central University (Babu 2019; Teltumbde 2019: 209–12).

In the post-2014 regime shift, however, a discernible crackdown against social justice organizations within public higher education institutions became palpable. Based simply on an 'anonymous' complaint made to the Union Human Resources Ministry, for example, sometime in 2015, the Ambedkar-Periyar Study Circle (APSC) in the Indian Institute of Technology (Madras) was derecognized by the authorities (Yamunan 2015). In the anonymous complaint, the APSC was accused of instigating students against the central government by 'creating hatred . . . in the name of caste and against the Prime Minister (Modi) and Hindus' (Sudhir 2017; Yechury 2018). Though the notification against the APSC was subsequently withdrawn after strong protests, the IIT(M) campus was soon turned into a battleground of sorts over questions such as beef-eating festivals and Brahminism (Thangavelu 2017).

In fact, since 2015, with almost chilling regularity, a cycle of hysterical accusations followed by violence against so-called 'anti-nationals' have been made to play out at Jadavpur University (West Bengal), Ramjas

College (Delhi), the Film and Television Institute of India (Pune), Aligarh Muslim University (Aligarh) and the Benares Hindu University (Varanasi). Nandini Sundar describes these attacks as being made up of the 'multiple batteries of privatisation, Hindutva and bureaucratic indifference' (Sundar 2018). In a subsequent study based on the parameters that were spelt out in the Academic Freedom Index (AFI) developed by the V-Dem Institute of the University of Gothenburg (Sweden), Nandini goes on to provide us with an even more detailed list of how a range of what should have been ordinary-taken-for-granted freedoms within Indian campuses – political expression, institutional autonomy, right to dissent, faculty hiring and course design – were put under different levels of threat with the ever-present danger of mob violence (Sundar 2020).

Following an equally decisive electoral victory in the seventeenth Indian general elections of 2019, the Modi-led government initiated a deeper round of actions on higher education. The focus this time around was on students' fees, and it began with the implementation of a steep hike in JNU (Pandey 2020). A decision that was almost immediately challenged with determined protests erupting saw students in large numbers taking to the streets and even paralysing life in various parts of the capital city.[27] The agitation proved so stunningly robust that the government's own narrative about the need for higher fees to dissuade uninterested students from wasting time in higher learning soon lost its bite. On the reverse, the agitating students were able to forcefully make it clear that the public university system genuinely addressed the aspirations of most economically underprivileged and socially marginal communities (Shankar, Nagpaul and Dwivedi Johri 2019); an accessible and affordable higher education was, in fact, the best bet for many to improve their lives and raise the standards within their families and communities.

While the tenaciousness of the JNU students enabled them to win several concessions and some temporary reprieves on 5 January 2020, a hitherto unprecedented round of violence was unleashed. Beginning at 6.30 pm that day, masked club-wielding mobs began streaming into the campus. They not only remained entirely unchecked by campus security but strangely enough, the local Delhi police, in seeming coordination, proceeded to simultaneously block the entry and exit points to the university. Mysteriously as well, street lighting along roads adjoining the university and street lamps on the main arterial campus roads were suddenly switched off. And it is amidst this eerie and ominous darkness that the masked mob was given free rein to beat up and thrash students and teachers at will.

During the mayhem, which lasted for several hours, worried residents and friends alerted by phone calls and messages were not allowed into the campus while the entire university administration went conveniently missing (Tantray 2020). At the time of writing this essay, not a single one of the masked assailants had been arrested nor had any action been taken on the complaints by the JNU students and teachers (Krishnan 2020). One can thus only conclude, on the facts available, that to have such levels of violence within the premises of a university that lies well within the heart of the nation's capital (only subsequently dwarfed by the Delhi riots of 2020, a month or so later) suggests that this planned and premeditated criminal assault could only have been carried out through collusion and support at the highest levels.[28]

In sum, the public university system in India is being dismantled. Not only by a raft of regulations and a corporate university-inspired imagination that has been spelt out in the National Education Policy of 2020 but even more aggressively through violence. In other words, by eroding the public university's capacity to produce political citizenship, the Indian government (especially from 2014 onwards) appears to be aiming to radically reorient the mission of higher education.

The Covid-19 pandemic has, however, put a pause button on a simple turn towards adopting a corporate university model. The emergence of online education in the context of social distancing and health safety has suddenly and profoundly begun to impact the higher education debate and makes it clear that virtual teaching is not simply a logistical response. The ed-tech industry, in fact, has helped further elaborate the notion of the platform university – a paradigm shift for higher education, a new unity between computer hardware, software and education theory.

The platform heralds a significant shift in contemporary capitalism. The big four of Amazon, Google (Alphabet), Facebook and Apple, for example, not only make up the leading platform firms in the world today[29] but when combined, their wealth, power and domination over our everyday living are most certainly unparalleled and unprecedented in recorded history (Galloway 2017). Platforms, for Nick Srnicek, refer to the digital infrastructure that serves to 'intermediate between different user groups'. A type of intermediation that, unlike traditional business models, is profoundly based upon the extraction and control of data. The platform, hence, essentially boils down to the 'ownership of software (the 2 billion lines of code for Google or the 20 million lines of code for Facebook) and hardware (servers, data centres, smartphones, etc.) (Srnicek 2017).

In a more pointed elaboration by media studies scholars Dijck, Poell and de Waal, the platform's architecture is described as being 'fuelled by data, automated and organized through *algorithms* and *interfaces*, formalized through *ownership* relations driven by business models and governed through *user agreements*' (Dijck, Poell and de Waal 2018: 9). Rigged and programmed thus, the platform then steers 'user interactions' towards generating 'data exhaust', which is the digital trail that Cukier and Schonberger, in their bestseller titled *Big Data,* refer to as being the 'by-product' that people leave in the wake of their online interactions (Mayer-Schonberger and Kenneth 2013: 113). Data exhaust, hence, is the raw material that is extracted from the user by the platform.

For Shoshana Zuboff in her much-acclaimed and authoritative *The Age of Surveillance Capitalism*, data exhaust is conceptualized as 'behavioural surplus', which is extracted through online interactions to feed the production of 'machine intelligence' or what is often referred to as 'artificial intelligence' (AI) (Zuboff 2019: 8). The AI by being able to automate a huge number of correlations and patterns can then essentially be purposed to anticipate and predict user behaviour. Prediction, in effect, enables the modification and control of the user's behaviour through a vast range of techniques such as the 'nudge, coax, tune' and the herding towards outcomes. We, as the user, consequently are the 'objects from which raw materials are extracted' and therefore become, as Zuboff argues, the *'means to others' ends'* (ibid.: 94). The platform, in other words, does not simply connect the service provider to the user nor does it naively set about organizing digital interactions. Rather, it is fundamentally wired up as 'machine intelligence' that is programmed through a suite of algorithms to extract, modify, steer, modulate and inevitably control human behaviour.

The persuasion that ed-tech as a platform holds for its advocates, investors and enthusiasts, hence, goes much beyond trying to develop capacities for online teaching. The online teaching platform, more pointedly, intends to be a 'disruptive technology'. Its grand scope is no less than trying to 'Uberize' higher education by delivering a death blow to the remaining detritus of the Humboldtian ideal and by fatally downsizing a wobbling corporate university model.

The Many Persuasions of Ed-tech

Ed-tech, in fact, on the surface, offers both a convincing critique and a compelling set of solutions to the crisis that now engulfs higher education.[30] It correctly understands that student debt has not only become unsustainable but is also eroding the corporate university's initial claim that markets could help 'massify' higher education by broadening access.

There is a growing disconnect, moreover, between the degree that was paid for and the actual financial returns on the jobs that are available. In sum, degrees from the corporate university are not only pricing themselves out of the job market but in the context of rapid technological change, the very notion of competence and employability are undergoing significant shifts: the demand seems to be veering towards the need for a regular upgradation in skill-sets rather than from an intense three- or four-year degree programme.

Ed-tech has the capacity to radically cheapen higher education. For starters, the online can entirely sidestep the huge costs involved in maintaining brick-and-mortar legacy infrastructures such as libraries, dormitories and lecture halls. Tens of thousands of students can be simultaneously connected to an online module, as opposed to a relatively minuscule number that can be packed into a single classroom. In a similar vein, virtual instruction can dramatically abandon the need to maintain an expensive student-teacher ratio by carrying out instructions via pre-recorded lectures, interactive apps and on-demand digital content.

In 2012, two Stanford computer science professors, Andrew Ng and Daphne Koller, assembled an online teaching and e-learning platform called Coursera, which they designed for offering massive open online courses (MOOC). The Coursera strategy involves partnering [like Uber] with existing universities, colleges, governments and corporates and as of December 2019, their total number of collaborations is listed as comprising roughly 200 across twenty-nine countries.[31]

According to Dijck, Poell and de Waal, the Coursera and the MOOC in general are aimed at entirely upending existing academic conventions and designs. Instead of the curriculum-based diploma or degree programmes, the platform offers the 'course – a single unit that can be "unbundled" and "rebundled" into an online "product"'. That is, instead of the current focus on completing a comprehensive two- or three-year programme that is made of several linked and connected courses, the user-student can now simply partake in a slice of the education experience by attempting a single course. Akin to what, as the authors tell us, Facebook and Google have done to the newspaper industry by un-packaging them in a manner that allowed the circulation of single articles, feature pieces and news feeds. These unbundled courses, furthermore, can be accredited by the award of certificates of completion and proctored exams – versions of micro-degrees or nano-degrees that can be earned for acquiring specific skills (Dijck, Poell and de Waal 2018: 117–36).

The ed-tech platform as a decentralized, virtual and low-cost higher education model, however, already reveals inherent dangers. For one, the user-student's data (behavioural surplus), generated through digital interactions, can be repurposed by the platform for a range of unstated outcomes. An individual's learning curve, emotional states, psychological dispositions and learning abilities, for example, could be minutely mapped and tracked through the trail of data exhaust. Every digital indent, in the form of a like button, emoji use, a quiz, a survey or a simple click, could be graphed to size up as a behavioural analysis that, in turn, could be then be conveyed as a score to a potential employer or authority.

Secondly, by dispensing with the *aura* of classroom solidarity, the online grinds away at attaining individualized and personalized outcomes. The gradient for learning is thus individual-centric and steered by predictive analytics – algorithms that can replace the teacher's professional judgement with 'learnification'. The learnification paradigm is the 'idea that learning can be managed, monitored, controlled and ultimately modified in each student's personal mind'. In effect, the user-student will be encased within a filter bubble, a self-referential niche that will be digitally reinforced by corroding social solidarity, public value and knowledge through collectives (ibid.: 124) – in sum, the undermining of political citizenship and the devaluing of democracy.

Towards a Conclusion

But how will the loss of the Humboldtian ideal and the corporate university actually play out? The impacts of ed-tech might, in fact, be far more perverse with the platform university consolidating a new type of social and economic hierarchy that is built around different levels of educational inequalities. The always perceptive and future-looking Scott Galloway, professor of marketing at the prestigious NYU Stern School of Business, in a stock-taking interview on the future of higher education in a post Covid-19 world, offers us an unnerving assessment. For Galloway, the shift to the platform university will first begin manifesting as:

> . . . a dip, the mother of all V's, among the top-50 universities, where the revenues are hit in the short run and then technology will expand their enrolments and they will come back stronger. In ten years, it's feasible to think that MIT doesn't welcome 1,000 freshmen to campus; it welcomes 10,000. What that means is the top-20 universities globally are going to become even stronger. What it also means is that universities Nos. 20 to 50 are fine. But Nos. 50 to 1,000 go out of business or become a shadow of themselves. Ultimately, universities are going to partner with companies to help them expand. I think that partnership will look something like MIT and Google partnering. Microsoft and Berkeley. Big-tech companies are about to enter education and health care in a big way, not because they want to but because they have to. . . . The strongest brands are MIT,

Oxford, and Stanford. Academics and administrators at the top universities have decided over the last 30 years that we're no longer public servants; we're luxury goods. (Walsh 2020)

Clearly, the Galloway prophecy is that higher education in the pre-Covid-19 world will become virtually unrecognizable in the not-too-distant future. The big brand universities are going to gobble up the small guys, online education will massify access and, finally, expect a defining role for tech giants such as Google and Microsoft in shaping the platform university. Despite this dramatic churn, however, Galloway still believes that the four-year liberal arts campus experience might survive, but only because it will be populated by the really rich. Brick-and-mortar higher education, hence, will spur a caste system, the triumph of aristocratic entitlement over malodorous merit.

In all likelihood, the coming years will see continued frictions, tensions and abrading wars between the Humdoltdian ideal, the corporate university and the ed-tech-driven platform. Three souls will haunt and agitate campuses: that of the student-citizen, the customer-consumer and the user-student. The winner, for sure, will not take all.

Notes

[1] See the dynamic *Oxford Covid-19 Government Response Tracker* (OxCGRT), which collects and updates information on policy measures that governments had taken to tackle Covid-19. The different policy responses are tracked from 1 January 2020 onwards, cover more than 180 countries and are coded into twenty-three indicators, such as school closures, travel restrictions and vaccination policies. Available at https://www.bsg.ox.ac.uk/research/research-projects/covid-19-government-response-tracker, accessed 14 December 2021.

[2] 'Online Education in India 2021: A Study by KPMG in India and Google', May 2021, available at https://kpmg.com/in/en/home/insights/2017/05/internet-online-education-india.html, accessed 20 September 2021. At the time of this article going to press in 2023, the Indian ed-tech sector has begun to unravel following a mix of a huge global funding slowdown and a spate of mass-layoffs. Clearly, at heart, is the financial unsustainability of the ed-tech business model. See Soni (2022). Also see Khan (2023).

[3] The report underlined that there were several existing Government of India initiatives that could provide infrastructural support and help drives for online education, notably, SWAYAM, E-Basta, Rashtriya Madhyamik Shiksha Abhiyan (RMSA), Skill India and Digital India. See 'Online Education in India 2021', p. 12.

[4] For a critique of the NEP, see D' Souza (2022a).

[5] See a bullet-point assessment of the NEP after a year in the *India Brand Equity Foundation* portal, available at https://www.ibef.org/blogs/new-educational-schemes-one-year-completion-of-nep-the-road-ahead, accessed 16 December 2021.

[6] See 'Colleges to Conduct 40 Percent Courses Online, says UGC', *The Telegraph*, 23 November 2021, available at https://www.telegraphindia.com/edugraph/news/colleges-to-conduct-40-percent-courses-online-says-ugc/cid/1840251, accessed 16 December 2021.

[7] 1991 is often marked as the year when 'economic liberalization' was initiated in

India. The previous Nehruvian paradigm for pursuing a self-reliant and relatively closed economy was steadily dismantled through a set of economic reforms that sought to institute market-led economic growth. For an excellent discussion on how the economic and political 'caesura' of 1991 was ideologically legitimated, see Bajpai (2018). Also see Balakrishnan (2010) and Kohli (2009).

[8] For a discussion on Humboldt and his ideas on education, see David Sorkin (1983), 'William von Humboldt: the Theory and Practice of Self-formation (*Bildung*)', *Journal of the History of Ideas*, vol. 44, pp. 55–74. Also, for a succinct summary on how Humboldt's call for intimacy between the nation-state and the modern university was debated, see D. Bhattacharya, ed. (2019, pp. 2–12).

[9] GATS refers to the 1995 General Agreement on Trade in Service.

[10] Some of the university rankings (with different metrics and criteria) are carried out by the *Times Higher Education Supplement, Shanghai Jiao Tong, US News and World Report* and *Princeton Review.*

[11] An emphasis that is also underlined by Michel Sandel, who suggests that higher education from the 1990s in the US and the UK was talked up as a response to inequality, stagnant wages and the loss of manufacturing jobs. See Sandel (2020, pp. 81–112).

[12] See the lucid and crisply written *Consuming Life* (Bauman 2007a) and *Liquid Times: Living in an Age of Uncertainty* (Bauman 2007b).

[13] On what the neoliberal turn has meant for the liberal arts, see Brown (2011).

[14] For insightful and accessible discussions on the processes and politics that drove liberalization in India see Balakrishnan (2010); Balakrishnan, ed. (2011); Kohli (2009), Mukherji (2014). For an empathetic and celebratory account, see Ramesh (2016) and Kochar (2016).

[15] The educationist Pankaj Chandra similarly suggests that the Indian public higher education system was in 'institutional decay' from poor governance, uninspired teaching, lack of funds, infrastructural collapse and even a loss of moral direction. See Chandra (2018).

[16] The college admission scandal that dramatically broke out in March 2019 in the United States has once again brought home the harsh contrast between an education that reinforces privilege and status from that which challenges the status quo. From a host of available press writings on the subject, see Wadman (2019).

[17] See the introduction, and especially pp. 7–8, in Rawat and Satyanarayana (2016).

[18] For an introduction to the politics of the BJP, see the excellent essays in Hansen and Jaffrelot (2001 [1998]). Also see Sharma (2015) and Ananthamurthy (2016). On the RSS, see Basu *et al.* (1993). Also see Patel (2020).

[19] For some indication of JNU's rich legacy of student politics and ideological diversity, see the document brought out by the JNU Students' Union (JNUSU) titled *30 Years in Defence of Progressive, Democratic and Secular Culture, Jawaharlal Nehru University Students' Union,* Delhi: J.K. Offset Printers, 2004. Also see Bhattacharya *et al.*, eds (2020) and D'Souza (2022b).

[20] 'What Really Happened on the Night of Feb 9: A JNU Student Recounts', *Hindustan Times,* 16 February 2016, available at https://www.hindustantimes. com/india/what-really-happened-on-the-night-of-feb-9-a-jnu-student-recounts/ story-Hz3USZC3NwntZFwKpF2g1M.html, accessed 29 September 2020.

[21] Note the resignation of Vishwa Deepak on the biased reporting of the Zee News channel; see Hafeez (2016).

[22] For the arrest in his own words and the events leading up to it, see Kumar (2016).

[23] A fairly detailed record of the agitations and arguments on the 'JNU Sedition Row' are available at online sites such as *Kafila* (https://kafila.online/) and *The Wire* (https://thewire.in/).

24 The JNU teaching community initiated a public lecture series on nationalism which was uploaded on YouTube and subsequently several lectures were published in a collection: Azad *et al.*, eds (2017).

25 See, for example, Dutta (2019). Also see Ajantha Subramanian's (2019) path-breaking study of the famed Indian Institute of Technology (IIT), where she convincingly shows how the pursuit of an exclusive and elite education strategy can end up further consolidating the privileges of India's already powerful upper castes.

26 Anand Teltumbde was arrested in February 2019 by the Mumbai police on various trumped-up charges, including a supposed plot to kill the Prime Minister of India. He is currently out on bail. See Sampath (2019).

27 'JNU: Protesters bring top India university to its knees', 22 November 2020, available at https://www.bbc.com/news/world-asia-india-50498890, accessed 20 July 2020. Also see Sharma (2019).

28 The JNU administration and the pro-government media were keen to claim that the violence of 5 January 2020 was essentially a 'clash' between left-leaning students and those on the right such as the ABVP. The detailed report by Chitranshu Tewari, however, claims that it was the ABVP that had carried out a one-sided and systematic assault. See Tewari (2020).

29 Somewhat comparable but nowhere near in terms of global reach are the Chinese BAT firms: Baidu, Alibaba and Tencent. See Wade and Shan (2017).

30 Increasingly, one notes how regular the failings of the corporate university are being written about. See, for example, Farrelly (2020).

31 See the *Wikipedia* page on Coursera, available at https://en.wikipedia.org/wiki/Coursera.

References

Ambani, M. and K. Birla (2000), 'Report on a Policy Frame Work for Reforms in Education', Special Subject Group on Policy Framework for Private Investment in Education Health and Rural Development, Prime Minister's Council on Trade and Industry, Government of India, New Delhi; Executive Summary printed in the *Journal of Indian School of Political Economy,* vol. 15, no. 4, October–December 2003, p. 840.

Ananthamurthy, U.R. (2016), *Hindutva or Hind Swaraj*, Harper Collins India.

Azad, R., J. Nair, M. Singh, M. Sinha Roy, eds (2017), *What the Nation Really Needs to Know: The JNU Nationalism Lectures*, Harper Collins India.

Basu, T., P. Datta, S. Sarkar, T. Sarkar and S. Sen (1993), *Khaki Shorts and Saffron Flags: A Critique of the Hindu Right*, Hyderabad: Orient Longman.

Bajpai, A. (2018), *Speaking the Nation: The Oratorical Making of Secular, Neoliberal India*, New Delhi: Oxford University Press.

Balakrishnan, P. (2010), *Economic Growth in India: History and Prospect*, New Delhi: Oxford University Press.

Balakrishnan, P., ed. (2011), *Economic Reforms and Growth in India: Essays from Economic and Political Weekly*, Hyderabad: Orient BlackSwan.

Bauman, Z. (2007a), *Consuming Life*, Cambridge: Polity Press.

———— (2007b), *Liquid Times: Living in an Age of Uncertainty*, Cambridge: Polity Press.

Bell, D. (1999 [1973]), *The Coming of the Post-Industrial Society: A Venture in Social Forecasting*, New York: Basic Books.

Berg, M. and B.K. Seeber (2016), *The Slow Professor: Challenging the Culture of Speed in the Academy,* London, Buffalo, Toronto: University of Toronto.

Bhalla, K. (2021), 'From Byju's to Eruditus – India Now Has Four Edtech Unicorns, Thanks to a $4 Billion Fund Flowing in Since 2020', *Business Line*, 14 August, available at https://www.businessinsider.in/business/startups/news/india-now-has-four-edtech-unicorns-byju-unacademy-eruditis-upgrad/articleshow/85300757. cms, accessed 16 December 2021.

Bhattacharya, D., ed. (2019), *The Idea of the University: Histories and Contexts*, Routledge (South Asia Edition).

Bhattacharya, N., K. Chakrabarti, S. Gunasekaran, J. Nair and J.L.K. Pachuau, eds (2020), *JNU Stories: The First Fifty Years*, New Delhi: Aleph.

Brown, W. (2011), 'The End of Educated Democracy', *Representations*, vol. 116, no. 1, pp. 19–41.

Chamie, J. (2017), 'As Student Debt Rises Worldwide, An Education Crisis Could be on the Horizon', *Scroll.in*, 22 May (originally carried in *Yale Global Online*), available at https://scroll.in/article/838078/as-student-debt-rises-worldwide-an-education-crisis-could-be-on-the-horizon, accessed 15 June 2020.

Chandra, N. (2019), 'The Surplus University', in D. Bhattacharya, ed., *The Idea of the University: Histories and Contexts*, Routledge (South Asia Edition), pp. 66–67.

Chandra, P. (2018), *Building Universities that Matter: Where Are Indian Institutions Going Wrong*, Hyderabad: Orient BlackSwan, pp. 221–56.

Collini, S. (2012), *What are the Universities for?* London: Penguin.

Cote, J. and J.L. Buller (2010), *Lowering Higher Education: The Rise of Corporate Universities and the Fall of Liberal Education*, Toronto: University of Toronto Press, 2011.

Davies, W. (2017), *The Limits of Neoliberalism: Authority, Sovereignty and the Logic of Competition*, Los Angeles, London, New Delhi: Sage Publications.

Dev, A. (2016), 'A History of the Infamous Section 124A', *The Caravan*, 25 February, available at http://www.caravanmagazine.in/vantage/section-124a-sedition-jnu-protests, accessed 9 July 2018.

Di Leo, Jeffrey R. (2013), *Corporate Humanities in Higher Education: Moving Beyond the Neoliberal Academy*, New York: Palgrave Macmillan.

Dogra, C.S. (2010), 'A Lovely Story Indeed', *Outlook,* 23 August, available at https://www.outlookindia.com/magazine/story/a-lovely-story-indeed/266660, accessed 6 July 2018.

Donoghue, F. (2008), *The Last Professors: The Corporate University and the Fate of the Humanities*, New York: Fordham University Press.

D'Souza, R. (2015), 'Hardly the Soft Sciences', *The Hindu,* 10 June, available at https://www.thehindu.com/opinion/op-ed/hardly-the-soft-sciences/article7298891.ece, accessed 21 November 2021.

——— (2021), 'What Lies Behind China's Crackdown on Ed-tech Companies', 8 September, *The Indian Express*, available at https://indianexpress.com/article/opinion/columns/china-crackdown-ed-tech-companies-7495277/, accessed 16 December 2021.

——— (2022a), 'The Coming Disruption in Higher Education in India', in N. Narayanan and D. Dhar, *Education or Exclusion: The Plight of Indian Students*, New Delhi: LeftWord Books, pp. 102–13.

——— (2022b), 'Why the Idea of JNU is Still Worth Fighting For', *Scroll.in*, 28 September, available at https://scroll.in/article/1033717/why-the-idea-of-jnu-is-still-worth-fighting-for.

Dutta, Y. (2019), 'The IITs Have a Long History of Systematically Othering Dalit Students', *The Print*, 17 February, available at https://theprint.in/pageturner/excerpt/the-iits-have-a-long-history-of-systematically-othering-dalit-students/193284/, accessed 30 December 2021.

Farrelly, E. (2020), 'The Decline of Universities, Where Students are Customers and Academics Itinerant Workers', *The Sydney Morning Herald*, 30 May, available at https://www.smh.com.au/national/the-decline-of-universities-where-students-are-customers-and-academics-itinerant-workers-20200528-p54xbd.html, accessed 1 June 2020.

Ford, M. (2015), *The Rise of the Robots: Technology and the Threat of Mass Unemployment*, Great Britain: Oneworld Publication, pp. 145–46.

Gabriel, K. and P.K. Vijayan (2016), 'The Discontents of a Seditious Nation', *Countercurrents. org*, 6 March, available at https://www.countercurrents.org/vijayan060316.htm, accessed 10 July 2018.

Galloway, S. (2017), *The Four: The Hidden DNA of Amazon, Apple, Facebook and Google*, London: Corgi Books.

Ginsberg, B. (2011), *The Fall of the Faculty: the Rise of the All-Administrative University and Why it Matters*, Oxford: Oxford University Press, 2011.

Giroux, H.A. (2007), *The University in Chains: Confronting the Military–Industrial–Academic Complex*, CO: Paradigm.

Gupta, A. (2017), 'Emerging Trends in Private Higher Education in India', in N.V. Varghese and G. Malik, eds, *Higher Education Report 2015*, p. 360.

Hafeez, S. (2016), 'Zee News Producer Quits: Video We Shot had No Pakistan Zindabad Slogan', *The Indian Express*, 22 February, available at https://indianexpress. com/article/india/india-news-india/zee-news-producer-quits-video-we-shot-had-no-pakistan-zindabad-slogan/, accessed 7 July 2018.

Hansen, T.B. and C. Jaffrelot (2001 [1998]), *The BJP and the Compulsions of Politics in India*, New Delhi: Oxford University Press.

Hany Babu, M.T. (2019), '"The Convergence of Unequals": Struggle for Rights in the University Space', in D. Bhattacharya, ed., *The Idea of the University: Histories and Contexts*, Routledge (South Asia Edition), pp. 217–29.

Harvey, D. (2007), *A Brief History of Neoliberalism*, Oxford, New York: Oxford University Press.

Kakkar, R. (2020), 'Digital Earning: Can Online Education Replace the School Classroom in India?', *India Today*, 6 June, available at https://www.indiatoday.in/education-today/featurephilia/story/digital-learning-can-online-education-replace-the-school-classroom-in-india-1697474-2020-07-06, accessed 28 July 2020.

Kapur, D. and E.J. Perry (2015), 'Higher Education Reform in China and India: The Role of the State', Harvard-Yenching Institute Working Paper Series, January.

Kaur, R. (2020), *Brand New Nation: Capitalist Dreams and Nationalist Designs in Twenty-First-Century India*, Stanford, California: Stanford University Press.

Khan, S. (2003), 'Massive Layoffs in the Indian EdTech Industry (2022 Lookback)', *Ed-Tech Review*, 20 January, available at https://www.edtechreview.in/trends-insights/insights/massive-layoffs-in-the-indian-edtech-industry-2022-lookback/, accessed 15 April 2023.

Kochar, S. (2016), *The Untold Story: Indian Reforms (1991–2016)*, Gurgaon: SKOCH.

Kohli, A. (2009), *Democracy and Development in India: From Socialism to Pro-Business*, New Delhi: Oxford University Press.

Krishnan, R. (2020), '23 Days and Counting: No FIRs in JNU Violence Even After 40 Complaints by Students, Faculty', 29 January, available at https://theprint.in/india/23-days-and-counting-no-firs-in-jnu-violence-even-after-40-complaints-by-students-faculty/356058/, accessed 24 July 2020.

Kumar, K. (2016), *From Bihar to Tihar*, Delhi: Juggernaut Books.

Mayer-Schonberger, V. and K. Cukier (2013), *Big Data: A Revolution That Will Transform How We Live, Work and Think*, UK: John Mayer.

McKenzie, L. (2020), 'India Opens the Door Wide for Online Learning', *Inside Higher Ed*, 17 February, available at https://www.insidehighered.com/news/2020/02/17/indian-government-opens-market-online-higher-education, accessed 20 July 2020.

Minhaz, A. (2017), '"It Feels Stifling": A Year after Rohith Vemula's Suicide, Hyderabad

University is Still Tense', *Scroll.in*, 17 January, available at https://scroll.in/article/826891/it-feels-stifling-a-year-after-rohith-vemulas-suicide-hyderabad-university-is-still-tense, accessed 8 July 2018.

Mukherji, R. (2014), *Political Economy of Reforms in India*, New Delhi: Oxford University Press.

Muller, J.Z. (2018), *The Tyranny of Metrics*, Princeton and Oxford: Princeton University Press.

Nussbaum, M. (2011), *Not for Profit: Why Democracy Needs the Humanities,* Princeton: Princeton University.

Pandey, A. (2020), 'Keeping India's Universities for the Rich', *JACOBIN,* 27 January, available at https://jacobinmag.com/2020/01/jawaharlal-nehru-university-india-fee-hike, accessed 28 July 2020.

Patel, A. (2020), *Our Hindu Rashtra: What It Is, How We Got Here*, Delhi: Westland.

Pednekar, P. (2020), 'Can Online Learning Replace the School Classroom?', *The Hindu,* 26 June, available at https://www.thehindu.com/opinion/op-ed/can-online-learning-replace-the-school-classroom/article31917964.ece, accessed 28 July 2020.

Pushkar (2017), 'It Makes Little Sense to Blame Students for India's Growing Loan Default Problem', *The Wire*, 31 July, available at https://thewire.in/education/serious-indias-student-loan-default-problem, accessed 8 July 2018.

Ramesh, J. (2016), *To the Brink and Back: India's 1991 Story*, New Delhi: Rupa Publications.

Rapanta, C., L. Botturi, P. Goodyear, L. Guàrdia and M. Koole (2021), 'Balancing Technology, Pedagogy and the New Normal: Post-pandemic Challenges for Higher Education', *Postdigital Science and Education*, vol. 3, pp. 715–42.

Rawat, R.S. and K. Satyanarayana, eds (2016), *Dalit Studies*, Durham and London: Duke University Press.

Readings, B. (1996), *The University in Ruins*, Cambridge: Harvard University Press.

Rider, S (2009), 'The Future of the European University: Liberal Democracy or Authoritarian Capitalism?', *Culture Unbound*, vol. 1, pp. 83–104.

Rodgers, D.T. (2012), *Age of Fracture*, Harvard: Harvard University Press.

Sainato, M. (2021), '"Killing the middle class": Millions in US Brace for Student Loan Payments after Covid Pause', *The Guardian,* 9 December, available at https://www.theguardian.com/us-news/2021/dec/09/us-student-loan-crisis-payments, accessed 21 December 2021.

Sampath, G. (2019), 'Who is Anand Teltumbde and Why was He Recently Arrested?', *The Hindu*, 16 February, available at https://www.thehindu.com/news/national/who-is-anand-teltumbde-and-why-was-he-arrested-recently/article26292219.ece, accessed 25 February 2019.

Sandel, M.J. (2020), *The Tyranny of Merit: What Becomes of the Common Good?*, New York: Farrar, Straus and Giroux.

Shankar, A., D. Nagpaul and A. Dwivedi Johri (2019), 'Not Just JNU: How India's Public Univer-sities Becoming Costlier Hurts the Most Vulnerable', *The Indian Express*, 1 December, available at https://indianexpress.com/article/express-sunday-eye/jnu-fee-hike-protest-students-underprivileged-sections-tiss-presidency-college-jamia-millia-islamia-hostel-fee-6141302/, accessed 30 July 2020.

Sharma, J. (2015), *Hindutva: Exploring the Idea of Hindu Nationalism*, India: Harper Collins (2003, Penguin).

Shanta, S. (2018), 'Rohith Vemula's Suicide Triggered a New Political Wave', *The Wire*, 19 January, available at https://thewire.in/caste/rohith-vemula-suicide-triggered-a-new-political-wave, accessed 8 July 2018.

Sharma, V. (2001), 'Reject Ambani-Birla Report on Education', *People's Democracy*, vol. 25, no. 12, March, p. 25, available at http://archives.peoplesdemocracy.in/2001/march25/march25_vijender.htm, accessed 5 July 2018.

Singh, S. (2020), 'The Future of Education: Indian Startups chase $10 Bn Edtech Opportunity', INC42, 8 October, available at https://inc42.com/datalab/the-future-of-education-indian-startups-chase-10-bn-edtech-market/, accessed 16 December 2021.

Singh, M. and R. Dasgupta (2019), 'Exceptionalizing Democratic Dissent: A Study of the JNU Event and Its Representations', *Postcolonial Studies*, vol. 22, no. 1, pp. 59–78.

Soni, Y. (2022), 'Is Indian Edtech's House of Cards Collapsing? *Hindu Business Line*, 9 June, available at https://www.thehindubusinessline.com/info-tech/is-indian-edtechs-house-of-cards-collapsing/article65509810.ece, accessed 15 April 2023.

Sorkin, D. (1983), 'William von Humboldt: the Theory and Practice of Self-formation (*Bildung*)', *Journal of the History of Ideas*, vol. 44, pp. 55–74.

Srnicek, N. (2017), *Platform Capitalism,* Cambridge: Polity Press.

Steger, M.B. and R.K. Roy (2010), *Neoliberalism: A Very Short Introduction,* Oxford, New York: Oxford University Press.

Subramanian, A. (2019), *The Caste of Merit: Engineering Education in India*, Cambridge, London: Harvard University Press.

Sudhir, T.S. (2017), 'Beef Politics to Fighting Brahminism: IIT Madras's APSC is One Hell of a Disruptive Element', *Quartz India*, 5 June, available at https://qz.com/997283/from-beef-politics-to-fighting-brahminism-iit-madrass-apsc-is-one-hell-of-a-disruptive-element/, accessed 4 July 2018.

Sundar, N. (2018), 'Academic Freedom and Indian Universities', *Economic and Political Weekly,* vol. 53, no 24, 16 June, pp. 48–56.

——— (2020), 'Academic Freedom in India', *The India Forum*, 4 September, available at https://www.theindiaforum.in/article/academic-freedom-india, accessed early preview 1 September 2020.

Tantray, S. (2020), 'JNU Violence: Students Recount Attack by a Masked Mob, said Delhi Police Watched', *The Caravan*, 6 January, available at https://caravanmagazine.in/education/jnu-abvp-attack-5-january, accessed 15 July 2020.

Teltumbde, A. (2019), 'The University as Passivity?: The Role of Students' Political Activism', in D. Bhattacharya, ed., *The Idea of the University: Histories and Contexts,* Routledge (South Asia Edition), 2019, pp. 199–216.

Tewari, C. (2020), 'Lies, False Equivalence, Diversions, Ad Hominem Attacks: That's TV Media's Spin on JNU Violence', *NewsLaundry.com*, vol. 55, available at https://www.newslaundry.com/2020/01/10/tv-media-spin-jnu-violence, accessed 29 September 2020.

Thangavelu, D. (2017), 'IIT Madras Students Hold Protest Against Assault on PhD Scholar Over Beef Fest', *Live Mint*, 31 May, available at https://www.livemint.com/Politics/xQqYQoRkqJgG1DUVt7gmgK/IIT-Madras-erupts-on-demand-for-action-against-assault-at-Ph.html, accessed 2 July 2018.

Thorat, S. (2017), 'Higher Education Policy in India: Emerging Issues and Approaches', in N.V. Varghese and G. Malik, eds, *Higher Education Report 2015*, Routledge (South Asia Edition), p. 17.

Unnikrishnan, D. (2020), 'Why have Indian banks stopped lending to students?', *Money Control,* 27 January, available at https://www.moneycontrol.com/news/economy/policy/why-have-indian-banks-stopped-lending-to-students-4862821.html, accessed 21 December 2021.

van Dijck, J., T. Poell and M. de Waal (2018), *The Platform Society: Public Values in a Connective World,* Oxford: Oxford University Press.

Varghese, N.V. and G. Malik, eds (2017 [2016]), *Higher Education Report 2015*, Routledge (South Asia Edition).

Wade, M. and J. Shan (2017), 'The Chinese Digital Giants – Coming to a Store Near You!: Europe and North America Beware of the BATs – Baidu, Alibaba and Tencent', *IMD*, December, available at https://www.imd.org/research-knowledge/articles/

the-chinese-digital-giants-coming-to-a-store-near-you/, accessed 28 May 2020.

Walsh, J.D. (2020),'The Coming Disruption Scott Galloway Predicts a Handful of Elite Cyborg Universities will Soon Monopolize Higher Education', *Intelligencer*, 11 May, available at https://nymag.com/intelligencer/2020/05/scott-galloway-future-of-college.html, accessed 18 July 2021.

Yamunan, S. (2015), 'IIT-Madras Derecognizes Student Group', *The Hindu*, 28 May, available at https://www.thehindu.com/news/national/tamil-nadu/iitmadras-derecognises-student-group/article7256712.ece, accessed 6 July 2018.

Yechury, S. (2015), 'Ban on IIT-M Students' Group Part of Larger Design of an RSS Project', *Hindustan Times*, 2 June, available at https://www.hindustantimes.com/columns/ban-on-iit-m-students-group-part-of-larger-design-of-an-rss-project/story-IFmwddCCJOVic3SjzFSmMM.html, accessed 1 July 2018.

Zuboff, S. (2019), *The Age of Surveillance Capitalism: the Fight for the Future of the New Frontier of Power*, London: Profile Books.

11

Higher Education in NEP 2020

Rhetoric and Realities

Maya John

In July 2021, the Indian Cabinet approved the National Education Policy (NEP) 2020[1] despite vehement opposition to several of its provisions that were earlier circulated as draft policy documents.[2] The formal adoption of the 'new' policy framework was rolled out at a time of festering problems like the second wave of the Covid-19 pandemic, widening economic disparity and marked socioeconomic ruination triggered by lockdowns, the disruption of direct classroom teaching and the inability of a large number of children and youth to access education through the online mode.

A close engagement with the key thrusts of NEP 2020 reveals their sharp contradiction with the aspirations for quality education that the vast majority of youth harbours, the fulfilment of which depends on unfettered access to public-funded education. A long-term aspiration of socially and economically disadvantaged groups, in particular, has been accessing quality education without discrimination – a right which can facilitate a change in inherited and existing circumstances of deprivation. However, despite the repeated verbose rhetoric on 'increased access, equity and inclusion' in NEP 2020, it is precisely such aspirations which are dangerously compromised by the new policy framework.

Verbosity, Ambiguity and Exclusionary Agenda

The politics of words in NEP 2020 is hard to miss. The approved policy document is infused with newer terminology and a conscious play of words which strive to conceal the exclusionary principle-cum-ideology and the privatization agenda of the ruling regime. Cautioned by the incisive critiques of the proposals of 'financial autonomy', 'public–private partnerships' in higher educational institutions (HEIs), the downsizing of the number of undergraduate colleges, etc., which were made in the 2019 draft report submitted by Dr K. Kasturirangan Committee (GoI 2019),[3] the policy framers of NEP 2020 have strategically replaced these terms with 'financial robustness' and 'public–*philanthropic* partnerships'. Likewise, they have couched the bid of downsizing the number of public-funded degree colleges by emphasizing the creation of 'large', 'multidisciplinary' HEIs in place of a multitude of institutions.

In a graded society marked by differential access to quality education, the aspiration and struggles on the question of access to such education have been crucial for social upliftment. Unfortunately, constitutional safeguards like a proportionate reservation for Scheduled Castes (SCs) and Scheduled Tribes (STs) in public-funded institutions or piecemeal provisions like a quota for the economically weak sections in private schools have not displaced the rampant inequality. In this light, the NEP 2020 has little to offer. While the policy document provides for feewaivers and scholarships for 'talented' and 'meritorious' students from socioeconomically deprived sections, it strategically creates a category of students within the underprivileged for whom there would be no feewaivers, thereby, slyly evading the need for creating and expanding the educational infrastructure to enable access to quality education for all. In fact, NEP's use of ambiguous terminology like 'socioeconomically disadvantaged groups (SDGs)' or 'under-represented groups' and the special emphasis on providing them, in particular, 'multiple pathways to learning' reflects the marginalization of precisely those sections of society whose need for *formal*, quality education should be made the backbone of any education policy.

Indeed, the politics of words is well-inscribed in the policy framework's conscious emphasis on the 'multiple pathways to learning involving both formal and non-formal education modes' (GoI 2020: 10). Multiple pathways, especially when earmarked as a necessity for the 'SDGs', represent little more than the veiled promotion of ruling elite's agenda of greater informalization of education imparted to the deprived and underprivileged sections of youth. The mainstreaming of informal modes of education, such as open and distance learning (ODL) and online learning, in addition to the promotion of a 'blended mode', is a marked agenda of the ruling dispensation. This agenda is conveniently cloaked behind the jargon of improving the accessibility of education, retention of students, enrolment ratios, etc. The hollowness of such projections is an issue elaborated on later.

Reading between the lines and recognizing the politics informing NEP's terminology and the proposed 'forward-looking vision for India's higher education', we find the desperate attempt to sugarcoat and repackage already unfolding processes of institutional restructuring, informalization of education for the poor and enhanced privatization of education that completely betrays the aspirations of the most vulnerable sections of society. These implications of NEP 2020 are best comprehended whilst engaging with earlier drafts of the policy framework, as well as recently introduced regulations that have paved the way for rapid privatization. Take for example the executive orders by which the new autonomous body – Higher Education Financing Agency (HEFA) – was created in 2017 to extend loans in place of grants to HEIs, as well as the 2018 regulation of the University Grants Commission (UGC) which allows high performing HEIs to apply for autonomy based on whether they are ranked among top 500 of reputed world rankings or have National Assessment and Accreditation Council (NAAC) grades above 3.26.

An era of policy discourse has clearly developed in which the now dominant opinion holds that the state cannot be expected to pay for the education of all. As a consequence, there has been a serious lack of development of educational infrastructure to meet the rapidly increasing demand for higher education amongst the country's youth, the majority of whom see such education as a tool for moving up the social ladder. Indeed, as observed by the 'Report of the Committee to Advise on Renovation and Rejuvenation of Higher Education', chaired by Professor Yash Pal:

> As more youngsters from different segments of society enter the universities, they look at higher education as a means to transcend the class barriers. Consequently, university education is no longer viewed as a good in itself, but also as the stepping stone into a higher orbit of the job market, where the student expects a concrete monetary return. (GoI 2009a: 10)[4]

In response to the widening gap between the demand and supply for education, successive governments have pushed through measures that have largely allowed for greater penetration of private capital in higher education and its corollary, the persistent decline in per capita government allocation of funds towards education. Expectedly, the inadequacy of public funding has fuelled the growth of private colleges and universities, as well as the rapid expansion of the largely self-financed mode of ODL offered by public-funded universities. The larger consequence of such developments has been the perpetuation of a highly segmented and hierarchical structure of higher education – one which NEP 2020 reinforces.

Pre-existing Hierarchization

The education system in post-colonial India has unfortunately proved exclusionary since its very inception. A *dual* education structure has been allowed to flourish at the school level, whereby poorly funded and ill-equipped government schools have coexisted with private schools. With the shunning of *common schooling*, educational inequality has been bred from the school level onwards with a majority languishing in run-down government schools and distance learning programmes of the National Institute of Open Schooling (NIOS), while the more privileged purchase quality education through private schooling and expensive coaching centres. This dual system of education at the school level is complemented by a higher education system that has been developed in an exceedingly uneven manner, resulting in a decidedly segmented, hierarchical educational structure.

The education commissions instituted by Indian governments such as University Education Commission (Radhakrishnan Commission), 1948, and Indian Education Commission (Kothari Commission), 1964, made certain recommendations, which led to the creation of a handful of 'centres of excellence' for higher education. At the time of these recommendations, the country had only three universities that had been sanctioned as per imperial legislation passed by the Central Legislative Assembly. These included the University of Delhi (DU), Aligarh Muslim University and Banaras Hindu University. Rigorous academic standards have been maintained along with full financial support from the central government in these universities, in the new central universities established as per Acts of Parliament and in institutions of national importance for technical education such as the Indian Institutes of Technology (IITs), National Institutes of Technology (NITs), Indian Institutes of Science Education and Research, Indian Institutes of Management (IIMs), National Law Schools, etc.

In these centrally funded, premium HEIs for research and teaching, a *limited* percentage of India's youth, that is, those from affluent and upward-mobile segments of society who have had access to all-round school education, are successful in procuring admission. They are provided either an advanced scientific education of a professional or research-oriented nature or advanced education in the social sciences. Consequently, these few 'centres of excellence' have enabled the privileged to gain greater access to well-paying professional jobs as well.

Alongside these centrally funded premium HEIs, a corpus of regional universities funded by state governments has also existed. Apart from a handful of quality institutions like the University of Calcutta, the University of Bombay, Madras University, etc., the bulk of such regional universities has seen rapid deterioration soon after their establishment. A great divergence between central and state universities was particularly evident from the 1980s onwards. In a bid to respond to the skewed quality and opportunity of growth in higher education across semi-urban and remote areas, the central government introduced the Central Universities Act 2009, which launched sixteen new central universities; some of which were regional universities that were incorporated as central institutions. The policy has had a checkered outcome and it is questionable whether this has provided a new lease of life to erstwhile regional universities that were upgraded to the status of central institutions (Bhattacharya 2019). Significantly, the uppermost segment of the regional elites has rarely depended on regional universities. Increasingly, regional elites are known to have prioritized admission into premium central-funded HEIs in metropolitan cities.

A large section of the country's youth, meanwhile, has been simultaneously relegated to *vocational* courses (polytechnic and industrial training), kept out of the *regular academic* stream of university education by the cut-throat competition encapsulated in soaring cut-offs and entrance tests or pushed into distance education offered by public-funded universities. Notably, this vast majority has been skilled in arduous, menial and less remunerative occupations in the Indian economy.

In reality, even before NEP 2020, the earlier-mentioned inequality in access to quality higher education and hierarchy among HEIs has been bred by prior strategic shifts in policy measures that have largely benefitted premium central universities and institutions identified as having national importance. The corollary to this trend has been the decline of regional universities run by state governments and the growth of private colleges or relatively substandard grants-in-aid institutions.[5] In this regard, a landmark policy shift was in 1976 when the 42nd Amendment in the Indian Constitution was introduced whereby education as a subject of administration was transferred from the State List to the Concurrent List. However, instead of remedying the uneven growth of HEIs and improving the quality of higher education imparted across HEIs, this administrative man oeuvre furthered the disparity.

For one, using the powers under the Concurrent List, successive central governments, and thereby, all-India level ruling parties/coalitions, have sought to gain a foothold in unfolding regional politics by constituting central universities in various states. Very often, central governments have consciously overlooked demands for upgrading the status and funding of existing regional universities to that of a central university; a relevant example is Patna University. The opening of altogether new central universities was consequently part of populist political ploys of the ruling elite and went a long way in fuelling persistent competition for the establishment of central universities within various states. Of course, this policy trend came at the cost of drawing attention away from the need to bridge the gap between regional universities and centrally funded universities in the first place.

In such a context, several regional universities ran into disarray. This was also expected, given that many of the regional universities were set up as part of politically rewarding, popular measures resorted to by state governments in order to meet democratic pressures for the expansion of mass higher education at the state level. Usually, state governments responded to such pressure by expanding general, less expensive and even *low-quality* HEIs (Carnoy and Dosani 2013). The continuous fall in the rankings of regional universities as per the parameters set by central agencies, which regulated institutional standards, legitimized greater levels of neglect of these universities. Thus, while the central universities, especially metropolitan ones, have thrived post-1976, the bulk of regional universities have grown more and more decrepit and backward (ibid.). A widening disparity in funding between HEIs became the order of the day.

This apart, many educationalists and political commentators have also argued that the basic federal structure inscribed in the Constitution has been constantly undermined with the centre pushing forth with over-centralization of decision-making, using the Concurrent List. However, the growing role of the central government in the planning/development/ design and funding of educational development at the state level is not the problem, given the divide between rich and poor states and the consequent differential capacity of state governments to contribute to educational development. Significantly, the composition of the union–state shares in funding has rapidly changed in recent decades. Though the union/central government's funds under 'central schemes' for the promotion of primary, secondary and higher education have constituted a significant corpus, the share of the centre and the state governments has varied greatly. In more recent years, of the total public expenditure on education in the country, the union government's contribution is less than one-quarter (20 to 25 per cent) while the rest three quarters are shouldered by state governments (Motkuri and Revathi 2022). Various reports also reveal the overall low level of public expenditure on education as a share of the country's GDP. When it comes to *public* expenditure on education, less than 1 per cent of the GDP is borne by the union government while approximately 3 per cent is borne by states together.[6] Overall, the process of placing education in the Concurrent List has *not* bridged the wide gap between central and state/regional universities.

Even lower down in the higher education hierarchy, ODL institutions affiliated with regional universities and central universities have gone from bad to worse, with some of the biggest ODL institutions becoming self-financed institutions altogether. Ironically, the weakest and most disadvantaged students, who flock to ODL institutions, have been paying full tuition fees in order to finance the operational and other running costs of ODL institutions. This is in marked contrast to the subsidized education provided through the regular mode by public-funded HEIs (John 2020a).[7]

One way in which NEP 2020 furthers unequal access to quality higher education and the hierarchy between institutions and streams is by accelerating the push towards the quantification of institutional performance in ways that prioritize funding for premium public-funded HEIs where the privileged youth are concentrated, while starving low-ranked institutions, which cater predominantly to poorer students, of requisite funds.

Imposed over this pre-existing structure of hierarchy, NEP 2020 fails altogether to chart out a new terrain. Instead, it strives to provide an institutional policy backing and formal framework to what has already unfolded in a haphazard manner in terms of differentially placed HEIs vying for funds and rankings, efforts of crème de la crème public-funded institutions to become autonomous, the introduction of massive open online courses (MOOCs) and short-term self-financed courses in public-funded HEIs, imposition of homogeneous university curriculum in the name of the choice based credit system, etc. Epistemologically speaking, NEP 2020 and preceding education policies have rarely provided a 'new' vision or direction for education. The underlying thrust of national education policies tends to be towards providing a framework for what persists on the ground and intensifying and consolidating existing practices and trends.

Clearly, every 'new' education policy implemented so far has strengthened the hold of the privileged sections of society on elite (metropolitan central government-funded) universities – several of which may soon be made 'autonomous'. At the same time, education policies of successive governments have relegated the lower middle class to the lower segment of institutions, that is, poorly funded provincial central universities, second-grade regional universities and private institutes. They have simultaneously kept the bulk of the socially and economically disadvantaged youth out of the university system while pushing a section of them into run-down regional universities, low-grade private institutes and the lowest rung of institutions, that is, ODL centres run by some public-funded universities.

Instead of bringing in reforms aimed at making higher education accessible and inclusive and, in turn, facilitating an equal opportunity for entry into higher-paid segments of the labour market, state policies have steadily prized opening the education sector to rapid privatization and bred unequal access to quality higher education. Indeed, the inclusion of education in the General Agreement on Trade in Services (GATS) and India's participation in GATS-related talks in Nairobi in 2015 is indicative of how the ruling elite of different countries are reaching a consensus on the need to increase the scope of a profitable investment by domestic and global corporates in the education sector. On the one hand, the growing talk of facilitating the setting up of offshore campuses by foreign universities points to the Indian ruling elite's commitment to allowing foreign investment in the Indian education market. On the other hand, the meteoric growth of large private universities and autonomous colleges vying for high accreditation scores, in addition to the mushrooming of low-grade private colleges, reveals the unfettered diversification of domestic private capital into high-demand sectors like education.

Such consensus stems from a process initiated in the 1990s via the Bologna Congress. The Bologna Process, initiated in 1999 through a series of ministerial meetings and agreements between European countries, was designed to ensure comparability in the standards and quality of higher education qualifications. Its principles also strove to ensure that the degrees offered by European universities equip students for employability as per emerging requirements of employer lobbies. Taken together, the Bologna Process and GATS have had far-reaching influences (de Weert 2011).

Thus, the recent educational 'reforms' in India in the form of a four-year undergraduate programme with multiple exit options, 'multidisciplinary' undergraduate education, cluster innovation centres, knowledge hubs, research parks, incubation centres, semesterization, growing emphasis on vocational education, etc., represent an assortment of recently developed models that now exist across the world, and which have been envisaged to facilitate the movement of elite students, teachers and private capital (John 2013). Importantly, the accelerated globalization of capital in recent decades has also created a global labour market which triggers the need for a homogeneous education and uniform educational degrees across countries. These wider international developments and lobbying are precisely what has fuelled the NEP's provision of a four-year undergraduate degree in India and the growing thrust towards curriculum revision to suit 'global standards'. Such homogenous education, needless to say, also stands to detach education and pedagogical practices in India from the concrete Indian setting.

Institutional Restructuring

NEP 2020 accelerates the processes of a major restructuring of educational institutions and curricula that were already set in motion via piecemeal measures introduced in the recent past. Amongst the contentious provisions of restructuring in higher education is the phasing out of the system of affiliated colleges over the next fifteen years and the grant of greater autonomy in academic, administrative and financial matters to premium colleges and, essentially, to the top-ranked universities of the country.

This measure has used the long-standing anxieties about the perils of over-centralization; namely, the alleged constraints imposed on the potential for premium affiliated colleges to innovate and evolve. Likewise, concerns have long existed about politico-bureaucratic interference in the internal functioning of universities and concerns about the substantial burden on universities which have to regulate admissions, set curricula and conduct examinations for a large number of undergraduate colleges. Drawing on such concerns, the earliest inclinations towards autonomy were reflected in the recommendations of different education committees and commissions from the 1960s onwards. In its report, the Mahajani Committee on Colleges, 1964 (GoI 1967), for example, took the position that one way of improving the standard of higher education in India was by selecting a few colleges 'on the basis of past work, influence, traditions, maturity and academic standards and give them what might be called for want of a better phrase an 'autonomous' status with the freedom to develop their personalities'.

Even while solutions to apprehensions about over-centralization were being discussed by stakeholders such as the teaching community, educationalists, etc., these came to be used by successive governments to build a case for the promotion of autonomous colleges. Correspondingly, the National Policy on Education (NPE) 1986 stated: 'Autonomous colleges will be helped to develop in large numbers until the affiliation system is replaced by a free and more creative association of universities and colleges' (GoI 1986).[8] Even before NPE 1986, the recommendations of prior committees like the Mahajani Committee paved the way for autonomous colleges to be established. The first such college came into existence in Tamil Nadu in 1978 and the number of autonomous colleges progressively grew.

In the early 1990s, faced with an unprecedented balance of payment crisis and forced to borrow heavily from the World Bank, the Indian state increasingly pushed forward with the liberalization of the economy. It began implementing 'structural adjustment reforms' as mandated by the World Bank. These 'reforms' included the deregulation of many sectors of the economy and a reduction in state expenditure on education, health and development programmes. In light of these larger structural changes which aimed at creating a free-market economy and facilitating an enhanced flow of foreign direct investment in the Indian economy, *graded* autonomy with its inbuilt potential for privatization steadily became a buzzword in policy discourse.

However, the model of graded autonomy has not synced with what educationalists and other stakeholders have envisaged as solutions to the problems of over-centralization and the need for the upgradation of HEIs. It also harbours grave implications for the accessibility, equity and quality of higher education. Nonetheless, graded autonomy has steadily been pushed into the centre stage of education policy. Recommendations of recent education commissions have promoted the already existing unequal structure

of funding for higher education and perpetuated the prevailing hierarchy in
higher education along the lines of 'centres of excellence' or metropolitan central government-funded universities, provincial central government-funded
universities, regional universities and colleges funded by state governments,
etc. For instance, the National Knowledge Commission (2005), headed by
Sam Pitroda and other pro-corporate lobbyists, argued that:

> undergraduate colleges are constrained by their affiliated status . . . the
> problem is particularly acute for undergraduate colleges that are good, for
> both teachers and students are subjected to the 'convoy problem' insofar
> as they are forced to move at the speed of the slowest. . . . In fact, the
> design of courses and examinations needs to be flexible rather than exactly
> the same for large student communities. (GoI 2009b: 70)

Rather than bringing lower grade affiliated colleges at par with premium
colleges, recent commissions and high-powered committees have strategically taken to projecting as a fetter the relatively *equitable* funding extended
by the central and/or state governments to HEIs under expenditure heads
like salary and other operational costs.[9] Other so-called fetters include the
structure of common syllabi and evaluation systems, standardized rules for
teacher recruitment, etc. The now dominant policy discourse vocally propa-
gates the quantification of the performance of HEIs that paves the way for
graded autonomy for better-performing HEIs. In 1994, NAAC was set up
to determine grades for institutions, based on their performance. By the
early 2000s, the ranking of public and private HEIs was steadily enforced.
Apprehensions soon surfaced that the grading system would eventually
be used to allocate differential funds to different institutions, which has
increasingly become a reality. Brushing these concerns aside, newer ranking
systems have been envisaged, culminating in the National Institute Ranking
Framework (NIRF) that was launched in September 2015 by the Ministry
of Human Resources Development (MHRD).

The graded autonomy paradigm, which allows greater power to
such institutions to grant degrees, start new self-financed courses, decide on
the fee structure for such courses, hire and fix the pay of non-tenured teachers independent of the regulatory authority, etc., has been cemented with
the release of the UGC Regulations, 2018, on the categorization of HEIs.
Such measures go to show just how much restructuring of higher education
has been pushed through via executive decisions and bypassing the scrutiny
by the Parliament. Implications of such executive orders have a bearing on
the fundamental structure of central universities, which were constituted
as per Acts of Parliament, making it imperative to gain the assent of the
Parliament for any proposed restructuring of such institutions.

The crucial point of concern is that the model of graded autonomy is far from based on the universalization of educational resources and equal access to quality higher education. Instead, it perpetuates the prevailing hierarchy that exists between different colleges within a public-funded university and between different universities across the country. In real terms, the merit of an educational policy lies in its scope to transform existing unequal structures, which will do away with the uneven development of educational infrastructure and opportunities in the country. Against this yardstick, NEP 2020 fairs poorly.

For those who believe that NEP 2020 offers a safe exit from over-centralization while still guaranteeing institutional accountability, it is vital to examine the provisions of the 'light but tight' regulatory framework under a single regulator, as proposed in the policy. The term 'light' in the oft-repeated oxymoronic formulation 'light but tight' may as well be seen as referring to the fading responsibility of the state towards the funding of education while the term 'tight' points to the enhanced centralized control on key facets of university administration, curriculum and research offered by HEIs. In its current form, NEP 2020 encompasses overt centralization of decision-making, embodied in a plethora of new central agencies that eat into the powers and responsibilities of the state/UT governments as well as local bodies. The thrust towards deeper centralization is indicated in the constitution of the government-nominated umbrella institution, Higher Education Council of India (HECI) with its four wings or 'verticals': (1) the National Higher Education Regulatory Council (NHERC) for single point regulation of 'financial probity, good governance, and the full online and offline public self-disclosure' of key information by all HEIs, except those associated with medical and legal education; (2) the 'meta-accrediting body', called the National Accreditation Council (NAC); (3) the Higher Education Grants Council (HEGC), which will carry out funding and financing of higher education based on pre-announced criteria, etc.; and (4) the General Education Council (GEC), which is tasked with framing expected learning outcomes, also referred to as 'graduate attributes'.

Likewise, the centralization thrust of NEP 2020 is manifested in the corporate-style board of governors with powers hitherto assigned to governing bodies of colleges and other statutory bodies of HEIs, leading to a concentration of power away from any democratic scrutiny at the local level. Overt centralization is further evident in the new apex body, the National Education Commission (Rashtriya Shiksha Aayog, RSA), which is responsible for 'developing', 'implementing' and 'evaluating' the 'educational vision of the country'. Importantly, the policy makes it amply clear that the allocation and channelization of the budget for education will be reviewed and approved by the RSA. Further, the RSA represents nominated, extra-constitutional people, whose very 'act of 'constitution is based on bypassing the Parliament. It is estimated that appointments to the RSA will be politically motivated and will expedite the massive misuse of public money for consolidating the specific interests of the ruling dispensation. Even the creation of a separate research supervisory body, the National Research Foundation (NRF), to seed research in universities and colleges is indicative of the centralization thrust envisaged by the current regime. Needless to say, the NRF, to be headed by the Prime Minister, manifests a covert effort to shape the agenda of research, and thereby, manipulate public opinion.

Commenting on the current structure of affiliated colleges, the NEP 2020 document strategically makes no reference to systemic inequalities which have been bred between affiliated colleges, and essentially criticizes the affiliation system for representing undue 'fragmentation' (GoI 2020: 34). The policy calls for phasing out the affiliation system by 2035. In turn, it refurbishes and sugarcoats the entire model of graded autonomy by pushing for the creation of 'large multidisciplinary universities, colleges, and HEI clusters/Knowledge Hubs, each of which will aim to have 3,000 or more students' (ibid.).

A close and critical examination of the choice of words like 'large, 'clusters' and 'hubs', should caution us to the implications of such stipulations, that is, the *merger* of several existing colleges and HEIs – a term cautiously avoided by the policy and its framers. Such 'defragmentation' does not guarantee enhanced accessibility to higher education by actually increasing the number of HEIs. Instead, it paves the way for the mere carving out of autonomous 'large research-intensive and teaching-intensive universities' (ibid.) from the existing pool of HEIs, while expanding the layer of autonomous degree-awarding undergraduate colleges by facilitating the breakaway of affiliate and constituent colleges from existing universities (ibid.: 36).

The proposed restructuring is best contextualized within the existing collegiate university system whereby the bulk of colleges and stand-alone institutes function under central and state universities. Typically, in several public-funded universities, the main functions are divided between the academic departments of the university and affiliated or constituent colleges. Given the overall segmented nature of higher education, collegiate university systems have their *internal gradations* as well. For instance, in DU, out of the 90 constituent colleges, there are some institutions which are maintained by the university and are 100 per cent funded by the central government. There are other DU colleges which depend on the university for legitimizing their academic and administrative processes but are fully funded by the Delhi government or partially funded by a private trust or society. In the case of colleges partially funded by a trust or society, there are some which exercise a minority status. The structure of governing bodies and the constitution of recruitment/selection panels for appointments, among certain other administrative facets, is different in the Delhi government, trust and minority colleges.

This overall structure is sought to be transformed with the enforcement of NEP 2020. The new policy framework's restructuring agenda is based on criticizing the 'fragmented' nomenclature – constituent, affiliate, trust, recognized, aided, deemed, etc. – which is used for various kinds of institutions. Showcased as a rational measure, the discourse on restructuring conceals the inherent tendency of privatization written into the logic of making existing public-funded colleges 'opt' for the status of autonomous degree-granting colleges (ibid.: 35). In fact, the hidden agenda of privatization or steady withdrawal of public funding from higher education has been well-exposed in the Draft National Education Policy 2019 of the Kasturirangan Committee.

The addendum in the said draft policy carried a blueprint of what the supposed 'defragmentation' endeavour would entail. Speaking of three types of institutions, the committee recommended 300 institutions in the Type I category of HEIs that will focus equally on research and teaching, 2,000 institutions in the Type II category that will focus primarily on teaching but conduct significant research as well and just 10,000 institutions, namely, undergraduate colleges in the Type III category. For a country still grappling to provide equal access to higher education, the reduction of the existing 50,000-odd colleges to a mere 10,000 colleges represents a marked threat to public-funded, quality higher education.

Vanishing Public Funds and Accelerated Privatization

The institutional restructuring envisaged in Section 10 of the NEP 2020 document consolidates, if not intensifies, the hierarchical, deeply segmented educational structure, as well as the push towards privatization. Take, for instance, the provisions that speak of a 'robust system of graded accreditation', which essentially compels existing HEIs to prove their worth in the next fifteen years. All HEIs are hereby expected to chalk out 'Institutional Development Plans (IDPs)' for the period of the next fifteen years. Herein the policy reads:

> . . . a robust system of graded accreditation shall be established, which will specify phased benchmarks for all HEIs to achieve set levels of quality, self-governance, and autonomy. In turn, all HEIs will aim, through their Institutional Development Plans (IDPs), to attain the highest level of

accreditation over the next 15 years, and thereby eventually aim to function as self-governing degree-granting institutions/clusters. (GoI 2020: 47)

Moreover, the passing references to 'incentivized' expansion of HEIs' capacity (ibid.: 35), coupled with the elusive talk of public funding based on
'graded accreditation', point towards furthering the existing system of unequal funding for HEIs. For instance, the NEP 2020 policy document states
that the system for 'determining increased levels of public funding support
for public HEIs . . . will give an equitable opportunity for all public institutions to grow and develop', but in the same breath, it also points to the
oft-critiqued linking of funding with accreditation scores – a measure that
will fail to bridge the gap between premium, middling and lower grade
public-funded HEIs. Overall, funding for the fulfilment of IDPs, as well as
future financial support after the lapse of the prescribed fifteen years, will
depend on *outcomes* quantified through accreditation. This brings the fate
of institutions which have lagged due to prior neglect, under the cloud.
Undoubtedly, it is precisely the more backward institutions that will be
rendered deficient of funds with the enforcement of NEP 2020.

In real terms, NEP 2020 asserts a 'new' normal with respect to *differential* access to public funding. The policy framework speaks of extending equal opportunity to all HEIs but does so by strategically reducing the
concept of equal opportunity squarely to the procedures of 'transparent'
accreditation. This approach imbibes the reactionary technocratic assumption that the procedures for accreditation by themselves ensure a level
playing field in spite of historically constituted disparities and hierarchies
nurtured between HEIs by the current political economy. The so-called failure to make the most of a transparent system of accreditation and to 'take
off' as an institution in the next fifteen years is a paradigm of quantification
of HEIs' performances which easily shifts the blame onto individual institutions rather than calling out the system itself. The new normal is nothing
but a covert form of victim blaming.

Significantly, the NEP 2020 document states that the system of enhanced public funding, 'will be based on transparent, pre-announced criteria from within the accreditation norms' (ibid.), and that 'HEIs delivering
education of the highest quality as laid down in this Policy will be incentivized in expanding their capacity' (ibid.). The latter statement, in particular,
harbours the prospect that the lion's share of funding will be eventually
directed to crème-de-la-crème research-intensive and teaching-intensive
universities. Such provisions are to be read along with the earlier 2019
draft policy which emphasized self-funding for new development goals
and with pronouncements made in recent times like in May 2020 that the

government will facilitate top-ranking HEIs to launch their online courses without prior approvals.[10] The framework of incentivization provided by NEP 2020, thus, also indicates that premium HEIs will be 'encouraged' to launch self-financed (online) courses in order to fund components of their institutional development goals – the cost of which will be passed onto the individual learner.

It is doubtful whether the claims of NEP 2020 to 're-energize the higher education sector' and talk of 'deliver[ing] high-quality higher education, with equity and inclusion' is possible given the model of institutional restructuring to be enforced. For one, graded autonomy can be expected to trigger a massive spurt in expensive self-financed courses as premium colleges, as well as struggling affiliated colleges threatened by phasing out, will strive to chalk out their financial self-sufficiency and fulfilment of their IDPs. This will expectedly lead to significant expenditure by the individual learner, who will be compelled to pay higher fees for such courses and for a sizeable share of the development costs of individual institutions that strive to fulfil their IDPs. Apart from this, the intensification of privatization will also manifest itself in the numerical growth of autonomous degree-granting colleges from the existing pool of high-ranking public-funded colleges that opt out of the provision of becoming or remaining constituent colleges of a central or state university.

The prospect of accelerated privatization in higher education is also likely, given the serious cause of doubt on whether the Indian state will actually enhance public investment in this educational sector in the long run. While much is being made of the policy's ultimate goal to increase the public investment in education to 6 per cent of the country's gross domestic product (GDP), there is a tendency to downplay three important facts. These facts point to the double-speak engrained in the government's claims about its commitment to enhancing public funding for education.

For one, the present National Democratic Alliance (NDA) government awkwardly restricts the benchmark of public expenditure on the education sector to a target set by the Kothari Commission way back in the 1960s, conveniently sidestepping what the current context of educational disparity actually demands. Importantly, it has been a long-standing demand of the education movement in India that at least 10 per cent of the budgetary allocation should be earmarked for public education. Second, NEP 2020 seeks to formalize and consolidate the somewhat dispersed efforts of previous dispensations to promote private investment in education. The policy, consequently, represents the road map of massive private investment in education. It neither stipulates anything concrete about fund allocation for education by the central and state governments in their budgets nor does it spell out the share of funding to be shared by the central vis-à-vis state governments. If we follow the expenditure pattern of the union government on education in the previous years, it has shrunk significantly. The share of the Union Budget allocated to education fell from 4.14 per cent in 2014–15 to 3.4 per cent in 2019–20 (Centre for Budget and Governance Accountability 2020), which is the period of the NDA government's tenure at the centre. The trend points to a grave misuse of public money collected as a dedicated education cess. In fact, recent reports of the comptroller and auditor general of India (CAG) have shown that in the case of the Secondary and Higher Education Cess, Rs 94,036 crore collected since the financial year 2007 has been retained in the Consolidated Fund of India instead of being transferred to the special fund for secondary and higher education created in August 2017 (Centre for Budget and Policy Studies 2019).

Third, although the new policy framework eschews any mention of the HEFA and the reference to loans rather than the allocation of grants to HEIs, it is expected that HEFA will continue to function in tandem with the Higher Education Grants Council (HEGC) – the third vertical of the HECI, which will be responsible for disbursements of scholarships and development funds. Since 2017 the HEFA, which is a non-banking financial venture of the MHRD and Canara Bank, has been tasked with financing the building of educational infrastructure and R&D infrastructure of top-ranking institutions like the IITs, IIITs, NITs, IISCs, AIIMS, etc., in a bid to propel them 'to reach top rankings globally'.[11] Notably, the HEFA represents a PPP model that facilitates *competitive* funding by privileging the goals of infrastructure expansion of already well-funded and top-ranking HEIs instead of channelizing public funds towards resource-starved HEIs.

Facilitation of the entry of private corporate social responsibility (CSR) funds into the higher education sector and the extension of loans with significant interest rates are themselves an embodiment of the state's withdrawal from the responsibility of subsidizing educational services. Top-ranking HEIs that avail of HEFA loans are being made to return the principal sum and the interest by linking their institutional earnings to an escrow account from which the HEFA adjusts its repayment of infrastructure loans over a period of ten years. While officials in the MHRD project that the interest on HEFA loans is payable by the government, the realities of financial accounting cannot be overlooked. For instance, the interest money 'payable' by the government is eventually generated through investment of the borrowing HEI's earnings that are deposited in the escrow account.

The repeated use in NEP 2020 of terminology like 'philanthropic private participation' represents a foiled reference to the government's intention to facilitate a greater quantum of private capital investment in school and higher education. Policy framers consciously deploy the terms private and philanthropic *interchangeably*. For all purposes, 'philanthropic' is a simile for *private* interests. It is thus to be expected that the so-called philanthropic organizations will strategically further the interests of private players seeking to gain a foothold in the education sector through the CSR route. We cannot erroneously overlook the logic of cost recovery and the diktats on research, administration, curriculum design, etc., which private organizations investing in research projects or the running of HEIs will unleash.

Further, NEP 2020 not only speaks approvingly of pilot initiatives for the installation of public-philantrophic partnership models in higher education (GoI 2020: 48) but categorically promotes the growth of private HEIs themselves. Significantly, the policy framework allows for 'reasonable recovery of cost' (ibid.: 49) by private institutions via a 'transparent' fee-determining mechanism. Indeed, the stipulations that private HEIs should run as 'not for profit' entities barely challenge the logic of existing practices, given that such institutions have been known to charge high fees whilst simply projecting their 'surpluses' as 'reinvestment' in the education sector. This apart, the framework justifies cost recovery through high fees by linking the determination of the upper limit of fees to the accreditation level of the private HEIs. This measure is justified as a way of ensuring that 'individual institutions are not adversely affected' (ibid.). In the convoluted discussion on transparent disclosure of fee structure and a broad regulatory mechanism, the right of private HEIs 'to set fees for their programmes independently' is undeniably reinforced. Such reinforcement of existing practices of private HEIs will only facilitate the rapid growth of private HEIs.

The accelerated thrust towards privatization of the higher education sector is further substantiated by the provisions that lay the ground for the setting up of offshore campuses of foreign universities. This development is unsettling to say the least, considering that existing educational disparities can hardly be bridged by foreign universities offering expensive and lengthier (four-year) undergraduate programmes. For one, these foreign universities will cater essentially to the elite, privileged section of youth. Second, the questionable quality of higher education imparted by offshore campuses of foreign universities is a question that warrants close scrutiny.

The 2000 report of the joint task force of the World Bank and UNESCO should amply caution us in this regard. The said report revealed that 'there are prestigious universities from developed nations offering shabby courses in poor and developing countries . . . using their renowned names, without assuring equivalent quality' (Singh 2020). However, in no uncertain terms, NEP 2020 paves the ground for foreign HEIs to set up shop in India (GoI 2020: 39). Again, in a strategic move to blunt criticism, the framework simultaneously emphasizes that high-performing HEIs of the country will also be encouraged to set up campuses in other countries. Such a proposal is nothing short of bitter irony, considering the dire need for expansion of public-funded education infrastructure that is essential for closing the ranks of educational disparity within the country itself. This apart, the new policy framework provides ample scope for such foreign universities to be 'given special dispensation regarding regulatory, governance, and content norms on par with other *autonomous* institutions of India' (ibid.), thereby diluting the possibility of proper regulation of the quality and cost of education imparted under brand names of foreign HEIs.

Educational Inequality Magnified and Institutionalized

On 12 May 2020 during the lockdown imposed in the country, Prime Minister Narendra Modi proclaimed that the stimulus package of Rs 20 lakh crore announced by the Union Finance Minister would lead to growing self-reliance (*atmanirbharta*) for Indians. For the majority of Indians, this simply meant that they have to fend for themselves. For the majority of the labouring poor, who have borne the disproportionate brunt of the unprecedented crisis, the government's Covid-19 relief package remained a complete hoax. The logic of this *atmanirbharta* was duly extended to the education sector, which as discussed, is characterized by gross inequalities.

The Union Finance Minister's announcements on 17 May 2020, detailing the final tranche of the Covid-19 relief package, clearly reflected the agenda of the ruling dispensation. The pronouncements made it amply clear that the current dispensation is committed to facilitating the top 100 universities and 'institutes of eminence' to start running *online* degree courses without any prior approvals. With this purpose, guidelines were formulated by the UGC in 2020 and by June 2021 a total of thirty-eight universities were identified as free to offer online degree courses.[12]

While the augmentation of digitally accessible learning has been increasingly paraded as the sure shot 'democratic' route to making knowledge available to all, the entrenched hierarchy in the education sector, the significant degree of privatization already in existence, as well as the propensity of both these trends to intensify with online learning, are conveniently overlooked. NEP's creation of more varied categories of educational access – formal, informal, mainstream, alternative, online and offline education – will not close the socioeconomic divide that exists on the ground and determines access to quality education. Ironically, rather than the extension of formal education to all who aspire for quality education, it is the mainstreaming of the provision of multiple, or namely, *differential* paths to higher education that is paraded as equal opportunity.

The claims of multiple streams or pathways to learning represent a cover-up diversionary tactic that draws attention away from the need for universal and undifferentiated access to school and higher education. To comprehend such genuine concerns, it is important to draw attention to the pathetic state of pre-existing forms of informal education, such as ODL, which have long been mooted for the less privileged sections of society. The decrepit state of ODL institutions and the poor quality of education imparted through them make it imperative to question current projections about e-learning as a credible 'alternative' solution to meet the needs of the neediest students, that is, those who do not have the marks or financial condition to enrol in formal education. Clearly, what one form of informal education – the ODL mode – has failed to achieve in terms of bridging the social and economic divide cannot be miraculously fulfilled by online learning.

For one, the mainstreaming of online learning is sought to be imposed on a structure of educational inequality in which the most marginalized sections of youth are left with no option but to settle for informal modes of education. This is due to their systemic exclusion from the hallowed realm of the formal, regular mode of education offered by public-funded universities – a point discussed earlier in terms of the hierarchical, deeply segmented education system that has long been in existence. Second, there is no doubt that e-learning, particularly in the form of MOOCs which a substantial number of premier public-funded HEIs will be pushed into offering in order to facilitate their self-sufficiency, is just another channel through which the average per capita government allocation of funds to higher education can be reduced. This reduction will not translate automatically into reduced expenditure by the individual learner (John 2020b).[13]

In the bid to touch higher gross enrolment ratios (GER), the so-called credible alternatives to formal, public-funded education, such as e-learning and the ODL mode, are precisely the pathways of learning that NEP 2020 will aggressively promote. In fact, the enhanced GER rate of the country in the past decade has been mostly concentrated in the informal education or ODL mode. More importantly, ODL institutions, such as the vast Indira Gandhi National Open University (IGNOU), have seen a huge growth in the enrolment of students from poorer sections of society, especially historically disadvantaged groups like SCs and STs. According to a 2019 news report in the *Times of India*, IGNOU in the last nine years saw a 248 per cent increase in the enrolment of SC students and a 172 per cent increase of ST students. We can expect this tendency to be further accentuated and legitimized under NEP 2020.

On the one hand, the possibility of enhanced exclusion looms large when we consider that the independent rules and regulations of autonomous colleges and universities shall curtail incumbent transparent admission procedures, which guarantee a section of underprivileged students – though limited – a share of seats in such prestigious institutions. On the other hand, the shrinking number of public-funded colleges due to the phasing out of affiliate colleges will further push out marginalized sections and relegate them to low-grade private colleges and/or to *informal* education in the ODL and online modes of education offered by multidisciplinary universities, HEI clusters/knowledge hubs and autonomous colleges. In fact, on reading together the NEP's assertions that 'ODL and online education provide a natural path' for enhanced access to higher quality education (ibid.: 39), and its directives on how HEIs are to graduate into multidisciplinary institutions with enhanced student enrolment, 'preferably by thousands' (ibid.: 35), a sinister push towards ODL education and mainstreaming of online modes of education is apparent.

The policy enjoins that 'all types of institutions will have the option to run Open Distance Learning (ODL) and online programmes, provided they are accredited to do' (ibid.). Going by the developments in the last decade which go to show that enhanced enrolment in higher education has been concentrated in the ODL mode, it can easily be argued that NEP's proposed target of attaining 50 per cent GER will be actualized via the ODL mode and online courses. This eventuality marks a tragedy, given the poor quality of education imparted through the ODL mode and the heavy concentration of underprivileged students in existing ODL institutions; most of whom are first-generation learners who require access to regular classroom teaching and quality instruction to overcome inherited educational, social and economic inequality (John 2020c).[14]

While the ODL mode stands to be expanded, it cannot be expected that it will be radically transformed under NEP 2020. Since it is not the privileged section but the underprivileged section of youth who will be 'opting' for such informal higher education, it is not wrong to estimate that the ODL mode will continue imparting substandard education. Further, the upgrading of the ODL mode is highly unlikely, considering that the bulk of existing ODL institutions has no substantial government funding, with many running as self-financed centres within public-funded universities. This is a discrepancy which has been perpetuated by successive governments, including the present government. The recorded decline in the Union Budget allocation for education under the current dispensation must alert us further to the eventuality of continued financial neglect of ODL institutions.

The overt promotion of vocational education is also hard to miss.

NEP 2020 strategically institutionalizes courses in partnership with industry and the corporate sector. For instance, the policy states that 'incubation centres' are to be set up in HEIs in 'partnership with industries' (GoI 2020: 44). Furthermore, a special committee constituted by the MHRD, that is, the National Committee on Integration of Vocational Education (NCIVE), will oversee 'skill gap analysis' and the 'mapping of local opportunities' (ibid.) so as to develop focus areas of vocational education.

Hailing an era of 'integration' of vocational education into all schools and HEIs, NEP 2020 has nonetheless to be contextualized within the existing structure of the lack of cross-migration between the academic and vocational streams and the compartmentalization of the underprivileged into vocational education. Hence, the various models of vocational education and apprenticeships to be experimented with by HEIs will largely be restricted to vocational educational institutions like polytechnic colleges where socially and economically disadvantaged youth are trained for manual, lower-rung jobs in the labour market.

The so-called integration of vocational education within all HEIs is also a sugar-coated way of saying that training will be offered by HEIs so as to occupy and skill that segment of youth which briefly enters formal education and tends to drop out. Such provisions in NEP 2020 simply seek to reproduce hierarchy and inequality rather than addressing the rising dropout rates from the school level onwards, which reflects institutional failures. The 2020 policy argues two things, distinctively: (1) that dropouts are a given and (2) that there is a supposed lack of adequate skilling for employability when it comes to the academic stream of higher education, thus, there is a need to blend in vocational educational courses, if necessary, in partnership with industry and non-governmental organizations (NGOs). The latter pitch of the policy framers assumes and implies that the problem lies in the lack of skilled labour in the economy rather than the massive unemployment created by the overexploitation of the employed labour force by the industry-corporate combine. In fact, the growing talk within policy circles on the 'necessity' of blending academic and vocational education comes at a time when the manufacturing and service sectors are swiftly changing their organizational practices towards more and more flexibility.

With the shift in recent decades towards the 'holistic' form of organizational behaviour based on multitasking, the key requirement of the manufacturing and service sectors is workers who can perform *different* tasks. It is now being argued by employers that participants in the labour market should possess transferable skills and knowledge that help reduce training costs and creates flexibility for capital in the work process. These concerns have found their way into the policy discourse and the new policy framework on education. The blended model will intensify prevailing educational hierarchy and inequality, for vocational courses will be introduced on the incumbent structure of unequally placed and ranked institutions.

Thus, as per the current structure and institutional practices, crème-da-la-crème HEIs can be expected to steer clear of such experimentation or they will keep their renowned, most sought-after academic courses in the pure sciences, economics, etc., distinctly *separate* from such 'blending'. Vocational courses or streams will either be relegated to less valued academic courses, especially in the social sciences and BA Programme (BA Pass) courses. Overall, the blended model will find itself most concretely enforced in lower-grade HEIs that see a heavy concentration of students from working-class and lower-middle-class backgrounds.

This brings us to the institutionalization of drop-out rates of disadvantaged sections through the *multiple exit options* implanted in undergraduate university education (GoI 2020: 37). The problem is not just the institutionalization of the phenomenon of dropouts but the delinking of the organic inter-connectedness of the subject matter of the disciplines, especially the social sciences. Over the past decades, various disciplines have evolved pedagogy and content according to the specific nature of the study. The disciplines have also developed specific inter-disciplinary connectedness with each other based on their requirements. Moreover, the subject matter taught in any given year in a course is organically connected to the subjects taught over the whole course. Thus, delinking the years by allowing for multiple exits would break the inter-connectedness of a given course, thereby penalizing the students and, by extension, jeopardizing the development of the discipline in the long run.

Conclusion: Ideational and Institutional Envisioning

Undeniably, the education system since the country's independence remains deeply segmented and hierarchical, nurturing social exclusion in turn. In this regard, it is ironic that NEP 2020 valorizes and seeks to return to the supposedly grand tradition of education in ancient times (GoI 2020: 4) and to Sanskrit knowledge systems (ibid.: 14).

For one, the agenda of NEP 2020 to redesign curriculum and pedagogy to suit 'the Indian ethos' (ibid.: 6) and to 'instill among the learners a deep-rooted pride in being Indian' (ibid.) dangerously enforces an idea of India that is based on an unchanging, monolithic, singular representation of the cultural traditions of the Indian subcontinent. Indeed, given the policy framework's overt focus on Sanskrit knowledge systems, the concept of an 'Indian ethos' amounts to being purposefully devoid of the myriad agnostic, materialist and atheistic philosophical or knowledge traditions of the subcontinent. Furthermore, the inequalities stemming from caste status, region, religious community, etc., in the ancient era are strategically over-looked by the policy document when highlighting the achievements of the ancient education system and 'world class institutions' such as Takshashila, Nalanda, Vikramshila, Vallabhi, etc. Likewise, we find the listing of well-known intellectuals produced by the Indian education system. In many ways, this talk of revival or the return to a 'glorious' past represents a far from innocent concealment of the inherited and current inequalities.

Gone, of course, is the acknowledgement of the essential fact that access to learning and 'the acquisition of knowledge . . . for the complete realization and liberation of the self' in the so-called glorious past was based on engrained caste inequalities of the time. Strangely, in a sweeping state-ment, the policy framers argue to the contrary, stating that 'world-class institutions of ancient India . . . hosted scholars and students from *across* [sic] backgrounds' (ibid.: 4). Moreover, historical evidence as encapsulated in the numerous strictures in the ancient literature proves the dissuasion of learning by the 'lower' caste and tribal communities, especially in elite centres of Sanskrit learning. Indeed, what of the numerous Eklavyas who were punished as per the rules of the ancient Indian education system for their efforts to acquire learning imparted to high-caste pupils of renowned teachers? Overlooking these historical realities, including the plurality in the philosophical traditions and challenges posed to Sanskrit knowledge, NEP's mainstreaming of Sanskrit learning and Sanskrit knowledge systems within both schools and the multidisciplinary higher education system (GoI 2020: 22.15) is strategically based on the *singular* focus on the 'vast and significant contributions' of Sanskrit and sweeping generalizations about its intrinsically 'scientific nature'.

At the ideational and institutional level, NEP 2020 also embodies much more. As discussed earlier, there has been a steady widening of the class divide in educational conditions and opportunities in the education system. NEP 2020 is a firm reassertion of hierarchy and inequality in edu-cation. Unlike earlier policies with their smatterings of pro-privatization provisions and legitimization of the dual education system that were bal-anced with proclamations of social justice, NEP 2020 lays down a compre-hensive road map for the acceleration of the widening gap and disparity in educational access and quality of education imparted. It takes for granted and therefore normalizes the hierarchy between institutions. It justifies the elitism and exclusion inbuilt into the premium HEIs. It normalizes the lack of common schooling, thereby leaving unquestioned the unequal competi-tion for entry into public-funded, formal university education. Instead of addressing the need for equal access to quality public-funded higher education, it makes differential access the new norm by emphasizing multiple pathways of learning and *notionally* drawing an equivalence between them, which in real terms does not exist. It grafts itself on the institutional failures of the education system to eradicate inherited and current social and economic inequalities and reproduces them by introducing multiple exit 'options' within school and college education.

In this light, the 2020 policy framework does not herald much-needed reforms in education. Educational measures are best assessed as *reforms* if they concretely enhance equal access to quality education and set new benchmarks for the inclusion of the last person in the line within the best institutions. It is precisely in this light that NEP fails to deliver when we consider the existing system of higher education. More than deliverance, NEP 2020 represents the media for greater privatization and enhanced hierarchization in higher education.

Today, the need of the hour is the liquidation of a segmented education structure through the establishment of the common school, uniform allocation of resources which equalizes the pre-existing disparity among central and regional universities, as well as the creation of more public-funded universities with *equitable* funding to facilitate entry of the last person in line into the formal, regular mode of higher education. From the perspective of the socially and economically marginalized sections of society, anything less than this amounts to a farcical repetition, albeit at a greater pace, of the educational inequality which they have inherited.

Notes

1 https://www.education.gov.in/sites/upload_files/mhrd/files/NEP_Final_English_0. pdf, accessed 2 September 2021.

2 In a bid to meet what the ruling elites identify as the country's contemporary educational needs, the Ministry of Human Resource Development of the Government of India began consultations for shaping a national-level policy in 2016. Subsequently, the Committee for Evolution of the New Education Policy was constituted under the chairmanship of former Cabinet Secretary T.S.R. Subramanian, which submitted its report in May 2016, titled 'National Policy on Education 2016' (GoI 2016). A 'vision document' or Draft National Education Policy 2019 that sought to offer a suitable road map for the next twenty years was prepared by a separate committee constituted in 2017 and headed by Dr Kasturirangan. The 'Draft National Education Policy 2019' (Dr Kasturirangan Report) was a 500-page document. On 29 July 2020, the Cabinet officially adopted a 66-page report, titled *National Education Policy 2020*.

3 https://innovate.mygov.in/wp-content/uploads/2019/06/mygov15596510111.pdf, accessed 30 July 2021.

4 https://www.education.gov.in/sites/upload_files/mhrd/files/document-reports/ YPC-Report_0.pdf, accessed 11 July 2021.

5 Grants-in-aid institutions are those which are extended financial assistance by the government to meet a certain proportion of their total expenditure. These institu-

tions in turn agree to submit to inspection by the government and to rules prescribed for grants-in-aid institutions.

[6] For details of public expenditure on education by the education departments of the
centre and the states, see Government of India's 'Analysis of Budgeted Expenditure
on Education, 2014–15 to 2016–17' (GoI 2018). For trends in total budgetary
spending on education by the central and state governments between 2004–05 and
2014–15, see GoI (2015).

[7] For an elaboration of the point of ODL institutions running in self-financed mode,
see the discussion on the School of Open Learning, University of Delhi, in John
(2020a).

[8] https://www.education.gov.in/sites/upload_files/mhrd/files/document-reports/
NPE86-mod92.pdf, accessed 15 September 2021.

[9] Salary is the largest component of public funds released by the state/central
government.

[10] 'Top 100 NIRF Institutes Don't Need Approval to Start Online Degree Programmes:
UGC Chairman', *The New Indian Express*, 11 June 2020, available at https://
www.newindianexpress.com/nation/2020/jun/11/top-100-nirf-institutes-dont-
need-approval-to-start-online-degree-programmes-ugc-chairman-2155357.html

[11] See 'About Us', Higher Education Financing Agency (HEFA), https://hefa.co.in/
about-us/. The agreed equity participation in this joint venture of the MHRD and
Canara Bank is 90.91 per cent and 9.09 per cent, respectively.

[12] See 'Top 100 NIRF Institutes Don't Need Approval' (note 10 above). Also see, '38
Universities Can Offer Online Degree Courses Now, Says UGC', *India Today*, 19
June 2021, available at https://www.indiatoday.in/education-today/news/story/38-
universities-can-offer-online-degree-courses-now-says-ugc-1816919-2021-06-19.

[13] For a detailed discussion on the costs borne by the individual learner with respect
to online education and the digitization thrust of the ODL mode, see John (2020b).

[14] For an elucidation of the institutional neglect of one of the largest ODL institutions
in the country, see John (2020c).

References

Bhattacharya, D. (2019), 'Of Feudal Intellectual Capital: The History of the New Provincial
Universities', in D. Bhattacharya, ed., *The Idea of the University: Histories and
Contexts*, New York: Routledge.

Carnoy, M. and R. Dosani (2013), 'Goals and Governance of Higher Education in India',
Higher Education, vol. 65, no. 5, pp. 595–612.

Centre for Budget and Governance Accountability (2020), 'Promises and Priorities: An
Analysis of Union Budget 2019–20', available at https://www.cbgaindia.org/
wp-content/uploads/2019/07/Promises-and-Priorities-An-Analysis-of-Union-
Budget-2019-20-2.pdf.

Centre for Budget and Policy Studies (2019), 'Education Cess and its Neglect of Education',
available at https://cbps.in/secondary-education/2019/07/01/education-cess-and-its-
neglect-of-education/ .

de Weert, E. (2011), 'Perspectives on Higher Education and the Labour Market: Review
of International Policy Developments', University of Twente: Centre for Higher
Education Policy Studies, available at http://www.utwente.nl/mb/cheps/publications/
Publications%202011/C11EW158%20Final%20version%20Themarapport%
20onderwijs%20-%20arbeidsmarkt.pdf.

Government of India (GoI) (1967), *Report of the Committee on Colleges*, New Delhi:
University Grants Commission, Ministry of Human Resource Development, Government of India.

———— (1986), 'National Policy on Education 1986', Ministry of Human Resource Development, New Delhi, Government of India, available at https://www.education.gov.in/sites/upload_files/mhrd/files/document-reports/NPE86-mod92.pdf

———— (2009a), 'Report of the Committee to Advise on Renovation and Rejuvenation of Higher Education' (Yash Pal Committee), New Delhi: Ministry of Human Resource Development, Government of India, available at https://www.education.gov.in/sites/upload_files/mhrd/files/document-reports/YPC-Report_0.pdf.

———— (2009b), *Report to the Nation 2006–2009*, National Knowledge Commission, New Delhi: Ministry of Human Resource Development, Government of India.

———— (2015), 'Budget Allocation for Education Sector in India', *Budgeted Expenditure*, New Delhi: Government of India.

———— (2016), 'National Policy on Education 2016: Report of the Committee for the Evolution of the New Education Policy' (T.S.R. Subramaniam Committee), New Delhi: Ministry of Human Resource Development, Government of India, available at http://www.niepa.ac.in/download/NEP2016/ReportNEP.pdf.

———— (2018), *Analysis of Budgeted Expenditure on Education (2014–15 to 2016–17)*, New Delhi: Department of Higher Education, Ministry of Human Resource Development, Government of India.

———— (2019), 'Report of the Committee for the Draft National Education Policy 2019' (Kasturirangan Committee), New Delhi: Ministry of Human Resource Development, Government of India, available at https://innovate.mygov.in/wp-content/uploads/2019/06/mygov15596510111.pdf.

———— (2020), *National Education Policy 2020*, New Delhi: Government of India, available at https://www.education.gov.in/sites/upload_files/mhrd/files/NEP_Final_English_0.pdf.

John, M. (2013), 'Critiquing Reforms in Higher Education', *Social Scientist*, vol. 41, nos 7–8, pp. 49–67.

———— (2020a), 'Fears and Furies of Online (Mis) Education: Lockdown and Beyond', *Kafila*, 22 May, available at https://kafila.online/2020/05/22/fears-and-furies-of-online-miseducation-lockdown-and-beyond-maya-john/.

———— (2020b), 'Online Education: The Latest Stage of Educational Apartheid', *Mainstream*, vol. 58, no. 26, New Delhi, 13 June, available at https://mainstreamweekly.net/article9480.html .

———— (2020c), 'Online Examinations: Towards Educational Genocide of Students of School of Open Learning', *Countercurrents,* 24 May, available at https://countercurrents.org/2020/05/online-examinations-towards-educational-genocide-of-students-of-school-of-open-learning/.

Motkuri, V. and E. Revathi (2022), 'Critical Need of Higher Outlays for Education Sector', *Hans India*, available at https://www.thehansindia.com/hans/opinion/news-analysis/critical-need-of-higher-outlays-for-education-sector-741554u.

Singh, P. (2020), 'Opinion Editorial: National Education Policy for the Elites', *The Indian Express*, 22 October.

Contributors

Debaditya Bhattacharya teaches literature at Kazi Nazrul University, Asansol. He has been working on a historical sociology of Indian universities, mapped against questions of policy. He has also been engaged in public conversations and debates around the new National Education Policy (NEP) 2020 and its intended futures. He has recently finished a manuscript on the relationship between the public university and its meanings of 'publicness', and is working on another on the histories and effects of NEP 2020. Two of his edited anthologies on critical university studies include *The Idea of the University: Histories and Contexts* (2019) and *The University Unthought: Notes for a Future* (2019).

Mohd. Bilal is a PhD scholar and a prominent activist in the field of school education and among students at the School of Open Learning, University of Delhi. His research interests include educational inequalities in India, labour history, and the relationship between constitutionalism and labour politics in early twentieth-century Bombay. His ongoing PhD research is examining the role of the Servants of India Society in the labour politics of Bombay, and the efforts of the colonial state to steer the workers' movement away from radical unionism and towards a constitutionalist path.

Saumen Chattopadhyaya joined the Zakir Husain Centre for Educational Studies, School of Social Sciences, Jawaharlal Nehru University (JNU) in 2004 and has been a Professor since 2010. He worked at the National Institute of Public Finance and Policy (NIPFP) during 1995–2004. His research areas include economics of education focusing particularly on policy-making in higher education, public finance specializing in the areas of tax evasion and black economy. His major publications are *Education* *and Economics: Disciplinary Evolution and Policy Discourse* (Oxford University Press, 2012); *Macroeconomics of the Black Economy* (Orient BlackSwan, 2018); and *Changing Higher Education in India*, co-edited with Simon Marginson, University of Oxford and N.V. Varghese, former Vice-Chancellor, NIEPA, New Delhi (Bloomsbury, 2021). He has been involved in many national and international projects, including funding of higher education, public–private partnership, capital flight and social science research and policymaking.

Rohan D'Souza is a Professor at the Graduate School of Asian and African Area Studies, Kyoto University. He is the author of *Drowned and Dammed: Colonial Capitalism and Flood control in Eastern India* (Oxford University Press, 2006). Among his jointly edited volumes are: (with Deepak Kumar and Vinita Damodaran) *The British Empire and the Natural World: Environmental Encounters in South Asia* (Oxford University Press, 2011), and (with Vinita Damodaran) *Commonwealth Forestry and Environmental History: Empire Forests and Colonial Environments in Africa, the Caribbean, South Asia and New Zealand* (Primus, 2020). He has been actively writing on the new shifts in higher education and the emergence of the 'platform university'.

Maya John, the editor of this volume, teaches history at Jesus and Mary College, University of Delhi. Some of her recent research and publications relate to fields such as mass social movements; educational inequalities in colonial and post-colonial India; evolution of India's labour laws; the impacts of labour segmentation in the Indian workforce; the relationship between caste, gender and the labour market; and histories of epidemics and epidemiology. She is a member of the Publications Committee of the Indian Association for Women's Studies. Her recent publication is a co-edited volume titled *Who Cares? Care Extraction and the Struggles of Indian Health Workers* (Zubaan Books, 2023). John has been writing on educational structures and policy developments. She is presently an elected member of the Academic Council, University of Delhi.

Anthony Joseph teaches in the Department of Elementary Education, Jesus and Mary College, Delhi University. As a teacher-educator and professional development consultant for Leadership in Education, he has served as Senior Consultant at the National Centre for School Leadership, NIEPA, New Delhi. His ongoing engagement with 'learning, reflexivity and interrogating assimilated educational perspectives' is a call to synchronize knowledge with lived reality based on deliberation, discernment and dedication.

L.R.S. Lakshmi taught history at Lakshmibai College, University of Delhi. She authored the book, *The Malabar Muslims: A Different Perspective*, which is a study of the social, economic, religious, theological, political and educational contexts informing the lives of the Muslim community, the Mappilas, of northern Kerala during the colonial and post-colonial periods. She was a Fellow at the Nehru Memorial Museum and Library (NMML) from 2015 to 2017, where she worked extensively on the education of Mappila Muslims.

Geetha B. Nambissan is a former professor of the sociology of education at the Zakir Husain Centre for Educational Studies, Jawaharlal Nehru University, New Delhi. Her research has focused on exclusion, inclusion and equity in education with particular reference to the schooling of marginalized sections of Indian society: Dalits, Adivasis and the urban poor. She was a partner in the Transnational Research Group on Education and the Urban anchored by the German Historical Institute, London. Her recent publications include 'Caste and the Politics of the Early "Public" in Schooling: Dalit Struggle for an Equitable Education' (*Contemporary Education Dialogue*, 2020) and 'Education and the Changing Urban in Delhi: Privilege and Exclusion in a Megacity' (*Perspectivia.net*, 2021). She is one of the associate editors of the *Oxford Encyclopaedia of School Reform* (Oxford University Press, 2022).

Madhu Prasad superannuated as an Associate Professor of Philosophy from the Department of Philosophy, Zakir Hussain Delhi College, University of Delhi. She is a founding member and presidium member of the All India Forum for Right to Education (AIFRTE). She has written widely on the history of education in the colonial period and the evolution of a national policy of education by the Education Commission (1964–66), and has been a steadfast critic of India's neoliberal policy in education. She has been for many years a member of the editorial board of the well-known journal, *Social Scientist*.

Jyoti Raina is Professor of Education at the Department of Elementary Education, Gargi College, University of Delhi. She has worked in the area of teacher education and school education for more than three decades. Her research interests include school education policy, psychology of education, cognitive education, action research and initial teacher education. She serves on the editorial board of the *Journal for Critical Education Policy Studies*. She has co-authored a number of popular articles on educational issues with her students. She has been a member of the Curriculum

Framework Committee for Bachelor of Elementary Education programme at the National Council of Teacher Education, a statutory body of the Government of India.

Kumkum Roy pursued her PhD in ancient Indian history at the Centre for Historical Studies, Jawaharlal Nehru University, New Delhi. She taught at the Satyawati Co-educational College, Delhi University, and at the Centre for Historical Studies, Jawaharlal Nehru University. Her specialization is in ancient Indian history. Her areas of interest include histories of political institutions and processes and issues of gender. Her publications include *The Emergence of Monarchy in North India*, *The Power of Gender and the Gender of Power* and *A Historical Dictionary of Ancient India* (Oxford University Press, 1994). She is also interested in issues of pedagogy at various levels.